REFRAMING THE FEUDAL REVOLUTION

The profound changes that took place between 800 and 1100 in the transition from Carolingian to post-Carolingian Europe have long been the subject of vigorous historical controversy. Looking beyond the notion of a 'Feudal Revolution', this book reveals that a radical shift in the patterns of

soc
unl
Fo
Ch
chr
tise
ref
anc
ele

CH
Sh

Cambridge Studies in Medieval Life and Thought
Fourth Series

General Editor:

ROSAMOND McKITTERICK

Professor of Medieval History, University of Cambridge, and Fellow of Sidney Sussex College

Advisory Editors:

CHRISTINE CARPENTER

Professor of Medieval English History, University of Cambridge

JONATHAN SHEPARD

The series *Cambridge Studies in Medieval Life and Thought* was inaugurated by G. G. Coulton in 1921; Professor Rosamond McKitterick now acts as General Editor of the Fourth Series, with Professor Christine Carpenter and Dr Jonathan Shepard as Advisory Editors. The series brings together outstanding work by medieval scholars over a wide range of human endeavour extending from political economy to the history of ideas.

This is book 90 in the series, and a full list of titles in the series can be found at: www.cambridge.org/medievallifeandthought

REFRAMING THE FEUDAL REVOLUTION

Political and Social Transformation Between
Marne and Moselle, c.800–c.1100

CHARLES WEST

CAMBRIDGE
UNIVERSITY PRESS

CAMBRIDGE
UNIVERSITY PRESS

University Printing House, Cambridge CB2 8BS, United Kingdom

Cambridge University Press is part of the University of Cambridge.

It furthers the University's mission by disseminating knowledge in the pursuit of
education, learning and research at the highest international levels of excellence.

www.cambridge.org
Information on this title: www.cambridge.org/9781316635506

© Charles West 2013

First published 2013

A catalogue record for this publication is available from the British Library

Library of Congress Cataloguing in Publication data
West, Charles, 1979–
Reframing the feudal revolution : political and social transformation between
Marne and Moselle, c.800 to c.1100 / Charles West.
pages cm. – (Cambridge studies in medieval life and thought. Fourth series ; book 90)
Includes bibliographical references and index.
ISBN 978-1-107-02886-9 (hardback)
1. Carolingians – France – Marne River Valley – History.   2. Carolingians – Moselle River
Valley – History.   3. Social change – Europe – History – To 1500.   4. Political
culture – Europe – History – To 1500.   5. Feudalism – Europe – History – To 1500.   6. Marne
River Valley (France) – Politics and government.   7. Moselle River Valley – Politics and
government.   8. Marne River Valley (France) – Social conditions.   9. Moselle River
Valley – Social conditions.   10. Europe – History – 476-1492.   I. Title.
DC70.W47 2013
944´.3014–dc23
2012042957

ISBN 978-1-107-02886-9 Hardback
ISBN 978-1-316-63550-6 Paperback

CONTENTS

Contents

ACKNOWLEDGEMENTS

If it takes a village to raise a child, it takes almost as many people to write a book, especially one as long in preparation as this. In first place, I should like to thank Rosamond McKitterick, who supervised the PhD thesis that was really this book's first draft, and who has continued to offer tremendous advice and support ever since; and Chris Wickham, who supervised the MPhil dissertation in which I first grappled with the Feudal Revolution and the Carolingians, who examined the PhD, and who has been very generous with his time subsequently. I am acutely conscious of my debt to Matthew Innes and Stuart Airlie, who acted as examiners at different stages and gave me much less of a hard time than I deserved, and from whose thoughts I have benefited on many other occasions besides. I am very grateful to Liesbeth van Houts, who over a decade ago supervised an undergraduate dissertation which first led me to think about the twelfth century in relation to the ninth, and to Régine le Jan, who facilitated a stay in Paris and made me feel very welcome there. I would also like to thank the anonymous Readers for this series, whose suggestions have greatly improved what follows. It need hardly be added that the errors in interpretation or detail that follow are entirely my own.

Many others have played a part in the slow gestation of this book, directly or indirectly. Lists are always invidious when incomplete, and this one is no exception; but it would be shameful not to register my gratitude to Aysu Dincer, Olga Magoula and Duncan Probert, all of whom I met in Birmingham; Helen Carrel, Thomas Faulkner, Julian Hendrix, Paul Hilliard, Christina Pössel, Christof Rolker and the GEMS in Cambridge; Rachel Stone in London; Christopher Tyerman in Oxford; Miriam Czock, Wolfgang Haubrichs, Sylvie Joye and Jean-Baptiste Renault in Germany and France; and Michael Raw and Mark Stephenson in Cumbria. Since 2008, Sheffield has provided a most convivial place to work, thanks to Sarah Foot, Julia Hillner, Simon Loseby, Amanda Power, Martial Staub and all my other colleagues in

Acknowledgements

the History Department, both academic and support staff, as well as its students, notably those of HST 3115/6.

Debts to institutions may not be as personally felt as those to supervisors, examiners, colleagues and friends, but institutions are vitally important in enabling a long-term project like this to come to fruition. The Arts and Humanities Research Board, and then the Arts and Humanities Research Council, funded the postgraduate work from which this book grew, with the University of Birmingham and Emmanuel College providing the scholarly environment; I am grateful, too, to the Fellows of Hertford College for electing me to a Research Fellowship, and to the Drapers' Company for providing the wherewithal for them to do so. I have also benefited from the resources of what I maintain to be the best library in the world, the Cambridge University Library, whose help in procuring the foreign-language material that research projects such as this require was invaluable: this book simply could not have been written without the University Library and its wonderful staff. Other libraries, archives and research institutes have also been very accommodating, particularly the Bibliothèque Nationale and the Institut de recherche et d'histoire des textes in Paris, libraries in Epinal, Nancy, Oxford, Rheims, Trier and Verdun and archives at Bar-le-Duc, Châlons, Metz, Rheims and Troyes: my thanks to them all.

My greatest debt is to Emma Hunter, who has patiently put up with early medieval history (and my files!) for so long, and who read almost all of the book's early drafts, which have been, I will admit, rather numerous. However, I should like to dedicate this book to the memory of my mother, who sadly did not live to see its publication.

ABBREVIATIONS

AASS	*Acta Sanctorum*, ed. Societas Bollandiensis, 68 vols. (Brussels, 1867–1925)
AB	*Annales Bertiniani*, ed. F. Grat, *Annales de Saint-Bertin* (Paris, 1964)
AD	Archives Départementales
Artem	*La diplomatique française du Haut Moyen Age: inventaire des chartes originales antérieures à 1121 conservées en France*, ed. B.-M. Tock, 2 vols. (Turnhout, 2001)
BEC	*Bibliothèque d'Ecole des Chartes*
BHL	Bibliotheca Hagiographica Latina
CCCM	*Corpus Christianorum, continuatio mediaevalis*
D(D)	Diplomas of rulers (see Bibliography for full details):

A	Emperor Arnulf
CB	King, later Emperor, Charles the Bald
CF	King, later Emperor, Charles the Fat
CM	King, later Emperor, Charlemagne
CS	King Charles the Simple
HIII	Emperor Henry III
HIV	Emperor Henry IV
LothI	King, later Emperor, Lothar I
LothII	King Lothar II
LP	Emperor Louis the Pious. In the absence of a critical edition, numbers are taken from *Regesta imperii. Die Regesten des Kaisserreichs under den Karolingern, 751–918*, ed. J. F. Böhmer, revised by E. Mühlbacher with J. Lechner, 2nd edn (Innsbruck, 1908)
LS	King Louis the Stammerer
LVI	King Louis VI (of West Francia/France)

LY	King Louis the Younger
Philip	King Philip I
Pippin	King Pippin the Short
Rod	King Rodulf/Raoul (of West Francia)
Z	King Zwentibold

EME	*Early Medieval Europe*
FMS	*Frühmittelalterliche Studien*
HRE	Flodoard, *Historia remensis ecclesiae*, ed. M. Stratmann, *Die Geschichte der Reimser Kirche, MGH SS*, vol. XXXVI (Hanover, 1998)
MGH	*Monumenta Germaniae historica*

Capit.	*Capitularia regum Francorum*, eds. A. Boretius and V. Krause, *MGH Leges, Sectio III*, 2 vols. (Hanover, 1883–97)
Concilia	*Concilia, MGH Legum, Sectio III*, 5 vols. (Hanover, 1893–2010)
Constitutiones	*Constitutiones et acta publica imperatorum et regum, Volume I, 911–1197*, ed. L. Weiland, Legum Sectio IV (Hanover, 1893)
Epp.	*Epistolae (in Quart)*, 8 vols. (Hanover, 1887–)
Formulae	*Formulae Merovingici et Karolini Aevi*, ed. K. Zeumer, *MGH Leges* Sectio V (Hanover, 1886)
SRG	*Scriptores rerum Germanicarum* (Hanover, 1871–)
SRM	*Scriptores rerum Merovingicarum*, 7 vols. (Hanover, 1884–1920)
SS	*Scriptores*, 32 vols. (Hanover, 1826–1934)

PL	*Patrologia cursus completus, series Latina*, ed. J.-P. Migne, 221 vols. (Paris, 1841–66)
Settimane	*Settimane di studio del Centro italiano di studi sull'alto medioevo* (Spoleto, 1953–)
TRHS	*Transactions of the Royal Historical Society*
UBMR	*Urkundenbuch zur Geschichte der jetzt die Preussischen Regierungsbezirke Coblenz und Trier bildenden mittelrheinischen Territorien, Volume I, Von den ältesten Zeiten bis zum Jahre 1169*, ed. H. Beyer (Koblenz, 1860)

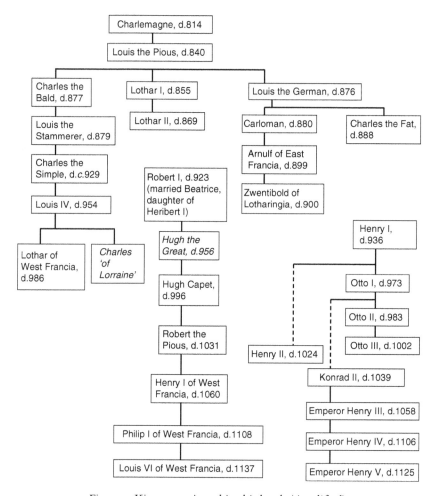

Figure 1 Kings mentioned in this book (simplified)

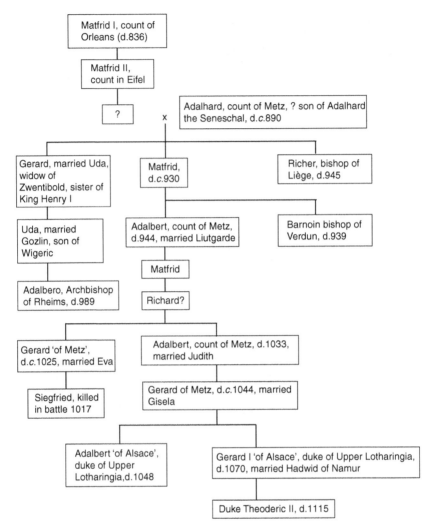

Figure 2 The ancestors of Duke Theoderic II of Upper Lotharingia (simplified).
The generations around Richard remain uncertain.

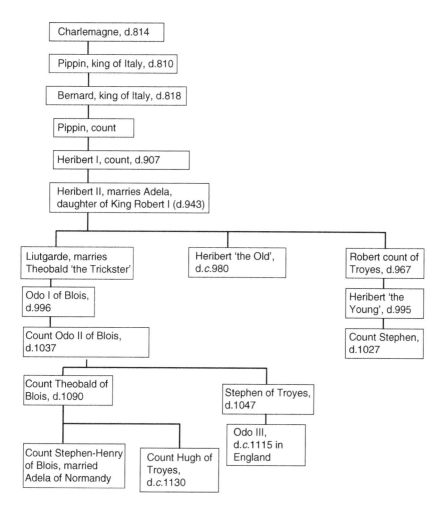

Figure 3 The ancestors of Count Hugh of Champagne (simplified)

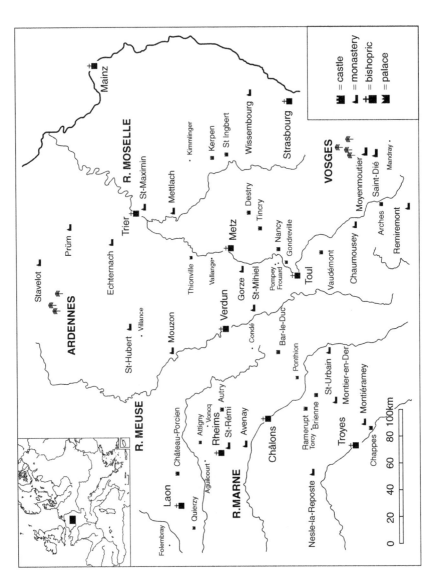

Map of places cited in the text

INTRODUCTION

This book sets out to reassess the changes that took place in the nature and co-ordination of social relations between around 800 and 1100 in Carolingian and post-Carolingian Europe, by means of a geographically defined case-study. Its overarching argument is three-fold. Firstly, it proposes that a radical shift in patterns of social organisation took place within this period of time. Secondly, it identifies that shift as primarily one of formalisation, working at different levels. Thirdly, it suggests that this shift, though radical, can nevertheless best be understood as a consequence, one might say continuation, of processes unleashed by the movement conventionally labelled as Carolingian reform. It is to the exploration of these ideas and the questions they raise that the pages that follow are devoted.

THE HISTORIOGRAPHICAL BACKGROUND

The broad issue to which this book is dedicated has hardly been neglected by historians. On the contrary, the challenge of defining the nature of the transition that took place from Carolingian to twelfth-century Europe is one of the most heavily scrutinised in medieval history, because it encodes a question about disciplinary division; that is, about periodisation. Most historians of medieval Continental Europe would locate the juncture between the early and the central Middle Ages during this time-frame, but at different points, and for different reasons. Historical distinctions of this kind may seem trivial, even tedious, exercises in arbitrary judgement that are best ignored; yet not only are such categorisations unavoidable, they also exercise a subtly far-reaching influence across a wide range of scholarship and even beyond, tacitly promoting certain interpretations and marginalising others.[1] Moreover, though this particular periodisation

---

[1] See the recent and stimulating study by K. Davis, *Periodization and sovereignty: how ideas of feudalism and secularization govern the politics of time* (Philadelphia, 2008).

I

might seem to be amongst history's more minor ones, it has often been invested with grander ambitions, for some marking nothing less than the end of the ancient world, for others intimating the first stirrings of a nascent modernity.[2]

Abbreviated textbook analysis aside, the most thorough, comprehensive and sophisticated engagement with this issue is to be found within the debate on the Feudal Revolution.[3] Though it can in fact be traced back further, the notion that a structural transformation of Carolingian society occurred is conventionally attributed to the French historian Georges Duby. Arguing primarily from Burgundian evidence, Duby suggested in a classic study that the formal disintegration of the Carolingian empire around 900 had relatively little impact on wider society.[4] For Duby, the real change came around the year 1000 with the rise of castellan power, a new form of violent lordship centred on castles and their lords, with which the traditional structures of Carolingian society were wholly incapable of dealing, and before which they crumbled away. This new order took little account of distinctions of free and unfree, of public and private. Instead, it revolved around the power of aristocratic lineage and the zone around the castle, the territorial expression of that power. This power was built not on simple land ownership (*seigneurie foncière*), but on judicial powers usurped from the king (*seigneurie banale*).

Duby's ideas exhilarated a generation of historians, who enthusiastically applied them to other regions in France, further developing their conceptual framework. Pierre Bonnassie provided a regional study more systematic than that sketched out by Duby, Robert Fossier's notion of *encellulement* enriched the conceptual apparatus and efforts were even made to use the criteria comparatively across great swathes of world history.[5] What turned out to be a culminating synthesis of this research was achieved by the publication in 1980 of Poly and Bournazel's magisterial restatement of

[2] D. Barthélemy, *La mutation de l'an mil, a-t-elle eu lieu?: servage et chevalerie dans la France des Xe et XIe siècles* (Paris, 1997), p. 26, 'La Renaissance du XIIe siècle n'aura pas lieu', *BEC* 154 (1996), 607–24, at p. 624; G. Bois, *La mutation de l'an mil: Lormand, village mâconais, de l'antiquité au féodalisme* (Paris, 1989).

[3] D. Barthélemy provides a judicious and succinct review of the debate: see 'Revisiting the "Feudal Revolution" of the year 1000', in his *The serf, the knight, and the historian* (Ithaca, 2009), tr. G. R. Edwards, pp. 1–11. Another aspect of the issue is the debate inspired by the work of Susan Reynolds; I address this below, pp. 199–206.

[4] G. Duby, *La société aux XIe et XIIe siècles dans la région mâconnaise* (Paris, 1953).

[5] For a summary of this regional work, see T. Bisson, 'La Terre et les hommes: a programme fulfilled?', *French History* 14 (2000), 322–34; P. Bonnassie, *La Catalogne du milieu du Xe à la fin du XIe siècle* (Toulouse, 1975–6); R. Fossier, *L'enfance de l'Europe X–XII siècles: aspects économiques et sociaux* (Paris, 1982). For the extension of the 'revolution' to the world stage, see J.-P. Poly and P. Bournazel, eds., *Les féodalités* (Paris, 1998), and more recently, R. I. Moore, 'The transformation of Europe as a Eurasian phenomenon', *Medieval Encounters* 10 (2004), 77–98.

Duby's original hypothesis.[6] Their book integrated arguments about the shape of the aristocratic family, the 'Peace of God', the rise of a new class of professional warriors, the usurpation of royal prerogatives and the smudging of legal categorisations which had hitherto sheltered the free peasant, ideas all adumbrated by Duby, into a single explanatory model of marvellous intellectual clarity.

However, in recent years the validity of that model has been increasingly called into question. Articulated in a growing series of diverse and lively interventions, such as the debates of the 1990s carried in the pages of *Past and Present* and *Médiévales*, these criticisms can schematically be classified into two strands, united only in the conviction that the Feudal Revolution model must be abandoned.

On the one hand is the position developed by Dominique Barthélemy across an array of publications.[7] Arguing that the image of feudal society implied by the Feudal Revolution, characterised by the dwindling away of the public in favour of personal bonds and an explosion of effectively unchecked violence, was intrinsically flawed, he suggested that the identification of the year 1000 as the moment this new society supposedly came into being derived merely from a naïve reading of monastic cartularies that fetishised particular words, notably *servus* and *miles*. In a conscious return to nineteenth-century approaches, Barthélemy has offered an alternative periodisation based on an alternative dynamic of change, concentrating on shifts he considers far more important than those emphasised by the Feudal Revolution. Some of these shifts he associates with the year 888 or 900, representing the collapse of the Carolingian empire and the emergence of principalities; others he suggests are linked to 1100 or the long twelfth century, these dates standing for a panoply of developments, including urbanisation, the bureaucratisation of government and the emergence of scholasticism.[8]

The second strand of critique is in a way more ambitious. Duby's model of the Feudal Revolution depended on privileging distinctions in how disputes and conflicts were resolved between the Carolingian and the post-Carolingian period. The interest which he helped stimulate in medieval disputes has if anything only increased over the past few decades, and there is now a thriving field of medieval conflict studies.[9] Yet the conclusions which this scholarship has produced have increasingly tended to contradict

---

[6] J.-P. Poly and E. Bournazel, *La mutation féodale, X^e–XIIe siècles* (Paris, 1980). tr. C. Higgitt as *The feudal transformation: 900–1200* (New York, 1991).

[7] D. Barthélemy, *La mutation de l'an mil* is the most convenient point of entry; the English translation, *The serf* contains additional material.

[8] D. Barthélemy, 'La mutation de l'an 1100', *Journal des Savants* (2005), 3–28.

[9] W. Brown and P. Górecki, eds., *Conflict in medieval Europe* (Aldershot, 2003).

not merely Duby's results but also his method. In the view of some historians, most notably Stephen White, the point is not simply that underneath the Carolingian rhetoric of peace and state order and the post-Carolingian monastic rhetoric of violence and disorder there lay essentially similar processes of dispute resolution; it is that we should expect pre-modern change to be tentative, and that a history of turning points with attention to structure is inherently misleading.[10]

The difference between these critiques is that the first merely seeks to shift the periodisation on empirical grounds, while the second more radically calls into question the grounds for any periodisation more subtle than that between modern and pre-modern. Nevertheless, it should not be forgotten that Duby's ideas, and the periodisation he championed, have also found defenders, though these have usually kept a certain critical distance from Duby's initial formulation.[11] Two historians working in the central Middle Ages are particularly prominent here. Thomas Bisson's increasingly refined restatements of Duby's hypothesis, emphasising an explosion of unrestrained power and violence that initiated an age of lordship, seem likely to continue stimulating debate – indeed it was Bisson who brought the Feudal Revolution model to Anglophone attention – though have as yet won few open adherents.[12] In contrast, the work of R. I. Moore, for whom the Revolution functions explicitly or implicitly to clear the ground for the exploration of a range of developments connected with the onset of modernity, has become hugely influential, eagerly adopted by many historians of later periods even as the assumptions on which it relies are being challenged by earlier specialists.[13]

THE PLACE OF THE CAROLINGIANS IN THE FEUDAL REVOLUTION DEBATE

If the Feudal Revolution debate has become quieter in more recent years, it is not, as one might think when reading the rather triumphalist rhetoric

---

[10] Many of White's most important articles are republished in his *Re-thinking kinship and feudalism* (Aldershot, 2005). See also his programmatic 'Tenth-century courts at Macon and the perils of Structuralist history: re-reading Burgundian judicial institutions', in Brown and Górecki, eds., *Conflict*, pp. 37–68.

[11] In addition to the two historians mentioned below, reference should also be made to D. Bates, 'England and the "Feudal Revolution"', *Il Feudalesimo nell'alto medioevo Settimane* 47 (2000), 611–46 and to A. Wareham's stimulating *Lords and communities in early medieval East Anglia* (Woodbridge, 2005).

[12] T. Bisson, 'The Feudal Revolution', *Past and Present* 142 (1994), 6–42; and see T. Bisson, *The crisis of the twelfth century: power, lordship, and the origins of European government* (Princeton, 2008).

[13] R. I. Moore, notably *The first European revolution, c.970–1215* (Oxford, 2000). For an example of the reception of Moore's general argument, a reception that shows no signs of slackening, see C. Fasolt, 'Hegel's ghost: Europe, the Reformation, and the Middle Ages', *Viator* 39 (2008), 345–86.

of certain participants, because one 'side' has proven its case to general satisfaction. Rather, it is because of deadlock, a growing sense that the debate stands before an impasse. This book proposes that one way out of the impasse is to reconsider the role of the Carolingians. For, notwithstanding the great diversity of approaches, one element that nearly all share is a strictly limited engagement with Carolingian material.

For proponents of the Feudal Revolution, whether in Duby's original formulation or in some modified form, the Carolingian ninth century is relevant only in proving the definitive nature of the decisive transition. Whether the Carolingians are imagined as the heirs (or perhaps creators) of a properly public state, or the ninth century is portrayed as an archaic age, impoverished and backwards, the separation from the post-1000 world is guaranteed. What is striking is that the critics of Duby's position have not substantially challenged this relegation of the Carolingian period. Rejecting the argument of radical change, the tendency has been to argue instead that the ninth century was not really as distinctive as it may seem. This is the central point of Barthélemy's influential notion of 'feudal revelation', suggesting that the most radical change was really just one of documentary practice that revealed established ideas and practices which Carolingian sources had veiled over.[14]

Setting aside the intrinsic merits or otherwise of these arguments for the moment, two underlying reasons for this pervasive neglect of the ninth century throughout the debate can be discerned. The first, and most obvious, brings us back to the question of historical disciplinarity. Most of those historians involved in the Feudal Revolution debate, or more broadly concerned with the beginning of the central Middle Ages, are naturally enough specialists in central medieval history, interested in characterising the origins and features of their field of study. Carolingian historians, by contrast, are usually early medievalists, whose interests often reach back to Late Antiquity but seldom extend much beyond the tenth century. These historians read different journals, attend different scholarly conferences, and engage in different debates.[15] With a couple of – notably stimulating – exceptions, contributions to the Feudal Revolution debate, and indeed analogous fields, have come from only the former set of historians, and this has inevitably shaped the way the debate has been conducted.

Compounding this disciplinary problem, and in a way even more serious, is the prevalence of sets of conceptual oppositions in this debate

---

[14] D. Barthélemy, *La société dans le comté de Vendôme de l'an mil au XIVe siècle* (Paris 1993), pp. 19–127; see also S. White, 'Debate: the Feudal Revolution: comment', *Past and Present* 152 (1996), 196–223.
[15] Cf. M. Innes, 'Economies and societies in early medieval Western Europe', in C. Lansing and E. English, eds., *A companion to the Medieval world* (Oxford, 2009), pp. 9–35.

and beyond it that effectively preclude a better understanding of the place of the Carolingians. Two of these, in their various forms, are particularly influential: one revolving around a Weberian distinction between pre-modern and modern, the other based on the apparently self-evident distinction between ideal and reality. The former identifies certain characteristics as aspects of a proto-modernity, or at least heading in the right direction, and identifies the emergence of these character-istics as the central measure of structured historical change. Along these lines, historians have used as indices of salient change issues such as the origins of the state, the increasing role of bureaucracy, processes of institutionalisation and sharpening differentiations between religious and secular authority.[16] The second set of oppositions in effect repro-duces the divide between cultural and social history, in which ideas and representations are kept carefully separate from practices and actions.[17] Examples of this kind of opposition at work are the distinctions made between rhetoric and the strategies of negotiating actors that inform much of the work on dispute settlement, between ritual (perceived as cultural) and law present in much legal history, and a tenacious under-lying assumption that historical change must always, at root, be triggered (and not merely influenced) by some 'external' material factor such as climate change, or autonomous demographic or economic growth.[18]

Of course, none of these oppositions finds explicit support from those engaged in the Feudal Revolution in quite such bald terms. After all, most of them have long since individually been brought into question, both in the wider theoretical literature and historiographically.[19] Nevertheless, they continue to exercise a tacit influence on analyses of medieval society, and this plays a crucial role in isolating the ninth century from later developments. For, as Matthew Innes has noted, if we analyse the Carolingians in classically Weberian terms we can only find an enigmatic failure: an attempt to build a state that failed, a bureaucracy that fizzled out, a premature institutionalisation of authority that was in due course

---

[16] For a thoughtful inquiry into these issues, see C. Symes, 'When we talk about modernity', *American Historical Review* 116 (2011), 715–26; more particularly on religious matters, see M. de Jong, 'Ecclesia and the early medieval polity', in S. Airlie, W. Pohl and H. Reimitz, eds., *Staat im frühen Mittelalter* (Vienna, 2006), pp. 113–32.

[17] Cf. now P. Joyce, 'What is the social in social history?', *Past and Present* 206 (2010), 213–48.

[18] For a critique of the latter two positions, see J. Bowman, 'Do neo-Romans curse? Law, land, and ritual in the Midi (900–1100)', *Viator* 28 (1997), 1–32; and J. Moreland, 'Going native, becoming German', *postmedieval* 1 (2010), 142–9.

[19] The bibliography here is huge, but the parameters of a still-incipient debate can be found in works ranging from T. Kirsch, *Spirits and letters: reading, writing and charisma in African Christianity* (New York, 2008), to B. Latour, *Reassembling the social: an introduction to actor-network theory* (Oxford, 2005) and A. Mbembe, *On the postcolony* (Berkeley, 2001).

re-personalised.[20] Meanwhile, any attempt to link Carolingian intellectual and conceptual developments to actual historical reality is blocked by an almost unconscious conviction that these fields must be studied separately; that perhaps the Carolingian 'reforms' were influential in their own way, but there can have been little connection with the power-games being played out on the ground, best analysed through studies of actors' interest. It is significant that the small number of studies that have consciously rejected both these types of categorisation have also been successful at bringing the early into relation with the central Middle Ages, such as Dominique Iogna-Prat's recent work on the church's nature and activities.[21]

This study, too, seeks to break with these categorisations, in order to bring out more clearly certain crucial connections between the ninth and the twelfth centuries. Up to this point, two representations of the Carolingian period have been brought to bear on the Feudal Revolution debate, and the issue of periodisation that it represents, namely the statist views that once held sway and still remain important, and the turn to practices of domination ('lordship'), often conceived of as somehow prior to discursive construction, which has recently won prominence. Historiographical positions on the Feudal Revolution are in large part determined by which of these representations of the ninth century is employed. As Part I will show, the standard versions of these two approaches are indeed superficially difficult to reconcile, yet the evidence that supports each is unassailable. This has created a deadlock that has hamstrung the Feudal Revolution debate. The solution to this deadlock is not to attempt to sidestep the evidence, it is to reassess the entire question, and above all, to do so on the basis of a serious and sustained engagement with Carolingian evidence.

The foundations for such an engagement have been laid by a remarkable reinvigoration of Carolingian studies in recent decades which has taken many forms: the work of McKitterick on literacy and, more recently, memory and the construction of the past; of Nelson, MacLean and Hen on liturgy and kingship; of Innes, Stone and Airlie on the aristocracy; and of de Jong, Noble and Smith on the church, to name but a small selection of historians writing in English, a list that could easily be doubled even before considering research conducted in French, German and Italian.[22] No longer

---

[20] M. Innes, *State and society in the early Middle Ages: the middle Rhine valley, 400–1000* (Cambridge, 2000), is the classic treatment of this particular problem.

[21] D. Iogna-Prat, *La maison Dieu: une histoire monumentale de l'église au Moyen-âge (v. 800–v. 1200)* (Paris, 2006).

[22] See the Bibliography for works of these historians cited in this book.

is Charlemagne's empire considered to have been conservative or backward-looking. Terms like the Carolingian Renaissance or the Carolingian reforms remain as difficult to define as always, but it is ever clearer that however we choose to label it, Charlemagne and his heirs presided over a cultural efflorescence that cannot be pigeonholed within the conventional categories of religious, or political or social, but was rather all of these together.[23]

So, we may indeed ask whether the Carolingians tried to create a state which then failed, or whether the ninth century was already permeated by lordship; and as we will see, asking such questions produces revealing answers. However, allowing the parameters of the Feudal Revolution debate to determine in this way the questions we ask of the ninth century eventually leads to stalemate. Instead, therefore, of peering back at the Carolingians from the Feudal Revolution and the central Middle Ages, this book is anchored in the Carolingian period and in approaches to that period, and looks forward. Building on the advances in scholarship won by the historians mentioned above and many others, and on the basis of a defined set of evidence, it proposes a new approach that both resolves contradictions in the existing literature and simultaneously offers a new perspective on the Feudal Revolution debate. The argument, put bluntly, is that the Carolingian reforms worked to formalise social interaction across the entire social spectrum, and that most of the phenomena associated with the Feudal Revolution, and the new social formations apparent from the later eleventh century, can be seen as in part the long-term consequences of this process.

I do not seek to prove that this is the only possible interpretation of the historical changes whose evaluation is at stake here; most of the arguments discussed above have something to be said for them, after all. I merely wish to show that this approach fits the evidence well, and therefore calls for a reappraisal of the role of the Carolingians in the dominant periodisation. Nor does this book attempt to argue that all post-Carolingian history was simply a pre-determined unfolding of a process previously set in motion; indeed it attempts to identify variations in how Carolingian legacies were realised, with profound implications for the organisation of social life, and moreover to account for them. It does, however, argue that the Carolingian period was of foundational importance for what followed, which is the point that has been denied, ignored, or neglected by almost all those involved in the Feudal Revolution debate.

---

[23] M. Costambeys, M. Innes and S. MacLean, *The Carolingian world* (Cambridge, 2011); and R. McKitterick, ed., *Carolingian culture: emulation and innovation* (Cambridge, 1993) are excellent introductions.

Introduction

Precisely because this approach is relatively novel, two interventions that anticipated elements of it should be mentioned. In an important paper, Chris Wickham suggested that the Feudal Revolution in the tenth century could be associated with a process of the formalisation of social relations.[24] Around the same time, Matthew Innes suggested that the patterns of formal authority prevalent in Western Europe post-1000 increasingly rested on a perception of power as property, and that such a perception articulated a highly formalised and reified system of social relations.[25] This book elaborates and modifies these observations, confirming that what they denote is vital to understanding the issues raised by the Feudal Revolution debate, but also connecting it directly with Carolingian innovations in social organisation, whose scope, it argues, was wider than has hitherto been appreciated.

METHODOLOGY

The methodology that underlies this broad argument is drawn from a number of sources. Foremost is the research produced by the explosion of attention to 'symbolic communication' in the early and central Middle Ages, a strand of scholarship commonly associated with Gerd Althoff and his many students, though there is also a distinguished anglophone contribution to the field.[26] Conceived as an alternative to a constitutional history which lacked purchase on medieval realities, and with roots in older traditions of the study of medieval symbolism as well as Geertzian anthropology, the study of ritual blossomed in the wake of pathbreaking work by Karl Leyser on Ottonian ritual, suggesting that it could help explain how order was maintained in the post-Carolingian East Frankish kingdom. Indeed, to an extent this literature can be seen as functionally analogous to the Feudal Revolution debate to which German historians have tended to give short shrift.[27] These studies concentrate on elaborating the ways in which social status was confirmed and consolidated by means of a repertoire of signs and symbols whose meanings

[24] C. Wickham, 'Debate: the Feudal Revolution: comment 4', *Past and Present* 155 (1997), 196–208. This is a point Wickham has also made elsewhere, e.g. in his *Courts and conflict in twelfth-century Tuscany* (Oxford, 2003), pp. 18–19.
[25] Innes, *State*, pp. 241–50.
[26] For example, the work of T. Reuter, e.g. '"Pastorale pedum ante pedes apostolici posuit": Dis- and reinvestiture in the era of the investiture contest', in R. Gameson and H. Leyser, eds., *Belief and culture in the Middle Ages* (Oxford, 2001), pp. 197–210. See also C. Pössel, 'The magic of early medieval ritual', *EME* 17 (2009), 111–25, 'Symbolic communication and the negotiation of power at Carolingian regnal assemblies, 814–40', unpublished PhD thesis, Cambridge 2004.
[27] H.-W. Goetz, 'Gesellschaftliche Neuformierungen um die erste Jahrtausendwende? Zum Streit um die "mutation de l'an mil"', in A. Hubel and B. Schneidmüller, eds., *Aufbruch ins zweite Jahrtausend. Innovation und Kontinuität in der Mitte des Mittelalters*, Mittelalter-Forschungen 16 (Ostfildern 2004), pp. 31–50, gives a good review.

were well known to contemporaries. As is widely acknowledged and will be further explored later, there are a number of difficulties with the model thus conceived, but its challenge to pay more attention to the forms of communication that underpin and indeed constitute all interactions has proved tremendously stimulating.[28]

This body of work can usefully be brought into dialogue with a broader set of ideas and approaches that can be loosely termed anthropological. Some of these focus on the concept and practice of property. Like lawyers, anthropologists have long recognised that property must be analysed not as a category of objects but as a set of social relations, whose scope and intensity vary over time and space, and that must be considered alongside other forms of social interaction. Christian Lund's study of Ghana is an exemplary exploration of these issues.[29] Other studies have concentrated on ritual, and not always in the same way, or for the same reasons, as historians have. Ritual has in fact become a little unfashionable in anthropology recently, yet work by Asad on the force of ritual practices in medieval Europe, and by Maurice Bloch, using Madagascan material to reflect on the extent to which ritual can be thought of as a deliberately impoverished form of communication, have much to offer the medievalist.[30] The same is true of research into the question of indeterminacy, which investigates how the irreducible polysemy of human interaction with each other and the material world is managed in practice, not least by means of processes of formalisation: here, the work of S. F. Moore is central.[31]

A final dimension is added by attention to how these processes unfold over time. A number of important studies could be cited here, but it is worthwhile to single out the Comaroffs' study of the missionary encounter amongst the Tswana, in what is now South Africa. Arguing that nineteenth-century missionaries there were attempting the 'colonisation of consciousness', the Comaroffs drew attention to the importance of conflicts over signifying practices in the creation of all forms of social domination, in particular noting the impossibility of clearly separating these issues from those over material resources.[32] Their book offers a case-study of a contestation over the scope, precision and content of symbolic practice that is very suggestive from a comparative point of view.

---

[28] P. Buc, *The dangers of ritual: between early medieval texts and social scientific theory* (Princeton, 2001); S. Patzold, '"... inter pagensium nostrorum gladios vivimus". Zu den "Spielregeln" der Konfliktführung in Niederlothringen zur Zeit der Ottonen und frühen Salier', *Zeitschrift der Savigny-Stiftung für Rechtsgeschichte, Germanistische Abteilung* 118 (2001), 578–99.

[29] C. Lund, *Local politics and the dynamics of property in Africa* (New York, 2008).

[30] T. Asad, *Genealogies of religion: discipline and reasons of power in Christianity and Islam* (Baltimore, 1993); M. Bloch, *Ritual, history and power: selected papers in anthropology* (London, 1989).

[31] S. F. Moore, *Law as process: an anthropological process* (London, 1978).

[32] J. Comaroff and J. Comaroff, *Of revelation and revolution*, 2 vols. (Chicago, 1991–7).

The intention in referring to this material is not to 'wedge Java into Francia', since there is much that is inapplicable and potentially highly misleading in anthropological scholarship – not least the specific colonial context that was the precondition for that scholarship.[33] These anthropological insights are used not as a discrete source of knowledge that can be applied to early and central medieval realities, but as a set of ideas that can help us question the assumptions whose influence on research is otherwise difficult to detect.[34] For example, the idea that property can be considered as a particular kind of social interaction, distant from but not entirely unrelated to unregulated and inchoate forms, helps make sense of the spread of property into new spheres of social life in the period in question, beyond tired appeals to immanent principles of heredity. The observation that human interaction is discursively constructed does not mean that the material can be ignored, but it does mean that we cannot treat people merely as transcendental actors strategising and negotiating in pursuit of their interests. Finally, the idea that formalisation is really a process of limiting the proliferation of meaning, effectively providing standards of interpretation, has enormous consequences for our evaluation of a range of developments in the period, as will become clear. In short, reference to this range of ideas allows a definitive break with the organising oppositions mentioned above, that phenomena can be defined with reference to some transcendental scale of modernity, and that ideas can be for all intents and purposes set aside when dealing with practice.[35]

GEOGRAPHY AND SOURCES

Though this book does not seek to offer a total history of the period, its analytical scope is avowedly wide-ranging, and ideally its arguments would be buttressed by material drawn from the whole of Western Europe. For pragmatic reasons, however, this book is based on a more restricted set of evidence, one defined geographically (see map, p. xiv). Such a geographical restriction inevitably (and justifiably) raises questions about the general validity of the argument. Yet regionally rooted research has its own advantages which should not be overlooked. It encourages the

---

[33] Cf. T. Asad, ed., *Anthropology and the colonial encounter* (London, 1973). For the phrase, B. Rosenwein, 'Francia and Polynesia: rethinking anthropological approaches', in G. Algazi, V. Groebner and B. Jussen, eds., *Negotiating the gift. Pre-modern figurations of exchange* (Göttingen, 2003), pp. 361–79.

[34] See Buc, *Dangers*, and J. Goodman, 'History and anthropology', in M. Bentley, ed., *Companion to Historiography* (London, 1997), pp. 783–804.

[35] Most work on concepts of modernity have not engaged much with the earlier Middle Ages; cf. C. Wickham, *The inheritance of Rome: a history of Europe from 400 to 1000* (London, 2010), pp. 5–6.

historian at least to aim at comprehensiveness, and to include material which might seem tangential but which can instead be read as challenging the categories on which relevance is decided. It also permits a much closer and more detailed engagement with these sources, generating thereby more rigorous analysis.

Still, though geographically focused, it bears reiteration that this book is not conceived as another regional study, but as a contribution, using a particular set of sources as its anchor, to a wider historiographical debate. The area in question is therefore a large one, consisting of the modern French *régions* of Lorraine and Champagne (a total of eight *départements*), together with parts of Belgium, southern Luxembourg, the German *Land* of the Saarland, and part of that of the Rheinland-Pfalz. Dominated by three rivers (Marne, Moselle and Meuse) and three great cities (Rheims, Trier and Metz), the area lies between the Ile de France in the west (Paris, Senlis), the Rhineland to the east (Mainz, Frankfurt), Aachen to the north and the Burgundian lands to the south. Geologically, most of it can be described as the eastern section of the great Parisian basin which extends to the hills of the Rhineland.[36] The western portion of this area was some-times called Champagne in the early Middle Ages, though this label did not imply any clear boundaries, while some of the lands of the east were intermittently labelled as the Moselle duchy. Together, these formed in the Merovingian period a large portion of the Austrasian heartland of the Frankish kingdom. The landscape included much good-quality farming land for both pasture and crops, separated by low ridges, as well as wide expanses of woodland, notably around the rugged uplands of the Ardennes, Eifel and Vosges, and the Brie and Langres plateaux.

This area was not selected as a field of study by chance. It offers an interesting scale of analysis: larger than that used by more conventional regional studies, and thus more suitable for the development of generalised arguments, but more manageable, empirically speaking, than a generic history of Frankish and post-Frankish society. It also crosses political and scholarly boundaries. Divided now between four different countries, it was divided then, in different ways at different times, between the kings of West and East Francia. Not only does the study of such an area bring French and

---

[36] For a basic description of the geography, see F. Cardot, *L'espace et le pouvoir. Etude sur l'Austrasie mérovingienne* (Paris, 1987); G. Chabot, *Géographie régionale de la France* (Paris, 1966); and E. Wightman, *Gallia Belgica* (London, 1985), pp. 1–5. Geographers use 'Parisian basin' to indicate a geographical unity between the Armorican Massif and the Vosges, and 'Paris basin' to label that part of the basin immediately around Paris itself: see Y. Dewolf and C. Pomerol, 'The Parisian basin', in E. Koster, ed., *The physical geography of Western Europe* (Oxford, 2005), pp. 251–66. The region under investigation is effectively therefore the eastern 'Parisian basin', though I refrain from using the term to avoid confusion.

German historiographical approaches into direct relation with each other, it also directs attention to the question of differentiation within an area that was relatively homogeneous in the earlier period. Finally, the bulk of recent work on the Feudal Revolution has been southern in focus, and indeed much of the most innovative recent work on early medieval Europe has skirted the heartlands of Frankish power.[37] This can be justified on good methodological grounds, but a contribution to the debates based squarely on northern Frankish material nevertheless seems timely. It should be noted that I have sometimes made use of evidence from beyond this area in the shape of material produced around royal courts, partly to provide consolidatory material, and partly to be better able to assess the interaction between centre and locality. I have, however, systematically excluded Italian sources, though not because the arguments I am proposing necessarily do not apply to the peninsula, but because I suspect the timing of developments there to have been sufficiently distinct as to require separate treatment.

As one might expect from an area of this size, there is a tremendous range of relevant evidence. Most of this is preserved in ecclesiastical archives, but this does not represent a serious problem when studying a society which invested so heavily in the church, and in which that church played a leading (perhaps dominant) role. At the heart of this study is what might be called administrative material. Taking pride of place here are charters, the documents of legal practice preserved mostly by monasteries that record transfers of land. The corpus is not as rich as that surviving from other neighbouring regions, but is nevertheless substantial. Particularly important in the ninth century are documents preserved in the cartularies of the monasteries of Prüm, Gorze and St-Mihiel, and in the substantial section of that of Wissembourg relating to the Saargau. In the tenth century, the archives of St-Vanne of Verdun and Montier-en-Der become more prominent, and a growing number of episcopal foundations produced much material from the eleventh century. A large proportion of these charters was issued by kings, and such royal diplomata were probably more likely to be preserved in one form or another than so-called private charters, but these more informal productions, attesting

[37] Apart from the synthesis of Poly and Bournazel, the most recent sustained contribution from a northern perspective was R. Fossier, *La terre et les hommes en Picardie jusqu'à la fin du XIIIe siècle*, 2 vols. (Paris, 1968), whose work is characterised by a notoriously minimalist view of the Carolingian period. The Rhineland that forms the focus of Innes, *State*, was a heartland of Frankish power, but in a quite distinctive way. For Brittany, see the still-definitive W. Davies, *Small worlds: the village community in early medieval Brittany* (Berkeley, 1988); for Bavaria, W. Brown, *Unjust seizure: conflict, interest and authority in an early medieval society* (Ithaca, 2001); for Alsace, H. Hummer, *Politics and power in early medieval Europe: Alsace and the Frankish realm, 600–1000* (Cambridge, 2005); for the region around Farfa in Italy, M. Costambeys, *Power and patronage in the early medieval Italy: local society, Italian politics, and the abbey of Farfa, c.700–900* (Cambridge, 2007).

transactions between churches and less exalted parties, nevertheless represent the bulk of the material.

These documents of practice can be supplemented with other kinds of administrative text, again overwhelmingly produced by ecclesiastical institutions. Particularly important here are estate management texts. The polyptychs of Prüm, St-Rémi, Montier-en-Der and Mettlach are especially useful since they come from the heart of the area considered, but other monasteries and institutions also had holdings here, for example St-Maur-des-Fossés and St-Germain des Prés.[38] Later material of this kind is provided by Chaumousey, St-Dié and St-Pierre of Metz, to name the most prominent institutions. Sources of this practical nature are supplemented by letters, many concerning routine matters of day-to-day business. In the ninth century, the letters are dominated by the collections of Carolingian bishops, of which Frothar of Toul (d.847), Adventius of Metz (d.875) and the notoriously prolific Archbishop Hincmar of Rheims (d.882) are the most important. Again, there is less material from the tenth century, with the important exception of Archbishop Gerbert of Rheims (d.1003), and again the eleventh century sees a renewed diversity, including letters sent by Count Stephen of Blois-Champagne (d.1102) from the crusade to his wife, Countess Adela, together with a great range of smaller, relatively neglected collections, like the letters of Abbot Walo of St-Arnulf (d. *c.*1097).

Though these 'practical' texts lie at this book's core, I have not neglected other material; after all, over-reliance on documentary material has been a criticism levelled at the Feudal Revolution model, so it is methodologically vital for any study to take a broad approach. Measured by sheer bulk, it is hagiographical production that dominates the records. Saints' lives and associated miracle collections are preserved in their scores, offering insight into almost every major ecclesiastical institution. Some ninth-century texts are justifiably renowned, like the revised lives of St Remigius and of St Goar, while others, although more obscure, can still cast light onto local conditions. Some, like the *Vita Dagoberti* from Stenay, are regrettably difficult to date, which considerably limits their usefulness.[39] In this field, the material does not dry up in the tenth century, and the region around Gorze and Metz was particularly active, though the work of Adso of Montier-en-Der (d. *c.*992) deserves mention too. The eleventh and early twelfth centuries saw another wave of *vitae*, some of

---

[38] I have excluded the polyptych of Wissembourg partly because the lands concerned are mostly beyond my region of interest, but also in view of the problems with the edition noted by M. Gockel in his review, which make it difficult to rely upon its datings: 'Kritische Bemerkungen zu einer Neuausgabe des Liber possessionum Wizenburgensis', *Hessisches Jahrbuch für Landesgeschichte* 39 (1989), 353–80.

[39] See C. Carozzi, 'La vie de saint Dagobert de Stenay: histoire et hagiographie', *Revue Belge de Philologie et d'Histoire* 62 (1984), 225–58.

which, like the Life of Bishop Godfrey of Soissons, are very considerable pieces of writing, whilst others can be thought of as parts of concerted hagiographical campaigns.[40] Alongside these texts, the work of the saints in the world was recorded by the compilation of miracle collections, some clearly part of the initial redaction of a life, others added at later dates. As well as offering information on monastic textual and spiritual strategies, these works provide a wealth of anecdotal detail unavailable elsewhere.

Perhaps more obviously useful is the body of more narrowly historio-graphical material produced in the area. It is particularly rich in episcopal histories known as *Gesta*, notably the account of Rheims by Flodoard (d. 966), which makes use of, and thereby preserves, much lost material, but the histories of the bishops of Verdun, Toul and Trier are also important. Monastic historical and annalistic writing is surprisingly diverse, ranging from short pamphlets like that produced for Werden to longer works including reference to charters, like those made at St-Mihiel and Mouzon. A number of historical texts with a wider remit have survived too. One might include in this category, for example, the histories of Richer of Rheims (d.998), or the chronicle of Hugh of St-Vanne/Flavigny (d. *c.*1114), or that of Regino of Prüm (d.915). These are invaluable texts, though often tantalisingly incomplete. Regino of Prüm's chronicle, for example, offers only clues for the first half of the ninth century, leaving many years blank and in others giving details only about the Loire region, where Prüm had some holdings.[41]

There is a wealth of what might be called theoretical literature, particularly legal, theological and liturgical texts. In the ninth century, Archbishop Hincmar of Rheims is the outstanding figure.[42] He produced a magnificent array of works tackling theological and legal points, was heavily involved in the production of west Frankish capitularies, and issued influential episcopal statutes (instructional texts for local priests) too. Whether, or how, one can generalise from what Hincmar says to the entire Frankish empire is a point which can be debated, but it is not essential here, where the primary stress is on Hincmar as a witness for his own region. In any case, the production of substantial discursive texts was far from monopolised by Hincmar. Quite apart from anonymous texts which are probably (though not certainly) from the area, we have ninth-century works from abbots like Smaragdus of St-Mihiel (d. *c.*840), monks like Amalarius of Trier (d. *c.*850) and Wandalbert of Prüm

---

[40] K. Krönert, *L'exaltation de Trèves: écriture hagiographique et passé historique de la métropole mosellane, viiie–xie siècle* (Ostfildern, 2010).

[41] On Regino's choices, see S. Maclean, 'Insinuation, censorship and the struggle for late Carolingian Lotharingia in Regino of Prüm's chronicle', *English Historical Review* 124 (2009), 1–28.

[42] See, still, J. Devisse, *Hincmar archevêque de Reims, 845–882*, 3 vols. (Geneva, 1975–6); M. Stratmann, 'Zur Wirkungsgeschichte Hinkmars von Reims', *Francia* 22 (1995), 1–43.

(d. *c*.870), all of whom made contributions to a great number of topics. There is rather less material of this kind from the tenth century, but our sources blossom again from the mid eleventh century. The work of Wenric of Trier (d. *c*.1090), Humbert of Moyenmoutier (d.1061), and more minor figures, like Hugo Metellus of Toul (d. *c*.1150), not to mention the voluminous output of Sigibert of Gembloux (d.1112) who spent time in Metz, all have close connections with the lands between Meuse and Moselle, and as a consequence, are potentially important witnesses to developments in a range of fields taking place there.

Needless to say, not too much faith should be put in the way this material has been categorised in the previous paragraphs, another reason why the whole range of evidence must be taken into account, rather than excising whole swathes on a priori grounds. Individual texts routinely defy any categories we choose to apply. Charters and collections of canon law, for example, are as much historical as legal, and theological texts were intended to have an impact just as real as more transparently administrative texts. Moreover, whenever appropriate, I try to bring in the manuscript context of these sources, which often sheds a great deal of light on how we should interpret what they have to say, and often challenges the ways historians organise their evidence.

One final kind of evidence that needs no justification for inclusion is the material traces left from the period. I have studied the local archaeology insofar as it is published in print or online, most notably relating to castles and rural settlements, not as a supplement for textual sources but in its own right. Here, though, the nationalist historiography is harder to put into context, since recent French research in this field, thanks to the remarkable surge in rescue excavations, has been more prolific than Belgian or German. I have also studied the published material on coins, which can be interpreted to give indications about economic activity and the distribution of political power, though by its nature, such evidence is not always well-placed to help with geographically weighted studies.

Analysis of the Carolingian evidence, central to the argument of this book and so discussed at length, is provided by the three chapters that form Part I. Part II, divided into two chapters, engages with the often recalcitrant but fascinating evidence from the tenth and early eleventh centuries, with Chapter 4 studying the decline in royal authority, and Chapter 5 devoted to indications of more subtle underlying changes. In Part III, based on the evidence from the mid eleventh century and later, Chapter 6 deals with lord–peasant relations, and Chapter 7 the forms of interaction within the elite, while Chapter 8 offers an account of how, and why, the lands on either side of the Meuse began to diverge. The conclusion finally provides a summary of the argument and suggests further areas for research.

PART I

The parameters of Carolingian society

Any understanding of the processes of change that took place between 800 and 1100 inevitably depends, explicitly or otherwise, on conceptions of the Carolingian period. The initial model of the Feudal Revolution provided by Duby, and indeed most subsequent reformulations, rested on an institutionalised vision of that world. These were Ganshof's, or, later, Karl-Ferdinand Werner's Carolingians: a centre controlling the locality through effective administration, where the public was distinguished from and dominated over the private, for all the world like a post-Westphalian nation-state, simply on a larger scale and more prone to corruption.[1] Most criticism of Duby's model has mobilised quite different visions of the ninth century. If that Ganshofian public order was illusory, if in fact the ninth century was always really suffused with 'lordship' and informal practices of domination that undermined the formal apparatus of government, then Duby's distinctions fail.

The logic here is impeccable, and though the starkness of the contrast can be rhetorically softened, it cannot be denied that to reconcile the two views of the Carolingian world on which these arguments rest seems awkward. The difficulty, as we shall see, is that both positions can be strongly supported from the Carolingian evidence, with recourse neither to special pleading nor to naïve face-value source interpretation. The problem is therefore not with the sources for one or either approach, but with our categories of analysis; consequently, the only way to escape the impasse is to bring an alternative perspective on the ninth century to bear.

This is the argument that the next three chapters will develop. The first two are dedicated to showing that the evidence from the lands between Marne and Moselle is indeed genuinely capable of sustaining both a top-down perspective and one centred on the local exercise of power in the ninth century, in order to

[1] F.-L. Ganshof, *Feudalism*, tr. P. Grierson (London, 1952); K. F. Werner, '*Missus – Marchio – Comes*. Entre l'administration centrale et l'administration locale de l'Empire carolingien', in W. Paravicini and K. F. Werner, eds., *Histoire comparée de l'administration (IVe–XVIIe siècles)* (Munich, 1980), pp. 191–239.

show that the interpretative difficulty is a real one. A resolution to this problem is provided by Chapter 3, focusing on the forms of symbolic and communicative practice. This chapter reinforces the arguments put forward by some early medieval historians that the Carolingian institutions of power should not be anachronistically interpreted as yearnings for a state, but as part of attempts to bring order to the world. That step allows us to see that the formal structures of Chapter 1 and the informal processes of Chapter 2 which jointly characterise this period must not be thought of as separate spheres, but as relational, and interacting, fields of activity. It is from this vantage point that we can then begin to consider in what ways Carolingian efforts to reform society gradually succeeded in changing it, the topic of the subsequent chapters.

Chapter 1

INSTITUTIONAL INTEGRATION

What his brother [Charles the Bald] had done badly in the kingdom, he [King Louis] would correct, and what his brother had let slip through negligence, he would make sure carefully to improve.
Archbishop Hincmar of Rheims, *On keeping faith with Charles.*[1]

For many historians, one of the most striking features of the Carolingian ninth century is the imposition of a rigorous and relatively centralised system of government upon the highly regionalised kingdom which Pippin and his heirs took over after the formal elimination of the Merovingian dynasty in the mid eighth century. Notwithstanding the cultural vitality of late Merovingian Francia, it can scarcely be doubted that 'the comprehensive and ambitious scheme of Carolingian administration' meant Frankish kingship impinged more on the provinces than hitherto: and if this was true anywhere, it was true for the area with which we are concerned, at the heart of the Carolingian empire ruled by Charlemagne and his successors.[2] The key figures in this reinvigorated administration were local office-holders, namely the count and the bishop, together with their various agents. In addition, the Carolingian king exerted influence through unmediated control of local resources, and through personal presence, whether indirectly, through palaces, or directly, by visiting the area. These aspects of ninth-century society can be considered the formal institutions of Carolingian rule.

Scepticism about the actual penetration of society by these formal institutions is a key part of the recent critique of the Feudal Revolution

---

[1] '[U]t quae frater eius in eo perperam egit ipse corrigat, et quod per negligentiam frater eius admisit, ipse per diligentiam emendare procurat': Hincmar of Rheims, *De fide Carolo servanda, PL*, vol. cxxv, col. 963.

[2] R. McKitterick, *The Frankish kingdoms under the Carolingians, 751–987* (London, 1983), p. 77. For the vitality, see Y. Hen, *Roman barbarians: the royal court and culture in the early medieval west* (Basingstoke, 2007). For centrality, see E. Ewig, 'Descriptio Franciae', in W. Braunfels, ed., *Karl der Grosse*, 5 vols. (Düsseldorf, 1967), vol. v, pp. 143–72.

model, which suggests a certain superficiality: these institutions look very impressive on paper, but left local society largely untouched in practice. The purpose of this chapter is to demonstrate that the evidence from the lands between Marne and Moselle for a thorough integration of the locality with the centre by means of these newly invigorated formal institutions is in fact substantial and cannot be ignored, and by implication that any analysis of the ninth century which does not do it justice is by that token necessarily incomplete. The aim is to prove that earlier approaches to the Carolingian period cannot be dismissed out of hand, though certain ideas sometimes to be found within these approaches, such as a priori division between church and state, cannot be justified and so will receive little discussion.[3] A relatively detailed assessment is therefore an integral part of the argument that is being proposed, even though in Chapter 3 we shall have cause to refine the standard interpretation of the evidence here set out.

COUNTS AND THE LOCALITY

In place of the regional duchies and dukes attested by Merovingian and early Carolingian sources in Champagne and around the Moselle, Carolingian rulers appear to have developed a finer-grained organisation, using officials named counts (*comites*) as their local representatives.[4] According to the edicts known as capitularies, it was the count who was tasked with channelling royal commands into the localities and with guaranteeing peace, tracking down thieves, implementing other decrees and reporting back to the emperor on progress achieved. They were endowed with resources, the *res de comitatu*, to give them the wherewithal to perform the arduous duties to which they were so vigorously exhorted.[5] The intention was to confine violence as far as possible to those holding office, as part of course of a general attempt to encompass social interaction within *ministeria*.[6]

At first sight, the evidence from the lands between Marne and Moselle showing that this system was no mere Aachen flight of fancy appears disappointingly slight. While historians have traditionally made use of geographical terminologies found in charters to estimate the number of counts and even reconstruct micro-political history, this is methodologically

---

[3] Cf. de Jong, 'Ecclesia and the early medieval polity'.

[4] For the Merovingian background, see I. Wood, *The Merovingian kingdoms 450–751* (London, 1994) and more specifically, Cardot, *L'espace*. Memories of the Moselle duchy are preserved in *DDCM* nos. 148 and 149.

[5] *DDCF* nos. 94 (Toul) and 152 (Langres).

[6] For example, Synodal letter of the Council of Paris 829, *MGH Capit.*, vol. II, ch. 29., p. 38.

unsound, as will be discussed in Chapter 5. In fact we do not know how many counts there were in this area (though an estimate of around a score at any one time would be probably of the right order of magnitude); nor do we know where they were based; nor do we know much about individual counts or their families. For example, we know the names of nine counts established by King Charles the Bald in 877 as a rotating retinue to attend his mistrusted son Louis when around the River Meuse, and we can be sure that these were powerful men in the region. Even so, only a couple can be positively identified.[7] For counts of rural areas, seldom documented other than as witnesses to occasional local charters or by passing reference in royal diplomas or capitularies, we can do little except gratefully accept the hints proffered by onomastics.[8] It should further be noted that we know very little about comital deputies, either. Enough evidence exists for viscounts and other figures like *centenarii* in some way subordinated to the count to suggest they existed, but compared to the count, they seem insignificant.[9]

It might seem, then, that we are reduced to making best use of anecdotal material to see whether counts truly exercised an efficacious authority on behalf of kings in the area. This kind of material is at least relatively plentiful. For example, Charlemagne's famous response to a count's series of eminently practical questions relating to collection of tolls, validity of charters of manumission, and problems in discipline, for all that it was probably produced at the centre, survives only in two manuscripts with connections both to Lotharingia and Rheims, suggesting that the puzzled count, and the problems he sought to overcome, came from the area.[10] Letters, formulae, and hagiography also preserve anecdotal documentation of comital responsibility for poachers, and the count's performance of his role.[11] The best anecdotal evidence, however, comes

[7] *MGH Capit.*, vol. II, no. 281, ch. 15.
[8] Cf. K. Schmid's discussion of the obscure, but apparently important, late-ninth-century Count Guntram, in 'Unerforschte Quellen aus quellenarmer Zeit: zur *amicitia* zwischen Heinrich I und dem westfränkisch König Robert im Jahre 923', *Francia* 12 (1984), 119–47.
[9] Ninth-century *vicecomites* are attested around Laon (*PL*, vol. CXXV, col. 1037 – Hincmar of Rheims's *Expostiones*); around Châlons (*HRE*, bk III, ch. 23, pp. 313–14, *c.*860s); and around Soissons (AD de l'Aisne, MS 455, f. 70r – the cartulary of St-Crepin, Soissons). *Traditiones Wizenburgenses: d. Urkunden d. Klosters Weissenburg: 661–864*, ed. K. Glöckner and A. Doll (Darmstadt, 1979), no. 201 (807) records *centenarii* from the Saargau.
[10] *MGH Capit.*, vol. I, no. 58, p. 145. The recipient was almost certainly a count, since one question was whether it was the count or the *cancellarius* who took the money from making a charter. The manuscripts in question are Paris BnF. lat. 9654 and Vatican Pal. lat. 582.
[11] Einhard, *Epistolae*, ed. K. Hampe, *MGH Epp.*, vol. V (Hanover, 1898–9), nos. 47 and 48; *Vita Nivardi*, ed. W. Levison, *MGH SRM*, vol. V (Hanover, 1896), pp. 239–341 for violence of the count. Compare 'Fragments du recueil perdu de formules franques dites "Formulae Pithoei"', ed. R. Poupardin, *BEC* 69 (1908), pp. 643–62 – a text linked to Laon – where at p. 656 someone is judged at a count's *mallum* for the theft of a horse (cf. below, p. 146); and *MGH Formulae*, p. 191 and p. 256 for murder, and p. 194 over status.

from Flodoard's *History of the Church of Rheims*, written in the mid tenth century but registering much earlier material. The letters that Flodoard records as having been sent by Archbishop Hincmar of Rheims to various counts on a whole range of issues in his capacity as royal envoy (*missus*) show that the mid-ninth-century counts around Rheims received letters from *missi* on a regular basis. For example, Hincmar noted that a certain Count Bertram in the Tardenois had made people in his county swear an oath to the king and summoned people to his court *per bannum*, 'by command', just as capitularies indicate he was supposed to.[12]

The evidence for public exactions

Ultimately, though, one cannot prove a systematic kind of control simply by reference to anecdotal evidence, however suggestive, for it can always be dismissed as exceptional or unrepresentative in some way. We need therefore to see whether more general points can be made if we approach our evidence more subtly. One possibility is to make use of the plentiful evidence from this area for exemptions and exceptions: anecdotal in a sense, but indicative nevertheless of broader realities. Exemptions from public duties were not always explicitly linked to counts, but they provide evidence for the framework in which counts were expected to be active, and therefore they help shift the burden of proof.

One particularly plentiful kind of source are charters of royal immunity given to churches, texts exempting the church from the activities of royal agents, and many of which explicitly indicate that free men resident on the church's lands remained liable to public exactions.[13] Immunities bestowed by Charlemagne upon the cathedrals of Metz and Trier are clear about the public services which were not exempted, specifically referring to army service, guard and bridge duty.[14] Whether these strictures were observed cannot be known from these texts, but this was not merely empty rhetoric. After all, immunities were even given to Rheims for certain named estates, showing that the texts were not simply generic, and one capitulary text directly discussed the practical implications of an immunity charter (*praeceptum immunitatis*) for the count's jurisdiction over landless free men resident on a church's estate.[15] A number of immunity-related

[12] *HRE*, bk III, ch. 26, p. 342. The underlying issue was that Haimo, Hincmar's *fidelis*, had set out on the king's *servitium* and could not attend Bertram's *placitum*.
[13] E.g., *DDCM* nos. 71 (St-Germain des Prés), 193 (Paris); *DLP* nos. 624 (Murbach) and 534 (Hornbach).
[14] *DDCM* nos. 66 and 91.
[15] For the Rheims immunities, see *HRE*, bk II, ch. 11, p. 158, and ch. 17, p. 170 for Juvigny, Crugny and Courville. There are some question marks over these texts, but they are certainly ninth

texts bring us still closer to practice, like the writs Emperor Lothar I sent to the counts around Prüm, reminding them of that monastery's immunity.[16] Evidence that the monasteries of St-Rémi and St-Maur-des-Fossés took dues linked to royal obligations from their tenants may give an indication of the concrete content of an immunity.[17] From a different angle, so does another text issued by Lothar for Prüm, stating that anyone who killed a dependant (*servus*) linked to the monastery was to pay the fine (*freda*) not to royal agents (*publici actores*), but to Prüm.[18] Exemptions from a system can, after all, point to that system's strength, not its weakness.

There is also evidence for public exactions not directly associated with the immunity. Three examples, relating to different forms of public obligation, are particularly instructive. A village community at Awans in the Ardennes, held responsible for the murder of a priest, had to pay his *leudis* or *wergild* to Prüm, to which the king had given the land, rather than to the royal agent, who would probably have been the count.[19] Another charter attests how in the time of Bishop Drogo of Metz (d.855), a certain Winebert had transferred his property to the monastery of St-Arnulf as part of an arrangement to free himself and his children of evidently effective public exactions. The charter, issued by King Lothar II in 856, barely survived, its verso side ominously marked 'useless charter' in a twelfth-century hand, so perhaps this arrangement was more common than it now seems.[20] Not everyone, though, sought to evade their duties. A little earlier, a certain Folcuin, probably a local free landowner around Remiremont in the Vosges, had gone with Frankish armies to fight the Slavs. His case is known only because he entrusted his lands to an unfortunately short-lived royal free man, whose estates automatically fell to the king on his death, as a dismayed Folcuin discovered on his return.[21]

There are signs, too, that formal legal status, though far from defining social status, certainly informed it, with implications for the formal distribution of authority. Much of the recent work on freedom has

---

century, at the latest. For the capitulary, H. Mordek, *Bibliotheca capitularium regum Francorum manuscripta: Überlieferung und Traditionszusammenhang der fränkischen Herrschererlasse* (Munich, 1995), Appendix II, no. 19, ch. 18.

[16] *DLothI* no. 57 (c.841), relating to the *potestas* of Prüm. Cf. *HRE*, bk II, ch. 19, p. 175.

[17] Specifically, the *bos aquensis* (Aachen ox) and the *heribannum*, mentioned in the polyptych of St-Rémi and the polyptych of St-Maur: *Le polyptyque et les listes de cens de l'abbaye de Saint-Remi de Reims (9ᵉ–11ᵉ siècle)*, ed. J-P. Devroey (Rheims, 1984), ch. 16 (p. 15); and *Das Polyptychon und die Notitia de Areis von Saint-Maur-des-Fossés*, ed. D. Hägermann and A. Hedwig (Sigmaringen, 1990), ch. 6 (p. 92). Cf. the *hostilicium*, mentioned throughout the polyptych of Prüm (*Das Prümer Urbar*, ed. I. Schwab (Düsseldorf, 1983) e.g. p. 166), and the polyptych of Montier-en-Der (*Das Polyptichon von Montierender*, ed. C.-D. Droste (Trier, 1988), e.g. ch. 27).

[18] *DLothI*, no. 137.   [19] *DLothI*, no. 132.

[20] *DLothII*, no. 6. The note *carta inutilis* was crossed out, which explains the charter's survival.

[21] *DLP* no. 739 (the charter survives only as a formulary).

rightly stressed negotiability, but sometimes the distinction between legally free and legally unfree was both sharp and significant, with certain duties and privileges resting on a stratum of free men, often labelled ethnically as Frankish. Carolingian texts from this area routinely distinguished between *Franci homines* and *coloni* along these lines, and a concrete example of what these distinctions meant is provided by a dispute from around Laon in the 870s. A certain Nivin claimed the right to defend himself with his weapons, a typical privilege of freedom, because 'he was a Frank'. In contrast, some of Nivin's followers were legally unfree, and so in theory, at least, could be subjected to the ordeal.[22] No wonder, then, that counts and their delegates presided over enquiries to establish individuals' formal legal status, as recorded in hagiographical texts and indeed through a good dozen references in various northern Frankish formularies, collections of sample documents preserved in Carolingian-period manuscripts.[23]

The mallum *court*

A second kind of approach to discerning the reality of comital power in this area concentrates on the conceptual significance of the Carolingian count's court, the so-called *mallum* or *mallum publicum*. Recent discussions about the *mallum* have been shaped by what has been thought to be Duby's implication that it was somehow more fair, legitimate, or binding than courts in later periods, because it meted out judgement rather than relying on arbitration. Historians working on conflict studies have discussed this idea, and their conclusions have been in general critical.[24] However, in the midst of this debate, a potentially rather important shift in what *mallum* actually meant has been neglected.

In the earliest uses of the word, in the pre-Carolingian Frankish law codes and particularly the *Lex Salica*, the meaning of the *mallum* is ambiguous but seems to label any judicial meeting, in particular those

---

[22] Hincmar of Rheims, *Epistolae Ad Ludovicum Germaniae*, MGH Concilia, vol. IV, ch. 14, pp. 422–3, for the *Franci/coloni* distinction. For Nivin, see Hincmar of Rheims, *Opusculum in LV Capitulis*, ed. R. Schieffer, *Die Streitschriften Hinkmars von Reims und Hinkmars von Laon 869–871*, MGH Concilia (Hanover, 2003), pp. 308–10.

[23] *Miracula Dionysii* (BHL 2201-), ed. J. Mabillon, *Acta sanctorum ordinis sancti Benedicti*, vol. III:ii (Paris, 1672), pp. 358–423, bk I, ch. 23. Formula references can be found in *MGH Formulae*, in the texts labelled as *Cartae Senonenses, Formulae Bignoniae, Formulae Senonenses recentiores, Lindonbrogianae* and *Merkelianae* (excluding evidence from Reichenau and St-Gall). The second largest category of comital enquiry concerned murder (four). For a recent discussion of these manuscripts, see A. Rio, *Legal practice and the written word in the early Middle Ages: Frankish formulae, c.500–1000* (Cambridge, 2009).

[24] S. White, 'Tenth-century courts'.

at village-level.[25] It was in other words a popular court, that institution which historians such as Wickham have been prepared to countenance as a genuine post- or non-Roman novelty in public life. In the later eighth and ninth century, however, the *mallum* came to describe a very different kind of court. In Carolingian-period texts, it was associated very strongly, indeed almost exclusively, with specifically comital or at least officially directed meetings, and clearly distinguished from lesser courts (*minora placita*). Of the twenty references to *mallum* courts in the Carolingian-period manuscripts of northern Frankish formularies, seventeen are linked to counts, the remainder to *missi* or *vicarii*. The association of comital activity with the *mallum*, and Carolingian promotion of the court, is particularly strong in late Carolingian capitularies, such as Charles the Bald's 873 Quierzy capitulary.[26] In texts like these, the *mallum* was identified as the only legitimate venue for certain kinds of court action. The Quierzy capitulary continued to remind its audience that the *mallum* should not be held in a church, 'because it is not right that men should be sentenced to death, dismembered and whipped, there where according to the capitularies they should have peace if they fled'.[27]

It appears, in short, that the *mallum* underwent a redefinition, moving from indicating a kind of 'bottom-up' traditional meeting of free Franks to a more specific, almost technical label for a meeting held under the aegis of the count or his representative: an attempt to integrate all political activity into a framework ostensibly legitimised by Frankish tradition, but practically speaking a creation of the Carolingian court. There was no room in this understanding of the *mallum* court for the kind of autonomous community justice that the word seems initially to have indicated. It is significant that the *mallum* in this Carolingian sense is also important in locally produced or locally specific texts too, not just anonymous and collective texts emanating from the court. For example, a diploma of Lothar I for Murbach, a monastery in the Vosges, exempted certain named men from their duty to attend it, and a charter from Wissembourg records the holding of such a court.[28] Moreover, a

---

[25] Cf. C. Wickham, 'Public court practice: the eighth and twelfth centuries', in S. Esders, ed., *Rechtsverständnis und Konfliktbewältigung: gerichtliche und aussergerichtliche Strategien im Mittelalter* (Cologne, 2007), pp. 17–30.

[26] *MGH Capit.*, vol. II, no. 278: ch. 3 (pp. 343–4) alone refers to the *mallum* court twelve times.

[27] Ibid., p. 346.

[28] *DLothI*, no. 45, transferring 'illud quod ad partem publicam facere', which included 'mallum custodire', and other duties owed to the count or his *iuniores*. Cf. *Traditiones*, ed. Doll, no. 160 (816), recording a *mallum* held at Brumath. There are plenty of others from Burgundian archives.

ninth-century vernacular text originating from east of the Meuse also associates counts with the *mallum* court. Probably composed at the monastery of Prüm, the Song of St George imagines the saint as a ninth-century count, riding along to his *mallum* court:

> *Gorio fluor ce malo / mit mikilemo herio* . . .
> *George rode to the* mallum */ with a great following.* . .
> *Dher mare crabo Gorio*
> *noble count George!*[29]

The fullest description of a specific Carolingian *mallum* court comes, however, from Hincmar of Rheims's account of a vision of the other world of a Rheims layman named Bernold, written around 880.[30] Amongst screaming bishops and wailing kings, groaning in regret for not having listened to Hincmar when alive, Bernold spotted a certain unshaven, filthy count called Othar. Vainly trying to hide from Bernold's gaze, Count Othar admitted that he had been motivated in his lifetime by an unnamed demon (perhaps pride, since the same demon had advised him to hide from Bernold). Now, Othar asked Bernold to return to tell his wife, retinue (*homines*) and friends to give alms and sponsor prayers for his benefit. Without ceasing to dream, Bernard complied, finding himself in an oneiric *mallum publicum* at Voncq (in Champagne). He passed on Othar's message to Othar's men, 'and the other people who were there' before returning to Othar, whom he found clean-shaven, washed and dressed in white. This was a *mallum* which was attended by the free men of the region, or at least not only by Count Othar's men, but which was nevertheless clearly associated with comital authority, and in this instance, with a count's misdeeds.[31] Needless to say, Hincmar's text does not document reality. We cannot claim that there was a real *mallum publicum* held at Voncq, and this Count Othar may never have existed (though in fact he probably did).[32] But in a way this account is more informative than an isolated empirical detail could be, giving an insight into the connection between formal authority and local society at the conceptual level.

---

[29] Edited in W. Haubrichs, *Georgslied und Georgslegende im frühen Mittelalter: Text und Rekonstruktion* (Königstein, 1979), pp. 370–4, with modern German translation: my translation is based on his, as is the identification of provenance.

[30] *HRE*, bk III, ch. 18, p. 256 (though the text also circulated independently: see following note). The vision is discussed in P. Dutton, *The politics of dreaming in the Carolingian empire* (Lincoln Nebraska, 1994), pp. 183–93.

[31] As also inferred by M. van der Lugt, 'Tradition and revision: the textual tradition of Hincmar of Rheims's Visio Bernoldi', *Bulletin du Cange* 52 (1994), 109–49, at 113.

[32] A Count Othar is mentioned in *DCB* no. 425 (877) as recently deceased ('olim'): he had held fiscal land at Sarcy in the Tardenois.

The Carolingian advocate

If the semantic shift in the (vernacular) word *mallum* appears to indicate a regearing of concepts of public justice, to centre them more firmly on the count and by implication the king, the concept of the Carolingian advocate points in a parallel direction.[33] As we have seen, Carolingian kings emphasised the importance of the count's court for dealing with local issues, and placed the *mallum* court at the centre of local society. However, canon law, like the sixth-century Council of Carthage, firmly forbade priests and especially monks from attending secular courts, and this was reinforced in ninth-century texts, too, since insulating clerics and monks from the outside world was a central objective of Carolingian reform.[34] The tension between these two priorities did not escape contemporaries' notice: a canon law reference to public courts (*publium iudicium*), to the effect that clerics should avoid them, was glossed as '*in mallo*' in one ninth-century Rheims manuscript, and Archbishop Hincmar made the connection perfectly explicit.[35]

Again, however, there is more than just anecdotal evidence to suggest that new conceptions of public courts were coming into conflict with older and reinvigorated ideas about clerical immunity. To ensure that the massive wealth and resources concentrated around monasteries were integrated into the formal court system, a systematic solution was devised – the ecclesiastical advocate. According to capitulary texts, abbots, abbesses and bishops were to appoint advocates to represent them in legal matters, implicitly, and sometimes explicitly, at the *mallum* court, rather than representing themselves. This command can certainly not be dismissed as hot air from Aachen, because these advocates are prominent in ninth-century archival evidence from the area of interest here. For example, a charter of Lothar I for St-Mihiel on the Meuse shows the exemption system in full working order, envisaging *missi* and advocates as co-operating with counts in inquisitions before *meliores*

---

[33] I have discussed this issue in greater detail in 'The significance of the Carolingian advocate', *EME* 17 (2009), 186–206.

[34] Defined at the Council of Mainz 813 as one of the many *negotia saecularia*: *MGH Concilia* vol. ii:i, p. 264 ('in placitis saecularibus disputare').

[35] See *HRE*, bk iii, ch.26, p. 335: 'quae de presbiteri et ecclesie causa ad episcopos et ad synodum diffinitio pertineat, non ad malli vel civilium iudicium dispositionem', repeated in Hincmar of Rheims, *Capitula*, ed. P. Brommer, R. Pokorny and M. Stratmann, *Capitula episcoporum*, 4 vols. (Hanover, 1984–2005), vol. ii:ii, ch. 21, extending the Council of Carthage proscription with a reference to the *mallum* court, again as representing secular justice. Regino does much the same: *Libri duo de synodalibus causis*, ed. and tr. W. Hartmann, *Das Sendhandbuch des Regino von Prüm* (Darmstadt, 2004), bk ii, ch.111: 'in seculari iudicio, id est in comitis placito'. A capitulary in Metz, Bibliothèque Municipale †MS 226, explicitly stated that monks should not go to *mallum* courts.

homines; and in fact most monastic archives preserve references to individual, named advocates.[36]

These ecclesiastical advocates were above all else mediating figures: not, or not primarily, mediating between the specialist knowledge of court and those seeking remedies (though in fact at least some advocates demonstrably had more than working knowledge of Frankish law), but rather between a secular form of judicial integration and a social *ordo* defined through separation from the world, but whose cultural and economic importance made total separation both impossible and undesirable. That this solution was to all intents and purposes novel, built essentially from scratch, shows the seriousness of purpose behind Carolingian ecclesiastical reform; but it also demonstrates the novel cultural importance allotted to the secular courts, and particularly the count's court in the locality. Ecclesiastical advocates, in other words, tell us just as much about secular courts as they do about monasteries. When placed alongside the evidence of the semantic shifts of the *mallum*, and its insistent association with the count, we have the impression of a conceptual realignment, quite clearly promoted from the centre, whose aim was to orientate local community justice with the formal Carolingian hierarchy of authority, and to iron out internal ideological tensions which might have impeded the development of the *mallum* court. This was a systematic project, for which there is systematic evidence in this area.

BISHOPS AND EPISCOPAL ORGANISATION

To concentrate solely on superficially 'secular' arms of government like counts in setting out the evidence for the formal institutions that integrated the lands on either side of the Meuse into Carolingian rule would be painfully anachronistic, blinding us to important ways in which ninth-century society was caught up in formal institutional authority.[37] The importance of bishops in Carolingian society at large is now well-acknowledged, as is their centrality to kingship and the exercise of power in the localities.[38] Accordingly, a survey of institutional authority between Marne and Moselle needs to consider bishops in some detail.

To some extent, this is an easier task, for if the Carolingian count in the region can best be seen side-on, the same is not true of Carolingian bishops and the institutions they headed. Even if northern Frankish bishops

---

[36] *DLothI*, no. 53. Cf. *DCB* no. 375 for Charroux.
[37] See de Jong, 'Ecclesia and the early medieval polity'.
[38] See the magisterial S. Patzold, *Episcopus: Wissen über Bischöfe im Frankenreich des späten 8. bis frühen 10. Jahrhunderts* (Ostfildern, 2008).

apparently sometimes still used papyrus in the ninth century, enough parchment has survived to give us a clear picture of the Carolingian church in this area.[39] The scale of the organisations centred upon bishops should not be underestimated. According to Hincmar himself, the Archbishop of Rheims had at his disposal the combined prayers of more than five hundred canons, monks and nuns, divided amongst ten monasteries.[40] The other cities in this area (with the possible exception of Trier) could not match that, but communities of canons, usually a few dozen men, were becoming organised everywhere in the ninth century, increasingly acquiring an independent share of the bishopric's wealth.[41] Still, the bishops remained dominant, keeping a controlling stake in their cities: there are no unequivocal references to counts of Rheims and even when we do hear of counts of cities, such as at Troyes and Metz, there is little evidence to suggest that they competed with bishops within the urban space. The Archbishop of Rheims had a prison, run by a *vicedominus*.[42] He probably also took responsibility for fortification, for notwithstanding the permission acquired in the early ninth century to demolish the ancient Roman wall, remnants of a Carolingian fortification around Rheims have recently been unearthed.[43] Though the precise scale of the commercial activity that went on in these cities remains uncertain, there is no doubt they were economic centres, too.[44]

Kings, history and Rome

This wealth of evidence should not lull us into supposing that we have a total view, for we know that much more has been lost.[45] Enough survives

---

[39] *MGH Epp.*, vol. VI, p. 214, with editorial note. A general survey covering most of the places in this region is provided by R. Kaiser, *Bischofsherrschaft zwischen Königtum und Fürstenmacht* (Bonn, 1981).

[40] *HRE*, bk III, ch. 26, p. 334: Hincmar encouraged Count Gerard to continue defending Rheims's lands by noting the power of prayer 'in Remensi ecclesia'. Cf. the comparable situation at Cologne, *DLothII*, no. 25.

[41] Organisation: *DLP* no. 658 (Tournai), confirmed by *DCB* no. 173. For Rheims, see *HRE*, bk, III, ch. 10. Cf. *DCB* no. 352 (Langres) and *DA*, no. 113 (Trier). Share in wealth: *DCB* nos. 125 and 477 (Châlons), 137 (Paris), and 150 (Langres), both confirming charters of Louis the Pious. St-Arnulf Metz, too, had a series of such grants, from Lothar I onwards. Scale: Toul counted sixty canons in 885 (*DA*, no. 124).

[42] *HRE*, bk III, ch. 28, p. 356.

[43] Unpublished excavations at the Médiathèque (1998–2000), summarised on the INRAP website, www.inrap.fr/archeologie-preventive/Sites_archeologiques/p-896-Mediatheque-Cathedrale.htm

[44] *Miracula Bertini* (BHL 1291), ed. O. Holder-Egger, *MGH SS*, vol.xv:i (Hanover, 1887), pp. 516–22, I, ch. 9, for Verdun merchants on their way to Spain. See in general O. Bruand, *Voyageurs et marchandises aux temps carolingiens: les réseaux de communication entre Loire et Meuse aux VIIIe et IXe siècles* (Brussels, 2002).

[45] W. Hartmann, 'Die Capita incerta im Sendhandbuch Reginos von Prüm', in O. Münsch and T. Zotz, eds., *Scientia Veritatis. Festschrift für Hubert Mordek zum 65 Geburtstag* (Ostfildern, 2004), pp. 207–26, is a good example.

from this area, however, to be able to show how bishops contributed to integrating their dioceses into wider networks, in several distinctive ways. Most obviously, bishops acted as points of contact with kings, who took a keen interest in matters of their appointment and management. The reason for this is not difficult to fathom. In addition to large amounts of moveable wealth, bishops between Marne and Moselle controlled large amounts of landed property, sufficient in extent to require justification based on innovative readings of awkward biblical passages.[46] The precise extent of these resources is more or less impossible to determine, not simply for lack of evidence, but because they might be temporarily depleted by the king and conversely expanded through bishops' considerable and often resented influence over local monasteries, in spite of the nominal autonomy bestowed through charters of immunity – indications of these kinds of conflicts survive from St-Bénigne, St-Médard and St-Denis.[47] Though an extension of episcopal responsibility to regulate saints' cults, bishops were also keen to acquire monasteries for less elevated reasons, and land granted by bishops to their followers, so-called 'precaria grants', was often drawn from monastic estates.[48]

Given such wealth, having a capable leader mattered not only to the particular church, it also mattered to the king.[49] Lip-service was paid to the principle of election, but ninth-century episcopal appointment was almost entirely a matter for royal assent, if not in fact outright royal initiative, so little wonder that the lobbying around appointments was intense.[50] Getting the

---

[46] Hincmar, *Opusculum*, p. 167. Council of Tusey 860, *MGH Concilia*, vol. IV, p. 22. For portable wealth, see Hincmar, *Epistolae*, *PL*, vol.CXXVI, col. 32. See D. Ganz, 'The ideology of sharing', in W. Davies and P. Fouracre, eds., *Property and power in the early Middle Ages* (Cambridge, 1995), pp. 17–30. Episcopal treasures are noted at Cologne (*AB* s. a. 864), Metz (*AB*, s. a. 882), Rheims (*HRE*, bk III, ch. 5, pp. 197–9 and *Vita Remigii*, ed. B. Krusch, *MGH SRM*, vol. V (Hanover, 1896), pp. 239–341, p. 262), and Châlons (*HRE*, bk III, ch. 23, p. 314).

[47] *MGH Epp.*, vol. V, pp. 363–8; *Vita Medardi*, ed. D. Papebroch, *AASS Junii*, vol. II (Anvers 1698), cols. 82–6, ch. 2, with a unmissable moral edge; *Gesta Dagoberti I regis Francorum*, ed. B. Krusch, *MGH SRM*, vol. II (Hanover, 1888), pp. 399–425, at p. 402. Cf. the criticism articulated in *DCB* no. 440 for Manglieu against the Bishop of Clermont.

[48] Precaria: for example, 'Die älteren Urkunden des Klosters S. Vanne in Verdun', ed. H. Bloch, *Jahrbuch der Gesellschaft für Lothringische Geschichte und Altertum* 10 (1898), 338–449 and 14 (1902), 48–150, no. 2 (771); 'Charte de Metz accompagnée de notes tironiennes', ed. J. Havet, *Bibliothèque de l'Ecole des Chartes* 49 (1888), 95–101.

[49] *Annales Xantenses*, ed. B. von Simson, *MGH SRG* vol. XII (Hanover, 1909), pp. 7–33, s. a. 869, detailing the troubles of *parvuli*, *sacerdotes* and *nobiles* in the absence of Gunthar. See *MGH Formulae*, pp. 549–50, for a letter of Louis the Pious about episcopal appointment perhaps connected with Verdun.

[50] Frothar of Toul, *Epistolae*, ed. and tr. M. Parisse, *La correspondance d'un évêque carolingien, Frothaire de Toul (ca 813–847), avec les lettres de Theuthilde, abbesse de Remiremont* (Paris, 1998), nos. 15–17, pp. 120–6; cf. *MGH Formulae*, p. 549. Cf. Hincmar, *Epistolae*, *PL*, vol. CXXVI, col. 112, about Louis the Stammerer's attitudes to the control of bishoprics and their property; and col. 267 on the case of Senlis. Cf. also *Metropolis Remensis historia*, ed. G. Marlot, 2 vols. (Rheims 1666), vol. I, col. 501 (883). Several bishops are known to have passed through the royal chapel or administration: for example, Hubert of Meaux was a

right man in the job was vital for the king: as King Charles the Bald wrote in
866 about a candidate he was promoting (a former priest of Rheims) to be an
archbishop of Bourges, 'if we did not have such a man in our kingdom, we
would have to drag him out from another'.[51] Compliance with the royal will
was advisable, because if the king did not get on with the bishop, the entire
bishopric would suffer, which is why one abbot, Lupus of Ferrières,
considered that contemporary bishops were degenerate, too willing to listen
to the king and too afraid to speak up to him.[52]

Chosen by the king, and regularly attending the king's councils, the
bishops therefore put their impressive resources at the king's disposal.[53] Not
the least of their duties was co-ordinating prayer in emergencies, as Bishop
Adventius of Metz did during a Viking attack in 867.[54] More concretely,
Toul and Rheims can also be shown to have contributed to the construction
and maintenance of royal palaces at Gondreville and Aachen.[55] Military
organisation was also important. The letters of Bishop Frothar of Toul
show the role allocated to bishops and archbishops in organising military
service, and their role in managing the episcopal contingents that formed the
backbone of Carolingian armies is widely recognised.[56] The king viewed
episcopal lands as a useful resource for rewarding his soldiers, and the
Carolingian kings introduced a formalised borrowing 'when necessary', in
which the church received recognition of its rights via payment of a regulated
census, an arrangement attested by evidence from Toul, Rheims, Châlons and
Beauvais.[57] Many bishops, like Archbishop Hincmar of Rheims, were
appointed to act as *missi dominici*, and some of the letters that responsibility
generated have been mentioned above.[58]

However, the integration of the diocese into the formal structures of
power was not simply a matter of the bishop acting as a conduit for royal

precentor palatii (Hincmar, *Epistolae, PL,* vol. CXXVI, col. 153). Cf. *HRE,* bk III, ch. 21, p. 275, bk III, ch. 24, p. 327; and bk III, ch. 28, p. 360. Some electoral permissions survive for monasteries (e.g. *DLothI,* no. 53 for St-Mihiel and cf. *MGH Formulae,* pp. 261–2).

[51] Council of Soissons 866, *MGH Concilia* vol. IV, p. 209.
[52] Lupus of Ferrières, *Vita Maximini* (BHL 5824), ed. B. Krusch, *MGH SRM* vol. III, pp. 71–82, p. 76. An example slightly out of our area is given by *DLothI,* no. 124, concerning Lyon.
[53] *DLothI,* no. 67.
[54] 'Mandement inedit d'Adventius de Metz à l'occasion d'une incursion normande (mai–juin 867)', ed. D. Misonne, *Revue bénédictine* 93 (1983), 71–9.
[55] *DLP* no. 801.
[56] J. Nelson, 'The church's military service in the ninth century', *Studies in Church History* 20 (1983), 15–30; Frothar, *Epistolae,* no. 26, p. 136.
[57] Toul: *DA* no. 112. Frothar, *Epistolae,* no. 9, pp. 104–6, complaining about forty-eight *mansi,* for most of which *census* was not being paid. Rheims: Hincmar, *Epistolae, PL,* vol.CXXVI, col. 813. *DCB* nos. 212 (Châlons) and 254 (Beauvais). For explanations based on necessity, see *DLothII* no. 9, referring to Lothar I and to himself; *DLothII* no. 17, for lack of land; *DCB* no. 75 likewise.
[58] For example, *HRE,* bk III, ch. 18, p. 255.

authority. Ninth-century bishops in this area also played a crucial part in consolidating cultural identities, again serving to promote a wider frame of reference for their diocesans. As individuals, they were often, indeed probably usually, highly educated. Some, like the bishops of Metz, acted as patrons to scholars, others, like the bishops of Laon, organised cathedral schools.[59] An 868 text from Archbishop Hincmar's Rheims gives a wonderfully vivid account of the interrogation a bishop-elect underwent before his consecration, showing Willibert of Châlons being put through his paces by questions about his faith and delicate theological matters.[60] Not all were as virtuosically learned as Bishop Hincmar of Laon, but he was probably not the only bishop to be presented with a book of canon law on his ordination, and at least one was refused consecration because he was found to be intellectually not up to scratch.[61]

Interesting in its own right, this point has an institutional dimension. Bishoprics, in this area all based in old Roman *civitates* (with the partial exceptions of Toul and Laon), were concentrations of spiritual and cultural resources as well as material ones, reservoirs of institutional memory.[62] The certainty of the past in Carolingian Francia was both highly prized and perceived as under constant threat. Collating old manuscripts of the works of St Augustine preserved in various cities and monasteries, Hincmar of Rheims was horrified to find that many of the oldest had been altered through the addition of new quires in a modern script.[63] Hincmar's panic reflects the duty of bishops and their clerics to maintain a continuity with the past. Lists of the names of former, often ancient, bishops were carefully preserved for ceremonial recitation.[64] Though the flowering of bishop-centred history-writing was yet to come, Metz was the first bishopric north of the Alps to boast a history of its bishops, and Verdun had one before the close of the ninth century. A lack of information about the distant past of a bishopric could be predictably attributed to the negligence of previous generations of clerics, arrestingly imagined at Rheims as wrapping up the pennies earned from

---

[59] J. Contreni, *The cathedral school of Laon from 850 to 930: its manuscripts and masters* (Munich, 1978). For Muretach's Metz connection, see the Introduction to his *In donati artem maiorem*, ed. L. Holtz, *CCCM*, vol. XL (Turnhout, 1977), pp. xxiii–xxviii.

[60] *MGH Concilia*, vol. IV, pp. 320–3.

[61] For the canon law manuscript (perhaps Paris BnF lat. 12445), see Hincmar, *Opusculum* p. 145 and Hincmar, *Epistolae, PL*, vol. CXXVI, col. 544 and col. 558. For the refusal to consecrate Gislemar on intellectual grounds, see *MGH Concilia*, vol. IV, pp. 239–40.

[62] The topographical and hagiographical history of the bishoprics is conveniently covered in a series of books edited by N. Gauthier, *Topographie chrétienne des cités de la Gaule: origines au milieu du VIIIe siètcle*, 8 vols. (Paris, 1986–), with volumes on Rheims, Trier and Cologne.

[63] Hincmar, *Collectio de una et non trina deitate, PL*, vol. CXXV, col. 473–618, at col. 512–13.

[64] Hincmar, *Epistolae, PL*, vol. CXXVI, col. 42, for references to lists in Trier, Cologne and Rheims.

illicit business in old charters and the pages of ancient books.[65] Nevertheless, there was enough left to allow episcopal clerics to posit a more or less continuous institutional history from around 600 onwards for most of the bishoprics in the area.[66]

Contemporaries, though, insisted on a still wider chronological frame, for most ninth-century bishops saw themselves as standing in a line of apostolic succession to their sees, and all viewed themselves as successors to the Apostles in a broader sense, integrating their dioceses into the remote past.[67] No wonder, then, that these were Rome-centred places. Already, by the ninth century, Metz had a reputation for formidable proficiency in Roman-style chant, recognised even in Rome, and indeed its *Gesta Episcoporum*, and in fact its liturgical organisation, were all based on Roman models, while its cultural ambitions tackled ancient Rome, too.[68] Rheims, for its part, had acquired by the 840s a map of Rome, consulted to verify the authenticity of recently acquired relics of St Helen, themselves brought from Rome.[69] Precious objects, like Remigius's phial of heaven-sent chrism or his chalice, encapsulated these claims and connected the present to the distant past, as did Rheims's impressive collection of relics;[70] as still more obviously did the huge Roman remains prominent then (as now) in the former Roman imperial capital at Trier. There was also a constant flow of people going to and returning from

---

[65] *Vita Remigii*, pp. 251–2, where Milo's depredations are blamed for the loss of knowledge about Remigius. Cf. Verdun's *Vita Pauli*, ed. J. Mabillon, *AASS Feb.*, vol. II (Anvers, 1658), col. 177, blaming the loss on *negligentia*.

[66] For example, Toul's records stretched back reliably to the seventh century: *Gesta episcoporum Tullensium*, ed. G. Waitz, *MGH SS*, vol. VIII (Hanover, 1848), pp. 631–48, at p. 635. Rheims archives appear to have been significant from the 590s onwards: see *HRE*, bk II, ch. 1, p. 132, no. 7, bk II, ch. 4, p. 141, ch. 11, p. 158; and above all, bk II, ch. 19, p. 175.

[67] Paul the Deacon is emphatic on this in his *Gesta episcoporum Mettensium*, ed. G. Pertz, *MGH SS*, vol. II (Hanover, 1829), pp. 260–8; cf. *HRE* bk I, ch. 3, p. 66, that gives the same origin to Châlons – cf. the ninth-century *Vita Memmii*, ed. J. Sollerius, J. Pinius, G. Cuperus and P. Boschius, *AASS Aug.*, vol. II (Antwerp, 1735), col. 11. Beauvais's case is also ninth-century, via the *Passio Luciani*, ed. J. Bolland, *AASS Jan.*, vol. I (Antwerp, 1664), cols. 461–6. Troyes's is less certain: on Potentius, see I. Crété-Protin, *Église et vie chrétienne dans le diocèse de Troyes du 4 au 9 siècle* (Villeneuve-d'ascq, 2002), pp. 69–79. Except Laon, they all would claim apostolicity by the twelfth century: Hugh of Flavigny, *Chronicon*, ed. G. Pertz, *MGH SS*, vol. VIII, pp. 280–503, at p. 289. The notion that bishops were the successors to the Apostles in a general sense was very common: see 829 Council of Paris, *MGH Concilia*, vol. II:ii, p. 629. Cf. T. Bauer, *Lotharingien als historischer Raum: Raumbildung und Raumbewusstsein im Mittelalter* (Cologne, 1997), pp. 347–76.

[68] Notker, *Gesta Karoli Magni*, ed. H. Haefele, *MGH SRG n. s.*, vol. XII (Berlin, 1959), ch. 10. For the liturgical organisation of Metz, see M. Claussen, *The reform of the Frankish church: Chrodegang of Metz and the Regula canonicorum in the eighth century* (Cambridge, 2004). For Roman recognition, see John the Deacon, *Vita Gregorii*, ed. *PL*, vol. LXXV, col. 59–242, at col. 91.

[69] *Historia translationis Helenae* ed. J. Sollerius, J. Pinius, G. Cuperus and P. Boschius, *AASS Aug.*, vol. III (Antwerp 1737), col. 601–3, at col. 602, 'profertur in medium mappa Romanae urbis'.

[70] *Vita Rigoberti* (BHL 7253), ed. W. Levison, *MGH SRM* 7, pp. 58–78, at p. 78, including various objects from the life of Christ, plus relics from the Apostles, nineteen martyrs and six confessors.

Rome, not least priests hopeful of their chances of persuading the Pope to revise disciplinary measures meted out by meticulous diocesan bishops.[71]

Pastoral care

If bishops integrated their dioceses into wider networks, they also played a role in integrating communities within their dioceses too. This took place most obviously by means of the bishop's physical presence. Bishops were by canon law obliged to travel around their dioceses as part of their episcopal duty, and these regions have some of the best evidence from Frankish Europe to show that they actually did. A late ninth-century Lotharingian manuscript, now in Munich, contains the earliest known account of an episcopal visitation of a village, involving the interrogation of the villagers and of the priest about questions of faith and morality. This episcopal visitation, or 'Sendgericht', was attested throughout the ensuing Middle Ages, but seems to have been a ninth-century innovation from east of the Meuse, indicating a very hands-on attitude to the saving of souls.[72]

Probably more important, though, in creating connections between the bishop and his diocesans were the episcopally supervised networks of local churches in the countryside. There may have been small communities of clerics engaged in pastoral work between Marne and Moselle, along the lines of the so-called 'minsters' of Anglo-Saxon England, perhaps using crosses set up in the countryside to focus local religiosity.[73] However, though the evidence is currently fragmentary, there are archaeological indications for ninth-century local churches, some even associated with burials, at Pompey (Meurthe-et-Moselle) and Kimmlinger, and there are standing buildings that may incorporate ninth-century elements, for example at Heiligenbösch near Trier.[74] The overwhelming impression from the contemporary textual evidence from this area is of individual priests serving in single churches for individual communities, which we should think of as

---

[71] This particularly bothered the (very meticulous) Hincmar of Rheims: see his *De presbiteris criminosis: ein Memorandum Erzbischof Hinkmars von Reims über straffällige Kleriker*, ed. G. Schmitz, *MGH* Studien und Texte 34 (Hanover, 2004).

[72] The manuscript in question is Munich, Bayerische Staatsbibliothek Clm. 3851. For context, see W. Hartmann, 'Zu Effektivität und Aktualität von Reginos Sendhandbuch', in W. Müller and M. Sommar, eds., *Medieval church law and the origins of the Western legal tradition* (Washington, DC, 2006), pp. 33–49.

[73] J. Semmler, 'Mission und Pfarrorganisation in den rheinischen, mosel- und maasländischen Bistümern 5–10 Jahrhundert', *Settimane* 28 (1982), 813–88. For crosses, *HRE*, bk I, ch. 25, p. 129; *HRE*, bk IV, ch. 41 p. 444; *Vita Medardi*, ch. 1.

[74] E. Peytremann, *Archéologie de l'habitat rural dans le nord de la France du IVe au XIIe siècle* (Saint-Germain-en-Laye, 2003), vol. I, p. 301; vol. II, pp. 249–50. On Kimmlinger, see B. Bienert, 'Zur frühmittelalterlichen Besiedlung Triers und des Trierer Landes', in H. Anton and A. Haverkamp, eds., *Trier im Mittelalter* (Trier, 1996), pp. 149–50. For a survey, see M. Polfer, 'Spätantike und

parishes.[75] Hincmar of Rheims's episcopal statutes assumed that individual priests staffed their own churches in a very agrarian setting, and there is good reason to assume that significant settlements were equipped with churches, and perhaps less significant ones too.[76] The Pseudo-Isidorian decretals, a canon law text widely disseminated in our area, demanded that a priest might only be accused by forty-four male witnesses, who should be without infamy, married with children and Christian. Archbishop Hincmar revealingly interpreted these witnesses as heads of peasant holdings (*mansi*), dryly observing that since many priests did not have so many parishioners (*parochiani*) as that, they would thereby be immune from accusation.[77] Assuming a family size of approximately five or six, it follows that some church communities around Rheims contained only around 250 or 300 people, an estimate further supported by texts relating to Langres.[78]

The level of episcopal interest in local priests and local churches was considerable and sustained in the ninth century. Complementing the attention paid to local priests in general church councils, and associated texts such as directions on how to hold diocesan synods (such as that preserved in Troyes Bibliothèque Municipale MS. 1979, a manuscript with a Lotharingian provenance), episcopal direction is demonstrated above all by the extraordinary series of statutes, many issued in this area.[79] The bishops who issued these texts intended nothing to be left unclear, laying out priests' duties with an eye to detail. Archbishop Hincmar, whose statutes have already been mentioned, wanted his priests to learn a number of texts by heart: expositions of the creed and Lord's prayer, the Athanasian creed, the canon of the mass and at least one sermon of

frühmittelalterliche Kirchenbauten der Kirchenprovinz Trier: einen Bestandaufnahme aus archäologischer Sicht', in *L'évangélisation des régions entre Meuse et Moselle et la fondation de l'abbaye d'Echternach (v^e–IXe siècle)* (Luxembourg, 2000), pp. 37–92.

[75] For Carolingian innovation, see J. Semmler, 'Zehntgebot und Pfarrtermination in karolingischer Zeit', in H. Mordek, ed., *Aus Kirche und Reich* (1983), pp. 33–44.

[76] E.g. Hincmar of Rheims, *Capitula*, vol. I, ch. 5, p. 36 ('quisque presbiter in sua ecclesia' ... 'per mansiones et agros ac vineas'); ch. 8, p. 38, recommending the priest undertake some *opus rurale*; *Capitula*, vol. II, ch. 1, p. 45, investigating which villages churches are in; ch. 11, p. 48, enquiring whether the priest has an assistant cleric, and ch. 17, p. 50, urging priests to support as *matricularii* the poor, not ploughmen or pigmen.

[77] Pseudo-Isidore, *Decretales*, ed. P. Hinschius, *Decretales Pseudo-Isidorianae et Capitula Angilramni* (Leipzig, 1863), p. 449. 'Sunt enim apud nos presbyteri, qui tot parochianos non habent, qui mansa teneant': Hincmar of Rheims, *De presbiteris criminosis*, p. 95.

[78] Discussed from a different perspective in my 'Unauthorised miracles at Dijon and the Carolingian church reforms', *Journal of Medieval History* 36 (2010), 295–311.

[79] The Council of Rheims 813 is a good example of a general council in which priests were instructed about the *ratio missarum*, the *ratio baptisterii*, and the *ratio paenitentiae*: MGH Concilia, vol. II:i, pp. 254–5. The episcopal capitularies have been helpfully studied by C. van Rhijn, *Shepherds of the Lord: priests and episcopal statutes in the Carolingian period* (Turnhout, 2007). It may be noted that the *Gesta episcoporum Virdunensium*, ed. G. Waitz, MGH SS, vol. IV (Hanover, 1841), pp. 38–45, implies that Berard of Verdun issued a set (p. 45), though if so they do not survive.

Gregory the Great, and further noted that priests might be obliged to show their books to bishops, an eventuality discussed in Metz too.[80] Hincmar was even prepared to promise a horse and cloak to anyone who caught a priest in a tavern.[81] The ecclesiastical hierarchy expected a full provision of religious services in the locality, and indeed relied on this as a conduit of information.[82] In the political crisis of 858/9, Hincmar sent texts to the priests throughout the villages to be read out to those causing trouble.[83] Communion three times a year was not thought to be enough, and it was for the dying newborns and the sick requesting the *viaticum* that Hincmar pleaded when one local priest announced he was considering leaving his parish to join a canonical community.[84]

One may legitimately question whether these normative sources reflected reality; yet even setting aside the considerable success of the texts that preserve them in manuscript terms – they were frequently copied – there is good reason to suppose that they did, in this area, anyway. Firstly, bishops often were visibly as concerned as they claimed to be. They really did refuse to consecrate churches with bodies in, and try to move parish churches to more suitable locations.[85] They really did distribute texts relating to canon law to local priests, and there is evidence too that liturgical requirements were carried out.[86] They really did introduce a network of archdeaconries to assist with the management of the diocese.[87] And though negligent priests tried to evade the bishop's control, for example supporting each other by oath, sometimes these priests really were deposed.[88]

---

[80] Hincmar, *Capitula* no. I, ch. I. Books: Council of Metz 893, edited in *UBMR*, no. 127 (wrongly attributed to Trier).

[81] Hincmar, *Capitula* no. II, ch. 20, p. 52.

[82] Cf. M. Stratmann, *Hinkmar von Reims als Verwalter von Bistum und Kirchenprovinz* (Sigmaringen 1991), pp. 6–7.

[83] Hincmar of Rheims, *De Coercendis militum rapinis*, *PL*, vol. cxxv col. 953–6, at col. 954. He sent an exemplar to the king too: the text survives, *MGH Epp.*, vol. VIII, p. 60–2. For the royal arbitration of parochial church status, see Hincmar of Rheims, *Collectio de Ecclesiis et Capellis*, *MGH Fontes iuris Germanici*, ed. M. Stratmann, (Hanover 1990), vol. XIV, p. 63; and ibid., p. 101 for prayer for the king.

[84] Hincmar of Rheims, *Opusculum*, p. 146 for Aguilcourt.

[85] *Vita Frodoberti* (BHL 3178), ed. M. Goullet, *Adsonis Dervensis opera hagiographica, CCCM*, vol. cxcviii (Turnhout, 2003), p. 44, referring to Bishop Prudentius of Troyes. Also for Troyes, see Hincmar's *Collectio de Ecclesiis*, p. 63. Heiric, *Miracula S. Germani*, ed. J. P. Migne, *PL*, vol. cxxiv, col. 1207–72 documents attempts by bishops of Langres to move a hilltop church at Larrey 'intra villae ambitum' (col. 1232).

[86] 'Neue Texte zur bischöflichen Reformgesetzgebung aus den Jahren 829/31. Vier Diözesansynoden Halitgars von Cambrai', ed. W. Hartmann, *Deutsches Archiv* 25 (1979), 368–94. For liturgies in practice, see *Collectio de Ecclesiis*, p. 81, where Hincmar cites the *Ordo Romanus* for the consecration of a church.

[87] See above, n. 82.

[88] Hincmar of Rheims, *De presbyteris criminosis*, pp. 86–7; and his *Epistolae, PL*, vol. cxxvi, cols. 231 and 254.

Secondly, we can often see that this theory of pastoral provision had been implemented in practice. Sometimes the evidence is negative: the absence of a local priest at the *villa* of Aguilcourt (in the diocese of Laon) led to babies dying unbaptised, and the sick passing away without the comfort of *viaticum*: deaths which not only could be, but actually were, totted up.[89] And there are a number of texts in which these local priests and the communities they served come more directly into the spotlight, showing parish priests fully integrated into the local communities. Priests were respectable local people, worth stealing from, and de facto village leaders, too. Many seem to have taken their task seriously, like the priest at Cond, a church on the Moselle, whose basic duties were carefully recorded in a mid-ninth-century charter from Stavelot.[90] The impression given by administrative texts that local churches were reasonably well stocked with all kinds of texts is confirmed by extant manuscripts, such as the penitentials that seem designed for the use of local priests – for example, London British Library Addit. 19725 from around Rheims, whose status as a pastoral handbook seems confirmed by marginal notes such as the remedy for pig-disease entered into f. 41r, or Verdun, Bibliothèque Municipale 69, a mid-ninth-century penitential manuscript from Lotharingia, into which penitential prayers were added in the late ninth and early tenth centuries (f. 11).[91] The texts that manuscripts of this kind contained, such as the Penitentials of Bede/Egbert or of Pseudo-Theodore, which themselves referred to priests' book collections, were often the product of compilation from, again, just this part of Francia, where they circulated widely.[92] Similar arguments could easily be mounted for the liturgical texts that local priests also needed, such as baptismal commentaries. Both Munich Clm 14508 and Laon

---

[89] Discussed briefly by van Rhijn, *Shepherd*, pp. 181–2, and in more detail by P. McKeon, *Hincmar of Laon and Carolingian politics* (Urbana, 1978), pp. 66–7.

[90] Cf. *Miracula Huberti* (BHL 3996–), ed. C. de Smedt, G. van Hooff and J. de Backer, *AASS Nov.*, vol. I (Paris, 1887), col. 819–29, at bk I, ch. 6, col. 820; and Heiric, *Miracula Germani*, *PL*, vol. CXXIV, col. 1237, the latter concerning a priest near Soissons. Note Regino's comment about priests rewarding those women who made donations at mass (*Libri duo*, bk I, ch. 202, source unknown): 'quidam presbyteri . . . calicem Domini mulierculis quae ad missas offerunt tradant'. This chapter incidentally includes one of the first references to oral delivery of communion, avoiding the recipients' hands. For Cond, see *Recueil des chartes de l'abbaye de Stavelot-Malmedy*, ed. J. Halkin and C. G. Roland (Brussels, 1908), no. 32 (857).

[91] The polyptych of St-Rémi gives occasional details on local churches' book collections. For example, the church in the village of Sault-Saint-Rémi had a missal, an antiphonary, a psalter, forty homilies of Gregory the Great, and a penitential of Bede (*Le polyptyque*, ed. Devroey, p. 53). The Verdun manuscript also has cryptographic ('magical'?) texts entered into the margins in an early medieval hand, for instance at f. 1v. Only thirteen folios in length, it is unclear whether it is a fragment of a larger manuscript or not.

[92] See L. Körntgen, 'Bußbuch und Bußpraxis in der zweiten Hälfte des 9. Jahrhunderts', in W. Hartmann, ed. *Recht und Gericht in Kirche und Welt um 900* (Munich, 2007), pp. 197–215.

Bibliothèque Municipale, MS 288, manuscripts originating from this area, have been identified as 'priests' readers', that is, as collections of texts that a local priest would have found extremely helpful.[93]

Inevitably, some priests became a little too much a part of local society. One priest from the area, a man named Trising, managed a hat-trick of offences, becoming involved in a brawl relating to an accusation of sexual misconduct as he made his way back from a tavern in Mouzon.[94] Yet such behaviour demonstrably provoked complaints. The outraged parishioners in Vanault (Marne), near Châlons, acted to prevent their priest Angelric from getting married to a certain Grimma in the late ninth century by complaining to their bishop.[95] Providing explicit testimony to the value placed on pastoral care, the parishioners of Folembray near Laon complained to the bishop that they were unjustly deprived of their priest, despite having given gifts and tithes to the church there for as long as anyone could remember, since at least the late eighth century (and the names of seven consecutive priests at Folembray could be given). It may well be that the priest was usually appointed in practice by the lord of the village – and that the Bishop of Laon's attempt to abolish the parish of Folembray, which sparked this particular dispute, was aimed at one of these lords. Nevertheless it was the residents, not the lord, who had complained, and it was the residents with whom the Bishop of Laon was exhorted to negotiate.[96]

Perhaps some of the reason that villagers in the area were so interested in their priest's morality was because they had themselves invested considerably in their church. The episcopal expectation of local pastoral provision was reciprocated. Villagers seem to have been keen to take holy water home from the local church with them, to sprinkle their houses, fields and vineyards, their cattle and the cattle's fodder, and their own food and drink, testifying to their faith in its efficacy, and they left their unwanted babies at the parish church.[97] It therefore comes as no surprise to learn that the Frankish inhabitants of the village of Aguilcourt had made a few small donations in order to be buried by the chapel, which, like the church at Folembray, was independently endowed, just as councils and

---

[93] S. Keefe, *Water and the word: baptism and the education of the clergy in the Carolingian empire*, 2 vols. (Notre Dame, 2002), vol. I, pp. 160–4.

[94] Hincmar of Rheims, *Epistolae, PL*, vol. CXXVI, col. 646.

[95] Mancio, Bishop of Châlons, *Epistola, PL*, vol. CXXXI, col. 23 (*c.*900).

[96] Hincmar of Rheims, *Epistolae, PL*, vol. CXXVI, col. 529: 'Sigebertus cui illud beneficium dedi a me secundum antiquam consuetudinem clericum petiit.'

[97] Theoretical prescription: Hincmar of Rheims, *Capitula* no. I, ch. 5, p. 36. Practice: *Historia translationis Germani* (BHL 3474–6), ed. *AASS Maii*, vol.VI, ed. G. Henschenius (Antwerp, 1688), cols. 788–96, at cols. 791–2. Cf. Regino, *Libri duo*, bk II, ch. 68.

capitularies envisaged.[98] Only one charter preserves a grant to a local church, from Wissembourg in the late eighth century, but small-scale donations are indirectly attested in many texts.[99]

Residents also paid for their church via their tithes. In 813, it was confirmed that *coloni* were to pay tithes not to a monastery or bishopric, but to the local churches where their children were baptised and where they regularly heard mass.[100] Again, there is evidence for this in practice in this area. The disputes about Aguilcourt and Folembray both revolved around the distribution of tithes to local priests and the mechanisms of these payments (such as tithe-barns), the only point of dispute being which priest benefited. It was at least plausible that monks should become priests precisely for the sake of, and perhaps profit from, parochial care.[101] Locals sometimes built their own church; very plausibly some of the three chapels at which Folembray's priest routinely sang mass, while remaining resident in Folembray, had been built by pious subscription, for they had not been granted parochial rights.[102]

As a result, attendance at episcopally supervised churches and contact with the liturgy seems to have been regular.[103] We can assume that the bulk of the population had the chance to listen to a sermon every Sunday (even if some left church early deliberately to avoid it, as Archbishop Hincmar grumbled), to have their children baptised and to die with a priest at their bedside.[104] The point does not relate simply to a bland

---

[98] Theoretical prescriptions: see the Council of Worms 829, *MGH Capit.*, vol. II. p. 12 (repeated in Benedict Levita, *Capitularia*, ed. E. Baluze, *Capitularia regum Francorum*, 3 vols. (Paris, 1667), vol. I, col. 801–1232, at vol. I, ch. 100). This *mansus* was exempted from all service: so too, however, were *terrulae ac vineoli* given 'pro loco sepulturae' (Council of Fimes 881, *PL*, col. 1080). The *Episcoporum ad Hludowicum imperatorem relatio* of the 829 Council of Paris worried about priests who had 'despoiled' their own churches, taking their lands 'in prediola sua propria' (*MGH Capit.*, vol. II, p. 33): cf. the Council of Meaux-Paris 845, ch. 63, concerning those who give land for their burial (Regino also worried about this, *Libri duo*, bk I, ch. 127). On Aguilcourt, see Hincmar of Rheims, *Opusculum*, p. 147.

[99] *Traditiones*, ed. Glöckner and Doll, no. 181, for Dauendorf (Alsace). Cf. Hincmar of Rheims's instructions for Gottschalk's eventual burial (*PL*, vol. CXXVI, *Epistolae*, col. 93 and col. 274), Hincmar's *Collectio de Ecclesiis*, which included gifts of 'terrulae vel vineolae' within their *oblationes*, p. 94. Such small donations are mentioned also in the polyptych of St-Rémi: *Le polyptyque*, ed. Devroey, e.g. ch. 15 (Ville-sur-Selve, p. 14) and ch. 22 (Sault).

[100] Council of Châlons 813, ch. 19 (*MGH Concilia*, vol. II:i, p. 277). Tithe disputes: Frothar, *Epistolae*, no. 31, p. 146. Hincmar's *Collectio de Ecclesiis* mentions a similar dispute around Soissons, p. 63.

[101] Hincmar of Rheims, *De una et non trina deitate*, col. 503, with special reference to monks' preaching. Hincmar, *Capitula*, no. IV takes a more critical angle, ch. 1, pp. 80–1.

[102] *Miracula Remacli*, ed. J. Pinius, J. Stiltingus, J. Limpenus and J. Veldius *AASS Sept.*, vol. I, cols. 696–721, at col. 700, mentions a church at Marche whose construction was co-ordinated by a certain *matrona* named Grimvara. Folembray: Hincmar, *Epistolae*, *PL*, vol. CXXVI, col. 537.

[103] Cf. D. Bullough, 'The Carolingian liturgical experience', *Studies in Church History* 35 (1999), 29–64.

[104] For avoiding the sermon, see Hincmar, *MGH Epp.*, vol. VIII, ed. E. Perels, (Berlin, 1939), p. 60: some people come to church 'non propter salutem, sed propter consuetudinem', and leave after the Epistle.

notion of 'Christianisation', but to a specific way of being Christian, the unflagging promotion of certain ways of seeing the world that were being explicitly and consciously promoted by bishops, who were themselves, as we have seen, in close contact with the king.[105]

ROYAL POWER

Both counts and bishops, and the institutionalisation they represented, can be understood as agents of royal authority, creating the systems of organisation that characterise many historiographical perspectives on the ninth century. However, royal authority was also directly asserted in our area. Charlemagne dispersed a village for killing a local official, and Lothar I fined another village for murder.[106] We have glimpses of direct taxation levied to pay the Vikings: King Lothar II was able to impose a levy on peasant holdings across his kingdom, including many of the lands we are concerned with, on at least one occasion.[107] Royal minting made royal power tangibly evident, as did tolls.[108] Yet the most obvious aspect of royal resources in the area was the control of substantial landed resources.

Royal resources

Many historians have attempted to reconstruct the extent of royal estates in northern Francia, known as the fisc.[109] The reconstructions rely chiefly on royal diplomata which mention fiscal sites in passing or at the moment of alienation, though other sources like chronicles, estate management

---

[105] Cf. on this J. Nelson, 'England and the Continent IV: bodies and minds', *TRHS* 15 (2005), 1–27.

[106] *Vita Remigii*, pp. 315–16, also in *HRE*, bk I, ch. 17, p. 95. *DLothI* no. 132; the land (Awans) was given to Prüm. Cf. *DLothI*, no. 137 (855).

[107] *AB*, s. a. 864.

[108] Christian 'of Stavelot', *Expositio super librum generationis*, ed. R. Huygens, *CCCM*, vol. CCXXIV (Turnout, 2008), pp. 407–8. On the iconography of Carolingian coins, see I. Garipzanov, *The symbolic language of authority in the Carolingian world (c.751–877)* (Leiden, 2008), pp. 208–16, with references to older approaches.

[109] J. Lusse, 'La presence royale en Champagne au Haut Moyen Age', in G. Clause, S. Guilbert and M. Vaisse, eds., *La Champagne et ses administrations à travers le temps* (Paris, 1990), pp. 69–92, provides a good survey of palaces and royal centres for Champagne, supplemented by J. Barbier, 'Rois et moines en Perthois pendant le haut Moyen Âge. A propos des origines et du temporel de Montiérender', in P. Corbet, J. Lusse and G. Viard, eds., *Les moines du Der (673–1790)* (Langres, 2000), pp. 45–81, who suggests that the land was inheritance from the Romans. For the Ardennes, see H. Müller-Kehlen, *Die Ardennen im Frühmittelalter. Untersuchungen zum Königsgut in einem karolingischen Kernland* (Göttingen, 1973) and for the Saarland, see H-W. Herrmann, ed., *Geschichtliche Landeskunde des Saarlandes vom Faustkeil zum Förderturm* (Saarbrücken, 1960). W. Metz, *Das karolingische Reichsgut: eine verfassungs- und verwaltungsgeschichtliche Untersuchung* (Berlin, 1960) analyses a few fiscal centres from the region, too: Barisis, Awans (referred to as fiscal in *DLP* no. 545) and Ponthion, at pp. 111–13.

documents preserved by monasteries and above all capitularies, contribute too.[110] For example, it is from a capitulary that we learn King Charles the Bald excluded his son Louis from the fiscal resources around Laon and the Ardennes, as well as from the palaces of Quierzy, Servais, Samoussey, Attigny, Ver and others, all in this region.[111] It is at first puzzling that none of the lands mentioned in the dower charter of Queen Theutberga, King Lothar II's ill-fated wife, was in Lotharingia proper, but this may point to the area's importance for the king and a consequential reluctance to alienate its assets, not to its lack of resources.[112] When all the evidence is taken together, there remains no room for doubt that kings could call upon enormous landed resources from this area. No wonder Smaragdus, abbot of St-Mihiel, congratulated the Frankish kings on their landed wealth.[113]

Most of the attention devoted to Carolingian royal lands has been framed, tacitly or otherwise, by the question of how and when these royal resources were dissipated, as fisc became benefice, and benefice *allod*. Quantifying this dissipation is a difficult business, since the distinction between restitutions and donations was much finer than it may seem from a superficial reading of the charter evidence. After all, St-Denis received two charters for the same piece of land in 766, one phrased as a restitution, the other as a donation.[114] Still, if we exclude those transactions explicitly described as restitutions or confirmations, or which deal with confiscated land, we are left with around a hundred transfers of royal land from 800 onwards in this area. Some were impressive in scale. The *villae* of Dodincourt, Fleury-la-Rivière and Villance, all objects of royal generosity, can be tracked in charters and polyptychs and shown to have been substantial.[115] Charles the Bald made donations of fifty holdings (*mansi*) to a Count Odo at Nogent in the region of Omois and sixty-eight *mansi* in the Laonnois to St-Germain-des-Prés, while Louis the Stammerer gave away ninety *mansi* in the Laonnois in one grant.

---

[110] Particularly informative charters include *DA*, no. 31, confirming a now-lost charter of Lothar II (*DLothII* no. 43), giving a proportion of the income of forty-three *villae*, and *DLP* no. 545, referring to Awans, Sinzig, Andernach, Thommen, Theux and Clotten, amongst others. Cf. *DLP* no. 995. For narrative reference, Regino, *Chronicon*, ed. F. Kurze, *MGH SRG* I (Hanover, 1890), s. a. 885 (p. 123).

[111] *MGH Capit.*, vol. II, no. 281, chs. 32–3.   [112] *DLothII*, no. 27.

[113] Smaragdus, *Via Regia, PL*, vol. CII, col. 933–70, ch. 27, observing that God had given Emperor Louis 'regna, parentumque multiplicia divisit et praedia; fiscorum plurima dedit vectigalia et multorum potentum honoravit munera unde regia fabricare possis palatia', so there was no need for palaces to be built from the 'tears of paupers'.

[114] *DPippin*, nos. 22–3, pp. 30–2, for the *villa* of Essones.

[115] Fleury was still in the hands of St-Maur in the early eleventh century: see J. P. Devroey, 'La "villa Floriacus" et la présence de l'abbaye des Fossés en Rémois durant le Haut Moyen Âge', *Revue belge de Philologie et d'histoire* 82 (2004), 809–38; *Vita Burchardi*, ed. C. Bourel de la Roncière, *Vie de Bouchard le Venerable* (Paris, 1892), ch. 8.

Yet these grants were exceptional. Only around twenty transactions seem to have been sizeable (larger than twenty *mansi*), of which only seven passed to laymen.[116] The great majority were on a small scale, a few *mansi* in a couple of *villae*, an impression confirmed by narrative texts.[117] It indeed seems to be the case that tenth-century kings had very little land, but this was not simply the result of a haemorrhaging of fiscal property in the ninth century due to royal profligacy. Admittedly, small grants might well have been cumulatively considerable, but then the movement of land was not only one-way. Confiscation was an eminently real possibility, as one count's family experienced in 874 when they were deprived of Neuilly-Saint-Front (Aisne), and as indeed attested in plenty of charters.[118] Often the blow might be softened by handing over the confiscated property to a relative, but this still left kings with room for manoeuvre.[119] Of course, confiscation might well be only the retrieval of royal property given out previously. Land was explicitly given on condition of loyalty in charters of Lothar I onwards, clearly implying the possibility of taking back what had been given.[120] But confiscation could also be rather more far-reaching. A few years before his death, Charles the Bald began a 'quo warranto' style procedure to reclaim land, a general enquiry demanding that aristocrats produce evidence for their claims to have acquired fiscal or church property. However unfeasible that may seem, demonstrably certain aristocrats really did lose land if they did not have a charter for it.[121]

This fiscal flexibility, the way in which the fisc was continually replenished by political means, reminds us that we should avoid becoming too fixated on formally identified royal properties. In fact, a great deal of royal influence rested on the control of non-fiscal royal resources. Church councils pleaded with the king to keep an eye on his fiscal resources, in

---

[116] *DCB* nos. 69 (845) Hannape to Nithard (Prüm), 119 (849) Nogent to Odo (St-Martin), 412 (876) Villeperrot to Conrad (St-Colombe), 416 (*c*.876) Chaource to Robert (Montiéramey); *DLothI*, no. 66 (842) *mansi* in six *villae* to Alpcar (Prüm); *DLP* no. 995 (839) Villance to Richard (Prüm); *DLS* no. 28 (879) Roubais and Autreppes to Aleran (St-Denis), and, though rather far to the south, *DRod* no. 26 (935).

[117] For example, *HRE*, bk III, ch. 10, p. 209, lists the donations made by Charles the Bald to Hincmar's Rheims: half a dozen *mansi*.

[118] For a narrative account, see Hincmar of Rheims, *De Noviliaco*, ed. H. Mordek, 'Ein exemplarischer Rechtsstreit: Hinkmar von Reims und das Landgut Neuilly-Saint-Front', *Zeitschrift der Savigny-Stiftung für Rechtsgeschichte. Kanonistische Abteilung* 83 (1997), pp. 86–112, ch. 4. Documentary evidence of confiscation: *DCB* nos. 196 (Corbie), 242, 323 (Everard), 347, 427 (around St-Germain) and 439; *DCM* no. 165, including fine paid by Alpad; *DLP* no. 995; *DLothI* no. 68 (Richard); *DLY* n. 17 (for Fulda, but concerning land in the Moselgau).

[119] E.g., *DLothII*, no. 32.   [120] *DLothI*, no. 66.

[121] Council of Quierzy 873, ch. 8 (*MGH Concilia*, vol. IV, p. 345). Those who held church or royal land were to prove their rights or lose it. Cf. *DCB*, no. 347.

fear that he would otherwise just take ecclesiastical lands.[122] Pre-eminent amongst this potential fisc, so to speak, were monastic lands. Already by the ninth century, there was a dense network of monasteries that continued to be thickened out by foundations, including, in the ninth century, Charles the Bald's establishment of St-Urbain and Compiègne.[123] Centres of literate practice though they were, we nevertheless have only a patchy view of this network overall, but as a rough estimate, we might suppose there were around fifty or so significant monasteries and convents in the lands between Marne and Moselle.[124]

The extent of monastic landholdings can only be known approximately, especially given that many donations may originally have been accompanied by now lost temporary restoration of the land for the donor's lifetime, while not all donations were necessarily recorded in writing.[125] Nevertheless, synodal decrees give a sense of the possible wealth of these institutions, and the figures are remarkable.[126] Small institutions were classed as those with a few hundred *mansi*, that is to say land nominally farmed by a few hundred households, whereas those with one or one-and-a-half thousand such farms were considered medium. Large were those institutions with three, four or even eight or more thousand *mansi*. Astonishing though it is, this sense of scale is supported in the documentary sources from this area. For example, the rich convent of Avenay, home to royal widows, certifiably controlled the lands on which perhaps a good seven thousand people lived, to support its twenty clerics and forty nuns; and the monastery of Prüm, certainly in the top rank but perhaps not the very wealthiest in the area, the lands of over eight thousand, if we conservatively assume an average household size of five people.[127]

In this area, as elsewhere, small monasteries were used by kings as profitable benefices. The disreputable Bishop of Soissons, Rothad, was offered on his deposition 'a really decent monastery . . . so that he who had always led a life full of delicacies might not be broken'.[128] Similarly, Montfaucon was given to Verdun, and St-Germer de Fly to none other

---

[122] Council of Meaux-Paris 845–6, ch. 20 (*MGH Concilia*, vol. III, pp. 94–5).

[123] On St-Urbain, see P. Gautier, 'Note sur des diplômes carolingiens des archives de la Haute-Marne', *Le Moyen Age* 16 (1912), 77–89.

[124] The will of Erkanfrida, *c.*853, lists twenty-five institutions as beneficiaries, of which fifteen were in the dioceses of Trier and Metz; just one, St-Eventius, cannot now be identified, though several are quite obscure. See J. Nelson, 'The wary widow', in Davies and Fouracre, eds., *Property and power*, pp. 54–82.

[125] Cf. *Traditiones*, ed. Glöckner and Doll, no. 271.

[126] Notably the Council of Aachen 816, ch. 122 (*MGH Concilia*, vol. II:i, p. 401).

[127] For Avenay's 1550 *mansi*, see *HRE*, bk III, ch. 27, p. 350. L. Kuchenbuch, *Bäuerliche Gesellschaft und Klosterherrschaft im 9. Jahrhundert. Studien zur Sozialstruktur der Familia der Abtei Prüm* (Wiesbaden, 1978) estimates that Prüm had at least 1,700 *mansi*, p. 49.

[128] Hincmar of Rheims, *Epistolae*, *PL*, vol. CXXVI, col. 30.

than a young Hincmar of Rheims. But the real prizes were the large monasteries. Many had at some point in the ninth century a lay, irregular, or titular abbot through the king's gift: Maingaud of St-Maximin (Trier) and Reginar 'Long-neck' of Echternach in the late ninth century are particularly well known, and there is good evidence to suggest that Count Adalelm of Troyes was a lay abbot of St-Lupus (Troyes) around the same time; and the practice can already be found earlier in the ninth century, too.[129] Sometimes it was the king himself who took the abbacy.[130] The titular abbot might impose a division of the monastery's assets into two parts, one reserved for the use of the monks, the second reserved for political engagement.[131] The appointment of titular abbots, men like Einhard, can be seen as an aspect of church reform, not decadence, indicating that it was no longer felt appropriate for professed monks to carry out the tasks required, and making it easier for the monks to concentrate on what they were supposed to be doing. Perhaps this is why the division of monastic assets into two parts was sometimes welcomed by monks.[132]

In any case, all monasteries, with or without a titular abbot, made important contributions to royal requirements. Prüm never had a titular abbot, and indeed acquired an impressive collection of immunities, but still kept back designated servants (*scararii*) for the service of the king in a transaction of 880, while its dependent cell of St-Goar seems to have functioned primarily to provision the king when in the Rhineland.[133] Kings did not, after all, have to take over a monastery, or keep a bishopric vacant, to exploit church resources. As already mentioned, both monasteries and bishoprics were billeted with royal vassals, who were obliged to pay nones and tithes as recognition of the church's rights, but beyond that had complete control of the property.[134]

---

[129] *Cartulaire de l'abbaye de St-Loup de Troyes*, ed. C. Lalore, Collection des principaux Cartulaires du Diocèse de Troyes, vol. I (Paris, 1878), no. I.

[130] *DLothI* no. 67 (regarding Mettlach). *DCB* no. 174.

[131] E.g. *DA* no. 12 (St-Maximin); *DCB* nos. 70 and 191 for Montier-en-Der, 326 for St-Bénigne, 431 for St-Mihiel, 304 for St-Vaast, 338 for St-Medard, and 433 for Nivelles. Often reconfigured, as at St-Amand (*DCB* no. 303) and St-Riquier (*DCB* no. 306); *DLothII* no. 17 for Stavelot (leaving them with just 245 *mansi!*); *DZ* no. 5 for Echternach; *Regesta Imperii. Die Regesten des Kaisserreichs under den Karolingern, 751–918*, ed. J. F. Böhmer, revised by E. Mühlbacher with J. Lechner, 2nd edn (Innsbruck, 1908), no. 857 for St-Germain; nos. 757 for St-Amand, 874 for St-Riquier and 906 for St-Denis, *inter alia*.

[132] Frothar, *Epistolae* no. 3, pp. 94–6.

[133] *UBMR*, vol. I, no. 118; Wandalbert, *Miracula Goaris*, ed. O. Holder-Egger, *MGH SS*, vol. XV:i, pp. 361–73, at p. 372 (and compare the entire *Vita Goaris*, ed. B. Krusch, *MGH SRM*, vol. IV (Hanover, 1902), pp. 402–23).

[134] *Regesta Imperii*, ed. J. F. Böhmer, no. 800; cf. nos. 615 for St-Mihiel (writ) and 801 for Rheims, echoed in *DCB* no. 99.

Assemblies, the written word and royal power

Royal power was not exercised only in terms of property, and the king, whose majesty demanded the royal 'we', was no mere landlord.[135] In large part, the king's power was demonstrated by the movement of the area's leaders to the royal court, where they offered gifts of both symbolic and practical significance.[136] One charter redacted in 820 at the palace of Quierzy, west of Laon, included a list of witnesses, which, though it did not necessarily reflect the composition of the assembly as a whole, is nevertheless tangible evidence for the potential composition of these royal meetings: of its thirty witnesses, eleven were counts, men who had come to Quierzy from areas across the Frankish kingdom, including Burgundy, Maine, the Rhineland, Bavaria, the Breton march and Alemannia.[137] General meetings like this structured the lives of important figures in the provinces. Bishops and abbots from this area anticipated seeing each other at general assemblies, spent much time travelling to and from these meetings and worried about how to present themselves properly when they arrived.[138] Hincmar of Rheims commented that he was rarely to be found at Rheims on feast days because of his association with the court, while Hincmar of Laon's route to and from court was traversed frequently enough to be well known by others.[139]

Conversely, the king and the royal court were often to be found at Rheims or in its environs.[140] In 869, Archbishop Hincmar dismissed the Pope's suggestion that he should avoid Charles the Bald following his unwelcome invasion of Lotharingia:

I don't know how I could avoid the presence, communion and company of this king … since the king and my neighbours often meet not just in my diocese, but in my city, and they stay there as long as the king wants to, with a great multitude from the kingdom which he used to have as well as the kingdom which Lothar had, indeed of people flocking together from other kingdoms, whom I look after in my city[141]

Kings often visited the areas around the Moselle and the Meuse too, as implied by dues mentioned in the Prüm polyptych, owed 'on the king's arrival'.[142] In

---

[135] Royal plural: Christian 'of Stavelot', *Expositio*, p. 301, 'in communi nostra lingua usus sit'.
[136] Ermold, *Carmen in Honorem Ludovici*, ed. and tr. E. Faral, *Ermold le Noir* (Paris, 1964), p. 16; Frothar, *Epistolae*, no. 22, pp. 130–2 (in this case horses).
[137] *Traditiones*, ed. Glöckner and Doll, no. 69, pp. 268–72.
[138] Frothar, *Epistolae* no. 8, pp. 102–4, and no. 24, p. 134. Lupus of Ferrières was cured on route to an assembly at Frankfurt, *Vita Faronis*, ed. B. Krusch, *MGH SRM* vol. v, pp. 171–203, at p. 198.
[139] Hincmar of Rheims, *Epistolae*, PL, vol. CXXVI col. 556.
[140] Hincmar of Rheims, *Epistolae*, PL, vol. CXXVI, col. 183.
[141] Hincmar of Rheims, *Epistolae*, PL, vol. CXXVI, col. 183.
[142] 'In adventu regis', a phrase first mentioned in ch. 6 of the Prüm polyptych (*Das Prümer Urbar*, ed. Schwab, p. 171).

view of all this movement, it is perhaps not surprising that for one ninth-century Lotharingian writer, music was no longer primarily associated with funerals, but with the processions of princes.[143]

Royal power was also mediated indirectly, again, in a variety of ways. The written word played a crucial role. Capitularies, for example, consensus documents produced in consultation with the king, represented efforts to control and constrain the king's agents. For example, the capitularies issued at Soissons in 853 directed *missi* to be sent to check on the localities, in terms of comital activity, monastic morality, benefice-holding and the like. Capitularies were probably read out in local meetings, and demonstrably impinged on real events in concrete ways.[144] But we should also consider the evidence for informal royal 'writs': terse documents of command, issued by the king without the formal characteristics of a diploma.[145] Though the likelihood of survival for these documents must have been low, monastic archives from this area have preserved ones issued by Louis the Pious, (probably) Charles the Bald and Lothar I. Others which do not now survive are mentioned in other sources.[146] Even the imposing, heavily formalised royal diplomata can be shown to have been genuinely valued in this area, particularly in cases of dispute, though in other contexts too, as mentioned above in the case of immunities.[147] Their precise wording could be crucially important.[148] Little wonder that secular recipients of royal favours hung

---

[143] Christian, *Expositio*, p. 206.

[144] See Benedict Levita, *Capitularia*, whose preface describes *capitula* as 'in diversis sinodis et placitis generalibus edita'; Benedict considered his purpose, in part, as one of *recordatio*. For local meetings, Council of Quierzy 857 (*MGH Concilia*, vol. IV, p. 397). For a specific case in which the capitularies were cited (about the murderer Luido), see Hincmar, *Epistolae, PL*, CXXVI, col. 97. Cf. Frothar, *Epistolae* no. 18, p. 126, and no. 29, pp. 142–4.

[145] M. Mersiowsky, 'Regierungspraxis und Schriftlichkeit im Karolingerreich: Das Fallbeispiel der Mandate und Briefe', in R. Schieffer, ed., *Schriftkultur und Reichsverwaltung unter den Karolingern. Referate des Kolloquiums der Nordrhein-Westfälischen Akademie der Wissenschaften am 17. /18.* Februar 1994 in Bonn (Opladen, 1996), pp. 109–66, is an excellent introduction.

[146] *DLothI* no. 57 (Prüm); *The cartulary of Montier-en-Der, 666–1129*, ed. C. Bouchard (Toronto, 2005), nos. 18 and 19; *DLP* no. 800 (St-Bénigne). Lost but attested: the *regis indiculum* presented to Hincmar of Laon, mentioned in Hincmar of Rheims, *Epistolae, PL*, vol. CXXVI, col. 495.

[147] *Cartulaire de l'abbaye de Gorze, Ms. 826 de la bibliothèque de Metz*, ed. A. d'Herbomez, Mettensia II (Paris, 1898), no. 60; *Cartulary*, ed. Bouchard, no. 18, where they were used to secure a writ; Frothar, *Epistolae*, no. 12, p. 114; Hincmar of Laon, *Rotula Prolixa*, ed. R. Schieffer, *Die Streitschriften Hinkmars von Reims und Hinkmars von Laon 869–871*, MGH Concilia (Hanover, 2003) pp. 367–8; *Vita Theodorici altera* (BHL 8060), ed. J. Sollerius, *AASS Jul.*, vol. I, cols. 64–70, at col. 68. The polyptych of St-Rémi refers to the *preceptum regis*, relating to dependants of a certain Sigibert *de Trepallo* (*Le Polyptyque*, ed. Devroey, pp. 66, 69).; cf. Hincmar's *De Noviliaco*, showing the use of *praecepta* on various occasions. Cf. Vandières and Douzy (*HRE*, bk I, ch. 24, p. 125; bk III, ch. 20, p. 267); and *DCB* no. 236 where charters are called upon to be inspected. Papal charters, too, were used 'in practice': e.g. *MGH Epp.*, vol. VIII, p. 215 (recited) and p. 216 (intended to terrify).

[148] For instance, *MGH Formulae*, p. 324, where a woman was enslaved because her *parentela* was not mentioned explicitly in the royal charter.

onto their charters, that ninth-century monasteries like Stavelot and St-Denis made up for a lack of material through forgery, and that diplomata might sometimes be the objects of targeted theft.[149] Little wonder, too, that much effort went into trying to get the right charter through lobbying at the royal court, reinforcing its centrality.[150]

Yet kings were not constrained by the written word, for oral commands could be just as effective. For example, Bishop Rothad of Soissons recalled how in 862 Charles the Bald had prevented him leaving to take a complaint to Rome. On hearing of his imminent departure, the king had sent an abbot post-haste, who arrived just as the bishop was leaving. Standing in the atrium of the church, the abbot publicly forbade the bishop to leave, by the king's command.[151] There are other concrete instances like this, showing that *missi dominici* and other ad hoc royal agents were prominent not just in the reign of Louis the Pious, but right through the period: altering the distribution of ecclesiastical land in Toul, protecting royal fiscal interests elsewhere, and insisting on their hospitality rights.[152] These *missi*, given letters of hospitality (*tractoria*) to ease their journey, were still prominent and active in the area into the 870s.[153]

CONCLUSION: STRUCTURES OF AUTHORITY

This chapter has brought together the secular and ecclesiastical material in order to assess the weight of evidence for the relevance of formal structures of Carolingian co-ordination in this area. This evidence requires subtle treatment and is sometimes indirect, but nevertheless is cumulatively impressive. It is apparent that the count, the bishop and the king, and their various agents, were real and influential presences between Marne and Moselle in the ninth century, representing an effective institutionalised authority.

The traditional interpretation built on this kind of evidence, that the Carolingians created a state, is still robustly maintained by many historians.[154]

---

[149] *DLP* no. 995 was passed over to Prüm three-and-a-half years later, and *DDLothI* no. 128 for well over a decade; while *DDLothI* nos. 69, 96, 138, and *DCB* nos. 10 and 119 were kept for longer still, beyond a generation, before passing into monastic archives. Theft: *HRE* bk III ch. 27 p. 351, for a charter stolen from Origny.

[150] *MGH Epp.*, vol. VI, p. 22

[151] Rothard, *Libellus proclamationis*, Council of Rome 864 (*MGH Concilia*, vol. IV, at pp. 183–4).

[152] Toul: Frothar, *Epistolae* no. 7, p. 102. Cf. *MGH Formulae*, pp. 293, 321 with *MGH Capit.*, vol. I, 151, p. 308. Protecting fiscal interests: *DCM* nos. 203 (Prüm); *DLP* nos. 638 (Prüm) and 699 (Hornbach). Cf. *DCB* no. 347, though, for an area a little to the south; and *DZ* no. 17.

[153] *MGH Epp.*, vol. VI, p. 63, using *tractoria*; cf. Council of Douzy 874, *MGH Concilia*, vol. IV, pp. 587–95, about an unnamed monastery.

[154] For instance, G. Althoff, *Die Ottonen: Königsherrschaft ohne Staat* (Stuttgart, 2000), p. 231. See the essays in W. Pohl and V. Wieser, eds., *Der frühmittelalterliche Staat – Europäische Perspektiven* (Vienna, 2010).

As we shall see in the next chapter, however, others have instead stressed the informal networks which underpinned or perhaps undermined these formal institutions, in order to criticise conventional models of the Feudal Revolution. Their critiques need to be taken seriously, and networks of kinship, landholding and patronage are the topic of the next chapter. However, as will be discussed again in Chapter 3, no matter how justified any critiques of an interpretative position may be, they must be considered incomplete unless they can make better sense of the evidence on which that position was founded.

Chapter 2

NETWORKS OF INEQUALITY

Struggling for these things in the world, we say and they say 'This is mine, and all these are mine.' They speak truthfully because it is, but then it is not. They have it, and they do not have it – they have it for a short while but not always.

Dhuoda, *Handbook*[1]

INTRODUCTION

It was easy to divide strangers arriving before the gates of the monastery of St-Mihiel on the Meuse into two categories. The powerful man (*potens*) who found the monastery's gate closed would pound on it with his fist or staff; the weak (*pauper*) would not dare to knock, instead crying out humbly. The monastery's gatekeeper was directed to act appropriately. To the latter, he was to respond with a reassuring 'Thanks be to God.' But if the stranger were a *potens*, the gatekeeper was to run out humbly to meet him, and to ask for a blessing.[2] The gatekeeper was not enjoined to enquire first about legal status or official position.

This chapter takes its cue from that advice, given in a commentary on the Benedictine Rule produced by St-Mihiel's abbot, Smaragdus. It pursues an alternative approach to ninth-century society, moving away from the previous chapter's focus on formal institutions towards a study of alternative forms of order and solidarity. In this way it replicates, in miniature, a wider historiographical trend away from institutionally dominated perspectives to

---

[1] Dhuoda, *Liber manualis*, ed. and tr. M. Thiebaux (Cambridge, 1998), bk 1, ch. 5, p. 66. Though Dhuoda wrote in the south, it has often been suggested that she came from, and was brought up in, northern Francia.

[2] Smaragdus of St-Mihiel, *Expositio in regulam S. Benedicti*, ed. A. Spannagel, *Corpus Consuetudinorum Monasticarum*, vol. VIII (Siegburg, 1978), ch. 66, p. 323, expanding on the Benedictine Rule. For the terms, see the incisive analysis of R. le Jan, '*Pauperes* et *paupertas* dans l'occident carolingien aux IX et x siècles', *Revue du Nord* 50 (1968), 169–87. For an example of gatekeepers in action, see *Miracula Remacli*, col. 702.

49

one self-consciously oriented to practice, not norms, and to 'lordship', not the state. In line with this trend, this chapter therefore sets out the arguments for characterising the elite that dominated the area, and particularly the secular elite, as a loose grouping defined by behavioural patterns, kinship networks, and a ready resort to violence, a very different impression from that given by looking at the formal sources alone. It puts forward the argument that not only were there certain aspects of society which demonstrably escaped the institutional apparatus, but even when this apparatus and its associated norms had some purchase, it was usually only because they were being harnessed to extrinsic ends. As a means of dispelling any illusion that Carolingian society was static – the impression perhaps given by the analysis of the previous chapter – it aims provisionally to characterise the dynamic of this society, and to show that it was underpinned by a logic of expanding aristocratic dominance apparently distinct from Carolingian ideals of reform.

ARISTOCRATIC SOLIDARITIES AND THE LIMITS OF CAROLINGIAN INSTITUTIONS OF RULE

Defining an elite

In spite of a vague theory of natural equality that occasionally surfaced amongst Carolingian thinkers, it was, and is, obvious that ninth-century society in the area was dominated by an elite, some of whose members were tonsured, some not. The Viking attacks caused periodic disruption, but that was ephemeral, and the elite's dominance was never seriously challenged in this area, as it briefly was in Saxony in the 840s.[3] As has been observed many times by historians, and as already suggested above, this elite was not defined by strictly formal criteria.[4] When King Lothar II encouraged everyone to make their criticisms to him bluntly 'as if he were one of the less honourable kind of people (*viliores*)', legal or formal criteria were not to the forefront of his mind.[5] This does not mean that we should minimise the level of social differentiation, simply that we should pay more attention to enactment than to typologies.

---

[3] Devisse, *Hincmar*, offers an interesting analysis of Hincmar's views on equality, derived from Gregory the Great: see vol. I, pp. 489–90. On Saxony, see E. Goldberg, 'Popular revolt, dynastic politics, and aristocratic factionalism in the Early Middle Ages: the Saxon stellinga reconsidered', *Speculum* 70 (1995), 485–96.

[4] See R. le Jan, *Famille et pouvoir dans le monde franc (vIIᵉ–xᵉ siècle): essai d'anthropologie sociale* (Paris, 1995) for the definitive study of elite kinship; and R. Stone, *Morality and masculinity in the Carolingian empire* (Cambridge, 2011), for insightful discussion of the performance of elite status from a gendered perspective. Stuart Airlie's forthcoming book will doubtless shed much further light.

[5] *MGH Epp*, vol. VI, no. 7, pp. 217–19.

Key elements of this differentiation were visible. Clothing was an obvious way of showing status, and indeed low-status dependants in this area dared not dress well for fear of attracting unwelcome attention, whilst for *pauperes* to take up weapons, the symbol of social importance, invited reprisals.[6] Physical activity was used to indicate, and indeed generate, status, too. One had to be humble when approaching the important, a humility to be demonstrated physically when the differentiation was particularly acute.[7] A beggar encountering a ninth-century bishop of Cambrai passing by on his mule bowed low with such vigour that the bishop's mule took fright, and fatally threw its rider.[8] Physical action distinguished different status more systematically, too. In the ninth, as in later, centuries, heavy agricultural labour was demeaning. If practised by a noble saint like Theodulf (Thiou), whose holy plough was displayed in the ninth-century parish church at Couleuvreux near Rheims, it could perhaps be praiseworthy; but this ascetic model was unusual in texts from this area, and presumably rarer still in practice.[9]

More generally, a hearty physicality was a central marker of elite status, which the occasional event such as the tragic death of Charles the Younger in 864, accidentally killed by a member of his own retinue in rough-and-tumble, allows us to glimpse.[10] There is abundant comparative archaeological evidence to show that elite sites consumed prodigious quantities of meat, and a miracle story from ninth-century St-Hubert in the Ardennes vividly makes the same point, describing aristocrats passing through a village whose demands for hospitality centred upon consuming it.[11] This elite sociability was all about generating at least the appearance of bonhomie. Refusing to share food, drink or a kiss was to reject this camaraderie, and was not to be done lightly.[12] None of this suggests that these elites were necessarily uneducated: indeed, some

---

[6] *Miracula Vedasti auctore Haimini*, (BHL 8510), ed. J. Bolland, *AASS Febr.*, vol. I (Antwerp, 1658) cols. 801–2, col. 802. For evidence of elite reprisals when *pauperes* took up armed-self defence against the Vikings, see the now-famous reference in *AB*, s. a. 859.

[7] Compare Dhuoda, *Liber manualis*, bk II, ch. 3, p. 76. Cf. *Miracula Dionysii*, bk I, ch. 10, when a *famulus* approaches a count 'ea reverentia qua maiores famuli adeunt'.

[8] *Gesta episcoporum Cameracensium*, ed. G. H. Bethmann, *MGH SS*, vol. VII (Stuttgart, 1846), pp. 402–88, bk I, ch. 47, p. 417. The fact that this striking anecdote does not have any obvious moral point, suggests that this might be a story that circulated near the time (863).

[9] Of Saint Theodulf's recorded miracles, one involved the rescue of a pig from a well and another two were ploughing-related. The *Vita Theodulfi* survives in *HRE*, bk I, ch. 25, pp. 127–9; another version in *AASS* is probably also ninth-century.

[10] *AB*, s. a. 864. Kings often feasted and stayed together to show their goodwill: e.g. Wandalbert, *Miracula Goaris* and *Annales Xantenses*, s. a. 850. On hunting, see the forthright opinions of Jonas, *De institutione, PL*, vol. CVI, col. 121–278, bk II, ch. 23; cf. e.g. *Miracula Richarii* ed. G. Henschius and D. Papebrochius, *AASS Apr.*, vol. III, cols. 447–57, bk I, ch. 1.

[11] *Miracula Huberti*, bk II, ch. 11, requesting it 'minis et verberibus', col. 825. The archaeology is chiefly Anglo-Saxon: see A. Gautier, *Le festin dans l'Angleterre anglo-saxonne* (Rennes, 2006).

[12] Council of Tusey 860, Text F, *MGH Concilia* vol. IV, p. 41. Refusing a goblet at a feast: *Gesta Dagoberti*, p. 403.

---

took a positively unhealthy interest, from the church establishment's point of view, in questions as abstruse as predestination.[13] Others took their duty as lay abbots very seriously, in fact altogether too seriously in the view of alarmed bishops gathered at the twin synod of Meaux-Paris in 845, who decided that the only thing worse than lay abbots acting like laymen was lay abbots acting like clerics.[14] Rather, it is simply to observe that being an aristocrat was at least in part a matter of acting like one, marking out the elite from the rest, in ways which transcended status definitions through office or *ministerium*.

Kinship was another important factor, though here some methodological caution is required. In the first place, representations of kinship for particular purposes, such as commemoration in Remiremont's ninth-century *Liber Memorialis*, a manuscript listing thousands of names, are easier to explore than more everyday or routine practices. It is likely that charter witness lists reflect family bonds, and we can use these charters to probe into a larger-scale sense of family consciousness, making use of the value contemporaries placed on naming their children.[15] However, it is nevertheless essentially impossible to distinguish in these witness lists between friends and relatives (*amici* and *propinqui*), not least because these may not have been clearly distinguishable anyway, as marriage connections tended to make family out of friends. Kinship networks were in any case never wholly free of conflict. Sometimes parents even disinherited their own children in favour of making gifts to monasteries, a disturbing topic discussed at a series of kingdom-wide royal councils in 813 by express royal command, though given the role of mon-asteries in providing a focus for kinship identity, such disinheritance might have been part of a wider strategy of kinship, with only the losers complain-ing.[16] Secondly, study of early medieval kinship has begun to focus on interactions between constructions of family community and wider socio-political developments. The implication, well known to many anthropo-logists, is that kinship is not 'fundamental' in that wider political configurations were not derivative of it. Irrespective of debates about the importance of wider kinship networks, kinship cannot be treated as a prior level of social organi-sation, for it too was 'socially constructed'.[17]

[13] For the appeal of Gottschalk, the renegade monk imprisoned in the diocese of Rheins, to educated Carolingian laymen, see P. Kershaw, 'Eberhard of Friuli, a Carolingian lay intellectual', in J. Nelson and P. Wormald, eds., *Lay intellectuals in the Carolingian world* (Cambridge, 2007), pp. 77–105.

[14] Council of Meaux-Paris 845–6 (*MGH Concilia*, vol. III), ch. 10, pp. 89–91.

[15] For example, *Cartulary*, ed. Bouchard, no. 13. For the practice of naming, see Dhuoda, *Liber manualis*, bk I, ch. 7, p. 70.

[16] Council of Mainz 813, ch. 6, *MGH Concilia*, vol. II:i, p. 262; but most notably, Council of Tours 813, *MGH Concilia*, vol. II:i, ch. 51, p. 293. On monasteries and kinship, see Hummer, *Politics and power*.

[17] See the useful comments by R. Barton, *Lordship in the county of Maine, c.890–1160* (Woodbridge, 2004), pp. 92–5; as a concrete example of kinship in construction, see Regino's account of the Megingaud feud, *Chronicon*, s. a. 892 (p. 140), 896 (p. 144) and 901 (p. 149).

Yet to say that kinship was socially constructed is not to say that it was not real or important. It is abundantly clear that the elite of the area drew part of their identity from an awareness of their kin, and not just from their place in a hierarchical chain of command stretching up to the king. Office-holders like bishops and counts, in this area as elsewhere, can often be identified, albeit only approximately, as belonging to an extended aristocratic family, extended both in time and space.[18] More specifically, particular offices tended to stay within particular families. Bishoprics often passed from uncle to nephew. In spite of Hincmar's protestations to the contrary, the appointment of his nephew Hincmar to the see of Laon was probably not unconnected to their kinship, while a single family occupied the bishopric of Verdun through three generations, starting from the later ninth century.[19] Counts called Reginar around the Meuse, Matfrid around the Moselle and Conrad around the middle Rhine: in few cases can precise relationships between the named individuals be pinned down, but the recurrence of names gives the impression of a strong and early family implantation (and one which persisted into much later periods).[20]

An illustration of this point is provided by the county of Troyes, which can be tracked using information provided by a series of (unfortunately fragmentary) charters from the nearby monastery of Montiéramey.[21] The first named Count of Troyes, Aleran, appears in 837. He was succeeded in the 850s by Odo 'of Châteaudun', who was eventually followed around 870 by another Aleran, probably the son of the first. This Aleran was succeeded *c.*880 by a Robert, probably the son of Odo, and then by Robert's nephew Adalelm, who died in the 890s. Ninth-century Troyes, then, saw two father–son successions, albeit interrupted, and at least one uncle–nephew succession. It is only, however, when one further realises that the Alerans and Odos were themselves in some way related that one understands the extent to which the county of Troyes was in the hands of a particular kinship group in the ninth century.[22]

---

[18] R. le Jan, 'Structures familiales et politiques au ixe siècle: un groupe familial de l'aristocratie franque', *Revue Historique* 265 (1981), 289–333, offers a tour-de-force investigation relating to a family based around the Moselle.

[19] Bishop Bernhard (d.879) was the uncle of Bishop Dado (d.923), himself the uncle of Bishop Barnuin (d.939). See G. Althoff, *Amicitia und pacta: Bündnis, Einung, Politik und Gebetsgedenken im beginnenden 10. Jahrhundert* (Hanover, 1992), pp. 210–17. For Hincmar's protestations, see his *Opusculum*, pp. 305–6.

[20] On the Reginar family, see C. Bernard, 'Etude sur le domaine ardennais de la famille des Reginar', *Moyen Age* 63 (1957), 1–21, and the table in le Jan, *Famille*, p. 453. On the Matfrids, see ibid., p. 444.

[21] See Crété-Protin, *Église*, pp. 297–308, for a careful reconstruction on which this paragraph draws. The charters are edited (from a lost cartulary) in 'Documents carolingiens de l'abbaye de Montiéramey', ed. A. Giry, *Etudes d'histoire du moyen age dediées à G. Monod* (Paris, 1896), pp. 107–36.

[22] Le Jan, *La Famille*, pp. 213 and 256.

That did not rule out occasional dramatic royal intervention. After all, Odo of Châteaudun was deposed in 859, and the charters suggest Troyes was held for around a decade by Rudolf, uncle of King Charles the Bald but directly related to neither Aleran nor Odo. On Rudolf's death, however, things returned to normal, with Aleran's son, then Odo's son, reasserting their family connections. Similar arguments for office in this area can be mounted for the counts of Metz, though with slightly less detail.[23] Carolingian kings had no interest in working against kin-based solidarity (or more precisely, solidarity articulated through kinship) when it was easier to work with it, and never campaigned against an abstract principle of heredity; it was just that events sometimes got in the way.[24] In short, even the formal offices discussed in Chapter 1 were infiltrated by less visible networks of kinship.

Aristocratic domination: violence and intimidation

Archaeologically, the ninth-century aristocracy in the area is practically invisible. Though doubtless defensible to a degree, there is no indication that their residences, wherever they were, were heavily fortified. Archaeologists have discovered fortified sites of refuge – including old Roman watchposts – and it might be naïve to assume that these had no links to the locally dominant, but these were not permanent residences.[25] Late ninth- and indeed early tenth-century aristocrats in rebellion usually fled to a *castellum* somewhere, rather than holing up where they lived.[26] The lack of fortified centres is at one level accounted for by the sheer range of the Carolingian imperial elite, whose interests stretched across the empire, and who were seldom around anywhere for very long. Tents played an important role in an aristocrat's life.[27] But it also reiterates the

[23] The counts of Metz have been studied in exhaustive detail by E. Hlawitschka, *Die Anfänge des Hauses Habsburg-Lothringen: Genealogische Untersuchungen zur Geschichte Lothringens und des Reiches im 9, 10 und 11 Jahrhundert* (Saarbrücken, 1969), who suggests (to summarise) that the descendants of Matfrid I (d.836) remained dominant around Metz into the tenth century and beyond, though the first Count of Metz specifically so-called is Adalhard II, active in the 870s. See the genealogy above, p. xii.
[24] Dhuoda, *Liber manualis*, bk III, ch. 2, p. 88.
[25] Other ninth-century refuge sites: Regino, *Chronicon*, s. a. 892; *Miracula Bertini*, bk II, ch. 13, which describes the ad hoc fortifications around the monastery of St-Omer made by the *incolae* from sticks, mud and turf; and ch. 12, referring to 'castella … recens facta' in the 'regno quondam Lotharii'. *DLothII*, no. 7 gave Utrecht a refuge site. Roman watchposts: Arlon, Ivois and Mouzon in the region between Rheims and Trier, all mentioned in *Vita Maximini*, pp. 78–9.
[26] Durfos is the classic example: Regino, *Chronicon*, s. a. 898, 899; in Flodoard, *Annales*, ed. P. Lauer (Paris, 1905), s. a. 928, it was being used as a refuge by Boso. Cf. Hincmar's example in his *De fide Carolo servanda*, ch. 16: 'aut igitur ad loca munita omnes transeant'.
[27] Hincmar's *De Coercendis militum* mentions the royal tent, col. 954 (*paramento vestro*); it is mentioned often in Thegan, too.

point that elite domination was not rigidly fixed, pivoting around particular places: things were simply more fluid, and more court-centred, than they would be later.

This domination was primarily exercised over people, and in the first instance, through and over lesser aristocrats.[28] The best evidence relates to bishops' retinues – the Archbishop of Rheims had nearly thirty *vassali* in 883, for instance – though what comparative evidence is available suggests that we are not dealing solely with an episcopal phenomenon.[29] Elite retinues were mounted, armed and, to judge from miracle stories, spoiling for a fight. Sometimes these followers might be of unfree status, but, like later *ministeriales*, they were functionally clearly differentiated from the peasantry. They were bound to their lords through a combination of ad hoc measures, including the allocation of land, gifts and basic loyalty, though this did not exclude a degree of calculation. This sort of relationship was widespread and normal: indeed, Hincmar of Rheims used this sort of relationship to explain to the young king, Louis the Stammerer, how he ought to act with God.[30] It was considered morally binding, and there are plenty of instances of lords outraged at their followers' infidelity, and conversely doing their best to protect more loyal followers from unpleasant consequences of their service.[31]

The violence these retinues implied was itself part of secular aristocratic identity. The removal of the sword-belt on entering a monastery should not be interpreted as showing that violence was perceived as un-Christian, as saints like Germanus, who appeared formidably arrayed in war-gear, demonstrate.[32] This sort of material should not be ignored in the quest to create a mythical *pax Karolina*, and to assume that this evidence indicates textual violence alone is as implausible as to assume that it transparently reflects physical violence. A figure given by Flodoard of Rheims perhaps transmits us a sense of the scale of this violence, albeit from the decades after 900: in the course of ravaging at Cormicy near Rheims, where Flodoard was for a time priest, pillagers (*praedones*) killed almost forty people.[33] It should be noted that this was in the context of struggles for control over Rheims, and that for the most part, occasional references to thieves (*latrones*) aside, the violence for which these retinues were employed was associated with larger-scale political conflict. King Louis the German's invasion of West Francia in 858 stands out as a particularly significant spark for local disorder.[34] Yet such an association with

[28] I am preparing an article treating this theme at greater length.
[29] *Metropolis*, ed. Marlot, vol. I, col. 501.
[30] Hincmar, *Ad Ludovicum Balbum*, *PL*, vol. CXXV, col. 983–90, ch. IX: 'Sicut enim homo subjectus vadit sollicite cum seniore suo', col. 988.
[31] E.g. *HRE*, bk III, ch. 26, p. 343.   [32] *DCB* no. 84.   [33] Flodoard, *Annales*, s. a. 948.
[34] Aimo, *De translatione SS. Martyrum Georgii monachi, Aurelii et Nathalie* (BHL 3409), ed. J. Sollerius, *AASS Jul.*,vol.vi (1729), pp. 459–69, col. 465 (around Sens). Cf. 857 Council

large-scale political conflict was by no means a limitation to levels of violence – indeed it could have been a positive stimulus, given the extent of political conflict.

Lower down, a background level of intimidation seems to have been part of everyday life, exacerbated by, but not restricted to, political crisis. As a contemporary commented on the exercise of influence, 'he who has power (*potentia*) easily bends the *inferiores* to his will'.[35] Authority, after all, required terror as much as love.[36] This intimidation is obviously hard to quantify, but we can at least surmise that it was taken for granted, and that it could be quite casually brutal. For example, one miracle collection relates a story about a gardener who, refusing to give some fruit to a member of a passing retinue, was unceremoniously beaten for his impertinence. His assailant was later punished by a saint, but another text portrays an aristocrat shaking an arrogant peasant by the head, and here it is the saint who is doing the shaking.[37] Accounts of the rough treatment of ninth-century peasants by aristocrats (or, the ecclesiastical equivalent, by saints on behalf of their monks) survive in abundance. At Montfaucon, an unpleasant *vicedominus* ordered the most honourable peasants to be beaten with sticks.[38] At Rheims, we learn of a certain Blitgarius who beat the peasants of St-Rémi.[39] At Prüm, we hear of a local magnate called Reginar who hated French speakers and Prüm so much that he attacked its *familia* through sheer spite.[40] Further examples could be adduced from Stavelot in the Ardennes, Toul in the south and Trier in the north-east.[41] If 'unjust customs' (*consuetudines iniustae*) appear 'already' in 845 and indeed thereafter in capitularies, that does not mean that they were then and later only simple rhetoric.[42] The early tenth-century lament of the Council of Trosly, near Rheims, in 909 –

---

of Quierzy, ch. 1, *MGH Concilia*, vol. III, p. 389. Cf. also Hincmar's comment in his *De coercendis*: 'Per villae in quibus non solum homines caballarii, sed etiam ipsi cocciones rapinas faciunt', and the Council of Savonnières, Synodal letter, *MGH Concilia* vol. IV, p. 485: 'agricolas quorum labore vivitis, fame torquetis'. For *latrones*, see Hincmar's *Collectio de Ecclesiis*, p. 82.

[35] Christian, *Expositio*, p. 500.
[36] Hincmar, *De ordine palatii*, ed. T. Gross and R. Schieffer, *MGH Fontes* 3 (Hanover, 1980), ch. 10, citing Pseudo-Cyprian.
[37] *Miracula Dionysii*, bk I, ch. 18; *Vita Theodulfi*, HRE, bk I, ch. 25, p. 129.
[38] Heiric, *Miracula Germani*, col. 1241–2.   [39] *Vita Remigii*, p. 325 (and HRE, bk I, ch. 20, p. 110).
[40] Wandalbert, *Miracula Goaris*, p. 365.
[41] Stavelot: *Miracula Remacli*, col. 700. Toul: Bishop Frothar, *Epistolae* no. 14, p. 118. Trier: Regino, *Libri duo*, bk II, ch. 434 talks about the illegal oppression of those who have fled from the Vikings. As often, his source here is unknown, which may imply local practice.
[42] Beauvais canons, repeated in Council of Meaux-Paris 845, ch. 19, *MGH Concilia*, vol. III: 'indebitas consuetudines et iniustas exactiones', p. 94. Cf. the Council of Koblenz 860, ch. 6, *MGH Concilia*, vol. IV, p. 158. Cf. Barton, *Lordship*, discussed below, at pp. 179–80.

'the more powerful man oppresses the weak, and men are like the fishes of the sea, who are devoured by each other in turn' – reflect late Carolingian as much as post-Carolingian conditions.[43]

Admittedly, Carolingian rulers expressed a qualified concern in protecting the *pauperes* from the oppression of the *potentes*.[44] Lords (*domini*) were frequently enjoined to be merciful to their dependants (*subditi*), though they were also held responsible for their actions.[45] But if these were efforts to mitigate oppression, they seem not to have enjoyed great success. Even counts and bishops were criticised for setting maximum prices at which they would buy grain and wine from the *pauperes*, and of beating them if they did not comply.[46]

Beyond comital reach

In spite of the energetic promotion of the *mallum* court documented in Chapter 1, it is clear that comital power did not reach as far into society as an uncontextualised reading of the sources could imply. Intimidation did not pass through formal channels and was not usually recorded; the few cases which are, mostly relating to royal agents, were preserved only because the targets of the intimidation were already spoken for. Sometimes, counts were so unpopular that they had to call in the king or emperor directly.[47] The hierarchies envisaged in Carolingian capitularies did not always speak to local audiences: the office of *centenarius* is, for example, systematically replaced by the more generic *iudex* in one capitulary manuscript, suggesting an impatience with the formalities of office.[48]

These problems are perhaps to be expected, so arguably more telling are indications for forms of local community solidarity apparently not integrated into the hierarchical schemata centred upon the royal court. The most visible evidence for these is through the abundant attestations of witnesses to charters, helping validate the transaction.[49] Often the groups

[43] Council of Trosly, *PL*, vol. CXXXII, col. 677.
[44] E.g. Council of Mainz 813, ch. 8; Council of Mainz 847, ch. 17; Council of Tours 813, ch. 44; *MGH Concilia*, vol. II:i, p. 262; *MGH Concilia*, vol. II:i, p. 292; *MGH Concilia*, vol. III, p. 170.
[45] Council of Tours 813, ch. 49, *MGH Concilia*, vol. II:i, p. 293; and 813 Concordia, ch. 31, *MGH Concilia*, vol. II:i, p. 301.
[46] Council of Paris 829, I, ch. 52, *MGH Concilia*, vol. II:ii, p. 645.
[47] *MGH Capit.*, vol. I, no. 155, p. 315 and vol. II, no. 287, p. 374.
[48] *Die Kapitulariensammlung Bischof Ghaerbalds*, ed. W. Eckhardt (Göttingen, 1955), p. 30.
[49] 'Cartam ... donarent et subscriptionibus coram testibus ex more firmarent', Hincmar of Rheims, *Collectio de Ecclesiis*, p. 85. Cf. the Council of Aachen 816, requiring that nuns giving land to convents should do so 'per scriptum publice roboratum' (*MGH Concilia*, vol. II:i, p. 444), and Regino *Libri duo*, bk I, ch. 414 on the witnessing of charters: 'nam sine horum

these reveal were associated with a monastery – witnesses frequently recur in monastic charters, implying some kind of association, as in charters from late eighth- and early ninth-century Gorze – and by that token integrated at least to a degree into formal structures of authority, as discussed in Chapter 1. Yet it is also possible to tease out other forms of solidarities too, and the most interesting, if most subtle, indication of these is through studying the places where meetings took place. As preliminary points of qualification, it should be pointed out that a large proportion of charters, especially those preserved in cartularies, do not record where the transaction took place, and secondly, that due to losses, Champagne is rather underrepresented. Nevertheless, there is a body of material sufficient to support the following observations.

Three kinds of meeting place can be discerned from the charter evidence recording transfers of land: the site that was being donated, the recipient institution, or some 'third place'.[50] Holding meetings on the land in question was very common, even for donations of value made by elites. This reflects a widespread tendency to lend as concrete a flavour to a donation as possible, particularly necessary when boundaries needed to be ceremonially paced.[51] If the ceremony could not be undertaken on the land in question, then it could be re-enacted later on, a common procedure for royal donations as attested by grants concerning Chaource (Aube), Condé (Marne) and Villance (Belgium).[52] Failing that, a token dependant could be handed over.[53] Holding the meeting in the church receiving the donation was more common still: hardly surprising, of course, given the archival context.

Yet we should remember that monastic archives are not a transparent window onto ninth-century practice. The 'public scribes' visible in the early ninth-century Saarland and in late ninth-century northern Burgundy, as elsewhere, must have acquired their expertise through more than the few charters which remain of their work.[54] So it is revealing that occasionally charters record meetings held at 'third sites', neither the recipient church nor

adstipulatione pagina auctoritate testium nudata pro nihilo deputatur' (Regino's own comment). Regino here incidentally assumes that the *nobiles laici* can write 'cum signis propria manu'.

[50] Cf. Innes, *State*, pp. 100–4 on similar 'intermediate centres'.   [51] Cf. *DLP* no. 638.

[52] Chaource: *DCB*, no. 416. Though a royal *fiscus*, Chaource may have been a local political meeting place. It had been the site of a donation for St-Bénigne in 760, and was the subject of a Montiéramey dossier: 'Documents carolingiens de l'abbaye de Montiéramey', ed. A. Giry, pp. 107–36, nos. 9 (i. and ii.), 14, 23 and 25. Condé: *Le Polyptyque*, ed. Devroey, 'coram testibus multis Francis videlicet atque colonis', p. 71. Villance: *UBMR*, no. 103.

[53] Token *ancilla*: *Cartulary*, ed. Bouchard, no. 13.

[54] Such scribes are abundantly evident at Redon in the early ninth century (see Davies, *Small worlds*); I am preparing a study of the lay scribe Moringus, active in northern Burgundy in the later ninth century.

the land in question. The archives of Wissembourg,[55] Prüm,[56] Gorze,[57] Montier-en-Der,[58] Stavelot,[59] St-Bénigne near Dijon,[60] and to a lesser extent St-Mihiel and St-Vanne near Verdun,[61] and St-Maximin by Trier,[62] preserve a certain number prior to the mid tenth century. Relatively speaking, these charters are very much in the minority. However, several deal with business only indirectly related to a particular monastery, and so they are probably substantially underrepresented as a whole. In the two instances in the cisalpine Frankish kingdom where substantial non-ecclesiastical archives have survived, there are many more instances of these 'third places'. The Rankweil documents are sometimes explained away as part of the unique heritage of Rhaetia.[63] Cluny, too, however, preserved about a hundred charters made prior to its foundation, largely by and for non-institutional parties, of which a relatively higher proportion were made in 'third place' sites.[64] Both Cluny's archives and the Rankweil collection may be more

---

[55] Meetings were held at Saarburg: *Traditiones*, ed. Glöckner and Doll, nos. 212 (818) and 273 (838), where earlier transactions are also attested; and at Marsal: ibid., no. 215 (833), where again earlier transactions are attested. Both are possible *pagus* centres; but meetings were also held at Hermelingen (n. 200, 847) and Mackweiler (n. 201, 807), in neither case connected with the land in question. Wissembourg's non-Lotharingian holdings fill out the picture: *Biberesdorph* was twice the site of meetings also in the ninth century, Hochfelden was used twice, Kirchberg three times, Waldhambach three times and Ungstein four times, while Brumath, the site of a *mallum publicum*, was also the location for two meetings, one from 816 and one from 771.

[56] A manumission charter made at 'Berg', and a meeting held at *Sugiaco*, neither identified: *UBMR*, nos. 30 and 79.

[57] For example, *Cartulaire*, ed. d'Herbomez, nos. 46 (822), 47 (824), 55 (856) and 82 (894).

[58] Notably a meeting at Rupt *c.*851 and at Bar (-le-Duc? 'actum barrense castro sive ad Maurimunt') *c.*828, without the participation of a count: *Cartulary*, ed. Bouchard, nos. 15 and 10. Both these sites are suspected to have had Carolingian-period mints. Bar's double name is similar to what one finds at Ste-Menehould and at Saarburg, both of which had alternative names (Saarburg as 'Churbelin', according to a charter of 964).

[59] Two were made at Namur: *Recueil*, ed. Halkin, nos. 27 (824) and 55 (922); three at Huy, of which two did not involve the monastery (n. 45, no. 46), the third was made by a lay abbot (n. 51). Inden/Cornelimünster also made a charter at Huy in the mid ninth century, 'Etude sur une charte privée redigée à Huy', ed. with facsimile by G. Despy, *Bulletin de la Commission Royale* (1960), 110–17. Another meeting was held at Waha: *Recueil*, ed. Halkin, no. 61, likewise does not directly concern Stavelot.

[60] E.g. *Chartes et documents de Saint-Bénigne de Dijon, prieurés et dépendances des origines à 1300*, ed. G. Chevrier and M. Chaume, 2 vols. (Dijon 1943–86), vol. 1, nos. 24, 28 and 45.

[61] St-Mihiel's cartulary preserved records of a meeting held at Nancois in 943 about land at Boviolles and Marson: *Chronique et chartes de l'abbaye de Saint Mihiel*, ed. A. Lesort, Mettensia 6 (Paris, 1909), no. 26. The charters of St-Vanne record a similar meeting at Peuvillers in 882 ('Urkunden', ed. Bloch, no. 6), though this involved a count.

[62] Viz. the Erkanfrida testament: *Urkunden und Quellenbuch zur Geschichte der altluxemburgischen territorien* ed. C. Wampach, vol. 1 (Luxembourg, 1935), no. 89, though again involving a count.

[63] For these documents, see the excellent edition, without a whisper of explaining away, of P. Erhart and J. Kleindinst, *Urkundenlandschaft Rätien* (Vienna, 2004). On Rankweil, see K. Bullimore, 'Folcwin of Rankweil', *EME* 13 (2005), 43–77.

[64] *Recueil des chartes de l'abbaye de Cluny*, ed. A. Bruel, 6 vols. (Paris 1876–1903), vol. 1. Many of these early charters survive as originals and are best consulted in H. Atsma and J. Vezin's ongoing edition of the originals, *Les plus anciens documents originaux de l'abbaye de Cluny* (Turnhout, 1997-). See also

representative, and more relevant to the lands between Marne and Moselle, than first appears to be the case.

These 'third place' sites do not always recur, and they were not usually dominated by counts or known aristocrats, so we simply do not know what made these sites particularly appropriate for local meetings. The implication, though, is that these meetings took place flexibly, in the absence of formal hierarchies or organisations. Needless to say, this does not exclude the possibility of a looser aristocratic dominance, mediated by patronage or clientage; nor should these meetings be seen as in outright opposition to comital authority. It would be more straightforward to see them simply as not fully integrated into it. It is not necessary to imagine a free republic of peasants to see that the institutions of power had their limits.

Instrumentalising institutions

The limited reach of formal institutions implied by these third places is reinforced by the abundant evidence that even when the 'rules' were obeyed, it was more in the letter than the spirit. We need to consider how far the formal institutions, insofar as they were effective, were instrumentalised, and in this way rendered incapable of imparting any qualitative difference to local society. As Hincmar of Rheims complained, talking about the west Frankish elite in general, 'When they hope to make some illicit profit, they turn to the law. And if they don't think they can get it through the law, they turn to the capitularies: so it happens that neither the capitularies nor the law are properly maintained, but instead both are brought to nothing.'[65]

There is certainly abundant evidence to suggest that Carolingian counts could be wholly unscrupulous in pursuing their interests, which might not be specifically those of the king.[66] Texts from this area accused counts of engaging the *pauperes* in unnecessary building projects, taking money from them for war at times of peace, and fining them if they did not come to the

M. Innes, 'On the material culture of legal documents: charters and their preservation in the Cluny archive, ninth to eleventh centuries', in W. Brown, M. Costambeys, M. Innes and A. Kosto, eds., *Documentary culture and the laity in the Early Middle Ages* (Cambridge, 2012).

[65] Hincmar of Rheims, *Ad Episcopos regni Admonitio Altera*, PL, vol. CXXV, col. 1016, 'Quando enim sperant aliquid lucrari, ad legem se convertunt: quando vero per legem non aestimant acquirere, ad capitula confugiunt: sicque interdum fit, ut nec capitula pleniter conserventur, sed pro nihilo habeantur, nec lex. Omnia enim mala lex Veteris Testamenti damnat' (cf. 'Eine Übersehene Schrift', in 'Eine übersehene Schrift Hinkmars von Reims über Priestertum und Königtum', ed. R. Schieffer, *Deutsches Archiv* 37 (1981), 511–28, at p. 526).

[66] Cf. J. Fried, 'Elite und ideologie, oder die Nachfolgeordnung Karls des Grossen vom Jahre 813', in R. Le Jan, ed., *La royauté et les élites dans l'Europe carolingienne: début IXe siècle aux environs de 920* (Villeneuve, 1998), pp. 71–109.

placita: in short, abusing their comital authority for their own interest.[67] Little surprise, too, that, irrespective of formal criteria, not all counts were equal. Their status depended upon their connections with the king and other 'imperial aristocrats' and their semi-autonomous social position. For instance, extant charters show very clearly that Count Matfrid II, son of Matfrid I and rich in his own right, built up a considerable patronage network, making use of his access to Emperor Lothar I.[68] Of course, *missi* were sent by the king to oversee the counts in the locality; but from an early date these *missi* were themselves local figures, with their own interests to pursue, and dependent in any case on local communities for their information. The picture drawn by Paschasius of Corbie of one roving *missus* (the king's cousin) who was actually both impartial and (to an extent) effective condemns the rest in comparison.[69]

An analogous point could be made concerning the institutions of the church. Bishops were themselves members of this elite, and as we have seen, they often seem to have used their position to assist their kin.[70] Closer to the ground, the institutions of pastoral care were themselves liable to instrumentalisation. This is not the place to rehearse arguments about *Eigenkirchen*, the relations that aristocrats had to churches that they had built or claimed to own, but it must be noted that there is evidence – mostly normative, it is true – to suggest that aristocrats in our area of varying levels were busily constructing churches whose integration into diocesan systems of parochial care was half-hearted, and whose main function seemed to be to endow the family cleric, perform services for the count's household and return a steady profit.[71] In this way, the effort early Carolingian rulers had put into ensuring regular tithes were paid to local churches went to enrich the pockets of these churches' lords.

---

[67] Hincmar, 'Übersehene Schrift', pp. 52–3 (an important distinction between *banniti* and *manniti*). Cf. *Ad Episcopos regni Admonitio*, blaming counts: 'excogitaverunt quidam, ut per bannos venirent ad placita, quasi propterea melius esset, ne ipsas manninas alterutrum solverent', col. 1016.

[68] Matfrid intervened for secular aristocrats in *DDLothI* nos. 83, 84, 96 and *DDLothII* nos. 5, 11 and 31, all his own *vassali*, though also royal *fideles*. For his Italian connections, see *DLothI* no. 100. For comparable behaviour, cf. *DCB*, no. 98.

[69] Paschasius, *Vita Walae, PL*, vol. cxx, col. 1557–650, at I, ch. 16, col. 1601–3.

[70] For example, Gunther of Cologne's intrigue on behalf of his niece with Lothar II, Regino, *Chronicon*, s. a. 864 (pp. 80–2); cf. s. a. 869 for Adventius's lobbying on behalf of his nephew.

[71] There are plenty of examples of counts installing clerics into their churches: e.g. counts Liuthard and Teudulf (*HRE*, bk III, ch. 26 pp. 336–7). The normative evidence is to be found scattered across the Carolingian councils: see S. Wood, *The proprietary church in the medieval West* (Oxford, 2006) for a thorough analysis, particularly pp. 789–821, and Hincmar's *Collectio de Ecclesiis et Capellis* for the most informative contemporary discussion (including reference to burials within the church). Enthusiasm for building churches is well attested; for instance, Gerhild's church at Bachen, *DLothII*, no. 26. Cf. though *Miracula Dionysii*, bk I, ch. 3, a vivid example of a benefice holder using a church as stables.

Even apparently direct royal influence was necessarily 'mediated' through the locally dominant, as a glance at the fisc shows. The previous chapter gave the impression of a coherent and well-defined royal estate, and this is also the kind of impression given by hagiography depicting generous Merovingian kings granting away great tracts of land, texts which have influenced later historians to make generous estimates of the 'original' extent of these lands. In reality, things were less clear-cut. Sometimes, as at Epernay (near Rheims) or Vandières-sur-Marne, it was not actually clear whether a *villa* was royal property or not.[72] Even directly managed royal estates, like Verneuil, appear to be surrounded by a cloud of scattered dependent holdings, the precise status of which might vary.[73] While these holdings might sometimes have thickened to make a fiscal 'zone', that should not be assumed. Places like Ars-en-Moselle contained fiscal land, but there were other interests at places like Ars too, sometimes subjacent, sometimes not.[74] Fiscal rights were often in fact superimposed on other rights, so the definition of what was fiscal and what not reflected partly local opinion, and partly local power relations.[75] No wonder kings sometimes, and perhaps often, gave away what was not really theirs to give.[76] When we add to this the problem that large amounts of royal properties were held in benefice, it becomes clear that fiscal land simply cannot be counted up as a kind of independent variable.[77] When Charles the Bald claimed that he had given fully two thousand *mansi* to the bishopric of Laon, it would be absurd to

---

[72] *AB* s. a. 872; cf. *HRE*, bk I, ch. 18, p. 98; bk II, ch. 19, p. 182; and with *DCB*, no. 87, made at Epernay. For Vandières, see *HRE*, bk I, ch. 24, p. 125. Cf. *DLothI* no. 67, which was issued on a *villa* previously donated to Prüm by King Pippin III.

[73] Apart from the *Brevium Exemplum* (*MGH Capit.*, vol. I, no. 128), see *DCB*, nos. 230, 248 and 342; cf. *DA* no. 33 (six *mansi* in six *villae*). Two *mansi* at Pont-a-Mousson, for example, were attached to Gundolvesdorf (not identified): *DA* no. 95. The fisc at Seffent had another, similar floating *mansus*, *DZ* no. 11. For submission of a *villa* to a fisc, see *Miracula Richarii*, bk II, ch. 2, and cf. *DLP* no. 847, concerning wine dues.

[74] Ars: *DA*, nos. 56 and 99. *Cartulaire*, ed. d'Herbomez, no. 75 shows that Gorze had a *mansus* here. Cf. Chaource, discussed in n. 52 above.

[75] The case of a royal *potestas* around Sacy mentioned in *Die Urkunden der Merowinger*, ed. T. Kölzer (Hanover, 2001), no. 103, for St-Bénigne is illuminating: it involved thirteen *villae*, but it is clear from St-Bénigne's charters that there were layers of land control underneath this overarching royal power. The editor deems it *unecht*, because the cartulary copyist seems to have used an eleventh-century copy: but the undoubtedly genuine *DCB* no. 326, which survives in an original, was also recopied in the eleventh century. If the Sacy charter is a forgery, might it be a ninth-century one?

[76] Council of Meaux-Paris 845–6, ch. 20, *MGH Concilia* vol. III, pp. 94–5. A concrete example: *DCB* no. 236, concerning land in the Lyonnais, claimed by a vassal *mendaciter*. Nones and tithes had been paid all along. *DCB* no. 235 (for Auxerre) is very similar. For a case of a courtier (*aulicus*) asking for land which did not in fact belong to the king, see *HRE*, bk I, ch. 24, p. 125 (Vandières); cf. *HRE*, bk III, ch. 26, p. 341.

[77] *DLothII* no. 31. Cf. *DCB* no. 157 for Fosses.

imagine that this land had come from the remnants of Roman fiscal estates, untouched for the past five centuries: the Carolingian fisc was considerably more dynamic than that.[78]

It follows that the best way to study royal property in this area is through accounts of it 'in action'. Doing this shows that local administrators were, more often than not, acting in their own interests, rather than the king's.[79] Documentary evidence showing how fiscal agents had exceeded their brief is particularly forthcoming from the reign of Louis the Pious, a concentration of evidence which might point more to the vigour of Louis's scrutiny than to any increase in intensity of appropriation. We learn that fiscal agents at Thommen seized land belonging to Prüm, that a royal *villicus* called Robert illicitly acquired land at Hornbach, that the *actor* of the Frankfurt fisc did much the same, and that agents at Theux also caused problems, all necessitating the king's intervention.[80] The prize was not always land: fisc managers at Remiremont and Andernach unjustly enslaved freed women.[81]

There is more of this kind of documentary evidence, and it can be readily backed up by contemporary hagiography.[82] From all this evidence, what comes across most clearly is the energy and influence of the local fiscal agents, who did not just maintain fiscal sites, but in a sense actually created them. Sometimes they faced opposition which is recorded; often, presumably, they did not. However, the only alternative to having locally powerful figures running the royal fisc in their own interests was not to have any fisc at all. Fiscal dependants easily moved into the dependence of local counts or of local churches.[83] A weak, distant or imperilled king would soon have little fiscal property on which he could rely, as Charles

---

[78] Charles the Bald, *Epistolae*, PL, cxxiv col. 879. Charles added that during Bishop Hincmar's period of office (from 858) alone, he had given a total of six hundred *mansi*. Cf. J. P. Devroey and N. Schroeder, 'Beyond royal estates and monasteries: landownership in the early medieval Ardennes', *EME* 20 (2012), 39–69.

[79] Cf. S. Airlie, 'Bonds of power and bonds of association in the court circles of Louis the Pious', in P. Godman and R. Collins, eds., *Charlemagne's heir* (Oxford, 1990), pp. 191–204.

[80] Prüm: *DLP* no. 638 (816). Thommen is mentioned as a fisc in *DLP* no. 545 (Stavelot). Robert: *DLP* no. 699 (819, Ingelheim). Frankfurt: *DLP* no. 770 (823). For *actores*, see Hincmar, *De Ordine Palatii*, ch. 23. Theux: *DLP* no. 841 (827).

[81] Remiremont: *DLP* no. 823. Andernach: *DLP* no. 815.

[82] *DLP*, no. 881 for fiscal acquisitiveness under Pippin III (Barisis); *HRE*, bk I, ch. 24, p. 125, re: Vandières; and *MGH Capit.*, vol. II, no. 148, ch. 2, p. 300, 'De rebus sive mancipiis, quae dicuntur a fisco nostro esse occupata'. Hagiography: for example, Wandalbert, *Miracula Goaris*, p. 367 and *Miracula Dionysii*, bk II, ch. 33.

[83] Astronomer, *Vita Ludovici*, ed. E. Tremp, *MGH SRG* vol. LXIV (Hanover, 1995), bk I, ch. 6, on how public lands are changed into private properties. Cf. *MGH Capit.*, vol. I, no. 46, ch. 6, p. 131.

the Bald found out in the crisis of 858.[84] An association of royal power and land stands assured, but as Martindale commented in an important article, it is not clear which was primary.[85] The thirteenth-century abbot Caesarius of Prüm observed that monastic piety generates wealth, and its absence destroys it, and the analogy works for royal power too: royal wealth was a consequence, as much as an origin, of power.[86] This has significant implications for how we view the disappearance of royal property in this area after the ninth century, as we will see. The point here, however, is to show that royal resources cannot be understood as working as a potential counter-balance to local community: they could be best mobilised only through, and with, that local community.

THE LOGIC OF ARISTOCRATIC DOMINANCE

It could therefore be argued that not only were Carolingian formal institutions more limited in reach than might seem the case, but that wherever they had purchase on local society, it was at the price of compromise with local elites. Those in royal favour had a free hand in the localities, and even if they paid attention to the institutional or legal framework, they were not constrained by it. The implication must be that if we want to grasp the way in which local society was changing, we should turn to the logic of aristocratic dominance, not the logic of law.[87]

Blurred status, fuzzy property

The first point to be made is that by 800, the lands between Marne and Moselle were already thoroughly caught up in networks of aristocracy control. There is no indication from this area of free peasant settlements to match those fleetingly identified by the polyptych of St-Germain des Prés at the moment it acquired interests in certain estates west of Paris, or indeed to match the villages on the middle Rhine.[88] On the contrary,

---

[84] For the 858 crisis, see Hincmar of Rheims, *De Coercendis militum rapinis*, col. 956, about the *capitalia loca*. Cf. J. Martindale, 'The kingdom of Aquitaine and the dissolution of the Carolingian fisc', *Francia* 11 (1984), 131–91.

[85] Martindale, 'The kingdom of Aquitaine', p. 169.

[86] Cited in E. Wisplinghoff, 'Lothringische und Clunyazensische Reform im Rheinland', *Rheinische Vierteljahrsblätter* 56 (1992), 59–78: 'religio peperit divitias, divitiae religionem destruxerunt, qua destructa simul et divitiae perierunt' (p. 184).

[87] Cf. the comments of A. Guerreau on *dominium* in his 'Quelques caractères spécifiques de l'espace féodal européen', in N. Bulst, R. Descimon and A. Guerreau, eds., *L'état ou le roi. Les fondations de la modernité monarchique en France (XIV⁰–XVII⁰ siècles)* (Paris, 1996), pp. 85–101.

[88] Cf. *Miracula Gisleni*, ed. O. Holder-Egger, MGH SS, vol. xv:ii (Hanover, 1888), p. 583: 'quandam villulam Alamannis … libere colebatur ab indigenis terrae sine alicuius respectus pretio'. The *villa*

Wandalbert of Prüm's *On the Twelve Months*, a beautiful ninth-century description of the agricultural year in the Moselle valley, evokes in passing a peasant community deeply enmeshed in aristocratic control.[89] The archaeology, too, suggests village communities were thoroughly integrated into elite domination, and indeed increasingly so in the ninth century, if the prevalence of nucleated settlements, which had been increasing since the seventh century, can be read in that way (and some archaeologists would suggest that it can).[90] The only evidence that could be interpreted as showing a relatively uninhibited peasantry relates to the *fiscalini*, inhabitants of royal estates who apparently enjoyed considerable leeway in the ninth century, perhaps indicating that the fisc could denote places submitted to the king in the absence of alternative control (reminding us once again of the fisc's intangibility).[91] Their freedom of manoeuvre points to the absence of leeway permitted to the rest.

In the absence of entirely free communities, a kind of independence of action is visible from time to time, for example through apparently harmonious, 'horizontal' rural co-operation, often expressed through co-operative veneration of saints (for instance jointly donating a barrel of beer), but sometimes through more prosaic matters like guarding granaries, or haymaking, and perhaps too in the meetings whose traces are preserved in some of the charters discussed above.[92] We can even glimpse, perhaps, the occasional micro-history of a particular community, a kind of local history preserved through hagiography.[93] Yet none of this really implies an insulation from aristocratic power. After all, domination could work to enhance village coherence, imposing communal fines for theft, and using those micro-histories to integrate the village to ecclesiastical lords. Village communities

---

in question was around Soissons. On the middle Rhine, see Innes, *State*, pp. 49 and 105–11. Cf. *Gesta Episcoporum Tullensium*, p. 638, for a reference to *ingenui homines* from certain villages commending themselves to the bishopric in the late ninth century.

[89] Wandalbert of Prüm, *De mensium duodecim nominibus*, ed. E. Dümmler, *MGH poetae Latini aevi carolini*, vol. II (Berlin 1884), pp. 604–33: of particular interest is how Wandalbert separates out hunting, an aristocratic pastime proper to the Franks (p. 613), from the labours of the *agricolae* and *coloni* (e.g. p. 607), who carry *vitea munera* on wagons (p. 613) – cf. pp. 81–2 on gifts, below.

[90] See in general the Cartes archéologiques de la Gaule series, particularly R. Chossenot, ed., *La Marne*, Cartes archéologiques de la Gaule 51/1 (Paris, 2004); L. Denejar, ed., *L'Aube*, Cartes archéologiques de la Gaule 10 (Paris, 2005); G. Hamm, ed., *La Meurthe-et-Moselle*, Cartes archéologiques de la Gaule 54 (Paris, 2004), as well as details on the INRAP internet site (see www.inrap.fr). German archaeology in this region is less forthcoming: see Bienert, 'Besiedlung'. Only two settlement sites have been dug, at Oberbillig and Nittel, neither of which are particularly informative.

[91] E.g. *HRE*, bk I, ch. 20, p. 110 and *Translatio Germani*, ch. 5. Cf. *DCM* 109, and the Council of Quierzy 858, ch. 14 (*MGH Concilia*, vol. III, p. 423).

[92] Barrel of beer: *Translatio SS. Chrysanthi et Dariae*, ed. H. Floss, 'Romreise des Abtes Markward von Prüm und Übertragung der hl. Chrysanthus und Daria nach Münstereifel im Jahre 844', *Annalen des historischen Vereins für den Niederrhein* 20 (1869), 172–83, at pp. 182–3. Guarding the granary: polyptych of Prüm, ch. 113, relating to communal fines of the villa in event of theft (*Prümer Urbar*, ed. Schwab, p. 251: 'component omnes de villa'). Haymaking: *DCB*, no. 191.

[93] *Miracula Richarii*, bk I, ch. 1.

were certainly socially differentiated – *mansi* holders needed to be prosperous to run their holdings, and often commanded the labour of others – but most of this differentiation was oriented to aristocratic control.[94] Village officers plausibly emerged as a response to that control, and so far as we know were appointed with the lord's consent.[95] *Maiores* and the like indicate differentiation at the lord's will.

Judging from our evidence, the fine distinctions of legal status did not determine this domination. Even a cursory glance at the sources from this area suggests that legally based distinctions of status did not entirely frame ninth-century society.[96] Although most administrative sources express an interest in telling the free and unfree apart, the practical implications seem frankly rather muted.[97] For instance, the polyptych of St-Rémi, like most others, notes whether peasants were free or not, but there was no attempt to keep *ingenui* and *servi* restricted to free and servile tenures respectively, which implies that the question was not decisively important from the monastery's point of view.[98] This mingling appears, too, in narrative texts. For example, the late ninth-century *Vita Rigoberti* from Rheims described the obligations of the people who worked the land at Courcelles and Neuville-en-Laonnois, *servi* who were to be 'ready for all servile works allocated to them'. If, it continued, the family of serfs/slaves (*familia servorum*) died, and a free man (*ingenuus*) received the land, then he had to perform these servile works in their place.[99] That *ingenuus* might not have greatly cared, since the difference in the dues demanded from free and unfree was not always significant. Servile status was associated with three-day week-work (that is, working at the lord's service for three days), as Caesarius of Prüm, a later, but informed, witness who copied out Prüm's polyptych, pointed out.[100] But the free were often obliged to

---

[94] Labour of others: polyptych of Prüm, ch. 6 (*Prümer Urbar*, ed. Schwab, p. 171). Cf. the *seniores villae* attested in *Miracula Huberti*, bk II, ch. 10, col. 824, as well as the *villicus*. Requirement for *mansi*-holders to be prosperous: *Le polyptyque*, ed. Devroey, p. 74.

[95] Adalard, *Consuetudines corbeienses*, ed. J. Semmler, *Corpus consuetudinum monasticarum*, vol. I (Siegburg, 1963), pp. 355–420, at p. 391. Cf. *Die Sendgerichte in Deutschland*, ed. A. Koeniger (Munich, 1907), pp. 191–4 discussing the *maior*, seven elders and also a *iudex*, all summoned to account for the village to the visiting bishop; and Regino's description of the otherwise unknown lay *decani*, who are to encourage the rest to go to church (*Libri duo*, bk II, ch. 69).

[96] See A. Sigoillot, 'Les *liberi homines* dans la polyptyque de Saint-Germain des Prés', *Journal des Savants* (2008), 261–71.

[97] Hincmar, *Capitula*, no. II, ch. 3, p. 46. Cf. V. Henn, 'Zur Bedeutung von "mansus" im Prümer Urbar', in G. Droege, W. Frühwald and F. Pauly, eds., *Verführung zur Geschichte. Festschrift zum 500. Jahrestag der Eröffnung der Universität Trier* (Trier, 1973), pp. 20–34.

[98] Polyptych of St-Rémi, Petit-Fleury (*Le polyptyque*, ed. Devroey, ch. 3, p. 6): 'Hunoldus ingenuus tenet mansum I servilem'; and sometimes the inverse (Chèzy, ch. 16, p. 15).

[99] *Vita Rigoberti*, p. 64.

[100] *Prümer Urbar*, ed. Schwab, p. 164; cf. also the *Brevium exempla*, MGH Capit., vol. I, p. 252.

offer two days, and actually it is easy to find free tenants under a three-day labour obligation.[101] In the context of estate variation, then, the distinction between free and unfree was heavily relativised. Very possibly it meant much more to the peasants at a symbolic level than it did to those who dominated them.[102]

However, aristocratic 'lordship' could do more than merely ignore distinctions of legal status. It also appears sometimes to have nuanced the apparently firmly established category of property itself.[103] It is conventionally understood that ninth-century landed property came in units of the *villa*, always ambivalent in meaning but often equating to a unit of settlement, in other words a village; and the *mansus*, indicating in this period a peasant holding, together with the peasants on it. Holdings were often managed as 'bipartite estates', in which the land was divided between the lord's reserve and tenanted plots, whose tenants worked the reserve, sometimes at least according to a three-field rotation.[104] Traditional interpretations of this organisation as economically defensive or autarkic are no longer sustainable. Notwithstanding occasional famines – notably in 868 – agricultural activity was developed and prosperous, and infrastructural improvements, such as water mills, were springing up on all sides.[105]

Some historians have ventured to identify more specific patterns. Chris Wickham has noted that estates around Paris often encompassed entire villages, judging from early charter evidence, but that around the Rhineland villages were divided between literally hundreds of independent small-holders, and that estates here often consisted of non-contiguous patches

---

[101] In the polyptych of Prüm, *ledilia* are associated with two-day week-work, *servilia* with three; but ch. 76 (for Güsten, p. 232) has implicitly free *mansi* owing three-day week-work, and ch. 45 (Villance) has explicitly free (*ingenuales*) owing three-day service (e.g. p. 202). Some servile *mansi* paid very little (e.g. ch. 76, p. 232: just linen and chickens), others were subject to arbitrary commands (e.g. ch. 10, p. 175: 'quiquit precipitur').

[102] This might explain why peasants might kill family members to avoid being proven unfree: Ansegis, ed. G. Schmitz, *Die Kapitulariensammlung des Ansegis, MGH Capitularia* (Hanover, 1996), bk IV, ch. 27, p. 638.

[103] Cf. M. Innes, 'Practices of property in the Carolingian empire', in J. Davies and M. McCormick, eds., *The long morning of medieval Europe: new directions in early medieval studies* (Aldershot, 2008), pp. 247–66, and J.-P. Devroey, *Économie rurale et société dans l'Europe franque (VIᵉ–IXᵉ siècles)* (Paris, 2003), ch. 7.

[104] *Das Polyptychon* ed. Hägermann and Hedwig, p. 72.

[105] *Annales sanctae Columbae*, ed. G. Pertz, *MGH SS*, vol. I, pp. 102–9, s. a. 868 (predictably leading to rumours of cannibalism). The text also offers a small price index. The famine was also noted in the *Annales Xantenses* and in the *Annales Fuldenses*, ed. F. Kurze, *MGH SRG*, vol. VII (Hanover, 1891). A good example of a Carolingian mill is that at Audun-le-Tiche near Metz, dated to 851 (see Devroey, *Économie*, p. 135, though hand-mills can still be found e.g. in *HRE*, bk I, ch. 24, p. 126. See, in general, E. Champion, *Moulins et meuniers carolingiens: dans les polyptyques entre Loire et Rhin* (Paris, 1996).

of land, scattered across different settlements. The evidence from our area, between Paris and the Rhineland, appears to fall somewhere in between. There are references to single-owner *villae*, particularly but by no means only to the west, yet donations by different people of land in a single village are also attested, as is the presence of several estate centres in one and the same settlement.[106] Just as settlements were divided between different property portfolios, estates were likewise scattered territorially.[107]

There is certainly a difference here. Yet to conclude that this reveals different property regimes is perhaps to take the charters too much at face value. Rankweil, though a village considerably outside our area of interest, provides a rather suggestive illustration. In 823, Lothar I described Rankweil as Count Hunfrid's *villa* ('villa Unfredi comitis') when a charter was made there. It is, however, hard to square this with the charters which reveal Rankweil's dozens of independent landholders.[108] If Hunfrid had donated Rankweil to a monastery, what exactly would have been given? On a broader canvas, Bruand has recently demonstrated from evidence at three sites across the empire that donations of stretches of land might be followed by donations of more land physically within the earlier grant by different donors.[109] He rightly observes that this makes large estates rather intangible, just as Durliat argued in the 1980s from the same kind of evidence, though to different effect.[110]

A relative lack of evidence from the region west of the Meuse makes it hard to test Bruand's arguments there, but they do seem relevant to

---

[106] Multiple estate centres: *Prümer Urbar*, ed. Schwab, ch. 25, and chs. 36–7. Multiple donations: *Cartulaire*, ed. d'Herbomez, nos. 24, 45, 36 and 46. B. Isphording, *Prüm: Studien zur Geschichte der Abtei von ihrer Gründung bis zum Tod Kaiser Lothars I. (721–855)* (Mainz, 2005), p. 14, identifies five places in the *Carosgau* where there were multiple *Grundherren*. *Geschichte der Grundherrschaft Echternach im Frühmittelalter*, ed. C. Wampach (Luxembourg, 1930), produces similar evidence for Echternach, citing Bollendorf, Edingen, Itzig and several others, pp. 347–91. Müller-Kehlen, *Die Ardennen* demonstrates multiple holdings at a range of sites in the Ardennes on the part of the institutions of Prüm, St-Mary Aachen, St-Maximin, Stablo, St-Hubert and Pfazel, e.g. at Amel (pp. 116–21). M. Pitz, 'Der Frühbesitz der Abtei Prüm im lothringischen Salzgebiet. Philologisch-onomastische Überlegungen zu den Brevia 41–3 des Prümer Urbars', *Rheinische Vierteljahrsblätter* 70 (2006) 1–35, points to more sharing between St-Maximin and Mettlach at Tincry, Prévocourt and Ménil, pp. 13–14.

[107] Villance: *Prümer Urbar*, ed. Schwab, ch. 45 (pp. 201–8); cf. also chs. 46 and 47. Petit-Fleury: *Le polyptych*, ed. Devroey, ch. 3, pp. 6–7. Cf. ch. 19 (Bouconville) where the *mansus indominicatus* seems coherent, but the dependent *mansi* not, as at Sault-Saint-Remi (*Le polyptych*, ed. Devroey, ch. 22, pp. 48–54) and Condé (*Le polyptych*, ed. Devroey, pp. 64–9). Cf. also *Das Polyptychon*, ed. Hägermann ch. 10; and *Das Polyptichon*, ed. Droste, chs. 18, 32, 46, 47 and 55. See in general Devroey and Schroeder, 'Beyond royal estates'.

[108] Erhart and Kleindinst, *Urkundenlandschaft Rätien*, edit the relevant documents.

[109] O. Bruand, 'La villa carolingienne: une seigneurie? Réflexions sur les cas des villas d'Hammelburg, Perrecy-les-Forges et Courçay', in D. Barthélemy, ed., *Liber largitorius: études d'histoire médiévale offertes à Pierre Toubert par ses élèves* (Geneva, 2003), pp. 349–73.

[110] J. Durliat, *Les finances publiques de Dioclétien aux Carolingiens (284–889)* (Sigmaringen, 1990).

68

Lotharingia. For example, later landholders appear at a number of *villae* that had already been given outright to Gorze, as at Varangeville, Moivron and Sponville, landholders whose rights were sometimes robust enough to allow exchanges to be made.[111] Similar arguments could be made from northern Lotharingian evidence, but also from Montier-en-Der, St-Maur-des-Fossés and perhaps Wissembourg.[112] There is no reason to suspect that this was a feature only of ecclesiastical property, either.[113]

A number of explanations could be advanced for all this, but the most plausible is that ownership of land meant different things to different people at different times: whatever Roman law might say, property was sometimes, and perhaps often, a matter of degree.[114] Lords might own, or claim to own, a *villa* in which others also owned or claimed smaller estates, without much tension or indeed interaction between these two levels. Such lower-level rights are brilliantly exposed by an exceptional Prüm charter made around 870 concerning the settlement of Mehring.[115] There is no doubt that the monastery owned the entire settlement, but nevertheless, as part of its efforts to consolidate wine production, Prüm produced a charter to document exchanges of land made with a score of local residents. The property rights of the local inhabitants did not exclude Prüm's '*Obereigentum*', but they were real enough to be materially consequential.[116] We should remember, then, when reading our charters that these texts were certainly describing a reality, but there must often have been other contemporary perspectives, too.

[111] E.g. Varangeville: *Cartulaire*, ed. d'Herbomez, nos. 12 and 53. Moivron: ibid., nos. 5, 68 and 83. Moivron is incidentally mentioned in the *Miracula Gorgonii* ch. 5, p. 240, where there are two brothers who have a *praedium* which they donate. Sponville: *Cartulaire*, ed. d'Herbomez, nos. 2, 67 and 89.

[112] On northern Lotharingia see the evidence accumulated in E. Linck, *Sozialer Wandel in klösterlichen Grundherrschaften des 11. bis 13. Jahrhunderts: Studien zu den familiae von Gembloux, Stablo-Malmedy und St. Trond* (Göttingen, 1979) who details the holdings (*villa* by *villa*) of Stavelot, St-Trond and Gembloux: see for example Ernage, p. 27 and Grand-manil, p. 30. Montier-en-Der: Braux, Ville-sur-Terre, Baudrecourt. St-Maur des Fossés: Boissy-Saint-Leger was given in the seventh century, but an exchange of land took place in 847, and Count Stephen owned land here in 811 (Hägermann, *St-Maur*, p. 42). Wissembourg: Einville, Waldhambach and possibly Preuschdorf are *villae* given to Wissembourg at which smaller grants of property can be subsequently identified.

[113] Count Bivin's interest in Doncourt (where Gorze had had property for several decades, e.g. *Cartulaire*, ed. d'Herbomez, no. 46) is a good example: *Cartulaire*, ed. d'Herbomez no. 77.

[114] Devroey and Schroeder, 'Beyond royal estates', identify similar patterns; they interpret the ambivalence a little differently from the approach essayed here, though their concept of 'loose lordship' is helpful.

[115] *UBMR*, no. 98; see F. Irsigler, 'Mehring. Ein Prümer Winzerdorf um 900', in J. M. Duvosquel and E. Thoen, eds., *Peasants and townsmen in medieval Europe* (Weimar, 1995), pp. 65–86.

[116] As Irsigler, 'Mehring', trenchantly puts it, 'auf jeden Fall war es erblicher Besitz, über den die Hörigen weitgehen frei verfügen konnten, auch wenn sie sich hier dem Druck des Abtes beugen mussten', p. 304. Cf. Innes, *State*, on Schwannheim, pp. 74–5.

These findings are confirmed by comparisons with non-documentary evidence. Archaeological excavations have revealed the great diversity in the organisation of rural settlement, with a bearing on local relations of power. At Torcy-le-Petit (Aube), for example, traces of a somewhat sprawling settlement have been discovered, whose eight similarly sized buildings, each with two rooms, suggest a roughly egalitarian social environment, occupied since the seventh century. At Frouard (Meurthe-et-Moselle), another old settlement where there were plentiful traces of artisanal work, the ninth century saw a new house constructed resting on stone pads, perhaps representing a lord or his agent. At Vallange, a lost village near Vitry-sur-Orne (Moselle), archaeologists have suggested there was a whole-scale reorganisation of the rural settlement pattern in the eighth century, and they have not hesitated to talk of a planned village. Of all these, it is in fact only for Torcy-le-Petit that there is good evidence that it was 'owned' in the ninth century (by Montier-en-Der), but clearly the plain language of ownership in charters or even polyptychs does not do justice to the qualitative differences suggested by excavations such as these.[117]

Hagiography offers another corroboratory angle. In his *Vita Remigii*, Hincmar of Rheims records that a king granted to St Remigius as much land as he could walk around while the king was taking a siesta.[118] Hincmar, however, writing for a ninth-century audience, did not content himself with this description, but included, too, a revealing passage about the saint's altercation with a mill-owner as he strolled. The usually steely Remigius for once entered into discussion: would it really be so bad to share the mill?[119] This ninth-century Remigius is not made to ask the mill-owner to hand over his mill for salvation, or to sell it; Hincmar did not envisage Remigius's grant wholly eradicating the miller's rights. Indeed, Hincmar actually specified that the royal grant was not so much land itself as 'what was owed to the king, they were to pay to the church of Rheims'.[120]

---

[117] The excavations at Torcy and Frouard are discussed in Peytremann, *L'archéologie*, vol. II, pp. 123–6 and pp. 247–9; Vallange, in *Vallange, un village retrouvé: les fouilles archéologiques de la Zac de la Plaine*, no editor given (Vitry-sur-Orne, 2006): see pp. 34–5 for the apparent 'planification'. For similar comparisons, see F. Bougard and G. Noyé, 'Archéologie médiévale et structures sociales: encore un effort', in D. Barthélemy, ed., *Liber largitorius: études d'histoire médiévale offertes à Pierre Toubert par ses élèves* (Geneva, 2003), pp. 331–46. Torcy is probably the settlement mentioned in the polyptych of Montier-en-Der, ch. 35, detailing the dues of five peasant holdings: see N. Béague-Tahon and M. Georges-Leroy, 'Deux habitats ruraux du Haut Moyen Age en Champagne crayeuse: Juvigny et Torcy le Petit', in C. Lorren and P. Périn, eds., *L'habitat rural du haut Moyen Age: France, Pays-Bas, Danemark et Grande Bretagne* (Rouen, 1995), pp. 175–83, though their suggestion that Juvigny is mentioned in Hincmar of Rheims's letters is unlikely.

[118] In the *Vita Remigii*, p. 306, reprised in *HRE*, bk I, ch. 14, pp. 91ff.   [119] Ibid., p. 307.

[120] *Vita Remigii*, p. 306, 'quod regi debebant, ecclesiae Remensi persolverent'.

The implication is that owning large tracts of land could be less an abstract 'property' than a claim to exercise power. Indeed, occasionally control over land was articulated precisely in the language of *potestas*, contrary to any assumption that this is a phenomenon only of the later period.[121] Chapter 1 showed that free men (*franci*) had made donations of their own land at Aguilcourt, but it is significant that this land remained nevertheless part of the *potestas* of the cathedral of Laon.[122] Other sources make use of the concept of *potestas*, explicitly or implicitly, for lands of Rheims,[123] Soissons,[124] Inden,[125] perhaps Stavelot,[126] and though a little later, Gorze.[127] This *potestas* cannot unequivocally be translated as ownership, as Hincmar of Rheims indeed hammered home in his treatise *De Ecclesiis et Capellis*, effectively an extended gloss on *potestas episcopi*, to prove that it did not exclude other rights.[128]

Formal criteria played a role in controlling a village in a dialectic with informal ones: indeed, the very mechanism on which estate management was predicated, the *corvée*, was only semi-formalised, still being referred to as a 'request' in some sources.[129] A ninth-century poem compared the tribute paid by a Breton leader to a Frankish peasant's *census*. Timothy Reuter interpreted this as showing that tribute relations could imply ownership: but an inverted reading, that ownership was a form of tribute-taking, might work just as well.[130] No wonder peasants were so nervous about agreeing to ostensibly one-off requests: irrespective of formalities, binding customs could develop very quickly.[131]

It now becomes easier to see how aristocratic power could penetrate and transcend the legal categories with which our documentary evidence attempts to order reality. *Villae* were in reality not so much owned as dominated: still very much a real relationship, but much more fluid, and

---

[121] Cf. Bisson, 'Feudal'; M. Bur, 'Menre, speculum temporis', in E. Mornet, ed., *Campagnes médiévales. L'homme et son espace: études offertes à Robert Fossier* (Paris, 1995), pp. 135–43.
[122] Hincmar, *Opusculum*, ch. 1, pp. 146–7.
[123] *HRE* bk III, ch. 26, p. 340. Cf. *Miracula Dionysii*, bk III, ch. 11 (St-Rémi). Hincmar, *Capitula*, no. II, ch. 17, p. 50, even makes a throw-away comment about the village as a *dominium*, though this is very rare.
[124] *Miracula Dionysii*, bk III, ch. 7.   [125] Frothar, *Epistolae*, no. 12, pp. 114–16.
[126] *Miracula Remacli*, col. 700: the *villa* of Marche is clearly linked to Stavelot, yet not unequivocally owned.
[127] 'Die Benediktinerabtei St. Arnulf vor Metz in der ersten Hälfte des Mittelalters', ed. E. Müsebeck *Jahrbuch für lothringische Geschichte und Altertumskunde* 13 (1901), 164–244, no. 1 (956): Rezonville, where St-Arnulf owned land 'intra potestatem sancti Gorgonii'. Cf. *UBMR*, no. 171 (929).
[128] Hincmar, *De Ecclesiis*: see particularly pp. 90 and 95.   [129] *MGH Epp.* vol. VI, p. 56.
[130] The poem is Ermold the Black's *In honorem*, p. 112; T. Reuter, 'Plunder and tribute in the Carolingian empire', *TRHS*, 5th ser. 35 (1985), 75–94, at p. 87.
[131] 'Quod renuentes non propter superbiam, sed ne in consuetudinem haberetur', *Miracula vedasti* (BHL 8513), ed. J. Bolland, *AASS Feb.*, vol. 1 (Antwerp, 1658), col. 807.

hard to build into complex systems of tenure.[132] As Devroey and Kuchenbuch have already argued from the evidence of St-Rémi and Prüm's estates respectively, estates were not simply aggregates of anodyne landlord/tenant relationships. Irrespective of practices of documentary representation, relations with the peasantry were only partially mediated through land ownership, and the direct exercise of power was never far away.[133] Carolingian landed property was a complex, multi-layered phenomenon, a means of articulating and modifying social relations which always maintained a varying element of flexibility and subjectivity. Ninth-century aristocratic landholding seems scarcely distinguished in this respect from either the royal fisc, whose intangibility was discussed above, or indeed from the notion of the church immunity.[134] Perhaps all these were far more similar than decades of specialised scholarship has made them seem.

The dynamic at work

Characterising local domination as essentially fluid entails space for man-oeuvrability and negotiation. In theory, this might have benefited those who cultivated the land, allowing them scope for an independence of action, and perhaps even the chance to break out of the direct control of the elite. The Edict of Pîtres – a massive piece of legislation, strongly represented in Rémois manuscripts – contains a clause in which King Charles the Bald worried about *villae* being 'destroyed' because *coloni* were selling their lands, not to their peers but to clerics, which would make it far more difficult to control.[135] That such fears were not restricted to royal estates is suggested by the author of a fragmentary polyptych from Verdun of which only the introduction survives, written in the early tenth century, who complained that villagers were escaping from seigneurial control

---

[132] Cf. F. Theuws, 'Landed property and manorial organisation in northern Austrasia: some considerations and a case study', in N. Roymans and F. Theuws, eds., *Images of the past: studies on ancient societies in northwestern Europe* (Amsterdam, 1991), pp. 299–40, for a parallel argument; for direct exploitation, see Innes, *State*, p. 253.

[133] J-P. Devroey, *Puissants et misérables: système social et monde paysan dans l'Europe des Francs (vi^e-ixe siècles)* (Brussels, 2006), pp. 455–6; Kuchenbuch, *Bäuerliche*, pp. 182–94.

[134] Hincmar, *Collectio de Ecclesiis*, p. 91.

[135] *MGH Capit.*, vol. II, p. 323, ch. 30: 'non solum suis paribus, sed et clericis canonicis ac villanis presbyteris et aliis quibusdam hominibus vendunt'. It was no longer possible to tell which lands had formed *villae*, or even *mansi*, 'et hac occasione sic destructae fiunt villae'. Cf. Ansegis, *Capitularia*, bk III, ch. 36, p. 589, banning donations; *coloni* are not meant to sell things *alicubi* (based on the see *Capitularia Missorum* of 803). Fears about disintegrating *villae* are quite common: Ansegis, *Capitularia*, bk I, ch. 106, p. 498.

altogether.[136] In this light, perhaps *coloni* said to have 'deserted' Rheims's control had not actually left the settlement.[137]

But given the inequalities which are already apparent, what the flexibility of Carolingian property relations meant in practice was the lack of restraint upon an aggressively expansionist domination.[138] Moralists noticed this, and commented on it. In the section on the sin of avarice in his *De Cavendis Vitiis*, a patchwork from quotations of Gregory the Great but woven together to form a coherent argument, Hincmar of Rheims comments that 'there are worldly-rich people who would have enough possessions, if they only were prepared to set limits to their avarice'.[139] Instead, they extend themselves at the cost of their neighbours, as if they could not bear to have partners in this world. This was not done through formal mechanisms: Hincmar describes their acquisition as devious, performed with 'sweet words and threats'. When Amalarius of Trier talked about the importance of distracting laymen at church from their preoccupations with acquiring *villae*, five-oxen plough-teams and a wife, he was probably right to be worried about where their thoughts were wandering.[140] No wonder Pseudo-Isidore considered property, and not the love of money, to be the root of evil.[141]

Most of the direct evidence relates to lords expanding at each other's expense, suggesting that expansion was not just an option but a necessity. Far-flung lands were exchanged not as a sanitised 'estate-consolidation', but because of threats from rivals. When Hincmar of Rheims fretted about Rheims's *mancipia* at Douzy becoming *servi* or *ancillae*, he was clearly anxious that they might just fall under someone else's control, and that Rheims's claims would simply dissolve.[142] The Council of Meaux-Paris in

---

[136] *Gesta episcoporum Virdunensium*, p. 38 (in fact a fragment of a polyptych): 'ne institutio antique et redditus villarum atque census earum prorsus ignorando aboletur'.

[137] *HRE*, bk II, ch. 19, p. 175. However, the Edict of Pîtres does suggest that some peasants had physically run away, as does *MGH Capit.*, vol.I, no. 33, ch. 4, p. 92 ('fugitivos fiscales . . . qui se . . . liberas dicunt').

[138] Cf. E. Renard, 'Genèse et manipulations d'un polyptyque carolingien: Montier-en-Der, IXe–XIe siècles', *Le Moyen Age* 110 (2004), 55–77.

[139] Hincmar, *De Cavendis vitiis et virtutibus exercendis*, ed. D. Nachtman, *MGH* Quellen zur Geistesgeschichte des Mittelalters, vol. XVI (Munich 1998), p. 135. This is a theme on which Ansegis's capitularies also grow prolix: e.g. Ansegis, *Capitularia*, bk I, ch. 64, p. 464.

[140] Amalarius, *Liber officialis*, ed. J. M. Hanssens, *Amalarii episcopi opera*, Studi e testi 138–40, 3 vols. (Rome, 1948), vol. II, bk III, ch. 11, p. 295, 'vacantes ab emptione villae, ab emptione boum quinque iugorum, a ductu uxoris'.

[141] Pseudo-Isidore, *Decretales*, Ps. Clement 5, 'Communis enim usus omnium quae sunt in hoc mundo omnibus esse hominibus debuit, sed per iniquitatem alius hoc suum dicit esse, et alius illud, et sic inter mortales facta divisio est', p. 65.

[142] *HRE* bk III, ch. 26, p. 332, 'ipsa villa in alodem vertatur et ecclesiastica mancipia in servos et ancillas disperciantur'. Note the rhetorical force of the terms of slavery. Cf. the complaint of the Abbot of Murbach to Charlemagne, recorded in the *Formulae Morbacenses*, in *MGH Formulae*, p. 331

845 tried to ensure that church dependants on land allocated by the king's will to his *fideles* carried out twenty days' labour a year for the church, a reminder more concrete even than nones and tithes of whose authority they were really under.[143] But it was not just the church which faced the problem: for example, we know that a certain Nivin, mentioned in Chapter 1, was prepared to give some lands to Hincmar of Laon in exchange for political support – lands that were unimportant for him because they were too distant from his centres of interest.[144] As Nivin must have known, land, if neglected, could slip out into someone else's control, irrespective of the attempt to fix power through charters, which could, despite everything, be interpreted in different ways.[145]

However, some of this expansion was at the expense of peasant communities, a slow encroachment upon relatively independent communities and a greater infiltration of those that were already partially dominated. For example, the visible growth in Montier-en-Der's holdings in the ninth century plausibly reflects growth of control as much as clearances.[146] The same seems to be true at Vanault, where a number of late ninth-century peasants (perhaps those who complained to Bishop Mancio about their priest – see above, p. 38) vainly tried to prove that the land they worked was theirs, not the monastery's.[147] Further west, we know that the village of Favières, near Melun, had been moved away from something that looks like tribute towards something that looks rather more like rent at some point prior to the 870s.[148] And we know, too, that lords were capable of pushing through demands for exacting new obligations, such as marling, the spreading of clay on fields to combat soil acidity.[149] These measures were accomplished partly, one suspects, by physical intimidation – the rough handling mentioned above – but adroit use of the written record played a role, too. Polyptychs, like charters, were instruments not for a benign estate management, but for an extension of practical control, as Barbier has shown with reference to the dispute at

(discussed in C. Wickham, *Framing the early Middle Ages* (Oxford, 2005), p. 257). On the distinctions, see E. Renard, 'Les *mancipia* carolingiens étaient-ils des esclaves?' in P. Corbet, ed., *Les moines du Der, 673–1790* (Langres, 2000), pp. 179–209.

[143] Council of Meaux-Paris 845–6, ch. 62, 'servi autem ecclesiarum quibuscunque potestatibus subditi, ...saltim xx diebus in anno eidem ecclesie ad reficiendas ipsius ruinas absque molestia servire sinantur', *MGH Concilia*, vol. III, p. 114.

[144] Hincmar of Laon, *Epistolae, PL*, vol. cxxiv, col. 980.

[145] For example, the arguments about the *villae* of Neuilly (Hincmar of Rheims, *De villa Noviliaco*) and Poilly (Hincmar of Laon, *Epistolae*, col. 1029–31).

[146] Renard, 'Les *mancipia*'.

[147] *Cartulaire*, ed. d'Herbomez, no. 78. J. Nightingale, *Monasteries and patrons in the Gorze reform: Lotharingia c.850–1000* (Oxford, 2001) suggests the charter needs to be redated to c.918, p. 67, but this does not unduly affect the argument here.

[148] *Das Polyptychon*, ed. Hägermann, ch. 16 (p. 96).   [149] *MGH Capit.*, vol. II, p. 323, ch. 29.

Courtisols recorded in the polyptych of St-Rémi.[150] To call these changes in 'estate organisation' is somewhat euphemistic. It was these changes that were responsible for breaking up the *Rentenlandschaften*, broad zones characterised by particular patterns of exploitation that are still dimly visible in ninth-century sources, but which were rapidly being fragmented into a patchwork of estate exploitation, whose rich variety cannot be explained in terms of formal institutions.[151]

It could in fact be argued that formal institutions won most importance insofar as they too were integrated into the dynamic in question. Perhaps the best example here is that of the distinction between free and unfree, already touched on in Chapter 1. Sometimes lords essentially ignored this distinction, and thereby in effect obliterated it. Dues which must have been unequivocally public, that is, connected with the king and raised from the free population, were incorporated into estate revenues, sometimes even when the royal obligation had been waived.[152] Meanwhile, letting the unfree take over free tenures surely worked to blur the legal status of that land. It is no surprise that the legally defined rights to which dependants sometimes clung could not resist the corrosive effect of immediate interpersonal relations with more powerful people. A capitulary pondering how far a count might discipline free people residing within church lands but holding no land of their own (there were similar populations of the free on royal lands too) has already been mentioned.[153] The status of such people was at risk, and in fact a capitulary issued at Worms in 829 noted that they suffered some legal restrictions.[154]

Formal resistance was seldom an option, or at least not an advisable one. Almost invariably north of the Alps, those who contested their treatment at the hands of their betters on grounds of legal categories found that these categorisations offered no irrefragable defence.[155] Whether one appealed direct to the king, as did the peasants of Mitry near Meaux, or whether

---

[150] J. Barbier, "De minimis curat praetor': Hincmar, le polyptyque de Saint-Remi de Reims et les esclaves de Courtisols', in G. Constable and M. Rouche, eds., *Auctoritas: Mélanges offerts à Olivier Guillot* (Paris, 2006), pp. 267–79. Barbier draws attention to *nota* marks next to the Courtisols section of the polpytych; I can confirm that Oxford Bodley Eng. Hist., c.242, another early modern copy of the polyptych of St-Rémi (whose original is lost), also contains these marginal notes, further supporting her argument.

[151] H-W. Goetz, 'Herrschaft und Recht in der frühmittelalterlichen Grundherrschaft', *Historisches Jahrbuch*, 104 (1984), 392–410.

[152] Notably the *bos aquensis*, in the polyptych of St-Rémi: see p. 27, n. 17 above.

[153] '[D]e liberis hominibus, qui super terram ecclesiae sedent et de proprio nihil habent, in quantum eos comes vel centenarius distringere debeat, quia praeceptum immunitatis eos in totum excusat'. Edited in Mordek, *Bibliotheca*, Appendix 1, no. 19. The *Capitulare de villis* supposes that there are *familia* and *Franci* on royal estates.

[154] *MGH Capit.*, vol. II, p. 19, ch. 6; also in Benedict Levita, *Capitularia*, ch. 301.

[155] For peasant revolts, see Wickham, *Framing*, pp. 578–88.

merely to the lord, as did the peasants of Courtisols (Marne), the result for those claiming their formal freedom was the same, for victory only came when peasants were able to play off one set of lords against another.[156] It is hardly surprising, then, that a kind of informal resistance was the most frequent response to an insidiously amorphous domination: petty theft, sabotage and non-cooperation, the sort of thing that made watches over monastic granaries a necessity.[157]

Sometimes, though, lords paid lip-service to these distinctions in status, the better to drive aristocratic power deeper into local communities. A passage in the polyptych of St-Maur shows how the division of labour was arranged to chime with local status hierarchies: the free *mansus*-holder held the elevated role of throwing the dung off the cart, the servile one was obliged to pile it up from below; along similar lines, the polyptych of Prüm records how only free peasants were obliged to make a ceremonial gift of a suckling pig to the lord.[158] These measures must have made the domination in question seem more natural, aligned with pre-existing divisions. The entire notion of dues differentiated between those of free and unfree status perhaps points to lords playing off, manipulating and working to their own advantage distinctions of status within local communities. Whether it was in a landlord's interests to ignore the finer points of social status presumably depended on the context: maybe in a very securely controlled settlement, it would convenient to gloss over them, whereas in one less under the thumb, it could be safer to hang onto the technicalities.

CONCLUSION: THE DOMINANCE OF LORDSHIP?

This chapter has shown that society between Marne and Moselle in the ninth century was dominated by an aristocratic elite, a finding that will occasion little, if any, surprise. However, it has also argued that this dominance was a little less clear-cut than might be supposed. As categories of office and property dissolve on inspection, we appear to be left with a tension between lordship and community, weighted towards the former. Local communities were not encapsulated by formal structures of power,

---

[156] *DCB* no. 228; *Le polyptych*, ed. Devroey, pp. 28–9.

[157] *HRE*, bk I, ch. 20, pp. 111–12 (forcing them to work on a Sabbath); *Vita Benedicti Anianensis*, ed. G. Waitz, *MGH SS*, vol.xv:i. (Hanover, 1887), pp. 200–20, ch. 10; Cf. *HRE*, bk I, ch. 17, pp. 94–5, for Sault-Saint-Rémi's resistance to Remigius. Granaries: *Prümer Urbar*, ed. Schwab, 'wactas', *passim*. This at least was Caesarius's opinion, 'ne comburatur a malis hominibus', *Prümer Urbar*, ed. Schwab, p. 164. Cf. the *wactas* set in the *Capitulare de villis*, *MGH Capit.*, vol. I, no. 32, ch. 27, p. 85, and cf. *Das Polyptichon*, ed. Droste, for 'vvaitas', *passim*, and *Le polyptych*, ed. Devroey, for 'uuagtas', *passim*.

[158] *Das Polyptychon*, ed. Hägermann, ch. 10 (p. 94) for Fleury-la-Rivière; L. Kuchenbuch, '*Porcus donativus*: language use and gifting in seignorial records between the eighth and the twelfth centuries', in Algazi, Groebner, and Jussen, eds., *Negotiating the gift*, pp. 203–56.

but were oriented by aristocratic power. The absence of a 'bureaucracy' meant that a strict modern distinction between public and private cannot hold. Social domination cannot be understood in terms of formal law, in terms of a public or private dichotomy, or for that matter in terms of property: all of these ideas were present, but they were harnessed in pursuit of an independent logic.

That does not mean that anarchy prevailed in the ninth century: but perhaps that was only because rivalry amongst the elite in itself generated a balance of power. Neither was there a barely suppressed mayhem lying just below irenically authoritative capitularies, nor was social stability generated by central fiat. In fact, just this balance is superbly illustrated by a passing comment of Archbishop Hincmar of Rheims. He had heard that his nephew Bishop Hincmar of Laon, bothered by troublesome neighbours and dependants, considered himself hampered by his ordination, and boasted of his athletic prowess and dreamed of battles: if only he were a layman, what might he do! Hincmar of Rheims took the pains to disillusion him:

Concerning the foolishness of your boasting about what you would do if you were a layman, I can reply to you concisely. You would do just as your compatriots and your neighbours do. That is, you would willingly and peacefully live among your neighbours and those living by you. Because if you did otherwise, you would find stronger and more powerful people who would resist your efforts, and who would cut you down to size.[159]

If even an archbishop and royal *missus* did not consider that social order was determined purely by formal institutions of power, then the implication is that the personal and social ambitions of the elite were conditioned by their role in a logic of aristocratic domination, and by extension, that what mattered during the ninth century was the central fact of lordship, and strategies for negotiating it. This has an obvious bearing on historians' view of the Feudal Revolution, whose 'classic' version is severely weakened by such revisionist readings of the ninth century. Yet while study of the formal institutions alone is evidently not enough to give us a sense of the dynamics of the period, a reliance on the concept of lordship is not in itself sufficient either, as will be discussed in the next chapter.

---

[159] 'De vanitate autem, qua te iactas qualiter faceres, si laicus esses, breviter tibi valeo respondere: faceres utique, sicut patriotae et propinqui tui laici faciunt, scilicet voluntarie viveres inter tuos conterraneos atque vicinos pacifice, quoniam, si aliter praesumeres, fortiores et superiores qui tibi resisterent teque reprimerent, invenires': Hincmar, *Opusculum*, p. 358.

Chapter 3

CAROLINGIAN CO-ORDINATIONS

Properly speaking, an interjection is an incoherent noise emitted from the secret depths of the mind which is uttered in public solely in order to reveal clearly the inner state of the person. It shows the motions of the inner mind clearly in a happy face, the guffaw of someone laughing, in clapping, stamping, winking, clearing the throat, shaking the head, wagging a finger, an angry face, a contemptuous look, a warning noise, an amorous stance, tears or in adapting the meaning of a spoken word. For the secrets of the mind within are not known to anyone but God unless some kind of utterance or sign is made. By making them known openly through a spoken sign, one person comes to know the secrets of another.

Smaragdus of St-Mihiel, *Liber in partibus Donati.*[1]

The previous two chapters explored two alternative perspectives on Carolingian society between Marne and Moselle in the ninth century. In part, this was to bring out certain topics which will be tracked in subsequent chapters, setting a base-line against which to measure later developments in fields such as charter practice, property-holding, royal authority and local domination. Yet they also represented, using the area between Marne and Moselle as a microcosm, the two approaches to Carolingian society that underpin opposing stances on the Feudal Revolution. Duby's original formulation was based on an understanding of the Carolingians akin to that set out in Chapter 1, whereas much recent critique of Duby and those following in his wake is founded on the approach to Carolingian society adopted in Chapter 2. Our problem is that both approaches find solid foundations in the evidence, and clearly speak to important aspects of the ninth century. It is methodologically not

---

[1] Smaragdus, *Liber in partibus Donati*, ed. L. Lofstedt, *CCCM* vol. LXVIII (Turnhout, 1986), p. 233; translation based on that of V. Law, 'The study of grammar', in R. McKitterick, ed., *Carolingian culture*, pp. 88–110.

possible to prioritise the evidence discussed in one chapter over that emphasised in the other, since the sources on which these chapters were based are fundamentally part of a single set of material, not two distinct ones of which one is somehow more authentic, reliable or truthful than the other.

Accordingly, if there is a temptation from the perspective of the Feudal Revolution debate to marshal the evidence of Chapter 1 to argue for the existence of, or at least for the intention to set up, a Weberian-style state (which could later collapse), or conversely to suggest that the material discussed in Chapter 2 reveals instead a society based on lordship (which never really changed), it is a temptation that must be resisted. The fact that convincing evidence can be mobilised on each side suggests that these mutually oppositional categories are flawed – as indeed historians are increasingly aware. The limitations of a state-centred approach to the medieval world are well known, but historians have also recently begun to question the concept of lordship, a category that is (at least in this period) equally artificial, suspiciously restricted in its use to 'pre-modern' societies, and always at risk of slipping into a shorthand for a mysteriously timeless, unchanging force that invisibly dominated 'medieval' societies.[2]

The aim of this chapter is therefore to identify an approach to ninth-century society that does justice both to those aspects of the evidence highlighted in Chapter 1 and to those emphasised in Chapter 2 without forcing the historian to prioritise one above the other; in other words, to see whether, looked at differently, the empirical contents of Chapters 1 and 2 can be understood as complementary rather than mutually exclusive, since there is no methodological grounds to discount either or to subordinate one to the other. Moving away from the categories of lordship or the state which together have led only to interpretatative deadlock, it will take its cue from recent work in attempting to sketch out a view of ninth-century society between Marne and Moselle that incorporates all the evidence, not merely some of it, and that sheds light, too, on the dynamics of change.

---

[2] For a recent appraisal, see S. Reynolds, 'Historiography of the medieval state', in M. Bentley, ed., *Companion*, pp. 117–38. For the cognate notion of *Herrschaft*, see L. Kuchenbuch, 'Abschied von der "Grundherrschaft". Ein Prüfgang durch das ostfränkisch-deutsche Reich (950–1050)', *Zeitschrift der Savigny-Stiftung für Rechtsgeschichte. Germanistische Abteilung* 121 (2004), 1–99; also useful here is M. Richter, *The history of social and political concepts: a critical introduction* (New York, 1995), pp. 58–70. Cf. P. Fouracre, 'The use of the term *beneficium* in Frankish sources: a society based on favours?', in W. Davies and P. Fouracre, eds., *The languages of gift in the early Middle Ages* (Cambridge, 2010), pp. 62–88, n. 76 at p. 80 for doubts about the value of the concept of honour, along similar lines.

CAROLINGIAN SYMBOLIC COMMUNICATION BETWEEN MARNE
AND MOSELLE: GIFTS, VIOLENCE AND MEETINGS

An important step towards that more comprehensive approach, though one
that suffers from its own difficulties, as we will see, is offered by the study of
symbolic communication. The history of this study is itself an intricate and
fascinating subject. It emerged from the interaction of a number of influences, of which especially important were a new sensitivity to cultural
practices inspired by the rise of cultural history, itself linked to certain strands
of cultural anthropology and a deep-rooted element of German-language
scholarship that considered medieval society to have been organised in ways
radically different from those of modern society.[3] The two have combined
to create a field of enquiry which sees 'ritual' (on which more later) as the
glue holding society together in the absence of more modern forms of
communication like writing, and one better suited to the peculiarities of
medieval society, characterised by a distinctive preoccupation with maintaining honour and social status.

Even from this brief sketch, it is apparent that there are a number of
methodological issues which require further discussion; but before we
tackle these it is necessary to see how far the study of symbolic communication finds resonance in the sources for the area between Marne and
Moselle. An investigation of three forms of 'symbolic' interaction makes it
clear that, like the approaches oriented to the centre and to the locality,
and in fact precisely as a way of bringing these within a single frame of
analysis, the field of symbolic communication has something to offer, just
as has been argued elsewhere (though to rather different effect) in innovative recent work by Ildar Garipzanov.[4]

Gifts and gift exchange

The centrality of practices of gift exchange to Carolingian society has been
explored in a number of recent studies, but these have usually concentrated on one or the other end of the social spectrum.[5] Florin Curta has
shown the importance of gifts for the exercise of kingship and the politics

---

[3] On these German traditions of scholarship, see J. Demade, 'The medieval countryside in German-language historiography since the 1930s', in I. Alfonso, ed., *The rural history of medieval European societies: trends and perspectives* (Turnhout, 2007), pp. 173–252.

[4] Garipzanov, *Symbolic language*, pp. 1–41. Taking its inspiration from Russian semiotics together with a dash of Weber, this stimulating book concentrates on the communication of royal authority in 'non-written' forms (though in fact much of its evidence is textual), and on the audience's reception or rejection of that message (its 'horizon of expectation'); as will become clear, my approach concentrates instead on the clarity and indelibility of what is communicated.

[5] Most recently, see Fouracre, '*Beneficium*'.

of the court, while Jean-Pierre Devroey and Ludolf Kuchenbuch have demonstrated that this is just as true of the micro-politics that can be faintly discerned from the material concerning local relations of domination.[6] In fact, what is interesting is how practices of gift exchange transcended the local and regional, and indeed infused the entire political edifice from top to bottom.

The importance of gift exchange amongst the elites can be addressed succinctly, not for lack of evidence, but because it is already so well known. After all, traces of the practice constitute a substantial portion of our evidence in this area as in others, in the shape of gifts to monasteries and to royal favourites. In the light of recent research on the ninth-century economy, it would be unrealistic to argue that this represents a 'gift economy', since there was plenty of commerce around already in the ninth century.[7] What it perhaps does reflect is a political system that was built around something other than fiscal extraction, an idea to which we will return. Whatever the case, it is striking that gift exchange is just as evident, if not indeed even clearer, at the local level. We know that elites in this area made gifts to their social inferiors. Bishop Frothar of Toul, for example, fed Toul *pauperes* during famines, later requesting reductions in his imperial obligations as a result.[8] Yet giving food was not restricted to emergencies; it was also a routine measure, part of the seigneurial relationship. Hincmar's St Remigius, as imagined in the *Vita* Hincmar wrote around 880, gave out food when he visited villages belonging to Rheims; more prosaically, ninth-century polyptychs, like that from Prüm or Montier-en-Der, sometimes specify when foodstuffs were to be given to dependants and in what quantity, and miracle collections depict this in action.[9]

As with all gifts, there was the anticipation of reciprocation. Bishop Frothar's patronage of the poor was repaid with their labour, and this is also the usual context for the polyptych references. Indeed, it is clear that gift-giving to the lord was as commonplace as the reverse. Several polyptychs, including that of St-Rémi, record the obligations of certain people, often the *maiores* of a *villa*, to make symbolic gifts to the monastery

---

[6] F. Curta, 'Merovingian and Carolingian gift giving', *Speculum* 81 (2006), 671–99; J.-P. Devroey, 'Communiquer et signifier entre seigneurs et paysans', *Settimane* 52 (Spoleto, 2005), 121–54; Kuchenbuch, '*Porcus*'.

[7] For an alternative view, more informed by Fossier's idea of the Carolingian period, see R. Keyser, 'La transformation de l'échange des dons pieux: Montier-la-Celle, Champagne, 1100–1350', *Revue historique* 628 (2003), 793–816.

[8] Frothar of Toul, *Epistolae*, no. 11, pp. 110–14.

[9] *Vita Remigii*, p. 273, depicts Remigius at Thugny, giving out 'cibum et potum in consolationem labori'. *Prümer Urbar*, ed. Schwab, for reference to the *pastum* 'qui dandus erat familie ex parte senioris' (ch. 54, p. 217); *Das Polyptichon*, ed. Droste, ch. 9 ('pro prandio'). *Miracula Remacli*, col. 703.

'in acts of veneration for the masters', but the *maiores* were not the only ones to be involved.[10] Several estate documents from the lands between Marne and Moselle specify that food renders from the demesne land were to be delivered to the estate centre; sometimes even a peasant's personal renders were to be delivered there and moreover in person, and there are records depicting this actually taking place.[11] Collective gifts were also made to the saint as lord of the community, particularly on festive occasions.[12] These compulsory gifts served to stage a relationship. Grateful peasants brought tokens of their gratitude in return for the lord's benevolence in letting them work their land.[13] Put differently, these gift exchanges, combined with the movement of the dependant, were central to performing the aristocratic control discussed in Chapter 2. Indeed, one wonders whether the cultivation of the lord's land that underpinned the entire bipartite system should itself be viewed in this gift-exchange nexus.

Thinking about gift exchange does not just help us think of 'secular' structures of authority; it also, perhaps, helps us make sense of the church's broader interaction with the world. The ninth-century insistence that parish priests go to the bishop's city each year to receive the chrism, holy oil necessary for a variety of pastoral uses, and the equal insistence that this chrism must be freely given by the bishop, can, for example, also be read as a form of highly staged gift exchange.[14] More mundanely, gifts appear to have played a crucial role in embedding parochial forms of authority in the countryside, too. As we have seen, local (parish) churches often received donations of parcels of land as tokens of gratitude, particularly for burial, already in the ninth century a sensitive marker of local social status. Even more interesting, there were efforts to capture the everyday circulation of foodstuffs within settlements and bring them within 'official' circuits. Hincmar of Rheims in his episcopal statutes promoted the negotiation of local community status via the local church, discussing how the *eulogiae* which the parishioners

---

[10] For example, Gerlaius, the *maior* of Aigny (Marne) was to bring two full bottles of wine, four chickens and three cakes or loaves (*fogatia*) at Easter and Christmas 'in veneration of the masters' (*Le Polyptych*, ed. Devroey, ch. 1, p. 4): at Courtisols, the *maior*, the priest and the deacon all had to take similar gifts 'to venerate the masters' to the monastery itself (p. 27); there are plenty more examples in the St-Rémi polyptych (e.g. pp. 29, 31, 35 and 53).

[11] *Miracula Remacli*, cols. 699 and 703.

[12] *HRE*, bk 1, ch. 24, p. 126; *Translatio SS, Chrysanthi et Dariae*, pp. 182–3.

[13] Cf. C. Dyer, 'Language of oppression: the vocabulary of rents and services in England', in M. Bourin and P. Martinez Sopeña, eds., *Pour une anthropologie du prélèvement seigneurial dans les campagnes médiévales, XIe–XIVe siècles: les mots, les temps, les lieux* (Paris, 2007), pp. 71–86.

[14] Roger of Trier, *Capitula*, ed. P. Brommer, *Capitula episcoporum*, vol. 1 (Hanover, 1984), pp. 57–70, at ch. 15, p. 67. His text is based on Radulf of Bourges's widely disseminated episcopal statute, who in turn drew on Ansegis's capitularies.

donated should be redistributed to the needy, framing thereby the priest as an authoritative intermediary.[15]

Violence

If gifts were a pervasive part of Carolingian political culture at every level, then the same could be argued for violence. Much recent study of violence has concentrated on its role as a means of communication, and though not the whole story – for the defining characteristic of violence, if it is to retain any meaning, is that it affects bodies, not just representations – the approach is fruitful.[16] Again, the role of violence at the higher levels needs be touched on only briefly, for even a cursory glance at material connected in some way to the royal court illustrates its prominence. Carolingian capitularies are frequently concerned with regulating violence, distinguishing between its legitimate and illegitimate forms, and some of the evidence adduced in Chapter 1 suggests that this discourse was not without practical effect, as discourses tend not to be.[17] The royal court was envisaged as a haven of peace, and indeed there is anecdotal evidence to suggest that prohibitions of violence within its walls had some impact, underpinned by the occasional execution by royal command.[18] Yet at the same time one kind of violence, that is warfare, was central to the Frankish view of themselves and their kings, to the extent that the early Carolingian assemblies could double as musters of the army, and paving the way for sharp criticism of those kings like Charles the Bald who bought off foes like the Vikings rather than aggressively facing them down.

Once again, the local level provides still more suggestive evidence. It is clear that beating peasants was a way of asserting control over land: this is why those who held church land illicitly, or against that church's will, could be readily accused of so much violence, as was discussed in Chapter 2. Texts from this region sometimes took on the defence of the powerless. Hincmar's Remigius cursed some recalcitrant peasants with hereditary impoverishment, but he also pointed out that the hungry will not listen to preaching, and Hincmar himself inveighed against the powerful's oppression of *coloni*.[19] Yet texts complaining about secular

---

[15] Hincmar, *Capitula* no. 1, ch. 7, p. 37 and ch. 16, p. 43.

[16] See G. Halsall, ed., *Violence and society in the early medieval West* (Woodbridge, 1998); for an interesting new angle, see L. Oliver, *The body legal in barbarian law* (Toronto, 2011).

[17] Cf. J. Nelson, 'Ninth-century knighthood: the evidence of Nithard', in C. Harper-Bill, C. J. Holdsworth and Janet L. Nelson, eds., *Studies in medieval history presented to R. Allen Brown* (Woodbridge, 1989), pp. 255–66.

[18] Regino, *Chronicon*, s. a. 892, p. 140 (execution of Waltgar for drawing his sword at a *conventum publicum*).

[19] *Vita Remigii*, p. 310; *HRE*, bk III, ch. 23, p. 3.

lords abusing their peasants might also, and more plausibly, be read as clerics championing the cause of their control of those poor.[20] Protection from the assaults of rival lords seems to have been a primary element of ninth-century domination, to judge from accounts in which oppressed cultivators made appeal to the saints through supplications, part of the self-justifying function of elite domination familiar from later periods, too.[21] We should assume that the miracles that followed were the functional (or at least imagined) equivalent of a similar protection exercised by secular lords, who we happen to know sometimes protected their dependants from episcopal punishment.[22] Particularly targeted by this kind of assault was the village elite, simultaneously using that group's prominence to highlight power whilst also conspicuously undermining potential alternative sources of social cohesion.[23]

The material discussed in Chapter 2 could be read as showing that 'lordship' is really a label, and an awkward one at that, for a composite of practices of violence combined with gift exchange, in which the lord, whether saint or secular, punished the recalcitrant, defended the obedient and rewarded the dependant. Put differently, these were mechanisms of communication, ways of articulating status and relative social positions. Without them, social domination could not be expressed, and if it could not be expressed, it threatened to dissolve, as the Edict of Pîtres and other texts imply: hence the insistence in our evidence on both aspects. Yet a final component also needs attention.

Formal meetings in the Carolingian world

The importance of public meetings at the highest political level cannot be doubted in the wake of recent research into royal assemblies, nor should the level of effort that went into orchestrating these meetings be underestimated.[24] It is generally acknowledged that Carolingian courts

---

[20] E.g. *HRE*, bk III, ch. 26, p. 336, in which Hincmar criticises Count Liuthard because 'famulos ipsius ecclesie inquietans cum pace non sineret degere' - presumably these *famuli* were on Rheims land, 'de qua multa bona habebat'. Hincmar refused to let some *coloni* of Rheims land around Worms be given hospitality duties: *HRE*, bk III, ch. 26, p. 332.

[21] See G. Algazi, *Herrengewalt und Gewalt der Herren in späten Mittelalter. Herrschaft, Gegenseitigkeit und Sprachgebrauch* (Frankfurt, 1996), for later medieval conditions.

[22] Council of Fimes, 881, *PL*, vol. CXXV, col. 1080, repeating an 853 capitulary and in turn repeated in Regino, *Libri duo*, bk II, ch. 5, no. 76. Cf. L. Feller, 'Les hiérarchies dans le monde rural', in D. Iogna-Prat, F. Bougard and R. le Jan, eds., *Hiérarchie et stratification sociale dans l'Occident médiéval (400–1100)*, pp. 257–76, at pp. 262–3 (citing work by Barthélemy).

[23] Attacking the elite: Heiric, *Miracula Germani*, col. 1241 (concerning Montfaucon), 'qui inter caeteros honoratior videbatur'.

[24] T. Reuter, 'Assembly politics in Western Europe from the eighth century to the twelfth', in P. Linehan and J. Nelson, eds., *The medieval world* (London, 2001), pp. 432–50.

were gorgeously ritualised places.[25] At the centre of this setting stood the king or emperor, whose gestures and comportment were carefully observed. Most attention has been devoted in this context to Emperor Louis the Pious, and secondarily to King Charles the Bald, but similar arguments could be mounted concerning King Lothar II of Lotharingia, on account of whose failed divorce case we have a wealth of evidence. We know that his public appearance at meetings of various kinds was the object of careful scrutiny. Bishop Adventius of Metz, reporting back to a stern Pope Nicholas I on the condition of his king's controversial marriage, hastened to prove that Lothar II had really taken back Theutberga: they were seen at church together, they feasted together and, 'as the report has it, he gives to believe that he happily pays the debt of conjugal convention'.[26] Lothar II's reign also reminds us that even apparently spontaneous actions were doubtless contrived. His appearance, tearful, barefoot and slightly out of control, before the assembled Councils of Aachen in 860 must have been remarkable, but given that we know that he had been briefed to cry on other occasions, it was probably not entirely off-the-cuff.[27]

Carefully orchestrated codes of behaviour of this sort were not, however, restricted to meetings involving kings. For example, we know that when King Charles the Bald left a council in the palace of Attigny in 870 and the synod was adjourned to the next day, the bishops stood around chatting by the windows of the palace. Hincmar of Rheims was talking to Bishop Odo of Beauvais by a window, when two other bishops approached, intimating that his younger nephew, Bishop Hincmar of Laon, wanted to talk to him, though up to this point they had been avoiding each other on account of a serious disagreement. The elder Hincmar was delighted – and turned round to where Hincmar the younger was talking with some other bishops by another window, and called him over. In a pantomime of ill-feeling, they had studiously been ignoring each other, within feet of each other. This must have taken a particular effort on the part of the younger bishop, for we are told elsewhere that he literally shook with anger whenever anyone

---

[25] An excellent contextualisation is provided by M. McCormick, *Eternal victory: triumphal rulership in late antiquity, Byzantium, and the early medieval West* (Cambridge, 1986), particularly ch. 9, pp. 328–87. Cf. also P. Depreux, 'Gestures and comportment at the Carolingian court: between practice and perception', *Past and Present* 203 (2009), 57–79.

[26] 'ut relatio innuit, coniugalis habitum debitum solvere hilariter praetendit': *MGH Epp.*, vol. VI, no. 16, pp. 233–6, at p. 235.

[27] Bishop Adventius specified that when Lothar II did his penance in 865, he had to cry as he did so: 'Et inter lacrimosa suspiria' (*MGH Epp.*, vol. VI, no. 15, pp. 232–3). Charles the Bald, too, had deployed penitential practice: Council of Quierzy 858, *MGH Capit.*, vol. II, p. 296. See the classic exposition of M. de Jong, 'What was public about public penance? Paenitentia publica and justice in the Carolingian world', *Settimane* 44 (1997), 863–904.

mentioned his uncle.[28] His anger found 'ritual' expression too, though. Hincmar of Laon's refusal at Gondreville in 869 to talk to or kiss Hincmar of Rheims, the 'required display of respect' (*debita obsequii veneratio*) which everyone else had carried out, had been a major (according to the elder Hincmar, a wretched) sign – *spectaculum* – but also a source of their ill-will.[29]

When it comes to the locality, the evidence is less forthcoming, but still suggestive.[30] Very plausibly the count's *mallum* was also a venue for this kind of behaviour. As with most discussion of comital power, the evidence is largely indirect. However, it would make sense of the developments discussed in Chapter 1, such as the increasing importance of the advocate, a concept and practice that implies a certain formality of action. The way *mallum* meetings were described in charters, in heavily formulaic language, also implies a certain staging; and indeed, signs of an increasing formality of procedure will be discussed in Chapter 5. The polyptychs are similarly inconclusive but suggestive, sometimes specifying that the gifts owed to those who controlled the land were to be brought on a feast-day, thereby implying a ceremonial meeting of sorts; but more than that cannot be said.

Overall, though, it could be argued that the Carolingian elites displayed a certain preoccupation with meetings of various kinds. We have texts describing the royal assembly, and indeed Hincmar's *De Ordine Palatii*, indicating in detail how it should be run. As already discussed, we have a greater emphasis on the distinctive nature of the count's *mallum* court, apparently increasingly differentiated from other kinds of meetings. We also have indications that the Carolingians were very interested in the form of synodal meetings. Whatever the date of the 'original' text, the oldest manuscripts of the *ordo de concilio celebrando*, setting out a basic framework for how synods should be run – as its editor points out, not so much a generic 'meeting agenda' as a format to guarantee the presence of the Holy Spirit – are all Carolingian. These manuscripts are ones of canon law, but the ninth century also saw a new redaction of the *ordo*, which introduced the genre into liturgical manuscript contexts.[31]

---

[28] 'frendentes motus cum de me loquitur': Hincmar, *Libellus Expostulationis* ed. *MGH Concilia*, vol. iv, pp. 420–87, at p. 460.
[29] Hincmar, *Opusculum*, Preface (the only source): 'pacis osculum dare noluisti ... non dicam magnum, sed miserum multis spectaculum praebuisti', p. 143. Cf. deliberate avoiding, ibid. p. 170. On Gondreville, see McKeon, *Hincmar*, pp. 70–2; cf. H. Fuhrmann, *Einfluss und Verbreitung der pseudoisidorischen Fälschungen: von ihrem Auftauchen bis in die neuere Zeit* (Stuttgart, 1972), vol. ii, p. 661. For kissing, cf. *Vita Benedicti*, ch. 32.
[30] Cf. the comparable arguments of McCormick, *Eternal victory*, on the percolation of imperial ritual throughout Byzantine society, pp. 252–8.
[31] *Ordines de celebrando concilio*, ed. H. Schneider, *MGH Leges* (Hanover, 1996), pp. 2–4. The manuscripts for *Ordo i* are listed pp. 125–35. The ninth-century redaction is edited as *Ordo vii*, pp. 296–315; textual revisions included adding specific instructions for each day of the synod, the insertion of some additional material, and above all, an attempt to 'Romanise' the text.

Finally, it should be noted that the institution of the monastic chapter, the daily meeting of the monastic community, was itself a Carolingian development, at least in its institutionalisation. Not mentioned in the Benedictine Rule, it took on a central importance in ninth-century monasticism, and indeed a chapter book from the monastery of Prüm represents some of the earliest evidence for the meeting as a kind of institution.[32] Together, these indications seem to show a sharpened interest in the importance of meetings, in distinguishing some from others, and in lending these a greater formality.

CHARACTERISING CAROLINGIAN SYMBOLIC COMMUNICATION

As already mentioned, much of the work on symbolic communication is associated with the pathbreaking research of Gerd Althoff and his students. The evidence discussed above seems to support part of Althoff's central argument, that Carolingian society really did lean heavily on symbolic communication, and moreover that it did so more than had Frankish society hitherto.[33] The intensification of interest in gifts, violence and orchestrated behaviour documented through, but also by, our evidence suggests that all this cannot be dismissed as a trick of the sources, and that some historical process was at work. That does not mean we have to claim that there was 'more' gift-giving, violence or formal ceremony in the ninth century than earlier, for if that is not altogether implausible, it is certainly immeasurable; we can, however, state that these forms took on a greater prominence in the co-ordination of social activity, and became the objects of greater scrutiny at a variety of levels.

This approach has the potential to help us out of our impasse, because it represents a means of grasping social action in a way which does not force us to separate, then compare, state and lordship. Instead, we can study the same practices distributed across Carolingian society. There is no incommensurable separation between state and lordship when we think about practices of gift-giving, or of the communicative power of bodily violence, or of ceremonialised meeting. Instead, we can see attempts to express and communicate in a variety of forms across the whole breadth of Carolingian society. However, in its current elaboration, the notion of symbolic communication tends to emphasis more the 'lordship' than the 'state' aspect of Carolingian society; two slight modifications are required

---

[32] See F. Lifshitz, *The name of the saint: the martyrology of Jerome and access to the sacred in Francia, 627–827* (Notre Dame, 2006), pp. 112–13, and p. 125 for the Prüm chapter book (Trier, Stadtbibliothek 1245).

[33] G. Althoff, *Die Macht der Rituale: Symbolik und Herrschaft im Mittelalter* (Darmstadt, 2003), particularly pp. 32–67.

if it is to realise its full potential for understanding the development of the Carolingian world.

Textual representation

The first of these is essentially an empirical point. Althoff himself noted that his model, honed on Ottonian material, did not perfectly suit the Carolingians, partly because Carolingian symbolic communication did not seem to have the binding quality, or the stability of meaning and effect, that it would later have, at least in his vision of the Ottonian court. This is an insight of great importance; but whereas Althoff saw it as a deficiency, a sign that the Carolingians lacked something or alternatively still relied on other means of social co-ordination, it might be preferable instead to see it as a specific characteristic.

That characteristic is perhaps most prominent in the ambivalence of reports of symbolic communication. In a series of iconoclastic interventions, Philippe Buc stressed that all historians know about the occasions classed as moments of symbolic communication throughout the Middle Ages comes from texts whose authors may have used their description as a means of passing judgement over the people involved. A hostile observer would claim that the choreography went embarrassingly wrong, where the well-disposed might record a ceremonial triumph. Buc's point is that we have no basis for establishing whether particular events unfolded as described or not, and that we would therefore do better to restrict our analysis to the level of the text; symbolic communication is thereby reduced to textual effect.[34] The argument is a strong one, and resonates with the material from Francia between Marne and Moselle. For example, after his deposition by a council in Francia in 863, Bishop Rothad of Soissons travelled to Rome to complain to the Pope. Requested to justify his actions, Hincmar of Rheims, who had presided over the deposition, argued that Rothad could not now reasonably be reappointed as bishop because five hundred people had witnessed the deposition, had seen him calmly arriving at the synod's door and leaving it like a madman: these people had come to the synod 'in truth as to a spectacle'.[35] It so happens

---

[34] For a discussion of Buc's work, and a generally thoughtful intervention in the debate, see the recent contribution of Pössel, 'Magic'.

[35] Hincmar, *Epistolae*, *PL*, vol. CXXVI, col. 32: 'sed et omnes urbis incolae ac populi, qui cum rege et episcopis ad synodum convenerunt, et ut revera ad spectaculum currentes, eum viderunt usque ad ostium synodi venientem, et mae ut maniaticum redeuntem'. It was 'amplius quam quingenti'. The letter is also cited in *HRE*, bk III ch. 13, p. 226. Similarly, the church of St-Medard, which in 833 had witnessed the deposition of Louis the Pious, was full to bursting: 'quotquot videlicet intra sui septum eadem continere potuit ecclesia' (*MGH Capit.*, vol. II, p. 53).

that Rothad himself also mentioned this same crowd, but put in rather a different interpretative light. For him, this crowd, composed of people from the city and the region around it, went to lobby in his favour the papal legates when they arrived, although they were dispersed by the threats and violence of Bishop Erchenraus of Châlons lest they disrupt events.[36] Were these people voyeuristic and impressionable bystanders, or Rothad's mustard-keen supporters? That depends whom you read, precisely the kind of dilemma to which Buc drew attention.

In fact, debate over the 'content' of symbolic communication is such a feature of Carolingian texts that it surely contributes to understanding their proliferation. It is quite possible (indeed likely) that different accounts of meetings and assemblies routinely circulated around the Frankish world, as suggested by the two versions of the Aachen 860 meeting over Lothar II's divorce preserved by Hincmar in his *De Divortio*, or the debates as to what exactly Pope Gregory was doing at the Field of Lies in 833, or what happened to Charles the Fat in the church at Frankfurt.[37] Indeed, it is differences of this nature which make Carolingian annals so revealing as a kind of source, for they disclose their carefully constructed nature by the differing way in which they represent certain pivotal events.[38] It is hardly any wonder there was concern to monitor those texts, as shown by Hincmar's concern over an early version of the Annals of St-Bertin that had in 866 passed into many people's hands and so threatened, in Hincmar's eyes, to promulgate an unfortunate interpretation of events.[39] We have, of course, only a fraction of the historical accounts that were composed; we know of dozens of texts drawn up in the rows between Hincmar of Rheims and his nephew Hincmar, Bishop of Laon, most of which seem to have been concerned to impose diverging interpretations on the same events, and virtually all of which are now lost.[40] We might well imagine conflicting reports of meetings as part of the

---

[36] Rothard, *Libellus proclamationis*, p. 186.

[37] Cf. Astronomer, *Vita Ludovici*, ch. 48 with Paschasius's rather different account, *Vita Walae*, bk II, ch. 16. For Charles the Fat, see S. Maclean, 'Ritual, misunderstanding, and the contest for meaning: representations of the disrupted royal assembly at Frankfurt (873)', in B. Weiler and S. MacLean, eds., *Representations of power in medieval Germany* (Turnhout, 2006), pp. 97–120. For Lothar II, cf. *Annales Fuldenses*, s. a. 864.

[38] For the careful construction of histories, see in general R. McKitterick, *Perceptions of the past in the early Middle Ages* (Notre Dame, 2006).

[39] Hincmar, *MGH Epistolae*, p. 196: a letter to Archbishop Egilo about Gottschalk, that refers to the Annals of Prudentius, 'iam in plurimorum manus devenerunt'. Hincmar was worried because Prudentius had written that Pope Nicholas had approved the theory of double predestination.

[40] Council of Aachen 860, *MGH Concilia*, vol. IV, pp. 3, 4. McKeon, *Hincmar*, 169–78 offers a register of Hincmar of Laon's output, most of which is lost.

'background noise' of textual exchange in the ninth century, circulating sometimes secretly, sometimes openly.

Symbolic fragility

Yet Buc's point about the instability of representation can perhaps be taken a little further, as has been suggested by a number of historians. There seems to be a more fundamental issue here, relating to a kind of immanent instability inhering in the events themselves.[41] For example, there is plenty of reason to believe that Carolingian *Inszenierung* ('stage-management') was less accomplished than it would be in Althoff's Ottonian court. We can take as an example an unusually rich account of a meeting at Worms in June 858, in the aftermath of King Louis the German's failed invasion of West Francia, between west Frankish and east Frankish legates. The western legates, led by Archbishop Hincmar, had been carefully briefed. Louis was to accept responsibility for his invasion, confess, promise to do better, agree to meet Charles and Lothar, promise never to invade again, and (the controversial part) to disassociate himself from those whose advice he had followed and publicly to punish them. If all these conditions were met, the legates were to offer him forgiveness and restore him to communion, and to give him not the years of penance he deserved, but a light sentence.[42]

However, King Louis commenced the meeting with a surprise, asking for forgiveness before he would discuss anything further. Caught off his guard – by his own declaration he was not good at thinking on his feet – Archbishop Hincmar 'standing first to his left', replied cautiously that 'this business can soon be settled, since you are seeking that which we are offering'.[43] Rather than asking what the conditions might be, as Hincmar surely hoped he would, Louis stayed silent and waited. Hincmar then added that he had no personal rancour sufficient to stop him performing the Eucharist. Louis stayed silent; another pause. Finally, Bishop Theoderic of Minden, one of Louis's bishops, burst out, 'Do as our lord has asked: forgive him.'[44] The consummate politician, Hincmar responded by forgiving him personally, but pointedly not as an archbishop whose church had been damaged. The meeting continued in a desultory fashion for a while, with each side trading accusations, until

---

[41] Cf. MacLean, 'Ritual misunderstanding'.

[42] Council of Metz 858, *MGH Concilia*, vol. III, p. 439, setting the conditions for *indulgentia*.

[43] Council of Metz 858, *Relatio Legatorum*, ed. *MGH Concilia*, vol. III, p. 443. Thinking on his feet: Hincmar, *MGH Epistolae*, p. 190. In his *Opusculum*, Hincmar also discussed how he feared he would be left literally speechless with anger (p. 144). Cf. the elaborate preparations he sent to Archbishop Egilo of Sens, going to the Pope, including the advice to find 'someone with a good memory'.

[44] 'dicente ipso Theoderico haec verba, "Facite, sicut senior noster precatur; parcite ille".' Ibid., p. 444.

Louis demanded a chance to consider the matter with his bishops. Here, Hincmar was outmanoeuvred: for when a king declared that he did nothing without the advice of his bishops, there was little Hincmar, of all people, could say.

It is inconceivable that this meeting was a pre-planned forum by which clear meanings were communicated, yet the references to who was standing where suggest that it was not entirely informal. Perhaps it could be argued that this is unusually good evidence of a 'behind the scenes' kind of meeting that Althoff thinks were pre-conditions for a proper *Inszenierung*, for which there is in fact considerable Carolingian evidence.[45] But there are also examples of unequivocally public meetings which seem to have come to an unexpected denouement. An obvious example is Lothar II's court in Aachen around 860, when the king put his wife Theutberga's champion to a public ordeal of boiling water as an initial attempt to get rid of her, and her champion astonishingly emerged 'uncooked', instantly plunging Lothar's court and kingdom into crisis.[46] Historians have speculated on the reasons for its failure, just as contemporaries did, but the point here is that Lothar had not realised it was going to fail, or he would not have arranged it.

Indeed, to take the point further, Carolingian symbolic practice itself often has an air of improvisation, making use of objects and ideas in a rather extemporaneous fashion. Pope Hadrian's gifts to King Lothar II in 869 of some cloth, a palm and a rod, offer an illustration. Archbishop Hincmar of Rheims, our only source, commented that Lothar II had wanted these gifts in particular, because the wool signified the reinvestiture of Waldrada, the palm Lothar's success, and the rod the punishment of some recalcitrant bishops. But we cannot assume that a gift of wool always signified reinvestiture of a queen: in fact quite the reverse, since Hincmar expressly presented this as Lothar II's innovative symbolic interpretation at play.[47]

In fact, the 'performances' that symbolic communication necessarily involved seemed, as Althoff indicated, to have had problems in achieving durable effect, or, to put it differently, problems in instilling a durable

---

[45] Notably in Hincmar's *De Ordine Palatii*. In the *De divortio*, Hincmar claimed that he had refused to attend a synod because he knew that he would lose the argument due to verbal trickery.

[46] Hincmar, ed. L. Böhringer, *De divortio Lotharii regis et Theutbergae reginae* (Hanover, 1992), p. 114. Recourse to the unpredictable ordeal was not unusual, of course: cf. the ordeal to which Louis the Younger put many of his *fideles* before fighting Charles the Bald at Andernach (*AB* p. 501, three sorts were performed), and Gottschalk's theatrical demand to be put through a particularly gruelling ordeal of successive buckets of pitch, tar, fat and water, then to be ignited (Hincmar, *Collectio de una et non trina deitate*, col. 495). The wife of Charles the Fat offered to walk over hot ploughshares, according to Regino, *Chronicon*, s. a. 887.

[47] *AB* s. a. 869: 'Quae munera ita ipse et sui interpretati sunt'.

meaning. This is evidently the case in the locality. For example, we can see that the significance of gift-giving was always vulnerable to conceptual slippage. Theodulf of Orléans's poem 'On judges' tried valiantly to distinguish between presents and bribes.[48] This might have been clear in the abstract, but evidently was not clear in practice. Charlemagne's *De Villis* capitulary attempted to forbid the giving of certain kinds of gifts to officials (*iudices*), lest these tokens begin to imply a more substantive relationship between fiscal manager and fiscal dependant. Just this slipping has already been discussed in Chapter 2, as one way in which the poor freeholders could be drawn into closer ties of dependence; that chapter also mentioned the risk that if control of lands was not symbolically affirmed, it was likely to vanish. Violence, too, was always liable to be interpreted in various ways by different parties. The very way in which these performances of local power seem to have taken on such significance does not imply a lack of intensity, but surely points to a certain fragility.

Much the same is visible even at the highest of political levels. Archbishop Ebbo's deposition at Rheims in 835 was, according to all the (admittedly later) evidence done literally by the book. Obliged to make his resignation speech from the pulpit in Metz, in 835, each bishop present, in turn, then commanded him to cease from his episcopal duties.[49] Reappointed, Ebbo was escorted to mass at Rheims in 840 by four bishops and two priests, holding his hands and clustering round him as he walked. However, even this splendid re-enactment of late antique canon law was not enough to eliminate all confusion (had he given rings out, or had he received them?), still less eliminate all doubt on the matter.[50] Questions about the legitimacy and efficacy of these procedures were still being raised thirty years later.[51]

It is surely only a pervasive uncertainty that can make sense of the remarkable whirl of rumour and gossip that characterised the ninth century. Admittedly, much of this rumour was the usual politicking one might expect in a court-centred society familiar with the potential of the

---

[48] See R. le Jan, 'Justice royale et pratiques sociales dans le royaume franc au IXᵉ siècle', *Settimane* 44 (1997), 47–86, at pp. 55–6.

[49] *HRE*, bk I, ch. 20, pp. 185–6 ('conscedens eundem locum . . . cunctique episcope . . . sigillatim ac viritim dixerunt illi'). The importance of Ebbo climbing to a higher place was reiterated in the *AB*, s. a. 835 ('conscenso eminentiori loco').

[50] *Narratio Clericorum Remensium*, MGH *Concilia*, vol. II:ii., pp. 791–814. Cf. de Jong 'What was public?' and Hincmar of Rheims's role in promoting *libelli proclamationis*, e.g. in Council of Soissons 853. For Ebbo's rings, see Hincmar, *Epistolae*, PL, vol. CXXVI, col. 258. Cf. the Council of Soissons 853, where the clerics appointed by Ebbo are depicted dutifully waiting *pro foribus* (MGH *Concilia*, vol. III, p. 266); equally common is the description of each bishop getting up, '*surgens*', to say what he wanted or was supposed to.

[51] Patzold, *Episcopus*, offers a brilliant analysis of the long-running controversy, 315–57.

written word. There was every reason to gossip, for those disgraced at court were vulnerable, and especially vulnerable to those in royal favour, as treatment of the disgraced Matfrid I demonstrated.[52] As a consequence of this intrigue, people fell and rose in favour with bewildering rapidity, and insecurity was a constant theme of ninth-century politics.[53] Some texts seem designed to encourage rumour, like Gottschalk's letters to his supporters (*fautores*). Archbishop Hincmar investigated these sadly now lost texts, finding to his astonishment that Gottschalk was prophesying that Hincmar would die in three-and-a-half years, and that he, Gottschalk, would become archbishop, but would be poisoned in seven years.[54] With messages like these, no wonder that sometimes sealed letters were broken into by the curious, and sometimes even by the king.[55]

One need but consult the letters of Lupus of Ferrières and Abbess Theuthild of Remiremont from this area to see how everyone was frantically trying to work out what everyone else was thinking, and floundering in a sea of unreliable report, gossip and hearsay, for the most part centred on the king's court or royal affairs. Indeed, all the ambiguity and rumour have led some to wonder whether historians have been misreading all the allusive and cryptic letter writing. As Dutton has noted, 'Perhaps the real problem is that we expect early medieval men and women to have hidden things in the way that we do, that is by scrambling a clear message that can be unscrambled at the receiving end. What if ... the goal was more often to send an oblique or ambiguous communication that required interpretation rather than decoding at the receiving end?'[56]

Symbolic clarification

In short, insofar as Althoff's depiction of symbolic communication rests on a presupposition that the meanings communicated through gift exchange, violence and ceremonialised meetings were both unambiguous and wholly congruent with the social order that was being consolidated, it does not seem quite to fit the Carolingian evidence. There were no 'transcendent' interpretations, and in fact it would seem that the articulation of social relations in the ninth century was consistently context-dependent, and

---

[52] *MGH Capit.*, vol. II, p. 10.
[53] Cf. Airlie, 'The aristocracy', in R. McKitterick, ed., *New Cambridge medieval history, AD 700–900* (Cambridge, 1995), vol. II, pp. 43–50. On insecurity, see also Innes, *State*, pp. 208–12.
[54] Hincmar, *Collectio de una et non trina deitate*, col. 613.
[55] *HRE*, bk III, ch. 17, p. 252: 'sigilla confringens'.
[56] P. Dutton, 'Whispering secrets to a dark age', in P. Dutton, *Charlemagne's mustache, and other cultural clusters of a dark age* (New York, 2009), pp. 129–50, at p. 147.

liable to sabotage. However, if Carolingian symbolic communication is characterised by a remarkable degree of ambivalence, an equally important characteristic is the vigour with which such ambivalence was contested. For not only did the Carolingians make greater use of symbolic communication as a means of consolidating authority, they also, on a very broad range of fronts, made efforts to 'codify' the interpretation of this symbolic array.

In a sense, this point is self-evident, and hardly in need of further discussion. The very texts whose diversity points to the struggle over interpretation by that token also represent specific efforts to clarify and narrow that interpretation. But the point can be elaborated, for example, with reference to the royal assemblies (many of which took place in palaces in this area, like Quierzy, Thionville, Ponthion or Attigny). These were not decision-making bodies, for the decisions had usually already been made behind closed doors; nor were they intended to promulgate these decisions, for that could be done through writing. Rather, their rationale was more communicative, their function more self-referential. Who was in favour, who was on the way out: these were the questions assemblies came together to decide upon, like a gigantic focus group analysing itself, with, as an outcome of each meeting, a slightly reconfigured social field.[57] In other words, the general Frankish assembly was largely about working out and communicating relative social status, a way of discerning the grain of consensus, to make a co-ordinated politics possible.

It is in this context that the stage-management discussed above can readily be interpreted as efforts to subdue secondary resonances, to ensure that the message put out was as non-misunderstandable as possible: an essential part of the exercise of power. As a contemporary put it, 'where there is variety, there is there discord'. In heaven, there would be no discord, because heavenly communication was perfect, but on earth, kings and their advisors had to help things along.[58] The attempt to iron out any possible discord by orchestrating a flawless communication could be taken to remarkable lengths, as at the assembly at Thionville in 835, where a detailed description of the meeting was collectively written, to be signed by all and then recited back.[59] Written accounts of this kind were carefully

---

[57] I draw here on the work of C. Pössel, 'Symbolic communication and the negotiation of power at Carolingian regnal assemblies, 814–840', unpublished PhD thesis, Cambridge 2004.

[58] Haimo of Auxerre's exegesis of Paul's letter to the Corinthians: 'et ubi est varietas, ibi dissensio', *PL*, vol. CXVII, col. 508ff. *Dissensio* was often identified as the root cause of problems in Carolingian councils.

[59] *AB* s. a. 835, and cf. *MGH Capit.*, vol. II, p. 55. Such signings were quite common: Amalarius of Trier claimed his works had been signed at a council (*MGH Concilia*, vol. II:ii, p. 769); Coulaines in 843 was signed by all (*MGH Concilia*, vol. III, p. 15); and Hincmar of Laon made his priests sign his legal treatises (Hincmar of Rheims, *Opusculum*, p. 155).

stored in order to be used again. Archbishop Wenilo of Sens's signature to some capitularies was brandished before a synod after his treachery in 858, while Bishop Theoderic of Cambrai's account of Archbishop Ebbo's deposition, written many years later, cited not only Ebbo's profession that had been kept in the Metz archive, but also the entry for 835 in the Annals of St-Bertin.[60] Capitularies can be interpreted in this light, too, as not just communicating a particular message, but also communicating assent to that message. In one of Charles the Bald's final capitularies, the participative assent of the people is built into the text, written as a form of proposals and responses: scripted in the most thorough sense of the word.[61]

On this reading, the distinction between the meeting and its textual (mis-)representation collapses. The meeting was only about representation, so written means were just another part of the struggle. Hincmar of Rheims tried to distinguish historical record from legal document, saying 'Some things are signed as a notice of a thing or a time, other things are bound with a signature so that a constitution, a profession, an accusation or a request is observed.'[62] But he must have known that this was really just a difference in register, not in nature, and that Carolingian texts worked at both levels at the same time, shaping the future by defining the past. If we want to characterise Carolingian symbolic communication, then, we have to combine both a certain persistent ambivalence and relentless efforts to reduce it: it is the process which is essential.

FROM SYMBOLIC COMMUNICATION
TO ECONOMIES OF MEANING

Viewing Carolingian symbolic communication as caught between ambivalence and unequivocity, and seeing this as a characteristic, not a deficiency which would by sheer dint of practice be remedied in the fullness of time, is the first modification to the notion of symbolic communication that seems necessary for the underlying approach to realise its full potential in relation to the ninth century, and for how we perceive the communities living between Marne and Moselle. The second is perhaps more far-reaching.

As mentioned previously, the concept of symbolic communication was developed in the context of questions about the maintenance of stability in post-Carolingian East Francia. To that extent, it is the historiographical

---

[60] Council of Soissons 853, 'Libellus Theoderici Cameracensis', *MGH Concilia*, vol. III, pp. 290, 292. For Wenilo, see Council of Savonnières 859, ibid., p. 465. Hincmar of Laon's signed oath of fidelity to the king was turned against him at Douzy.

[61] Council of Quierzy 877, *MGH Capit.*, vol. II, pp. 355–61. There is unfortunately no manuscript tradition.

[62] Hincmar, *Opusculum*, p. 295.

equivalent of the Feudal Revolution discussion that has always centred on west Frankish evidence. What has shaped both these paradigms is the contrast set up between the periods for which they were designed to account and a 'statist' reading of the Carolingian period. The way in which this has shaped the Feudal Revolution argument has already been discussed, but it has exercised an equally profound importance in shaping the field of symbolic communication, too. Ritual, or symbolic communication, has been understood as a form of social interaction opposed to the use of writing, or rather to a bureaucratic use of writing. In that respect, the idea of symbolic communication has traditionally been conceived as an alternative form of social organisation: on the one hand Carolingian bureaucracy, on the other post-Carolingian ritual. Indeed, the very reason Althoff gives for the supposedly tentative Carolingian recourse to symbolic communication is that they were still reliant on the written word instead.[63]

This helps explain why much research in the area has been marked by attempts to find in symbolic communication a functional substitute for written administration, searching for the unwritten rules that stood in for the written rules of bureaucratic communities. However, I would suggest that viewed from a broader perspective, the dichotomy that lurks here is profoundly misleading, for a number of reasons. First of all, and most obviously, it is not historically the case that writing and ritual, or administration and ritual, are remotely incompatible. The image of Louis the Pious, ceremonially stroking the scarf and sleeves of the patchwork-garbed Benedict of Aniane, established at the monastery of Inden near Aachen, to find the lists (*scheduli*) stuffed there, perfectly exemplifies this complementarity.[64] Indeed, forms of what Reuter called meta-languages are omnipresent in all societies, including those which are administered by the written word.[65] It is revealing that it was the prodigiously well-educated Bishop Hincmar of Laon, who knew so much Greek that he had almost forgotten how to speak Frankish (though he certainly used plenty of it in his writing) who writhed, gesticulated and rushed about.[66] Ritual processions might involve gospel books, and as we have already mentioned, Carolingian meetings were apparently increasingly choreographed according to textual models like the *Ordines de celebrando Concilio*, as

---

[63] Althoff, *Macht*, pp. 64–6.

[64] *Vita Benedicti Anianensis*, ch. 35. J. C. Schmitt, *La raison des gestes dans l'occident médiéval* (Paris, 1990), particularly p. 15, for trenchant discussion of the traditional opposition between gesture and writing.

[65] T. Reuter, '*Velle sibi fieri in forma hac*: Symbolisches Handeln im Becketstreit', in G. Althoff, ed., *Formen und Funktionen öffentlicher Kommunikation im Mittelalter* (Stuttgart, 2001), pp. 201–25.

[66] 'Qui enim linguam in qua natus es, non solum non loqui, verum nec intellegere nisi per interpretem potes', Hincmar of Rheims, *Opusculum*, p. 315. For rushing, *Opusculum*, p. 170; cf. *HRE*, bk III, ch. 22, p. 287, p. 288. Hincmar of Laon seems to have been fond of Frankish (*exonia, talamascas, manacta* and *scaz* all appear in his writings), though he also used plenty of Greek: Hincmar of Rheims, *Libellus expostulationis*, p. 456.

were, for that matter, royal ordinations, for which *ordines* were first set down on parchment in the ninth century.[67]

In itself, of course, these combinations do not show that the distinction lacks analytical value, since we are not compelled to analyse past societies in their own terms. Yet even if it has proved convenient in the past, the notion of a sharp distinction between writing, or written government, and ritual, or symbolic communication, is surely methodologically untenable. One scents the conviction that (modern) states are rationally organised, as opposed to being ritually organised – a conviction that needs to be tackled head on. What, after all, is writing, even (or especially) bureaucratic writing, if not a symbolic practice? And for that matter, what is a state of any kind, Weberian or otherwise, if not a bundle of regulated and policed symbolic practices?[68] It is a truism for some social analysts that 'politics is not merely about material interests, but also about contests over the symbolic world, over the management and appropriation of meanings'; and that this is the case in all places, at all times.[69] A similar point applies with particular force to our understanding of institutions: we tend instinctively to view these as entities, forgetting that 'organization, rather than being an entity, is a process of formation'.[70] In other words, even the most Weberian of bureaucracies should be understood 'as a precarious and ambiguous *process* revolving around the social construction, maintenance and re-construction of "formalized" organizational realities'.[71]

It follows that the distinction between symbolic communication and writing, that is to say between archetypes of ritual and bureaucracy, cannot be justified at a theoretical level, whatever its appeal to post-Reformation common-sense. Both were (and are) forms by which certain meanings may be communicated, in order to regulate, and indeed define, social interaction. That is not to say that we cannot make distinctions between different forms through which meaning is co-ordinated and imposed, of course; simply that these cannot be decided on a priori grounds. A more fruitful path of analysis would be to attempt to investigate the degree of ambivalence, and thereby the extent of 'semantic coercion', that characterises different forms of social interaction at different times and in different places. Sometimes occasions are unscripted and full of ambivalence (Hincmar's meeting with Louis the

---

[67] See above, n. 31. On coronation *ordines*, see *Ordines coronationis Franciae*, ed. R. Jackson, 2 vols. (Philadelphia, 1995), vol. I: *Ordo* XIII is a good example, pp. 142–53.

[68] T. Mitchell, *Colonising Egypt* (Cambridge, 1988), pp. 166–9 and 172–9, though his tacit premise of a pre-modern/modern 'break' could be questioned.

[69] L. Wedeen, *Ambiguities of domination: politics, rhetoric, and symbols in contemporary Syria* (Chicago, 1999), p. 30.

[70] T. Hernes, *Understanding organization as process: theory for a tangled world* (London, 2008), p. xxiii.

[71] Kirsch, *Spirits*, p. 7 (author's italics).

German), while others are not only exquisitely planned but are, relatively and at their core, immune from variant interpretations, like marriage or signing a contract (even though the significance of that core meaning can become in turn the object of interpretation).[72] We might accordingly investigate how far certain sets of meanings, for example those involved in controlling a patch of ground and those on it, become taken for granted and therefore effectively non-discursive ('landholding'), rendered into something like St Augustine's 'natural symbols', while others remain the object of discussion and contention.[73] Instead, then, of classifying practices as either ritual or bureaucratic, we might consider the ways in which certain processes take on the appearance of being stable through an effective management of meaning.

Codification: administration and institutionalisation

This argument offers a new perspective on Carolingian forms of organisation. For, once we have accepted that there is no inherent totalising difference to be made between 'bureaucracy' and 'ritual', as some historians have tended to assume, and that it would be better to see both as forms by which the natural polysemy of human interaction is channelled into something more discrete, and better suited for sustaining and reproducing inequalities in the distribution of power, then suddenly the relation between the material in chapters 1 and 2 is reframed. It is no longer a coincidence that as well as overseeing a kind of gestural politics at every level, the Carolingians also and at the same time promoted an effective 'bureaucratic' government involving writing, administration and institutions. These are two aspects of the same development, linked technologies of power.

The evidence for a heightened reliance on the written word by the Carolingians in a number of fields is irrefutable.[74] This has perhaps justifiably puzzled historians. It cannot be understood as some anodyne or self-evident 'rise in literacy', for literacy had never been forgotten in post-Roman Western Europe. Nor should we feel obliged to play down this evidence simply because it does not fit the narrative which ascribes to writing a single function, and a single set of consequences, in human society. Nor, finally, do we need tautologously to point to the role of writing in symbolic communication, for all texts are inherently and irreducibly symbolic objects. Rather, the written word was increasingly

---

[72] For a specifically Frankish interest in formalising marriage, based on Pseudo-Isidorian evidence, see P. Reynolds, *Marriage in the Western church: the Christianization of marriage during the patristic and early medieval periods* (Leiden, 1994), p. 409.

[73] Cf. Comaroff and Comaroff, *Of revelation*, vol. I, pp. 4–29.

[74] As amply demonstrated by R. McKitterick, *The Carolingians and the written word* (Cambridge, 1989).

promoted as a tool for use in the localities to mould social relations into a form that could be grasped, in parallel then to the use of gestural politics to communicate this new state of affairs. Whether we class it as bureaucratic or not, the massive promotion of written forms of communication in the ninth century can be understood as an attempt to stabilise social meaning.

The explosion in the number of documents of legal practice is particularly relevant here, attesting to an effort to impose a grid of legal meaning upon local society. It would be unsatisfactory to dismiss these texts as 'mere' administrative convenience. Writing in the 860s, Christian of Stavelot considered charters as primarily historical documents – these were narratives whose stories were formally acclaimed as truthful.[75] Charters, and for that matter, polyptychs too, were not just utilitarian estate tools, not just potential legal evidence,[76] and not just instruments of intimidation.[77] Though they were doubtless at times all these things, they were also attempts to instil certainty into a fluid situation, wholly in tune with the attempt to instil certainty and order in other fields. This is a topic which we will return to in Chapter 5; for the moment, it is sufficient to stress that we should think of *all* charters as documents of volition, as dispositive and not passively probative. Charters were attempts to change the social fabric, not simply to describe it; more than that, they were attempts to change it by literally rendering it legible.

Yet of course the most formidable means for categorising reality, making the incoherence of social interaction comprehensible, was the very institutional apparatus that formed the topic of Chapter 1. As we have seen, institutions of all kinds should be considered as processes rather than entities, as engines for the creation of a formal, recognised order. For example, like the other Carolingian *ministeria*, the office of the count can be read as an ongoing struggle to impose definition upon informal social relations. Comital power was itself an interpretation of social relation, the office of count a prefigured constellation of attributes and powers, a pre-thought out role which moreover implied other roles. *Comes* implied

---

[75] Christian, *Expositio*, p. 91 ('non solum in gestis sed etiam in chartis'). Various pasts were invoked in some 'eastern Parisian basin' charters of Louis the Pious: Pippin III's foundation of Prüm (*DLP* no. 638), Lantbert and Herard's construction of Hornbach and Charlemagne (*DLP* no. 699), Fulcric's participation in Slavic wars (*DLP* no. 739), the time of Charlemagne (*DLP* no. 770 and 815), Ingelbert's grandmother (*DLP* no. 823). I am grateful to Matthew Innes for conversations on this point.

[76] There are isolated instances of polyptychs being used in disputes: see p. 75, n. 150 above, and more generally, see J. Nelson, 'Dispute settlement in Carolingian West Francia', in W. Davies and P. Fouracre eds., *The settlement of disputes in early medieval Europe* (Cambridge, 1986), pp. 45–64, for the case of Cormery in 828.

[77] Though they probably were: cf. Caesarius's recommendation, admittedly from a later period, that his copy of the polyptych be taken to meetings, so that if peasants were reluctant to admit their duties, 'hoc eis prudenter audiantur, et ita magis sibi timebunt': *Prümer Urbar*, ed. Schwab, p. 175, n. 6.

paganus, the non-office holding inhabitant of a locality, in this way squeezing social relations more and more into particular definition. The *mallum* court was certainly intended to be more fair and just than alternatives, but it was also intended to embrace and contain all meaningful political activity, to the benefit of the count.

Similar points could of course be made about almost all the material discussed in Chapter 1. We cannot consider the count without his *mallum* court, the bishop without his liturgy, the parish priest without his books of ritual, the king without his assembly. These 'institutional' forms of power both reinforced and depended on particular communicative situations, whose meaning was set out by norms created by the centre, norms that oriented even if they did not compel. We must explicitly reject any assumption that cascades of Carolingian rhetoric simply bounced off battened-down local complexes of aristocratic power, because aristocratic authority was not an insuperable barrier, qualitatively different from and opposed to Carolingian royal power. 'Formal government' and 'property', 'written' and 'symbolic', or 'aristocratic domination' and 'institutions': these are not wholly different categories with radically different ontological status, insulated one from the other; they are related and relational.

Reconciling centre and locality

Strictly speaking, the argument above has proposed that there were two linked, but nevertheless parallel, processes at work, each responding to a slightly different challenge. At the level of the court, the evidence relating to the lands between Marne and Moselle reveals efforts to attain a greater and clearer definition of social status, in which everyone's political position was expressed and aligned, and the status of certain members of this elite raised and defined by means of formal title. In this way, an empire could be managed without the essential underpinnings of the Roman system, namely a fiscal base and an elaborated legal system – for the Carolingians did not regularly tax and had no professional lawyers, at least in the sense defined by historians working on later periods. At the level of the locality, we can see how the elite between Marne and Moselle strained to express its local domination ever more unambiguously, in the absence again of a totalising legal system, and without universally agreed and transparent practices of property, at least judging from the evidence of Chapter 2. In both instances, then, we can see the promotion of a more determinate form of authority, by means of a greater co-ordination of meaning, which underpins all forms of social hierarchy.

That there was some link between them is likely, for a number of reasons. Once the opposition between lordship and the state has been sidestepped, it is entirely unsurprising that the Carolingian kings promoted and supported their elite. As has been suggested by work on late medieval England, public and private power were seldom in opposition in the Middle Ages.[78] There are of course important differences between the England of Henry VI and the Francia of Louis the Pious, but the basic point is the same: for the most part, Carolingian king and aristocracy were not involved in a zero-sum struggle for power, but in a collaborative project better to anchor their collective authority, to create a more ordered world. There was every reason to co-operate. Secondly, the world of the court and the world of the locality were linked at a number of levels, as was true, too, of late medieval England, though in different ways. Studies of the Carolingian local elites that joined up the aristocracy to the world of the village, prominent in Italy, or the monastic networks that linked court and locality in Alsace and the Rhineland, make use of the remarkable wealth of documentary material from those areas, and perhaps reflect distinctive historical conditions, and so cannot be duplicated here, though we will return to localised elites in Chapter 6 when they do become more visible.[79] Nevertheless, in the end it was the production in the localities that funded the centre, so some kind of connection was always necessary.

The connections between these two levels, then, existed, and there is therefore no reason to suppose insuperable barriers between one and the other; indeed, the burden of proof must lie on those who would deny it. Surely the new formality of authority represented by the *mallum* court imparted something to the resolution of conflicts settled there, for example, with knock-on effects throughout the social field?[80] Surely the role of the royal court in spreading formulaic ways of writing about local domination (discussed further in Chapter 5) had some impact? Surely the efforts to ensure that everyone was exposed to the formal ritual every week in their local church had some consequences, even if not quite those anticipated, on how these people saw the world? Surely aristocrats accustomed to practices of gift exchange, concepts of violence and formalised meetings at court transferred these down to lower levels, to bolster their local authority? After all, we know that important men from this area like Archbishop Hincmar of Rheims, Abbot Lupus of Ferrières or Abbot Regino of Prüm were involved both in court politics and estate management at the same time.[81]

---

[78] For example, J. Watts, *Henry VI and the politics of kingship* (Cambridge, 1996).
[79] L. Feller, *Paysans et seigneurs au Moyen Age: VIIIe–XVe siècles* (Paris, 2007), pp. 86–96; Hummer, *Politics and power*; Innes, *State*.
[80] Cf. Brown, *Unjust seizure*.
[81] Regino is generally thought to have been responsible for the Prüm polyptych; Lupus, *Epistolae*, *MGH Epp.*, vol. VI, p. 56. For Hincmar, see p. 75, n. 150 above.

Names such as these give us a clue to a deeper link, should we wish to find one. For we should note firstly that the involvement of intellectuals in politics was a marked feature of Carolingian Europe that distinguished it from its contemporary neighbours;[82] and secondly, that these intellectuals were not merely religious figures, they were all intimately involved with a profoundly and perhaps increasingly liturgical form of religion, by virtue of their office as well as by disposition.[83] At the heart of this faith were a set of liturgical ceremonies, the sacraments, which, if rightly performed, were a source of anchored, God-given meaning: to quote a Lotharingian council, 'in the sacraments of the Church, there is nothing broken, nothing playful, but rather total truth, conjoined by its own verity and sincerity'.[84] If Carolingian kings and their advisors consciously pursued a political programme, it was one intimately connected to religious imperatives: the use of rhetoric to remake society as God wanted it to be. In such a context, what obstacles could there be between liturgical ideas and political or social ones? Little wonder that, as McCormick has noted, Carolingian royal ceremony breathed a distinctly liturgical air, in this way distinguishing itself from analogous Byzantine ceremonial.[85] Given such an imprint of theological and liturgical concern on Carolingian political thought and indeed society, with liturgical patterns of anchored thought intensifying at court, but also spilling out of the proliferating local churches discussed in Chapter 1, the attempt to orchestrate both empire and locality by means of co-ordinated symbolic communication must have seemed obvious: it was both the medium and the very stuff of power in the Carolingian world.

CONCLUSION

For the sake of grand historical narratives, the 'Carolingian moment' has been pigeonholed in various ways: as an initiative to reclaim and appropriate the

---

[82] Wickham, *Inheritance*, pp. 405–26.
[83] There is an enormous literature on the Carolingian engagement with liturgy. Studies from different angles are offered by A. Angenendt, *Das Frühmittelalter: die abendländische Christenheit von 400 bis 900* (Stuttgart, 1990); P. Cramer, *Baptism and change in the early Middle Ages, c.200–c.1150* (Cambridge, 1993); Y. Hen, *The royal patronage of liturgy in Frankish Gaul to the death of Charles the Bald* (London, 2001); J. Jungmann, *Mass of the Roman rite*, tr. F. Brunner, 2 vols. (New York, 1951); and R. McKitterick, ed., *The Frankish church and the Carolingian reforms* (London, 1977). There is still scope for yet more research, continuing to bring social and liturgical histories together and focusing on extant manuscripts (which are by and large all Carolingian) rather than reconstructing hypothetical ur-texts.
[84] 'Cum in ecclesiae sacramentis nihil sit cassum, nihil ludificatorium, sed prorsus totum verum et ipsa sui veritate ac sinceritate subnixum': Council of Valence (855), ch. 5; *MGH Concilia*, vol. III, p. 355.
[85] McCormick, *Eternal victory*, e.g. p. 385, 'The most striking aspect of Carolingian court ritual is its liturgical content and character, which far outstrip even the medieval court of Constantinople.'

Roman past inspired by Charlemagne's imperial ambitions, as an initiative stimulated by Anglo-Saxon missionaries to purify a corrupt church, or as an initiative to construct a state which was doomed to failure. Recent research has challenged the salience of the underlying categories of culture, religion and politics, instead highlighting the many-faceted nature of the reforming impetus, of a kind that defies any neat classification. As Devroey has put it, 'It is necessary to tackle the Carolingian Renaissance from a very broad perspective, which incorporates the relations of the *literati* with the material world, and the manner in which their capabilities were able to influence their capacity to analyse, put in order and describe'; one of the aims of that Renaissance was to put the world into order, and keep it there.[86]

It is in line with the thrust of this research that this chapter has suggested that certain aspects of that reform could be legitimately and helpfully construed as working to make social relations clearer, to make the interpretation of social action less potentially divergent, with implications for the efficiency and co-ordination of power both at the court and in the locality. In the Carolingian imagination, whatever the embattled practice, communication was perfectly transcendent and reliable, as Smaragdus of St-Mihiel's comment in his grammatical treatise with which this chapter began indicates. Clear communication was everywhere the aim, in the expectation, voiced by Dhuoda, that once this was achieved, all other problems would dissolve.[87] This communication could be achieved through the imposition of some sort of semiotic order on the complexities of social life, providing grids of orientation via the use of *ministeria*, an increasingly liturgised kingship, the imposition of oaths, a promotion of written forms of rule, and so on.[88] The institutions which are most visible to us are best viewed as conduits for an underlying process, not as categories in themselves. As S. F. Moore observed, 'in some underlying and basic sense social reality is fluid and indeterminate ... it is transformed into something more fixed through regularising process'.[89] The Carolingian reform represented a remarkably vigorous form of that regularising process. It is no wonder that a debate about the performative efficacy of words in the Eucharist was a ninth-century development: performative efficacy, making social reality immediately responsive to

---

[86] Devroey, *Puissants*, pp. 597 and 609.

[87] Dhuoda, *Liber manualis*, bk III, ch. 5: 'nichil deest obstans in rebus ubi assiduus militatur sermo eucarus', p. 96.

[88] Cf. S. Reynolds, *Fiefs and vassals: the medieval evidence reinterpreted* (Oxford, 1994), p. 89: 'oaths of fidelity that were taken so generally cannot have created a "personal bond between the subject and the king" or have been meant to do so': but this seems exactly what they were supposed to do. Kingship: W. Ullmann, *The Carolingian Renaissance and the idea of kingship* (London, 1969), pp. 71–110.

[89] Moore, *Law as process*, p. 52.

words, lending it a brittle formality, was at one level what the Carolingian reforms were all about in every sphere.

It follows that we do not need to see the Carolingian ninth century as characterised by a doomed attempt to create a state with a monopoly of violence, or as an elaborate confidence trick foisted upon contemporaries and historians through misleading rhetoric and discourse. Rather, the elite was interested in harnessing various kinds of forces to integrate a large empire and as a means of carrying out a political project, of bringing order to the world, by means of clarifying the communicative interaction that underwrites all authority: a kind of liturgisation of power. This mobilisation of forms of symbolic organisation of consensus and domination offered the Carolingian rulers a means of co-ordinating an empire without the mass taxation that was by the ninth century entirely unthinkable, and it offered the elite a means of sustaining its authority in the countryside too, on which control all political power ultimately rested in an agrarian economy.

The notion of the Carolingian system as an illusion depends on a reading of the evidence of Chapter 1 as implying the existence of a proto-modern state in a Weberian mode (bureaucracy, monopoly of violence, boundaries), which the material of Chapter 2 shows cannot have functioned as we might imagine it should have. Yet critiques based on *Realpolitik* ultimately miss their mark, because they require an entirely extra-discursive field of power. In fact, the Carolingian reforms reached deeper than merely setting up a state; they were about changing perceptions of the world, perceptions prior to the strategic choices of individuals. In this way, then, the impasse, the opposition between state and lordship, between top-down approaches and those centred on the local practice of power, which has shadowed the debate on the Feudal Revolution, can be dismantled. We need to think of symbolic practices reaching throughout society, with eminently practical consequences, while remaining oriented to the court. From this perspective, the evidence mobilised in chapters 1 and 2 is perfectly complementary.

As a force integrating together an empire, the harnessing of symbolic communication did not in the end succeed, as the Carolingian empire fragmented in the late ninth century. Yet does that mean that the attempt to hold it all together was without legacy? Not necessarily. Perhaps we should consider what we would expect to have happened had the Carolingian reforms, viewed in this double way, been successful. One might expect property rights to crystallise ever more sharply and to become more clearly layered, certain gestures and rituals to take on ever less controvertible meaning, and the role of the court as the clearing house for the performance of relations to begin to fade away, as its brokerage became less important. As the following chapters demonstrate, precisely these phenomena characterise the post-Carolingian period, at least in the lands between Marne and Moselle.

I have stressed that a view of the Carolingian reforms as concerned with a symbolic co-ordination of power is not the only one that can be sustained by the evidence, but as we shall see, it has the advantage of accounting well for what happened next, with obvious implications for the Feudal Revolution debate, which the following chapters will explore.

PART II

The long tenth century, c.880–c.1030

The following two chapters study the lands between Marne and Moselle in the aftermath of the Carolingian empire. They concentrate on the period from around 880 to the early eleventh century, though both chapters will sometimes reach beyond these termini. This 'long tenth century' should be treated neither as merely an appendage to the Carolingian era, nor as a prelude to the central Middle Ages. However, that does not preclude the application of a comparative perspective, and as will become clear, it is impossible properly to understand this area in the tenth century without taking into account both what came before and what followed. Many of the period's defining characteristics can usefully be viewed as extensions of earlier developments, representing a continuity, then, albeit one with disruptive consequences. Chapter 4 takes a top-down perspective, concentrating on the changing role of kingship in regional politics, and setting out a hypothesis to account for the changes that can be discerned; Chapter 5 offers a more bottom-up, synthetic approach, with the aim of supporting that hypothesis.

Alone among the sections of this book, something must be said here about the difficulties of the evidence. These difficulties do not rest in a lack of material as such; the problem is rather one of fragmentation.[1] The later tenth century saw a number of magnificent histories of near-contemporary events written in Western Europe, but their authors either cast only a passing glance at events in our area (Liudprand of Cremona and Widukind of Corvey), threaten to overwhelm with apparently undifferentiated detail (Flodoard's Annals), or resist anything beyond exploration of the author's intentionality (Richer of Rheims).[2] There are perhaps more private charters than in the ninth century, preserved in cartularies from Montier-en-Der and St-Vanne,

---

[1] T. Reuter, 'Introduction: reading the tenth century', in T. Reuter, ed., *New Cambridge medieval history 900–1024* (Cambridge, 1999), vol. III, pp. 1–26.

[2] Cf. J. Glenn, *Politics and history in the tenth century: the work and world of Richer of Reims* (Cambridge, 2004), p. 263.

yet the material can seem difficult to engage with in the absence of thicker context. There are fewer estate surveys, and those there are, like that preserved in Remiremont's famous *Liber Memorialis*, are thin and difficult to interpret. There are fewer letters too, with the great exception of those written by Gerbert of Rheims, later Pope Sylvester II, which are, however, hard to date and sometimes gnomic to the point of uninterpretability. Finally, it is notoriously difficult to attribute material evidence such as manuscripts or archaeological excavations securely and precisely to the tenth century. Yet insofar as these challenges encourage historians to work harder with the material they do have, and above all to make full use of the whole range of sources across genres, what appears to be a deficiency can be made into a strength.

Chapter 4

THE EBBING OF ROYAL POWER

The notion of a decline in royal power has long been vital to ideas about the Feudal Revolution, often conceived as the moment when the centre collapsed. It is evident therefore that an engagement with the questions posed by the Feudal Revolution debate requires an extensive investigation of the changing role of kings in this area after the ninth century. How far was kingship genuinely weakened, in what ways, for what reasons, and with what implications? These are the questions this chapter addresses.

THE DISTANCING OF ROYAL AUTHORITY
Marginalisation along the Meuse

The previous chapters left no doubt about the overall political centrality of the lands between Marne and Moselle. For much of the ninth century, this area formed part of the core lands of the Carolingian kingdoms. The Treaty of Verdun (843) saw, broadly speaking, the regions west of the Meuse become part of a western Frankish kingdom under Charles the Bald, and those to the east fall to Emperor Lothar I, but these lands continued to play a central role in these respective kingdoms.[1] That centrality was, however, brought into question by two key and essentially fortuitous events, which shaped the ensuing partition of the kingdoms.[2] The first was the death of King Lothar II in 869 without an accepted heir, which led to the division of his kingdom (Lotharingia) between his two uncles. One of them, King Charles the Bald, signalled his interest in fully integrating his windfall into his other territories by

---

[1] This division persisted, with minor changes, up to 869, when most of the area east of the Meuse was brought into Charles the Bald's kingdom; the Treaty of Ribemont (880) reversed this, and the area remained under the eastern kingdom's influence in the divisions of 888. From 911–25, Lotharingia was once again part of the western kingdom. For a discussion, see below, pp. 110–11.

[2] S. MacLean, 'The Carolingian response to the revolt of Boso, 879–887', *EME* 10 (2001), 21–48, is a convenient discussion of the tangled politics of partition.

means of a hurried coronation at Metz in 869; but, forced to share his spoils with his brother King Louis, Charles was anyway soon engaged in other adventures, crossing into Italy to seek the imperial throne. The outcome was that the lands between Meuse and Moselle, and indeed the whole of Lotharingia, were for the first time ruled by kings whose basis of power and focus of attention lay elsewhere. The second event was the deposition of Emperor Charles the Fat in 887, and the fact that the immediate beneficiaries of this deposition were powerbrokers whose networks lay around the peripheries of the Carolingian empire that Charles, more by luck than judgement, had reconstituted. The fate of Lotharingia now loomed in turn over the lands around Rheims, because the new ruler of western Francia, King Odo, was more at home further west, around the Seine and Loire.

Admittedly, a decade or so later, things might have seemed to be heading back to normal. In 895, the major winner from the division of Charles the Fat's empire, King (later Emperor) Arnulf, decided to endow his son Zwentibold with a kingdom, which by accident or design more or less replicated Lothar II's, confining another claimant, Rudolf, to the Jura and Swiss Alps and creating thereby the new kingdom of Burgundy. A couple of years earlier, the claims of a Carolingian too young to be heard in 888 had been made good when Charles the Simple was anointed king in 893 at Rheims. Significantly, both these new kings showed interest in controlling the lands on the other side of the Meuse. King Zwentibold launched a number of raids into western Francia, some of which were clearly intended as softening-up expeditions.[3] And though Zwentibold's kingdom lasted no longer than Zwentibold himself, who was killed by rebels in 900, Charles the Simple was able to win Lotharingia in 911, expelling for a while the Conradines, a family based along the Rhine which had begun to infiltrate to the west; and indeed it was Lotharingian resources, exemplified by the enigmatic figure of Hagano, Charles's unpopular Lotharingian favourite, on which Charles relied in his ultimately unsuccessful struggle against Odo's brother Robert.[4] In short, for a good twenty years the areas between Trier and Rheims were once again central to Western European politics, and knew strong kingship at first-hand.

Yet this moment of renewed centrality proved in reality only an interlude. Charles the Simple's Lotharingian followers grew progressively

---

[3] See for example, Regino, *Chronicon*, s. a. 895, p. 143.
[4] On Charles's takeover of Lotharingia, see M. Parisse, 'Lotharingia', in Reuter, ed., *New Cambridge medieval history*, pp. 310–27; cf. G. Koziol, 'Charles the Simple, Robert of Neustria, and the vexilla of Saint-Denis', *EME* 14 (2006), 385–6. On Charles's manoeuvring in Lotharingia even before Zwentibold's death, see H. Beumann, 'König Zwentibolds Kurswechsel im Jahre 898', *Rheinische Vierteljahrsblätter*, 31 (1966–7), 17–41. See Althoff, *Amicitia*, pp. 241–3 for a useful summary of the Conradine family.

less committed to supporting his campaigns further west, and though his rival Robert was killed at the battle of Soissons on 15 June 923, Charles was himself captured shortly afterwards, and never escaped imprisonment. One consequence was that the rulers of West Francia would thereafter no longer be anchored in the regions east and north of the Marne. Charles's successor, King Rudolf of West Francia, was based further to the south, and in spite of his best efforts, King Louis IV, the son of Charles the Simple who succeeded Rudolf in 936, was caught up in the patronage networks of Hugh the Great, whose authority was founded in the Robertian ascendency in Neustria, consolidated in the final decades of the ninth century (see Figure 1 for a table of the relevant kings). Louis's own son, King Lothar of West Francia, was considerably more independent, and indeed showed signs of raising the profile of the regions in question, including a bold attempt to bring the archbishopric of Rheims under firm control; but his premature death in 986, and Hugh Capet's successful, and perhaps desperate, bid for the throne in 987 ended these plans, and confirmed West Francia as a kingdom oriented to the west.[5]

The fate of Lotharingia, including its southern regions which concern us most closely, was not dissimilar. Following Charles the Simple's capture in 923, Lotharingia was gradually wrested away from West Francia by a determined and persistent King Henry I of East Francia, even if institutions at its furthest limits, such as St-Mihiel on the Meuse, occasionally toyed with French regnal datings.[6] Henry's descendants, the Ottonians, were a Franco-Saxon family but were by no means confined to Saxony: the East Frankish royal heartlands included the Rhineland and parts of Bavaria, and indeed the dynasty's control of Saxony was increasingly challenged by local leaders, just as the grip of the Capetian family on the Loire valley was loosened in the decades following, and probably also preceding, their accession to the throne. Yet though they made copious use of Lotharingian resources, now redirected to serve their ends north and south of the Alps, no east Frankish king would ever base himself in Lotharingia, whatever the allure of Aachen; and southern Lotharingia in particular, lacking the lure of Charlemagne's tomb, gradually sank into relative insignificance.

---

[5] O. Guillot, 'Formes, fondements et limites de l'organisation politique en France au xe siècle', *Settimane* 38 (1991), 57–116. On Lothar's independence, see B. Schneidmüller, *Karolingische Tradition und frühes französisches Königtum* (Wiesbaden, 1979), particularly pp. 156–70.
[6] *Chronique et chartes*, ed. Lesort, no. 25 (943x4) uses both Otto and Louis; no. 26 (943) uses just Louis. Still in 1068, no. 37 includes both Henry and Philip. B. Schneidmüller, 'Französische Lothringenpolitik im 10. Jahrhundert', *Jahrbuch für Westdeutsche Geschichte* 5 (1979), 1–32, offers analysis of the politics.

The extent of marginalisation

As a result of this entirely unpredictable sequence of events, the lands on either side of the Meuse had not only became more clearly divided than before, but they were also by *c*.930 both satellite regions: wealthy and by no means wholly insignificant, but peripheral to the polities of which they were part. However, the practical impact of this political development cannot be simply assumed from this bare statement of fact. Indeed, assessing the degree to which kings impinged on the locality in the tenth and eleventh centuries in this area requires a considerable degree of nuance, not least since any such comparison needs to work across time, in relation to the Carolingians, but also across space, comparing imperial with royal reach. It quickly becomes clear that by any definition, and marking a crucial difference with Frankish lands further south, the regions between Marne and Moselle can at no point be described as having been wholly kingless.

As far as the lands east of the Meuse are concerned, the indices of lingering royal authority were often rather unsubtle. In the eleventh and indeed twelfth centuries, emperors occasionally asserted their authority in the most dramatic fashion possible, coming with an army to besiege the disobedient. Emperor Henry II besieged Meilberg in 1003, Trier in 1008 and Metz in 1009 and 1012, the latter two as part of the so-called *Moselfehde*; while Emperor Henry V attacked Clermont in 1107, and Bar-le-Duc around 1114.[7] These were impressive projections of authority, even if they seldom met with unequivocal success. The tenth-century kings of West Francia, particularly Louis IV, sometimes ravaged the war-torn areas around Rheims, yet these campaigns were less ones of subordination of a rebellious province than parts of bitter struggle between the tenth-century Carolingians and their rivals: less projections of power, then, and more tokens of desperation.[8] The winners of these contests did not, in the eleventh century, intervene substantially in the lands west of the Meuse, because they did not assert their practical authority there; that changed only in the early twelfth century, with the campaigns, or raids, launched by a young King Louis VI.

However, royal power could be asserted in more mundane and routine fashion, too. The issue of military service is of importance here, and one that historiographically has again sharply distinguished the Ottonians from their late Carolingian and Capetian counterparts to the west. There are indeed some signs that the former were able to demand a little more from their

---

[7] For the siege of Clermont, see Laurentius of Liège, *Gesta episcoporum Virdunensium*, ed. G. Waitz, *MGH SS*, vol. x (1852), pp. 486–530, at pp. 499–500; for that of Bar, see ibid., p. 503. For the 'Moselfehde', see n. 45 below.

[8] See Glenn, *Politics*, pp. 216–34. For ravaging around Rheims, see, for example Flodoard, *Annales*, s. a. 944 and 945.

imperial subjects, including those in Lotharingia. This is suggested by fragmentary sources like the Mettlach *Güterrolle*, a (probably) tenth-century estate document implying that people around Valmünster (Moselle) were still subjected to public military service; and more spectacularly, the *Indiculus loricatorum*, a document from the 970s detailing Ottonian army contingents on their way south of the Alps.[9] Listing a number of Lotharingian contributors, the document omits Metz's contributions to imperial forces, but only because Metz's contingent was already serving in Italy: indeed we know from other sources that Metz soldiers played an important role in Otto II and Otto III's Italian expeditions. It would be misleading, though, to single out Metz, or to over-privilege the importance of the *Indiculus*: we know, for example, from other sources that Toul sent forces to assist Emperor Henry III, and that Trier helped Henry V.[10] Indeed, most archbishops of Trier seem to have helped with Italian expeditions, with some, like Henry (d.964) dying on them, and they demonstrably went to some lengths to raise the necessary armed forces, as shown by an agreement made with the counts of Arlon.[11] We have isolated instances, too, of secular military support for kings: for example, the Count of Luxembourg's assistance to Emperor Conrad II in the 1030s, recorded by a Stavelot charter.[12]

The west Frankish kings have little that can be compared with this sort of material. We know from sources from this region that King Henry of West Francia had problems compelling military service from his clergy, though it is interesting that he made the effort.[13] Later kings like Philip I, and still more so Louis VI, seem to have had more success, but were still relatively unimpressive

[9] 'Die Mettlacher Güterrolle', ed. H. Müller, *Zeitschrift für die Geschichte der Saargegend* 15 (1965), 110–46, see the entry for Valmünster, p. 117. On the Mettlach *Güterrolle*, see most recently O. Schneider, *Erzbischof Hinkmar und die Folgen: Der vierhundertjährige Weg historischer Erinnerungsbilder von Reims nach Trier* (Berlin, 2008), pp. 251–64, though his evaluation of the text is in part determined by his wider arguments. *Indiculus loricatorum*, ed, L. Weiland. *MGH Constitutiones*, vol. 1, no. 436, pp. 632–3.

[10] For Metz: *Vita Theoderici*, ed. G. Pertz, *MGH SS*, vol. IV, pp. 464–83, at pp. 474 (Theoderic in Rome) and (more ambivalently) *Vita Adalberonis* II, ed. G. Pertz, *MGH SS*, vol. IV (Hanover, 1841), pp. 658–72, at p. 667. For Toul: *Vita Leonis*, ed. M. Parisse and tr. M. Goullet, *La vie du Pape Léon IX (Brunon, évêque de Toul)* (Paris, 2007), bk I, ch. 7, p. 24. For Trier, Balderic, *Gesta Adalberonis archiepiscopi Treverensis*, ed. G. Waitz, *MGH SS*, vol. VIII (Hanover, 1848), p. 251 (Albero taking 67 *milites*). The evidence for Verdun is less forthcoming, probably because the mid-eleventh-century *Gesta episcoporum Virdunensium* was written at St-Vanne and takes remarkably little interest in the bishops' public activities.

[11] *Urkunden*, ed. Wampach no. 274 (Arlon). Robert (d.956) and Egbert (d.993) also went to Italy with the emperors. Udo of Trier, like Henry, died on military service, in his case, however, at Tübingen in 1078 (Bruno of Merseburg, *Liber de Bello Saxonico*, ed. W. Wattenbach, *MGH SRG* vol. XV (Hanover, 1880), p. 369).

[12] *Recueil*, ed. Halkin, no. 38; cf. 'Urkunden', ed. Bloch, no. 19 (968).

[13] Anselm of St-Rémi, *Historia dedicationis Ecclesiae sancti Remigii*, ed. J. Hourlier, 'Histoire de la dédicace de Saint-Remy', *Travaux de l'académie nationale de Reims* 160 (1981), p. 181–297: p. 218 describes an attempted general muster, but with mixed results. For Philip I, see the *Vita Arnulfi Suessionensis*, *PL*, vol. CLXXIV, col. 1389, concerning St-Medard.

compared with what the Ottonians could require.[14] Perhaps the major difference was that the kings in the west had in general less need for military support, since they were not conducting regular forays into Italy; but even if that is the case, that left them with less opportunity to assert their rights over local powerbrokers.

Another index for royal power is attendance at court. The presence or otherwise of secular magnates is hard to be sure about, not least because of problems of identification based on single names; but the evidence is better for bishops. Emperor Arnulf summoned Lotharingian bishops to councils, as at Tribur in 895 (attended by the bishops of Verdun and Trier), and so far as we can see, bishops from this region attended synods through the tenth century, for example Ingelheim in 972, or Frankfurt in 1001.[15] Bishops and archbishops from the province of Trier still attended the imperial court in the twelfth century, and though most royal charters east of the Meuse did not have witness lists, it seems almost certain that bishops attended the royal court between these dates too. While few historians still believe in the *Reichskirchenssystem*, the idea of an entirely systematic subjection of the institutional church to satisfy the needs of the emperor, still fewer would deny that Lotharingian bishops kept close relations with the Ottonian and early Salian emperors. It was after all a Lotharingian bishop, Bruno of Toul, who had raised funds for the rebuilding of the urban monastery of St-Evre, to which emperor and empress made generous donations, who was the emperor's choice to reform the church of Rome as Pope Leo IX.[16]

Correspondingly, even at the darkest moments of Capetian kingship, and notwithstanding Lemarignier's observations about the composition of the king's court, bishops from west of the Meuse were seldom figures genuinely distant from the king.[17] The bishops of Châlons represent a good illustration.[18] Châlons was significant enough for Odo and Charles the Simple to struggle over appointing a bishop there in 893–4, a struggle

---

[14] On the events of 1124, see G. Spiegel, '"Defence of the realm": evolution of a Capetian propaganda slogan', *Journal of Medieval History* 3 (1977), 115–25.

[15] Tribur: *MGH Capit.*, vol. II, p. 211; *MGH Concilia*, vol. VI, p. 330 (Verdun, Metz, Toul and Trier) and p. 626 (Trier).

[16] On the fundraising, see *Histoire ecclésiastique et politique de la ville et du diocèse de Toul*, ed. B. Picart (Toul, 1707), pr. col. 70, listing the donations. On the appointment, the main source is the *Vita Leonis*.

[17] In general, O. Guyotjeannin, 'Les évêques dans l'entourage royal sous les premiers Capétiens', in M. Parisse, ed., *Le roi de France et son royaume autour de l'an mil* (Paris, 1992), pp. 91–8. Charters are, of course, only one indication of a king's entourage and other texts can be useful too: for example, Helgaud's *Epitoma vitae regis Rotberti*, ed. and tr. R.-H. Bautier, *Vie de Robert le Pieux* (Paris, 1965), mentions the presence of the bishop of Langres at court, ch. 13.

[18] For a more exhaustive discussion of the bishops of Châlons mentioned here, see S. Benner, *Châlons-en-Champagne: die Stadt, das Chorherrenstift Toussaint und das Umland bis zur Mitte des 14. Jahrhunderts* (Trier, 2005), pp. 42–54 and pp. 123–39.

won by Charles's candidate, Mancio (894–908/9). Bishop Bovo (911–47) was just as close to the king as Mancio, and was in fact Charles's brother-in-law. Bishop Gibuin (947–99) was similarly long-lived and loyal to the late Carolingian kings who appointed his brother Richard as Count of Dijon, until the Capetian takeover, at which point he seems to have smoothly repositioned himself, supporting King Hugh against Charles of Lorraine. Bishop Roger I (1011–42) was in close contact with King Robert the Pious, whose charters he attested; his successor Roger II (1042–66) was sent to Russia in 1049 to negotiate King Henry's marriage to the Russian princess Anna;[19] and Bishop Roger III (1066–92) often witnessed the charters of King Philip, who lent him some assistance in a dispute with Pope Gregory VII. In the early twelfth century, Bishop William of Châlons plainly stated that he gave money and military support to the king, a claim that finds documentary support in charters showing King Louis VI demanding taxes from Châlons and holding important meetings there, foreshadowing later Capetian expansion.[20] Of course, there were variations in the relation between kings and bishops. Bishop Philip (1093–100) seems to have kept his distance from the royal court and sometimes we can be sure that elections in this region were not co-ordinated by kings; but in general, there is much here that seems familiar from 'imperial bishops' in the east, albeit with less intensity.[21]

Finally, more indirect forms of royal influence should be considered, too. People in these regions, for example, still had kings at the centre of their thinking. Richer of Rheims's king-centred history, which will be discussed in the next chapter, can be compared with the somewhat earlier first cartulary of Prüm, the *Liber Aureus*, composed entirely of royal charters.[22] Whether Adso of Montier-en-Der's celebrated treatise on the Antichrist was written with the West Frankish kings or the Ottonians in mind, its author was still looking to a royal court.[23] And in the eleventh century, Anselm of St-Rémi's account of the Council of Rheims in 1049, shot through with concerns about the king's absence and the reasons for it, can perhaps be compared with Thiofrid of Echternach's treatise on miracles written around the same time, within

---

[19] E.g. *DDPhilip*, nos. 26, 28 and 39. Reference to Bishop Roger's expedition is to be found in Rheims, Bibliothèque Municipale, lat. 15, f. 214v.
[20] Hesso, *Relatio de concilio Remensi*, ed. W. Wattenbach, *MGH Libelli de lite* vol. III (Hanover, 1897), pp. 21–8, at p. 22. For the taxes, *DLVI* nos. 77, 78, and 79. For the meeting, ibid., no. 80.
[21] For example Fulbert, *Epistolae*, ed. and tr. F. Behrends, *The Letters and Poems of Fulbert of Chartres* (Oxford, 1976), no. 52, pp. 92–4, where the election of the Bishop of Meaux seems to be a matter for the count (though the following letter calls the king to act).
[22] For Richer's king-centredness, see Glenn, *Politics*, 235–49. On the Prüm *Liber Aureus*, compiled in the 920s, see M. Willwersch, *Die Grundherrschaft des Klosters Prüm* (Trier, 1989).
[23] Adso of Montier-en-Der, *Epistola de ortu et tempore antichristo*, ed. D. Verhelst, *CCCM* vol. XLV (Turnhout, 1976). For this interpretation, see Schneidmüller, *Karolingische Tradition*, 61–4.

which Emperor Henry II takes a prominent role.[24] Late eleventh- and early twelfth-century hagiographers depicted archbishops of Trier in regular contact with court, whether summoned to attend or asking permission to conduct a relic translation, and something similar could be argued for the Champagne region too, at least in hagiographic imagination.[25] For example, mid-eleventh-century hagiographies of Elaphius and Leudomirus, two long-dead Chalonnais bishops from Late Antiquity, unhesitatingly depicted them as royal appointees.[26]

Kingship at a distance

Kings never really left the lands between Marne and Moselle entirely to their own devices. However, it is also clear that their presence was far less systematically asserted than it had been in the ninth century, and that kingship was a less intensive phenomenon. One way of demonstrating this is by using the evidence provided by royal charters, which not only show who received royal favours, but also where these favours were distributed, allowing us some idea of the extent of kings' personal presence in the area. It should be stressed that this is only a rough measure, not least in the absence of critical editions of the charters of the early Capetian kings, and that it would be perilous to put too much emphasis on a few documents; still, even from a empirical basis as precarious as this, a few observations can be ventured.

To begin with, King Henry I (of East Francia)'s and Emperor Otto I's concentration on regions other than that around the Moselle is striking.[27] Henry I visited the lands along the Moselle only to ravage, while, remarkably, Otto I can be shown to have visited the region of Upper Lotharingia just twice during his long reign, in 947 and 950. Judging from his extant charters, he usually dealt with Lotharingian business from the Rhineland,

---

[24] Anselm, *Historia*, pp. 216–8; Thiofrid, *Flores epytaphii sanctorum*, ed. M. Ferrari, *CCCM*, vol. CXXXIII (Turnhout, 1999), bk II, ch. 5, pp. 44–6.

[25] *Translatio Modoaldi*, P. Jaffé, *MGH SS* vol. XII (Hanover 1856), pp. 289–310, at pp. 297–8. Relic translation: *Translatio Celsi*, ed. J. Bolland and G. Henschen, *AASS Feb*, vol. III (Antwerp, 1658), cols. 397–9.

[26] *Vita Elaphii*, ed. H. Moretus, 'Catalogus Codicum Hagiographicorum Latinorum Bibliothecae Scholae Medicinae in Universitate Montepessulanensi', *Analecta Bollandiana* 34–5 (1915–16), 228–305; and *Vita Leodomiri*, both probably written by Stephen of St-Urbain. On these, see F. Dolbeau, 'Vie latine de Sainte Ame, composée au XIᵉ siècle par Etienne, abbé de Saint-Urbain', *Analecta bollandiana* 105 (1987), 25–63.

[27] The ground-breaking discussion is that of E. Müller-Mertens, *Reichsstruktur im Spiegel der Herrschaftspraxis Ottos des Grossen: mit historiographischen Prolegomena zur Frage Feudalstaat auf deutschem Boden, seit wann deutscher Feudalstaat?* (Berlin, 1980). Detailed discussion of Trier, Metz, Soissons, Laon, Troyes and Rheims can be found in C.-R. Brühl, *Palatium und Civitas: Studien zur Profantopographie Spätantike Civitates vom 3. bis 13. Jahrhundert*, 2 vols. (Cologne, 1975). Cf. also H. Zielinski, *Der Reichsepiskopat in spätottonischer und salischer Zeit, 1002–1125* (Wiesbaden, 1984), pp. 205–16.

at Cologne, Nijmegen, Ingelheim or Mainz, and this impression is confirmed by Flodoard's Annals. It was, for example, at Ingelheim that Otto 'met the Lotharingians' in 956.[28] Otto I apparently decided it would be best simply to delegate the management of Lotharingia to his brother Archbishop Bruno of Cologne: in fact, Bruno would seem to have been given responsibility for everything west of the Rhine, judging from his frequent and often heavy-handed interventions in the west.[29]

This pattern continued under these kings' successors. Emperor Otto II paid one or two visits to Trier, and went once to Thionville. Emperor Henry II likewise went once to Thionville, and when he passed through Verdun and Metz after meeting King Robert II at Ivois/Mouzon, it was a rare event, at which impressive gifts were made.[30] In total, the Saxon kings visited Trier seven times between 919 and 1024, the Salians twice from 1025 to 1125. After 1003, no more royal diplomas were made at Thionville; after 1023, no more were made at Verdun.[31] Using charters as a guide to royal visits is a very rough-and-ready measure, since kings might visit but not make charters, and perhaps vice versa.[32] Nevertheless, by the mid eleventh century, the marginality of the region for the kings and emperors was notorious. The author of the Life of Pope Leo IX noted that Toul was rarely visited by kings, and other eleventh-century writers also spoke of Toul's peripheral location.[33] Obviously the picture can be nuanced, since Trier, closer to the Rhine corridor, was not quite so peripheral as Toul or Verdun, but the general outlines are clear.

For their part, the West Frankish kings Louis IV and Lothar spent most of their time within the Ile-de-France and, to a lesser extent, around the Oise basin and Laon: they did visit Rheims, Soissons and Langres, but only rarely,

---

[28] Flodoard, *Annales* s. a. 951.

[29] On Bruno's role, see J. Ehlers, 'Carolingiens, Robertiens, Ottoniens: politique familiale ou relations franco-allemandes', in K. Leyser, '987: the Ottonian connection', in *Communications and power in medieval Europe, vol. 1, The Carolingian and Ottonian centuries*, ed. T. Reuter (London, 1994), pp. 165–79; Parisse, ed., *Le roi de France et son royaume*, pp. 39–45; L. Vones, 'Erzbischof Brun von Köln und der Reimser Erzstuhl', in *Von Sacerdotium und Regnum: Geistliche und weltliche Gewalt im frühen und hohen Mittelalter. Festschrift für Egon Boshof* (Vienna, 2002), pp. 325–46.

[30] *Gesta episcoporum Cameracensium*, bk III, ch. 38, pp. 480–1.

[31] Using *Regesta Imperii*, ed. J. F. Böhmer. Charters were made at Verdun four times by Ottonian kings, not once by Salian. Metz saw Ottonian charters made five times and Thionville three: neither of these places saw Salian kings at all. Salian kings also palpably retreated from Aachen, Mainz, Ingelheim and Frankfurt, making charters here a fraction of the number of times the Ottonians had.

[32] Emperor Henry III's important visit to Trier in 1044, for example, is mentioned by no charter, nor is Henry V's to Verdun in 1107 (a visit connected to the Pope's presence in Champagne at this time); cf. R. McKitterick, *Charlemagne: the formation of a European identity* (Cambridge, 2008), pp. 188–212.

[33] *Vita Leonis*, 'quod in extremis imperii sui finibus urbs illa posita, aut numquam aut rarissime aestimatur digna imperatoris diversorio', bk I, ch. 9, p. 34. *Vita Gerardis Tullensis*, ed. G. Pertz, *MGH SS*, vol. IV, pp. 485–520, at p. 493. Cf. Richer of Senones, *Gesta Senoniensis Ecclesiae*, ed. G. Waitz, *MGH SS*, vol. XXV (1880), pp. 249–348, at p. 270.

while no king can be shown to have visited Troyes between 901 and 1285.[34] The Capetian kings, particularly Robert the Pious, consciously and successfully extended their influence into Burgundy in the early eleventh century, but though the surviving evidence is far from satisfactory, appear to have attempted nothing on this scale in Champagne.[35] Under kings Hugh, Robert and Henry, few charters were issued in the Champagne region, and few were made for institutions from the region. Robert preferred to spend his time in Orléans, Paris and the surrounding area, and to a certain extent, Compiègne; the only difference visible from Henry's charters is an increase in attention to Laon. From the mid and later eleventh century, under King Philip, a greater concentration on the region around Rheims becomes visible, and this was accentuated under Philip's son Louis VI; but this region was not so much converted into royal heartland as gradually made into a better controlled outlier of early Capetian kingship's real base, the Ile de France. Essentially, then, these regions ceased to feature on the itinerary of kings as they travelled around their kingdoms: kings had become outsiders.[36]

This pattern may, of course, reflect the collapse in the number of royal charters issued for institutions in this region, though of course this collapse is itself indicative of the nature of connections between royal centre and locality. An even clearer diagnostic along the same lines are the more informal documents, the writs and royal letters which seem to have been relatively common in the late Carolingian period. There is, simply, none from the tenth century from this region. And there are other signs too of a relaxation of the royal grasp, and of a politics less firmly centred on kings. Bishops, for example, began now to add their names to royal coinage, and by the later tenth century the king's name was dropped on some episcopal coinages. Dukes and counts, too, began to mint coins in their own names in the tenth century.[37] Synods ceased to

[34] Brühl, *Palatium*, p. 147.

[35] Sources: the late, and unreliable *Vita Garnerii* (often used); Rodulf Glaber, but above all, the *Chronicon sancti Benigni Divionensi*, PL, vol. CLXII, col. 755–847, esp. col. 835, which the secondary literature sometimes simply paraphrases. The struggle turned around the duchy of Burgundy, and bishoprics of Langres, Sens and Auxerre.

[36] On itinerancy, see for this period, J. Bernhardt, *Itinerant kingship and royal monasteries in early medieval Germany, c.936–1075* (Cambridge, 1993), who devotes little time to southern Lotharingia, other than to note that it was increasingly seldom visited. On itinerancy in general, see McKitterick, *Charlemagne*. C. R. Brühl, *Fodrum, gistum, servitium regis: studien zu den wirtschaftlichen Grundlagen des Königtums im Frankenreich und in den fränkischen Nachfolgestaaten Deutschland, Frankreich und Italien vom 6. bis zur Mitte des 14. Jahrhunderts* (Cologne, 1968) offers some statistics, e.g. p. 117.

[37] On Duke Gilbert's coins, F. Dumas, 'La monnaie au xe siècle', *Settimane* 38 (1991), 565–609; D. Flon, *Histoire monétaire de la Lorraine et des Trois-Évêchés* (Nancy, 2002), pp. 339–41. The Bishop of Verdun began minting coins from the 970s: Flon, *Histoire*, pp. 162–3. For general overviews, see Kaiser, 'Münzprivilegien und bischöflichen Münzprägung in Frankreich, Deutschland und Burgund im 9–12 Jahrhundert', *Vierteljahrschrift für Sozial- und Wirtschaftsgeschichte* 63 (1976), 289–339.

be co-ordinated by the kings, at least in these lands; none is attested in the province of Trier, for example, between 929 and 1030.[38]

Another sign of political marginalisation is the thinning out of royal resources, such as palaces and fiscs. Kings who did not visit did not need infrastructures to support their stay, and the liquidation of these resources could produce valuable political capital, a realisation made already in the later ninth century. Famous Carolingian royal palaces quietly disappear from our sources, like Ponthion, last mentioned in 904. Zwentibold's opportunist interventions in the chaotic politics of western Francia were accompanied by substantial concessions in his charters, in which the traditions of Carolingian rule, rock-solid under Charles the Bald, began to bend.[39] It is a sign of the intense pressure Zwentibold was under as a king that he effectively barred himself from Trier in a series of extraordinary charters in favour of the archbishop, yet was also renowned for having struck the same archbishop with that archbishop's own crosier. But Zwentibold's alienations were only the beginning of a process which saw the dissolution of the royal fisc on both sides of the Meuse. Places like Attigny and Thionville reappear, later, in the hands of aristocrats, and texts like the famous, though ill-dated, *Tafelgüterverzeichnis*, a list of imperial properties, show that the scale of royal property in the east was on a very small scale by (probably) the early twelfth century. These losses were compensated for by occasional rashes of confiscation attested in some royal charters, but these seem largely to have been the reverberations from disputes which only touched on Lotharingia indirectly.[40] By the eleventh century, kings like Robert the Pious seem to have had little to give, at least according to his biographer Helgaud, who painted him as giving chiefly through authorising theft.[41] As discussed in Chapter 2, we do not need to suppose an array of lost charters collectively winding up the fisc. Given what we have seen of how that fisc worked in Chapter 2, it seems more likely it simply faded out, as kings ceased to pay it close attention. If there was pressing need, after all, there was always a monastery to tap.[42]

Finally, even the much-vaunted Ottonian control of bishoprics pales in comparison with Carolingian practice, at least as concerns these regions. Emperors seem to have been content with a fairly loose control of Lotharingian bishoprics, making sure they attended court and fulfilled

---

[38] H. Wolter, *Die Synoden im Reichsgebiet und in Reichitalien von 916–1056* (Paderborn, 1988), pp. 23–4.

[39] Notably *DZ*, nos. 18 and 27.

[40] R. Deutinger, *Königsherrschaft im Ostfränkischen Reich: eine pragmatische Verfassungsgeschichte der späten Karolingerzeit* (Ostfildern, 2006) discusses the East Frankish evidence for confiscations, pp. 258–9.

[41] Helgaud, *Vita Roberti, passim.*   [42] E.g. *Recueil*, ed. Halkin, no. 123; *UBMR* no. 382 (*c.*1083).

their obligations, but not supervising them closely. Most southern Lotharingian bishoprics, at least up until the later eleventh century and with the partial exception of Trier, were filled by Lotharingians, and not all of these were necessarily royal candidates.[43] Even before the 'Investiture Quarrel', emperors occasionally struggled to get their candidates in, despite considerable Ottonian success in appointing followers to sees in strategic western Frankish bishoprics. Henry I's appointment of a certain Benno to Metz in 927, against the wishes of the canons, proved disastrous.[44] Emperor Henry II was obliged to mount not one but three armed expeditions to Metz and Trier, as part of the so-called *Moselfehde*, to ensure that his appointees won out, and with only limited success.[45] Henry IV was capable of placing a Saxon named Pibo who had spent time at the imperial court into the bishopric of Toul in 1069, but in spite of Pibo's personal piety, the appointment proved controversial, and indeed Pibo faced an attempt on the part of the Toul clergy to have him deposed for simony in 1074.[46]

The bishops in the west are more obscure figures, for lack of episcopal *gesta* or other corroborative material that gives details for this period. For the most part, the appointment of bishops at cities like Troyes, Châlons, Laon and Rheims took place without registering in our sources in the tenth and early eleventh century. Sometimes we can be sure that kings had a say in the appointment of bishops. Hugh Capet's role in the appointment of Arnulf of Rheims in 989 after Archbishop Adalbero's death, for example, is made obvious by the material collected to prove Arnulf guilty of treason.[47] We know, too, that King Lothar of West Francia put the Rheims cleric Bruno into Langres, that King Louis IV appointed Gibuin

---

[43] See the detailed tables in A. Finck von Finckenstein, *Bischof und Reich: Untersuchungen zum Integrationsprozess des ottonisch-frühsalischen Reiches (919–1056)* (Sigmaringen, 1989), pp. 234–41. Cf. M. Parisse, 'L'évêque d'Empire au XIᵉ siècle. L'exemple lorrain', *Cahiers de civilisation médiévale* 27 (1984), pp. 95–105.

[44] Flodoard, *Annales*, s. a. 927 and 928. Cf. a little later the case of Rather of Verona, the Lotharingian appointed to Liège who was unable to hold onto his see.

[45] For the *Moselfehde*, Herrmann, ed., *Geschichtliche Landeskunde*, vol. 1, pp. 230–1. See Thietmar, *Chronicon*, ed. R. Holtzmann, *MGH SRG N. S.* 9 (Berlin, 1935), bk VI, 35 (p. 317), 51 (p. 339), 87 and bk VII, 54 (p. 379). Henry also besieged Metz in 1009 and then again in 1012, according to the *Annales Altahenses maiores*, ed. W. von Giesebrecht and E. von Oefele, *MGH SRG*, vol. IV (Hanover, 1891), pp. 16–17. According to the *Annales Quedlinburgenses*, ed. M. Giese, *MGH SRG*, vol. LXXII (Hanover, 2004), p. 526, Henry besieged the palace at Trier for sixteen weeks in 1008, before giving up.

[46] F.-R. Erkens, *Die Trierer Kirchenprovinz im Investiturstreit* (Cologne, 1987), pp. 10–12; the main source is a letter from Udo of Trier to Gregory VII in 1075, who had been tasked with investigating the accusation (the king had also sent a representative, Bishop Benno of Osnabrück). Ibid., pp. 110–12, arguing that resistance to Egilbert's appointment to Trier in 1078 was based not on principle but on unwillingness to accept a 'landfremden Bischof'.

[47] See below, pp. 163–5.

to Châlons and that King Henry placed Gervaise of Le Mans to Rheims in 1055 and at least consented to the appointment of Mainard to Troyes in 1034.[48] On other occasions, it is possible to be reasonably sure that the king was conspicuously not involved with appointments, such as that of Frotmund to Troyes in 1050, arranged by Pope Leo IX in the wake of the Council of Rheims (1049), and on occasions royal candidates flatly failed, such as Gervaise II's bid for Rheims in 1107.[49] In any case, the absence of any evidence comparable to the lobbying of kings documented in the ninth century (discussed on pp. 30–1) is surely indicative of a less closely monitored situation, even if these bishops were very far from representing challenges to royal authority.

POST-ROYAL POLITICS

If the extent to which royal power ebbed away should not be exagge-rated, it is nevertheless clear that both regions must have adjusted to a politics in which kings were markedly more distant. This represented a significant shift. As Chapter 1 showed, not only were ninth-century kings an unmissable presence in these regions, but ninth-century politics in the area had been resolutely court-centred to the extent that they cannot be said to have had a history distinct from the kingdoms, and so to write a political history of the area in the ninth century would be, like writing the history of medieval Belgium, plainly anachronistic. If, for example, a single extended family seems to have dominated the region of Troyes in the ninth century, as discussed above, it is equally true that members of this family, and sometimes the counts of Troyes in person, also held office around Chartres and Laon, and were active on royal business as far away as Spain.[50] In no way can families like this be said to have been based exclusively in this region, and in fact it can doubted whether they were really based anywhere at all other than the royal court. The relegation of that court, from the local perspective, must have been associated with significant change in the parameters within which political authority was wielded; and indeed something of this nature is evident from the sources.

---

[48] P. Demouy, *Genèse d'une cathédrale: les archevêques de Reims et leur église aux XIe et XIIe siècles* (Rheims, 2005), pp. 538–9; *Chronicon sancti Benigni*, col. 815; on Gibuin, see Richer, *Historiae*, p. 142; on Mainard, see Odorannus of Sens, *Opera omnia*, ed. and tr. R.-H. Bautier and M. Gilles (Paris, 1972), pp. 246–9.

[49] Frotmund: A. Becker, *Studien zum investiturproblem in Frankreich: Papsttum, Königtum und Episkopat im Zeitalter der gregorianischen Kirchenform (1049–1119)* (Saarbrücken, 1955), p. 40. Gervaise II: Suger, *Vita Ludovici*, ed. and tr. H. Waquet, *Vie de Louis VI le Gros* (Paris, 1964), pp. 86–8; cf. *The early councils of Pope Paschal II, 1100–1110*, ed. U.-R. Blumenthal (Toronto, 1978), p. 98.

[50] Crété-Protin, *Église*, pp. 297–308.

Tenth-century politics

The first signs of this change is a kind of regionalised politics that began to emerge more clearly in the tenth century. Admittedly, it is not altogether easy to reconstruct a coherent political narrative. The major narrative source for the first half of the century in this area is Flodoard's Annals, and modern readers are not alone in being overwhelmed by the sheer complexity of the politics he described, probably the impression he was trying to put across: as discussed below, Richer of Rheims's Histories, in all its idiosyncrasy, can be understood as a valiant effort to make some sense of Flodoard's brutally unadorned record of events.[51] Nevertheless, it is possible to elucidate patterns which speak to the evidence.

The first half of the tenth century saw kings chiefly concerned to ensure no new kings emerged in this region as a kind of political vacuum emerged, for there were several aristocrats who were potential candidates; when it is remembered that Lothar II's kingdom fell through political accident, not inherent weakness, there is no doubt that the lands could have supported such a bid. It is unrecorded whether the family of Matfrid, largely responsible for eliminating King Zwentibold, ever had royal ambitions, but the marriage of one of its leading figures, Gerhard, to Zwentibold's widow Uda was clearly a political gesture of some force.[52] Even before Charles the Simple was crowned, Reginar, a leading Lotharingian aristocrat, seems to have been angling for the greatest freedom of manoeuvre he could achieve, to judge from a charter he issued for an old royal church at Stenay, which mimicked the phrasing of a royal diploma; he had missed the opportunities of 888, but now perhaps weighed up the possibility of having himself crowned.[53] So too might have his son Duke Gilbert, identified as a key actor in Charles the Simple's takeover of Lotharingia, and with remarkably widespread interests through Lotharingia.[54] So too, it has been proposed, did Count Boso, brother of King Rodolf, who bestrode the Marne from his fortress at Vitry in the early tenth century, from where he launched ravaging expeditions which targeted Châlons, Dijon and Rheims, on one of which he was

---

[51] Richer of St-Rémi, *Historiae*, ed. H. Hoffmann, *MGH SS*, vol. xxxviii (Hanover, 2000), Introduction, p. 4.

[52] See most recently MacLean, 'Insinuation'.

[53] The charter is edited in *Histoire de Lorraine*, ed. A. Calmet, 6 vols. (2nd edition: Nancy, 1745–57), vol. ii, col. 144. It is assumed to be essentially genuine by F. Hirschmann, *Verdun im hohen Mittelalter: eine lothringische Kathedralstadt und ihr Umland im Spiegel der geistlichen Institutionen* (Trier, 1996), vol. i, pp. 355–6, though its transmission is decidedly weak. For Reginar, cf. Beumann, 'König Zwentibolds'.

[54] E. Hlawitschka, 'Herzog Giselbert von Lothringen und das Kloster Remiremont', *Zeitschrift für die Geschichte des Oberrheins* 108 (1960), 422–65.

eventually killed. Count Heribert II of Vermandois, the jailer of Charles the Simple, was yet another of these figures whose ambitions were potentially royal, in his case supported by his known descent from the Carolingian family.[55]

Each of these figures exercised an extensive domination over wide areas, and was only partially integrated into structures of power centred on the kings. They presented, in other words, an actual or potential threat to the exercise of royal authority, and indeed to individual kings. This threat must have been particularly acute in Lotharingia, given its history as an independent kingdom, and so it is revealing that the Ottonians seem deliberately to have avoided terming Lotharingia as a kingdom (*regnum*) in their charters, or its dukes as dukes of 'Lotharingia'.[56] Nevertheless, in one way or another, these major threats were all seen off. The Matfridings were marginalised in 906, Boso was eliminated in 935, the Reginar family's ambitions were broken in 936, and Count Heribert II died, fought to a standstill, in 943. Quite what accounted for this row of failures is still something of a puzzle: luck would seem to have played its part, but one could also speculate that the regions best integrated into the old system were those whose adaption to a new one was slowest; that these figures were akin to those who had emerged at the end of the ninth century elsewhere, but were simply a generation too late to win the same success.[57]

Thereafter more secure, the kings ruling from the old Carolingian peripheries began to engage more positively with the aristocracy of the region, though still at a distance. The form this engagement took in the tenth century was the promotion, and steering, of what we might call a particular 'constellation', a political network loosely based on kinship or alliance, though it should always be remembered that kinship was never an entirely stable platform for politics, not least because of cross-cutting marriage ties. In Lotharingia, the major constellation to benefit from the mid- and later-tenth-century politics of alliance was the Ardennes 'family', whose branches included counts of Verdun, dukes of Lower Lotharingia, and for a while, dukes of Upper Lotharingia too, not to mention numerous bishops.[58] After an experiment of ruling the region

---

[55] H. Schwager, *Graf Heribert II. von Soissons, Omois, Meaux, Madrie sowie Vermandois (900/06–943) und die Francia (Nord-Frankreich) in der 1. Hälfte des 10. Jahrhunderts* (Kallmunz, 1994). See genealogy, p. xiii above.

[56] Bauer, *Lotharingien*, pp. 18–20, 62–3.

[57] See R. le Jan, 'L'aristocratie Lotharingienne: structure interne et conscience politique', in H. W. Herrmann and R. Schneider, eds., *Lotharingia: eine europäische Kernlandschaft um das Jahr 1000. Une région au centre de l'Europe autour de l'an mil* (Saarbrücken, 1995), pp. 71–88.

[58] M. Parisse, ed., *La Maison d'Ardenne*, Publications de la section historique de l'Institut grand-ducal 95 (Luxembourg, 1981).

direct from the Rhine through Conradine intermediaries had failed in 955, Ottonian favour turned to related members of this group, whose interconnections underpinned the extent to which Lotharingia elites conceived of themselves of as a unit.[59]

Emperors also used this family to project their authority beyond Lotharingia, appointing clerics associated with this group to bishoprics at Rheims and Laon as well as Verdun and Metz.[60] Admittedly, it was not simply owing to the long-standing connections this flow of appointees generated that later tenth-century archbishops of Rheims co-minted coins with the emperor, for Rheims's lands in the empire must have played a role here too.[61] Nevertheless, these Lotharingian clerics in West Francia did not simply pass through; they also brought their secular cousins with them. Archbishop Odalric of Rheims, former titular abbot of Bouxières near Toul, seems to have rewarded his relatives, counts of Reynel, with Rheims lands still held by descendants of these relatives in the early eleventh century.[62] But closer relatives did better still. Thanks to Odalric's successor, Archbishop Adalbero of Rheims, a Lotharingian trained at Gorze, Godfrey of Ardennes and his clients became firmly established at various points in the diocese, creating networks that were still important in the mid eleventh century, even if their precise scope is difficult to establish with certainty owing to the usual perils of genealogical research.[63] The result was a pattern similar to Charles the Simple's policy of using Lotharingian resources to impose control on western Francia, now simply harnessed in the interests of the Ottonian political order, making West Francia into an extension of Lotharingia.[64]

The Heribert constellation, west of the Meuse, in some ways shadows that of the Ardennes.[65] Descended from Charlemagne via his son Pippin (as his

[59] The difficult question of Lotharingian self-consciousness is not directly relevant here; for positions on either side of the argument, see Bauer, *Lotharingien* and J. Schneider, *Auf der Suche nach dem verlorenen Reich: Lotharingien im 9. und 10. Jahrhundert* (Cologne, 2010).
[60] M. Bur, 'Adalbéron, archevêque de Reims, reconsidéré', in M. Parisse and X. Altet, eds., *Le roi de France et son royaume autour de l'an mil* (Paris, 1992), pp 55–63; Ehlers, 'Carolingiens'.
[61] P. Crinon and J. Lemant, 'Les deniers d'Otton III empereur et Arnoul archevêque de Reims (998–1021), émis pour la partie orientale du diocèse (Mouzon)', *Bulletin de la Société française de numismatique* 51 (1996), 166–71.
[62] M. Bur, *La formation du comté de Champagne: v. 950-v. 1150* (Nancy, 1977), pp. 140–1. Vatican Reg. lat. 1283, f. 63r–v contains a to my knowledge unedited agreement between the canons of Rheims and Odo II to help them remove these relatives from the Val-du-Rognon (1024).
[63] See M. Bur, 'La frontière entre la Champagne et la Lorraine du milieu du Xᵉ siècle à la fin du XIIᵉ siècle', *Francia* 4 (1976), 237–54. An example is provided by a charter of 1018, in 'Recueil des actes des archevêques de Reims d'Arnoul à Renaud II (997–1139)', ed. P. Demouy, unpublished thesis, Université de Nancy II, 1982, vol. I, n. 5, pp. 46–7; cf. *Metropolis*, ed. Marlot, vol. II, col. 169 (1075).
[64] See Leyser, '987: the Ottonian connection'.
[65] Essential reading: K.-F. Werner, 'Untersuchungen zur Frühzeit des Französischen Fürstentums (9–10 Jahrhundert)', *Die Welt als Geschichte* 18 (1958), 256–89; 19 (1959), 146–93; 20 (1960), 87–119;

descendants still knew in the twelfth century) Count Heribert II 'of Vermandois' negotiated a startling expansion of influence in the decades around 900, starting from the Oise valley.[66] This expansion was achieved partly by sheer aggression, but partly, too, by deft political manoeuvring, with Heribert steering his five-year-old son Hugh into the archiepiscopal seat of Rheims in the early tenth century, prior to the Ottonian-sponsored takeover. On Count Heribert's death in 943, his lands were divided amongst a number of successors, notably his son-in-law Odo of Blois, and his sons Albert of Vermandois, Heribert ('the Old') and Robert, who took control of Troyes via a marriage alliance with an ally of the dukes of Burgundy. While there is no firm indication that these heirs managed their interests collectively, they do seem to have maintained a loose alliance amongst themselves, much like the Ardennes group. King Louis IV intervened intermittently against them, sometimes even calling on Ottonian assistance to do so – usually in the form of Lotharingian armies – but did not try to abolish these dynamics of acquisition, merely to channel them, and gives the impression of having been more a rival than a king to these families.

Under King Lothar, things began to take a different shape, as he managed to bring Heribertine interests into alignment with his own, and Heribert the Old, whose interest in Lotharingia extended to visits to Metz, took on the title of 'count of the palace'.[67] Lothar attempted to drive back Ottonian influence, as shown by his attempt to depose Adalbero, the Lotharingian Archbishop of Rheims, a move which indirectly wrecked his brother Charles of Lorraine's subsequent hopes of becoming king. Equally unsuccessful, though even more spectacular, were Lothar's assaults on Aachen in 978 and then in 984 on Verdun: contesting control of Lotharingia, perhaps, but more certainly signalling a challenge to Ottonian hegemony.[68] The Heribert group offered crucial assistance in these endeavours. The attack on Verdun, in particular, was spearheaded by counts from the family, namely Odo I, son of Heribert II's daughter Liutgarde, and Heribert 'the Young', son of Robert of Troyes, who was also expanding his influence around Rheims.[69] Lothar jointly minted coins with this Heribert, and he continued

more recently, Schwager, *Heribert*, though vitiated by some errors. M. Bur, 'Léon IX et la France (1026–1054)', in G. Bischoff and B. Tocks, eds., *Léon IX et son temps* (Turnhout, 2007), pp. 233–57, also has a good account.
[66] Proven by Guido of Bazoches's letter to Count Henry the Liberal: *Liber Epistolarum*, ed. H. Adolfsson, *Liber Epistularum Guidonis de Basoches* (Stockholm, 1969), pp. 58–60 (the genealogy is actually taken back to Clovis).
[67] M. Bur, *La formation*, pp. 113–14. For the visit to Metz, *Vita Bercharii* (BHL 1178), ed. J. Vandermoere and J. Vanhecke, *AASS Oct.* vol. I (Brussels, 1845), cols. 1010–30, at bk II, col. 1024. Heribert also fostered connections with the monastery of Montier-en-Der, as the text goes on to relate.
[68] For the role of rivalry over Lotharingia, see MacLean, 'Boso', particularly 26–7.
[69] Gerbert of Rheims, *Epistolae*, ed. and tr. P. Riché and J.-P. Callu, *Correspondance*, 2 vols. (Paris, 1993), vol. I, nos. 17, 51, 58, 89, 93, 97, 103 and 129, showing Odo and Heribert working in collaboration.

later to support the claims of Lothar's family to the throne.[70] At the same time, these families were acquiring interests in Lotharingia at this time, expanding (like the Ardennes family) across political frontiers, to hold centres east of the Meuse at Vaucouleurs and elsewhere.[71]

Early eleventh-century politics

By the early eleventh century, however, relations between kings and the aristocracies of these regions were starting to build up to a crisis, largely because the dispersed networks promoted by kings began to throw up figures whose power once again posed a serious threat to royal authority. The emblematic figures here are Count Odo II of Blois (see Figure 3), whose Heribertine links came from his grandmother Liutgarde, the daughter of Heribert II, and Duke Godfrey the Bearded of Lotharingia, of the Ardennes family: two aristocrats whose control over the networks developed in previous decades allowed them to pursue more ambitious agendas, again by means of extensive, rather than intensive, forms of power.

Odo II's power came from his successful accumulation of securely held regional interests. Based initially around the middle Loire, Odo II profited from inheritance and application to acquire networks in the areas around Rheims and Châlons, and indeed further north, too.[72] These resources were marshalled solely in order further to expand. Though his takeover of the lands lying west of the Meuse in the 1020s succeeded, possibly in the teeth of royal opposition, for the most part these ventures failed. According to the (admittedly entirely hostile) set of sources, he was beaten out of Anjou and chased out of Burgundy, before meeting his end in the last of a number of raids, or arguably invasions, of Lotharingia in 1037. Yet the scale of his ambition is breathtaking. His major wars were fought against dukes and counts, and his struggle in the Swiss Alps against Emperor Henry III was surprisingly evenly matched. A Châlons charter in which Odo II promised not to build fortifications (*municipia*) within eight leagues of the city (around a hundred square miles) shows, if genuine, something of the breadth of his

---

[70] *Flodoardi Presbyteri Ecclesiae Remensis canonici historiarum eiusdem ecclesiæ libri* IV, ed. J. Sirmond (Paris, 1644), col. 405 (acquisition of Vertus). On the assault on Lotharingia, Richer, *Historiae*, bk III, ch. 100, p. 225. For the coins (five have been found), see M. Dhénin, 'Obole inédite de Lothaire (954–986) et Herbert II, comte de Troyes (967–983)', *Bulletin de la Société française de numismatique* 48 (1993), 473–4. For their support for Charles of Lorraine, see *MGH Concilia* vol. VI, pp. 420, 432.

[71] J. Schneider, 'Recherches sur les confins de la Lorraine et de la Champagne: les origines de Vaucouleurs', *Comptes-rendus des séances de l'Académie des Inscriptions et Belles-Lettres* 105 (1961), 270–4.

[72] Hariulf, *Chronicon centulense*, ed. F. Lot, *Chronique de l'abbaye de Saint-Riquier (Vᵉ siècle-1104)* (Paris, 1894), Appendix, p. 316 (for a charter issued by Odo); *Vita Leonis*, bk I, ch. 16, p. 54; Vat Reg. 1283: see n. 62, above.

power.[73] Little wonder that Odo II seems to have been considered by some a king.[74] It was a natural response to this development that by the 1030s, the west Frankish king was openly co-operating with the emperor to restrain Odo's ambition, leading to the co-ordinated ravaging of his lands.[75] King Henry certainly had reason to be satisfied with the division of Odo's territories between his two sons, Theobald and Stephen, with the former taking over the lands along the Loire, the latter the lands based on Troyes, and indeed west Frankish kings often seem to have attempted to divide and rule this family. King Philip may have offered some assistance to Stephen's son Odo III against the intimidation of his uncle Theobald, though Odo eventually decided that Anglo-Norman England was a more promising and probably safer place for his talents, allowing Theobald to expand into his nephew's territory.

Indirectly, it was the challenge posed by Count Odo II that lay behind the emperor's difficulties with Duke Godfrey the Bearded. Emperor Henry III had permitted Godfrey's father, Duke Gozilo I, based in the north of Lotharingia, to take on some kind of responsibility for the south too (that is, in the area of this book's concern) after the death of Duke Frederick III in 1033, in order to offer greater opposition to Odo II's increasingly serious assaults: the strategy proved its worth in 1037, when Gozilo led the army that defeated the count at Bar. On Gozilo's death in 1044, his son Godfrey was determined to retain his father's patrimony, that is, the whole of Lotharingia, but now that Odo II was dead, the emperor saw no advantage in this, and tried to force a division.[76] Nevertheless, he was prepared to honour the family's claims, dividing Gozilo's heritage between his two sons in the already traditional north/south fashion. It was only when one of these, Godfrey, rebelled, drawing considerable support although Lotharingian bishops continued to support the king, and began rampaging around Lotharingia (and in the 1050s moving down to Italy) that Henry reached out beyond the Ardennes family to another grouping, this one based rather more to the east of Lotharingia (see Figure 2).

Misled by Sigibert of Gembloux, historians have long given this family the epithet 'of Alsace', due to confusion with the (admittedly related)

---

[73] *Cartulaire du chapitre de l'église cathédrale de Châlons-sur-Marne. Par le chantre Warin*, ed. P. Pelicier (Paris, 1897), n. 28. For the ascription to Odo II and not Odo III, see Benner, *Châlons*, pp. 79–80. The cartulary is early twelfth century, giving plenty of scope for interpolation, but though the text is unusual, and there are similar documents from Toul that are certainly forged, it could perhaps be considered as analogous to Ottonian and Salian forest grants.

[74] C.-R. Brühl, *Deutschland – Frankreich: die Geburt zweier Völker* (Cologne, 1990), p. 178.

[75] I. Voss, 'La Lotharingie, terre de rencontres x^e–xie siècles', in D. Iogna-Prat and J-C. Picard, eds., *Religion et culture autour de l'an mil: royaume Capétien et Lotharingie* (Paris, 1990), pp. 267–72.

[76] E. Boshof, 'Lothringen, Frankreich, und das Reich in der Regierungszeit Heinrichs III', *Rheinische Vierteljahrsblätter* 42 (1978), 63–127.

Eguisheim family.[77] In fact, its leading figure in the early eleventh century, Count Gerard (uncle of the later Duke Gerard I), had interests throughout Lotharingia: independent sources document his influence around Heimbach in the north, near Toul in the south and around St-Mihiel in the west.[78] Increasingly, though, and unlike the Ardennes grouping, this family's interests were more clearly centred on the south, and the promotion of this group consolidated the divergence between north and south Lotharingia, mapping onto the archdiocese of Trier to create the region later known as Upper Lotharingia. Chance, too, played a role, though. The powerbase of another rival family, that of the Ezzonids, whose position in the heart of Lotharingia between north and south seemed strategically promising in the mid eleventh century, was eradicated largely through the opportunities that dynastic accident gave to capable archbishops of Cologne.[79]

In the absence of crises, kings and emperors were happy to let matters take their course. An indication of this abandonment of royal day-to-day intervention is the number of small-scale wars in the regions in the eleventh century, only indirectly related to kingdom-wide issues, and with which the kings tended not to become involved. The feud between counts Baldric and Wicman around the year 1000 north of Utrecht, involving participants from the region which concerns us, is one example, though here Otto III did intervene; others closer to this region include that between Count Gerard and Duke Godfrey c.1017, mentioned by the Deeds of the Bishops of Cambrai and Thietmar of Merseburg, that between Duke Theoderic I and the Pfalzgraf Ezzo at Odernheim around 1011 or 1012, mentioned only in the *Gesta* of the monastery of Brauweiler, or Duke Theoderic's assault on a certain Count Widric in 1017, mentioned only by the later chronicler Jean de Bayon.[80] Similar events can be perceived in Champagne too, such as the still-enigmatic 'surrender of Vitry' around

[77] The confusion was cleared up by Hlawitschka, *Anfänge*, particularly p. 151; it may be (as Parisse has argued) that Sigibert was not so much in error as referring to the family's interests in the area around Bitche, which he may have considered to lie in Alsace.

[78] Alpert of Metz, *De Diversitate Temporum*, ed. and tr. H. van Rij and A. Sapir Abulafia, *Gebeurtenissen van deze tijd; Een fragment over bisschop Diederik I van Metz; De mirakelen van de heilige Walburg in Tiel* (Amsterdam, 1980), p. 62; *Chronicon S. Benigni*, col. 829; *Chronicon S. Mihaelis*, p. 31. According to Jean de Bayon, *Chronicon Mediani monasterii*, ed. J. Belhomme, *Historia mediani monasterii*, pp. 228–77, at p. 219, it was Gerard's presence at the battle of Bar which caused the defeat of Odo II. Gerard of Metz is not to be confused with a Gerard of Alsace: see above, n. 77.

[79] See U. Lewald, 'Die Ezzonen. Das Schicksal eines rheinischen Fürstengeschlechts', *Rheinische Vierteljahrsblätter* 43 (1979), 120–68. The *Moselfehde* seems also to have strengthened Gerard's position by shaking the Luxembourger family: see n. 45.

[80] *Actus fundatorum Brunwilarensis monasterii*, ed. G. Waitz, *MGH SS*, vol. XIV (1883), p. 132; Jean de Bayon, *Chronique*, p. 217; *Gesta episcoporum Cameracensium*, bk III, ch. 11, p. 469; Thietmar, *Chronicon*, bk VII, ch. 62, p. 475 (the battle in which Gerard's son Siegfried died).

1070, and a battle of Bologne involving the Joinville family in 1055, mentioned by the later chronicler Alberic of Troisfontaines.[81] Little wonder that Archbishop Gervaise I of Rheims described his compatriots in the mid eleventh century as 'wild and untamed'.[82]

Patterns of power

As already suggested, it would be foolish to pretend that a coherent narrative can be forged from the events affecting two regions in different kingdoms. However, two crucial, overarching points do emerge. The first, and most obvious, is that these political developments can be seen as related to the retreat of royal authority. Kings could still intervene in these regions, and they were never forgotten; but their intervention took effort, and was more intermittent. It was generally easier to promote and channel the energies of broad-based networks based on extensive patterns of social domination, and hope that they did not coalesce too effectively. Only if they did, and a crisis loomed, were royal resources marshalled on a serious scale, with reasonable success on both sides of the Meuse.

The second is that up to the 1020s at least, the political characteristics of the lands on either side of the Meuse were certainly different, but nevertheless comparable. The western region would seem to have suffered more disruption in the tenth century than did the lands east of the Meuse, simply because the central politics of the western Frankish kingdom were more unstable (partly due to Ottonian policy to maintain a balance of power), and the lands around Rheims and Châlons were those where the battles were fought out. The lands that would later be known as Upper Lotharingia were not exactly tranquil, as discussed already, but were spared the almost structural quality of conflict familiar in the west. This perhaps had important consequences, to be discussed in Chapter 8; nevertheless, the difference was a matter of degree. The way that rulers on each side took a keen interest in these lands only when they began to pose a threat, intervening chiefly to prevent the concentration of authority, has long been identified as the key royal policy under the early Capetians, but their cousins across the Meuse acted similarly. The rhythm of these interventions was also linked, with a period of closer, though diversified, collaboration in the later tenth century followed by greater tension in the eleventh century. Only in the later eleventh century did the pattern diverge, as the higher levels of the aristocracy in Lotharingia definitively

[81] For Vitry, see P. Desportes and F. Dolbeau, 'Découverte de nouveaux documents relatifs au polyptyque de Saint-Rémi de Reims. À propos d'une édition récente', *Revue du Nord* 270 (1986), 575–607.
[82] Gervaise, *Epistolae, PL*, vol. CXLIII, col. 1361, 'infrenes et indomiti'.

fragmented, just as that of Champagne began, slowly, to coalesce, developments which will be further discussed in Chapter 8. Before this date, as Brühl has argued at considerable length, we should not simply assume differences along the lines of 'French' or 'German'.[83] This is not to say there were not sharp differences in the identities of the people concerned, though in fact that seems unlikely; it is to state that from the point of view of political process, much remained similar.

This is striking for two reasons. In the first place, Lotharingia is usually treated as a 'duchy', and indeed one which was divided into two in the tenth century (959 is sometimes given as the precise date of separation), creating Upper and Lower Lotharingia, whereas the region west of the Marne is thought in contrast to have been effectively unstructured until the twelfth century. Secondly, there were processes integrating the lands around the Marne and Moselle into the kingdoms to which they were joined. The Conradine dominance of Lotharingia, for example, tied the region to the Rhineland for a decade early in the tenth century, perhaps crucial for preventing the revival of Lothar's kingdom. Around the same time, the marriage alliance between Heribert II's daughter and the family of counts around Blois, former clients of the Robertians, created political links between the lower Loire and the Marne which would be sustained for centuries. These connections had ramifications in ecclesiastical terms (for instance, the influence of Marmoutier in southern Champagne); they also ensured that the politics of the region immediately west of the Meuse were at times subordinated to concerns focused on the Loire, leading to connections recently explored by LoPrete.[84] Nor should we restrict ourselves to 'secular' politics. Trier's battles over ecclesiastical primacy in the tenth century saw it largely competing with Mainz and Cologne, and only secondarily with Rheims, whose own fiercest battles over ecclesiastical hierarchy were fought out with Sens.[85]

However, the extent to which the duchy, or the duchies, of tenth-century Lotharingia, and for that matter of anywhere else in the East Frankish kingdom, provided coherent political frameworks has been brought into question by recent scholarship.[86] The difference between the ducal Lotharingia and the

---

[83] Brühl, *Geburt*. It should be noted that Brühl's arguments about the 'origins' of Germany are contested: W. Giese, *Heinrich I.: Begründer der ottonischen Herrschaft* (Darmstadt, 2008) pp. 34–8, offers excellent summary and counter-argument. A wider context is offered by J. Ehlers, *Die Entstehung des deutschen Reiches* (Munich, 1994): see pp. 19–23 and 75–6.

[84] J. Lusse, 'Marmoutier et Cluny en Champagne', *Etudes champenoises* 2 (1976), 27–44.

[85] E. Boshof, 'Köln–Mainz–Trier – Die Auseinandersetzung um die Spitzenstellung der deutschen Episkopat in ottonisch–salianisch Zeit', *Jahrbuch des Kölnischen Geschichtsvereins* 49 (1978), 19–48.

[86] H.-W. Goetz, *'Dux' und 'ducatus': begriffs- und verfassungsgeschichtliche Untersuchungen zur Entstehung des sogenannten 'jüngeren' Stammesherzogtums an der Wende vom neunten zum zehnten Jahrhundert* (Bochum, 1977). Cf. R. Barth, *Der Herzog in Lotharingien im 10 Jahrhundert* (Sigmaringen, 1990), applying these arguments to Lotharingia.

nascent region of Champagne can therefore probably be overstated. And moreover, there were countervailing processes at work bringing the lands between Marne and Moselle together. A surprising number of figures and groups had interests that crossed the Meuse frontier throughout the period in question: Boso from his frontier castle at Vitry in the 930s; Count Odo II's claims on the lands of Notre-Dame of Laon in Lotharingia in the 1020s; Count Theobald's meeting with the emperor in 1054; Mathilda of Tuscany's lands near Rheims, doubtless inherited from her ancestors, dukes of Upper Lotharingia; Count Godfrey of Ardennes's foothold around Mouzon; the counts of Dampierre's remarkable hold on the county of Toul into the eleventh century, to name but a few of these cross-cutting connections.[87] Still in the early twelfth century, King Louis VI's attempts to impose himself upon the region around Rheims were hampered by local marriage alliances with unnamed Lotharingians.[88]

These political connections were underscored by broader, underlying social ones, too. Some of these, like castles and counties, will be discussed in the next chapter. There are also anecdotal signs of continuing cultural inter-action. For example, the manuscript Vienna ÖNB cod. 529, an important element in the manuscript transmission of Einhard's Life of Charlemagne, was written in Trier in the tenth century from west Frankish exemplars, and moreover one of the hands is probably Rémois: indeed, Tischler has char-acterised the codex as in itself a manifestation of cultural contact.[89] Perhaps it was connected to the vigorous scholarly links maintained between Rheims and Mettlach, revealed by the letters of Gerbert of Rheims.[90]

Another especially important shared characteristic to note is the more than usually exiguous evidence for episcopal-sponsored peace move-ments, which according to Rodulf Glaber and Hugh of Flavigny never gained much ground in the area, even when entrusted to the capable abbot Richard of St-Vanne.[91] The closest that this region came to such phenomena was the still-mysterious council at Trier in 1044, reported in

---

[87] On Boso, Godfrey, Odo II, Theobald, Dampierre, see Bur, *Champagne*, pp. 94, 126–30, 165–7, 201, 264, respectively. On Matilda's Rheims lands, see Hugh of Flavigny, *Chronicon*, p. 419.

[88] Suger, *Vita*, p. 28. On the Roucy family, see B. Guenée, 'Les généalogies entre l'histoire et la politique: la fierté d'être Capétien en France au Moyen Âge', *Annales. Économies, Sociétés, Civilisations* 33 (1978), 450–77.

[89] M. Tischler, *Einharts Vita Karoli: Studien zur Entstehung, Überlieferung und Rezeption* (Hanover, 2001), pp. 1183–201, at p. 1197.

[90] Gerbert of Rheims, *Epistolae*, nos. 64, 68, 72, 134, 148, 162 and 169.

[91] Rodulf Glaber, *Historiae*, ed. and tr. J. France, *The five books of the histories* (Oxford, 1989), bk v, ch. 16, followed by Hugh of Flavigny, *Chronicon*, p. 403. Cf. Demouy, *Genèse*, pp. 476–7. For a brief discussion, see Barthélemy, *L'an mil*, p. 547, n. 3. The classic discussion for this region is R. Bonnaud-Delamare, 'Les institutions de paix dans la province ecclésiastique de Reims au xiᵉ siècle', *Bulletin philologique et historique du Comité des travaux historiques et scientifiques* 10 (1957), 143–200, though built on a very slender evidential basis.

only Lambert's Annals, and the rather better-known Council of Rheims in 1049.[92] Attended by great crowds, which proved very difficult to control, and marked by public speeches, edicts on peace, as well as relics, the Rheims council would seem to be almost a classic Peace Council, were it not that it cannot be construed as challenging social hierarchies: indeed, according to the mid-eleventh-century writer Anselm of St-Rémi, contemporaries apparently saw it as still another tool of imperial domination.[93] Perhaps, though, that does not make Rheims 1049 unusual, since even the earlier peace councils, like that of Héry, attended by monks from Montier-en-Der, can be read as not so much substituting for royal power as, potentially at least, supporting it.[94] Whatever the case, the point is that the conditions responsible for the peace movement further to the south, whether these be social or simply historiographical in nature, were essentially absent from the lands with which we are concerned, reflecting, perhaps, some shared characteristic.

THE CAUSES OF THE RETREAT OF ROYAL POWER

We have seen that though there is good reason not to exaggerate, royal power was less of an everyday reality in the lands between Marne and Moselle after the ninth century, and that this was accompanied by the emergence, and, moreover, ensuing development, of a regionally rooted politics. This was the case both in the lands around Rheims, where political disruption was particularly intense in the tenth century, and in the lands across the Meuse which, though far from peaceful, were politically more stable. The obvious, and appropriate, question to ask is: why? Why did kingship cease to play the kind of role it had in the ninth century?

Working from regional sources carries, of course, the potential that this shift might simply reflect the political marginalisation of these particular regions, as the middle Seine on the one hand and the Rhineland and Saxony on the other grew to overshadow these former centres of power, the result of political developments that were by no means inevitable. That possibility cannot be wholly ruled out from the perspective adopted here. Nevertheless, it should be noted that in spite of the region's importance in the ninth century, particular places, like Troyes and Toul, had never really been central to Carolingian royal itineraries; yet the reach of

---

[92] Cf., though, in the later eleventh century the Council of Soissons, edited in L. Delisle, *Littérature Latine et histoire du Moyen Age* (Paris, 1890), pp. 23–5.

[93] Anselm of St-Rémi, *Historia*, pp. 222–4, 228–230 and 238.

[94] T. Riches, 'The peace of God, the "weakness" of Robert the Pious and the struggle for the German throne, 1023–5', *EME* 18 (2010), 202–22, following an interpretation sketched out by Bonnaud-Delamare. For Héry, see *Vita Bercharii*, bk II, col. 1029.

royal government there seems to have been uncompromised by political marginality in a way which was not true of the tenth century. In other words, it is more likely that we are dealing with a wider structural change in nature of political interaction, rather than merely the decline in centrality of this particular part of the world: that this is the particular form taken of what is generally recognised as a broader phenomenon, the fading of royal power in the post-Carolingian world.

This question is one that has been extensively discussed, and a comprehensive review of this issue is hardly possible here, but nor can the problem be ignored, so we shall examine it in schematic form. In brief, three families of hypotheses have been developed to address this question. The first of these stresses the importance of external factors in bringing down royal power. Its earliest strand to achieve historiographical prominence was an emphasis on the Vikings, that last wave of barbarian invaders, as the agents for collapse. But Viking raids were not in fact that severe in this region, except for a brief spell of destruction in the 880s from which recovery appears to have been swift, and anyway the thrust of much recent work has been to emphasise that it is better to see these raids as a symptom of weak kingship, not its cause.[95]

In a different, but related, vein, historians have begun to investigate the connections between large-scale political change and changes in the climate, whose effect on a predominantly agricultural society can be devastating. However, analysing climate before 1800 remains a field fraught with difficulties because of the range of elements involved (temperatures, climactic variability, precipitation) and the inherent variability of the European climate.[96] Climatic changes have not been identified on a time-scale adequate to correlate with political change, and moreover do not appear to have been dramatic or indeed substantive enough either to disrupt or to accelerate what appears to have been a secular growth in economic production beginning in the ninth century, if not before.[97] Most of the effects of climate change would have been sharply regional as well as gradual, so it is particularly revealing that one case-study, using medieval tooth enamel from Lorraine, has shown little sign of marked variation over the medieval period

---

[95] See for example, J. Nelson, 'England and the Continent II: the Vikings and others', *TRHS* 13 (2003), 1–28.

[96] C. Schuurmans, 'Climate: mean state, variability, and change', in Koster, ed., *Physical Geography*, pp. 289–308.

[97] The field is fast moving, and both dates and degrees of climate change vary from one report to another. Important articles include M. Hughes and H. Diaz, 'Was there a medieval warm period?', *Climactic Change* 26 (1994), 109–42; M. Mann, 'Climate over the past two millennia', *Annual Review of Earth and Planetary Sciences* 35 (2007), 111–36; and R. Bradley, M. K. Hughes and H. F. Diaz, 'Climate in medieval time', *Science* 17 (2003), 404–5. Complicated by contemporary debates about global warming, no consensus is in sight.

at all.[98] In any case, putative shifts in climactic conditions, if further investigation were to confirm any kind of consistent effect, would have interacted with pre-existing fissure points, and cannot account for them.

These external factors share a common problem, then: they could plausibly explain timings or accelerations of historical developments of the Carolingian empire, but only in relation to processes already underway. Many historians, instead, have chosen to emphasise structural deficiencies within Carolingian kingship which can account for its collapse, forming a second family of explanations. One of these approaches identifies the late Carolingians' fiscal profligacy as the ultimate cause of the failure of Carolingian kingship.[99] However, although the royal fisc does seem to vanish away in this region in the tenth century, Chapter 2 argued that the power of the Carolingian kings did not rest on the amount of land they owned, but rather the opposite. Citing Cicero, the author of the 'Deeds of the Abbots of St-Mihiel' astutely observed that emperors do not have to be rich themselves, they merely have to command those who are.[100] While the loss of fiscal lands should certainly be associated with a decline in royal power, it should not be assumed to be prior to it.

An alternative structural flaw could be found in the particular balance between Carolingian emperor and aristocracy, which was upset as the latter began to claim more authority. This interpretation assumed an essential antagonism between king and aristocrat, and saw the collapse of the Carolingians as signalling that aristocracy's final triumph, suggesting that kings like Charles the Simple and Zwentibold were defeated by an aristocracy possessed of a swaggering new confidence. In a sense this is evidently true: both kings were in fact defeated by non-Carolingian opponents (though as we have seen, Zwentibold's opponent might have toyed with becoming king, and Charles's had already done so). This aristocracy was beginning, too, to experiment with castles in this region, which appear in the hands of the top echelons from the very late ninth, and more regularly from the middle tenth century, as will be touched on in the next chapter. The problem, of course, is that the Carolingian kings were not in fact opposed to a strong aristocracy; indeed, they had promoted it.[101]

[98] V. Daux, C. Lecuyer, F. Adam, F. Martineau and F. Vimeux, 'Oxygen isotope composition of human teeth and the record of climate changes in France (Lorraine) during the last 1700 years', *Climactic Change* 70 (2005), 445–64.
[99] J. Dhondt, *Études sur la naissance des principautés territoriales* (Bruges, 1948); cf., though in more complex fashion, Wickham, *Framing*, e.g. pp. 58–9 and pp. 106–7.
[100] *Chronicon S. Michaelis*, p. 30.
[101] P. Fouracre, 'Conflict, power and legitimation in Francia in the late seventh and early eighth centuries', in I. Alfonso, H. Kennedy and J. Escalona, eds., *Building legitimacy: political discourses and forms of legitimacy in medieval societies* (Leiden, 2004), pp. 3–26.

In view of this, many historians now prefer to emphasise the contingent, the coincidental and the unanticipated: the third family of approaches. Indeed, the dominant strand of explanation, particularly in anglophone historiography, for the collapse of Carolingian kingship in the late ninth century revolves around the twin notions of contingency and the ideology of dynasty.[102] According to this view (with which contemporary observers like Regino of Prüm would have had much sympathy) the Carolingian royal influence in local politics fell away because the dynasty itself fortuitously happened to die out in the male line. The growing disconnection between court and locality was simply the result of accidents of procreation. The Carolingian balance was broken by contingent dynastic failure, throwing the aristocracy back upon their own resources. An influential variant which fits into this overarching model is that the proliferation of adult Carolingians, and the concomitant proliferation of Frankish kingdoms, created an aristocracy which was accustomed to accessible royal patronage. The reverse process, as Charles the Fat inherited these kingdoms one by one, disoriented this aristocracy, who refused now to participate in the wider dynamics of empire. That Charles and Zwentibold may not have been the most politically adept of rulers did not help matters (Zwentibold in particular appears to have alienated his supporters by his capriciousness).

However, even this most recent set of explanations has some flaws. Firstly, it slips from the collapse of the Carolingian empire, which certainly took place, to the failure of the Carolingian political experiment, which is in a sense the argument to be proved. After all, the very notion of illegitimate birth which is deemed to have weakened the claims to rule of Zwentibold and Charles the Simple was itself in part a product of Carolingian reform, one of many proofs of the efficacy of the new rules of marriage which Carolingian bishops had been steadily implementing through councils in the course of the ninth century. We should be careful not simply to reproduce a king-centred narrative given by king-centred sources, nor to content ourselves with rebutting it. As the previous chapters have shown, there was more to Carolingian social reform than strong kings or a united empire.

More seriously, it concentrates heavily on problems with what we might call the 'push' factor, the insistence of kings to assert their

---

[102] S. MacLean, *Kingship and politics in the late ninth century: Charles the Fat and the end of the Carolingian empire* (Cambridge, 2003); see also Costambeys, Innes and MacLean, *Carolingian world*, pp. 386–88, 424–6, and pp. 431–5, balancing short- and long-term analyses of Carolingian society.

authority, and ways in which that might have been undermined. This
entirely neglects the 'pull' factor, ways in which the localities drew the
king in. It may be that more significant than Zwentibold's unalluring
personality is the fact that these supporters were so readily alienated.
After all, his installation by his father Arnulf should in theory have
resolved the tension which is often said to have brought down Charles
the Fat, the demand for a locally present king. Zwentibold was very
much locally present – but this turned out not to be what the leading
figures were looking for after all. The successful, large-scale rebellion
against a local, active king who tried hard, albeit ineptly, to follow
Carolingian traditions of rulership constitutes a significant step in the
gradual winding-down of Carolingian kingship, and much the same
could be argued of Charles the Simple. There was no shortage of
would-be strong kings between Marne and Moselle, at least before
923. But neither Charles nor Zwentibold won much support beyond
the bishops, loyal almost by nature to ruling kings before (and often
beyond) the later eleventh century.

In the light of this evidence, it seems appropriate to venture another
hypothesis to add to these, and to suggest that something was happening to make kings less necessary to the workings of local affairs. The
centrality of the royal court in the ninth century as the clearing house of
politics, at which attendance was politically essential, was already
discussed in Chapter 3. It is a plausible inference therefore to suggest
that local political standing had simply become, by the mid eleventh
century, less dependent on the court. Kings were less required, and
were accordingly given rather less assiduous support. When the region
east of the Meuse reacquired its own king, Zwentibold, its elites
decided that they would after all prefer a more distant figure, and
Zwentibold died fighting a rebellion, the first ruling Carolingian king
to be killed in battle.

In this hypothesis, the failure of old-style Carolingian kingship can be
read as in fact a result of Carolingian policies – not in terms of the excessive
promotion of the church or fiscal profligacy, but in terms of a successful
reorganisation of local patterns of domination. We have seen that the
Carolingian political system worked to bolster aristocratic authority; the
evidence here is congruent with supposing that this had in fact taken
effect. Rather than kings being unable now to coerce, we could argue that
aristocrats, and even regions, simply disengaged from courts which no
longer had anything substantial to offer. What changed was that aristocrats
no longer considered that their local and regional dominance needed to be
underpinned by royal authority: they felt their social dominance secure

enough to make its reinforcement through court ceremonies and patron-age redundant.[103] Kings perhaps lost their influence because they lost their appeal, not the other way round.

This chapter has sought to demonstrate that though kingship was never an entirely negligible factor in the politics of the lands between Marne and Moselle between the tenth and early eleventh centuries, there is indeed good reason, when compared with the kind of evidence assessed in Chapter 1 in particular, to believe that its practical impact had diminished, even in the lands of the Ottonian *Reich* where there was in general more political stability. It has sought also to characterise the kinds of political configurations that developed in association with that fading away, drawing attention to similarities on either side of the River Meuse, both in basic structure and in the dynamics that played out, notwithstanding certain differences. It has finally suggested that histor-ians trying to explain the impact of a decline in royal authority on wider society may have been working the wrong way round, because that decline could be more symptom than cause. Strong kingship can legiti-mately serve as a means of distinguishing Carolingian from post-Carolingian society, but to stop there is to stop with effects rather than causes.

This hypothesis proceeds on the basis that many of the problems that faced kings were really the logical culmination of the steadily crystallising power of an elite, a process initiated by Carolingian kings. If Carolingian kingship faltered, and to the extent that it did, it was perhaps because the Carolingian elite opted out. From this point of view, the decline of Carolingian kingship would itself, in an apparent paradox, be the best evidence for the success of elements of the political project they were driving. To the extent that a weakened (or perhaps simply less ambitious) kingship is an important part of the processes analysed in Feudal Revolution historiography, that weakening can be assessed not simply in terms of discontinuity, but also, in broader terms, as representing in a sense a deeper continuity.

This alternative approach remains of course only a hypothesis, just as reliant on assumptions as the others. Evaluating its strength, compared with the more traditional explanations that focus on external shocks,

---

[103] For courts as the centre for the generation of consensus, see most recently Deutinger, *Königsherrschaft*, pp. 383–7, and also 238–54.

structural weakness, or the sheer bad luck of individual kings as the causes of the transformation of the Carolingian world requires attention to be paid less to the way in which power was aggregated, the subject of this chapter, and more to how that power was constituted, embedded in the full discursive and social context, at the local level. An attempt to do this is the task of the next chapter.

Chapter 5

NEW HIERARCHIES

The previous chapter assessed changes in the workings of power between Marne and Moselle at the highest political levels in the wake of the Carolingian empire's fragmentation. Finding that kings did indeed become relatively more remote figures in these regions and setting out the extent of that shift, it discussed various arguments to account for it. Identifying the limitations of explanations based primarily on ideas of external shock, structural weakness or sheer dynastic accident, it proposed that the answer may lie not so much in a failure of the centre, as in processes at work lower down the social order which made the old court-centred structures redundant. The task of this chapter is to provide some substance for this suggestion. The evidence, fragmentary and diverse, presents a number of challenges, but provided we are prepared to stretch our net widely, it is capable of sustaining an interpretation which can be further developed in Part III using the more abundant later evidence.

The chapter looks at three particular manifestations of underlying social change that can be studied on the evidence available from this region: namely, the transformation of the county, changing patterns in how relations between lords and those who cultivated their lands were recorded, and, more abstractly, developments in the articulation between ritual practices and social order. Though these themes may appear at first sight to be rather disparate, it is this chapter's contention (following lines of argument sketched out in Chapter 3) that they are in fact all intimately connected, even though the precise nature of that connection becomes clear only when observed from the twelfth century.

THE TRANSFORMATION OF THE CAROLINGIAN COUNTY

As mentioned in the previous chapter, many historians have assumed, tacitly or otherwise, that the collapse of the Carolingian order was a consequence of the unleashing of hitherto suppressed aristocratic power, or at least that the collapse of the Carolingian dynasty permitted that unleashing. Both assumptions depend on a zero-sum conception of power as something that passed from king to aristocrats. In truth, however, the development seems to have been more complicated and subtle. The issue can most conveniently be addressed by studying the development of the office of count in this region; and this requires us to return, briefly, to the ninth century.[1]

The Carolingian pagus

Pagus is often translated as 'county', but might be better understood more neutrally as meaning 'area' or 'region'. Often referred to in narratives of various kinds, these *pagi* are particularly prominent in eighth- and ninth-century charters, which usually locate landed property with reference to a particular *pagus*. Historians used to assume that the *pagus* was an administrative unit, usually associated with a count, and that by aggregating these references, with the help of some regressive analysis using later medieval boundaries, it was possible to draw a map of the Carolingian *pagus* network, and thereby to reconstruct the basic lines of Carolingian administration. This perspective has had far-reaching implications for our understanding of the tenth and eleventh centuries, because *pagi* are less systematically referred to in post-ninth-century documentation, and secular power was more clearly associated with central places, classically castles. Historians have therefore inferred that a transformation took place from the neat, ordered lines of the Carolingian *pagus* to a very different kind of organisation of space, in which the old *pagi* had little influence. The transformation was therefore one of fragmentation, dislocation or *éclatement*, in the influential phrasing of Lemarignier.[2]

It is increasingly clear that this may not be the best way of approaching the issues at stake, at least as concerns the lands between Marne and Moselle.[3] The elaboration of carefully delineated maps of ninth-century *pagi* requires a considerable tidying-up of the evidence. *Pagus*-attributions for places at the fringes of *pagi* are noticeably inconsistent, in that the same

---

[1] I have discussed elements of this issue in 'Principautés et territoires, comtes et comtés', in M. Gaillard, M. Margue, A. Dierkens and H. Pettiau, eds., *De la Mer du Nord à la Méditerranée. Francia Media, une région au cœur de l'Europe (c.840–c.1050)* (Luxembourg, 2011), pp. 131–50.

[2] J.-F. Lemarignier, 'La dislocation du "Pagus" et le problème des "Consuetudines" (x^e–xie siècles)', in *Mélanges Louis Halphen* (Paris, 1951), pp. 401–10.

[3] For broadly analogous critiques of insufficiently rigorous approaches to early medieval space, see F. Mazel, ed., *L'espace du diocèse: genèse d'un territoire dans l'Occident médiéval v^e–xiiie siècle* (Rennes, 2008), particularly Mazel's Introduction, pp. 11–21. Also important in thinking about comital power is Innes, *State*, esp. pp. 118–24.

place is often located within various *pagi* by different documents, and sometimes even by a single one.[4] Naturally, these inconsistencies could be attributed to scribal error or even administrative change; yet it may be better to query the assumption that the ninth-century *pagus* must have been a unit with objectively verifiable limits like those of later medieval church jurisdictions. As the Germanist von Polenz argued several decades ago, historians' understanding of *pagi* has been influenced by an under-standing of these charters as legal documents akin to solicitors' deeds, administrative reflections of an administrative reality, whereas it is likely that the apparently systematic use of the term in these documents reflects a rigorous diplomatic more than a rigorous administration.

Were that to be the case, we should neither look for coherence in *pagi* networks, nor prioritise charters above other texts such as martyrologies, letters and miracle stories, all of which use *pagus* to give no more than an approximate sense of locality. The interpretation which fits the evidence most readily is that the *pagus* of the charters represents an awareness of landscape, imbued with a quasi technical meaning by the exigencies of charter diplomatic, but nevertheless primarily a socio-geographical, not a political or administrative, concept.[5] This is certainly how Alcuin described a *pagus*, as less an administrative unit than a space named by the locals.[6] We might think of them as spaces of sociability, rather than strictly defined communities. In this way, the *pagi* to be found in charters are simply smaller-scale equivalents of larger landscapes, like Brie or indeed Champagne itself, both of which are also referred to in contem-porary documentation.[7] This socio-geographical meaning would explain why many of these *pagi* between Marne and Moselle survived into the later Middle Ages. The chronicler Alberic of Troisfontaines, for example, was perfectly aware in the thirteenth century of the *pagus Pertinensis*, which he called the Perthois, and plenty of other examples could be adduced.[8] Indeed, many of the *pagi* of the regions that concern us, and

---

[4] T. Bauer, 'Die mittelalterliche Gaue', *Geschichtlicher Atlas der Rheinlande* IV/9, ed. Gesellschaft für Rheinische Geschichtskunde (Cologne, 2000), has produced an exemplary map, eschewing bound-aries altogether in favour of plotting attributions.

[5] On *pagi* in this sense, see M. Pitz, *Siedlungsnamen auf vilare (-weiler, -villers) zwischen Mosel, Hunsrück und Vogesen: Untersuchungen zu einem germanisch-romanisch Mischtypus der jüngeren Merowinger- und der Karolingerzeit* (Saarbrücken, 1997), vol. I, pp. 44–5, with further references.

[6] *Vita Vedasti*, ed. B. Krüsch *MGH SRM*, vol. III (Hanover, 1896) ch. 2, p. 418: 'quoddam pagum, quod incolarum terrae illius consuetudine Vunginse pagus dicitur'.

[7] *Gesta Dagoberti* p. 423; *Vita Faronis*, p. 201.

[8] Alberic Troisfontaines, *Chronica*, ed. G. Pertz, *MGH SS*, vol. XXIII (Hanover, 1874), pp. 631–950, at p. 742. The eleventh-century *Chronicon S. Michaelis* provides another example, talking of the *pagus* of Saintois, p. 30; Thiofrid's *Vita Willibrordi* ed. L. Weiland, *MGH SS*, vol. XXIII (Hanover, 1874), mentioned the *pagus Tulbiacensis* (p. 23); the twelfth-century *Gesta episcoporum Treverorum continuatio* talked of the *pagus Bedensis* (p. 182).

that first appear in Carolingian documentation, including the Perthois, Bassigny and the Saargau, survive to this day as unities of landscape readily appreciated by those who live within them.[9]

Secondly, we need to be careful about establishing how these socio-geographical regions related to the Carolingian office of being a count. There is no doubt that counts operated within *pagi*, but if we understand these simply as units of landscape, how could it have been otherwise? The evidence for a more systematic connection boils down to references in a few capitularies to the *comes pagi*, a phrase that could have a technical meaning, but could just as well simply express the sense that the local count was supposed to deal with local matters. There is no reason to imagine that every *pagus* mentioned in charter evidence always had its count, and it is revealing that Carolingian counts were conspicuously never called 'count of *pagus* X' in any of the surviving evidence. While it is likely that there was an approximate correlation in practice between spheres of authority and the landscape, natural enough in a pre-industrial agrarian economy, we must not elide a de facto, bottom-up development, with an anachronistic *de jure*, top-down constitution.

From pagus *to* comitatus

It is only from this revised understanding of the ninth-century *pagus* that a superficially obscure shift centred on the word *comitatus* takes on its full significance. Referring in tenth-century documentation to a region in which a particular comital authority was exercised, *comitatus* can in this context be unhesitatingly translated as 'county'. Indeed, the term was often explicitly contrasted with *pagus*, confirming an impression of the former as primarily geographical. For example, the same text (the Annals of Flodoard) records that in 927 Count Heribert entered into conflict over the *comitatus* of Laon, while in the same year a storm hit the *pagus* of Laon.[10]

Comitatus was first used in this sense, to describe the space in which a count exercised his authority, in Carolingian capitularies. From there, it steadily made its way into royal charters in the course of the early ninth century, identifying the location of pieces of property in just the same way that *pagus* did in texts produced in the localities. In other words, unlike *pagus*, the term *comitatus* was clearly linked to the court's view of the

---

[9] R. Puhl, *Die Gaue und Grafschaften des frühen Mittelalters im Saar-Mosel-Raum: philologisch-onomastische Studien zur frühmittelalterlichen Raumorganisation anhand der Raumnamen und der mit ihnen spezifizierten Ortsnamen* (Saarbrücken, 1999), gives a number of examples from the Moselle region: the Bidgau and the Saargau in particular (p. 484). Modern place-names like Fère-en-Tardenois, Fresnes-en-Tardenois, and Ville-en-Tardenois attest the unproblematic survival of *pagus* notions.

[10] Flodoard, *Annales*, s. a. 927.

Carolingian world. From around 900 onwards, however, *comitatus* began gradually to complement, rival, and even displace *pagus* as a means of providing contextual information about a particular location in non-royal charters too.[11] The implication is that charter scribes from the tenth century began to locate the property whose transfer they were recording not by landscape, but by territorialised political power, and that this was a development foreshadowed and perhaps promoted by court texts.

Initially, this understanding of comital power remained pegged to a sense of landscape, with the *pagus* defining a *comitatus* ('in the *pagus* of X, in the county of Y'). However, in the course of the tenth century, *comitatus* appear in this region whose link to a pre-existing, known geographical area was less immediate. A good example of these 'liberated' counties is Wallerfangen, which three late tenth-century charters associated with three different *pagi*, implying a kind of political authority that ignored or was superimposed upon landscape boundaries; other examples of something similar would include the counties of Bastogne in the Ardennes and Destry near Metz, and, though a little more complicated, Bar-le-Duc on the Meuse.[12] All these represented spaces of political authority without direct connection to any Carolingian-attested *pagi*. Though evidence west of the Meuse is scantier since there are fewer surviving charters, Ramerupt in southern Champagne in the later tenth century represents a very model of this new type of *comitatus*.[13]

There is, moreover, a further twist. Some *pagi* were clearly named after places (Perthois after Perthes, for instance), but there is no real evidence that these name-giving places were consistently of any practical political significance, and many *pagi* names in any case referred to landscape features, like rivers or hill ranges.[14] However, the names of the new *comitatus* always referred to a particular central site, and it would seem likely, and in some cases can be demonstrated, that this site was the residence of a count. This itself marks a significant move away from Carolingian practice, since there is no evidence that the counts between Marne and Moselle in the ninth century had had fixed, permanent residences at all, let alone that these had determined

---

[11] Cf. U. Nonn, *Pagus und Comitatus in Niederlothringen* (Bonn, 1983). M. Innes, *State*, n. 102, p. 109, suggests this development can be seen in pre-900 charters too, but there are question marks over the texts he cites, all of which survive only in cartulary copies, and at least one of which is in fact tenth-, not ninth-century.

[12] On Wallerfangen, see U. Nonn, 'Die Grafschaft Wallerfangen', *Jahrbuch für westdeutsche Landesgeschichte* 8 (1982), 1–12. On Destry, see below, pp. 145–6. On Bastogne, see A. Laret-Kayser and C. Dupont, 'A propos des comtés post-Carolingiens: les exemples d'Ivoix et de Bastogne', *Revue Belge de Philologie et d'Histoire* 57 (1979), 805–23. On Bar, see G. Poull, *La Maison ducale de Bar* (Rupt, 1977).

[13] See H. Arbois de Jubainville, 'Les premiers seigneurs de Ramerupt', *BEC* 22 (1861), 440–58.

[14] Cf. Nonn, *Pagus*, pp. 248–50, and Puhl, *Gaue*, who analyses the etymology of southern Lotharingian *pagus*-names.

political geography. Only from the tenth century did this begin to change. Castles as centres of lordship become prominent in Flodoard's Annals, written in the 960s, in marked contrast to typical Carolingian aristocratic practices.[15] The development was certainly not restricted to West Francia; political consolidation of this kind at the local level is beautifully demonstrated by the tenth-century case of the Lotharingian Frederick of Bar, whose efforts to develop a zone of lordship around Bar-le-Duc involved acquisitions from at least three churches.[16]

These textual indications are contextualised by the archaeological evidence, which indeed confirms that castles in the classic sense, fortified centres of lordship, though not nearly as numerous as those from the eleventh century, begin to be attested in this period, and that some of them at least appear associated with comital lordship.[17] They are also corroborated by tenth-century hagiographical sources. There was something of a boom in interest in mysterious saints buried in old *pagus* centres: for example, St Victor at Mouzon, St Leodegar at Perthes, Saint Elophe at Soulosse, St Livarius at Marsal and St Wulfoliac at Ivois.[18] Two cases are still more remarkable. The otherwise entirely obscure St Balsemius was taken from Arcis, the site after which the *pagus* of Arceois was named, to the new comital castle at Ramerupt; and the equally mysterious St Voulgis was taken from the *Orcisus* (unidentified but probably the nominal centre

---

[15] Cf. Nelson, 'Dispute settlement', p. 62.

[16] The *Chronicon S. Michaelis* offers the clearest description, pp. 11–12. On St-Denis's lands, see M. Parisse, 'In media Francia. St Mihiel, Salonnes et St. Denis', in *Media in Francia. Recueil de mélanges offert à Karl Ferdinand Werner à l'occasion de son 65ᵉ anniversaire par ses amis et collègues français* (Paris 1989), pp. 319–42.

[17] Examples of plausibly (late) tenth- or (early) eleventh-century residential castle sites with surviving archaeological evidence include St Ingbert and Humberg (Düren) in the Saarland (see H. Böhme, 'Burgen der Salierzeit in Hessen, in Rheinland-Pfalz und im Saarland' in H. Böhme, ed., *Burgen der Salierzeit*, 2 vols. (Sigmaringen, 1991), vol. II, pp. 7–80); Vaudémont, carbon dated to *c.*1000 (Meurthe-et-Moselle: see G. Giuliato, 'Le château, reflet de l'art défensif en Lorraine du Xᵉ au début du XIIIᵉ siècle', *Annales de l'Est*, 53 (2003), 55–76; and Chantereine (Ardennes: see M. Bur, *Inventaire de sites archéologiques non monumentaux de Champagne. I: Vestiges d'habitat seigneurial fortifié des Ardennes et de la Vallée de l'Aisne* (Rheims, 1980a), pp. 31–5). See also below, Chapter 6, pp. 191–4. The castle site of Harpelstein in the Hunsrück (Rheinland-Pfalz) is a little later in date (mid to late eleventh century), but has produced a plethora of finds, conveniently depicted in an exhibition catalogue: see C. Stiegemann and M. Wemhoff, eds., *Canossa 1077: Erschütterung der Welt* (2 vols., Munich, 2006), vol. II, pp. 179–83.

[18] Mouzon: *HRE*, bk IV, ch. 13, p. 405. Perthes: *Vita Leodegarii* (BHL 4857), ed. G. Henschenius, D. Pabebrochius, F. Baertius, and C. Janningus), *AASS Jun.*, vol. IV (Antwerp, 1707), 486–8, at col. 487–8. Soulosse: *Vita Gerardi*, p. 495, perhaps associated with Otto I's donation to Toul of rights here (*Gesta episcoporum Tullensium*, p. 640). Marsal: *Le souvenir des Carolingiens à Metz au Moyen Âge: le petit cartulaire de Saint-Arnoul* ed. M. Gaillard (Paris, 2006), pp. 24–6, which appears to be using a lost tenth-century translation about Bishop Theoderic of Metz. Ivois: *Vita Magnerici* (BHL 5149), ed. J. Sollerius, J. Pinius, G. Cuperus and P. Boschius, *AASS Jul.*, vol. VI, pp. 183–92, col. 190.

of the *pagus* of Orceois) to the new castle at La Ferté-Milon.[19] There is little evidence that these old *pagus* centres had had any real political importance, but the new sites certainly did. One could hardly hope for better evidence to show a shift not just in the location of political power, but in its structures, as diffuse networks articulated in terms of *pagi* were replaced by spatially more coherent patterns centred on comital residence.

Destry, the mallum publicum *and the* cancellarius

The transition from *pagus* to *comitatus* as reflected in the surviving evidence clearly speaks to some kind of change in the conception, and probably also practice, of comital authority in this region, and one which cannot be dismissed as simply a product of 'documentary mutation', since this evidence includes hagiography and archaeology as well as charters. However, the question remains how this transition should be conceptualised when compared with Carolingian precedents. Should it be seen as the failure of the Carolingian political project? The fact that the new terminology is foreshadowed first in Carolingian capitularies suggests that this might be a hasty inference. And indeed, close attention to a particular case-study brings rather a different interpretation to the fore.

In 957, two charters were made by a certain Count Regimbald for two different monasteries around Metz.[20] In spite of their late date, these texts appear thoroughly Carolingian in flavour. There may even be a connection between the precise phrasing of these charters and the translation into Old High German of a Carolingian capitulary text from around this time and place, relating to donations made outside one's own *comitatus*, precisely what Count Regimbald was doing.[21] Moreover, both charters were explicitly made at a *mallum publicum*, and were attested by witnesses identified as *scabini* – generally considered to be characteristically Carolingian institutions. The fact that both charters were explicitly, and obviously, written by the same *cancellarius*, the title for a scribe carrying some sense of official, public or communal responsibility, following a shared pattern, suggests that there was some institutionalisation behind the terminology, too. It may be noted that there is other evidence to suggest

[19] The source for Balsemius is the eleventh-century homiliary Paris BnF lat. 13784: *Vita Balsemii*, ed. J. Sollerius, J. Pinius, G. Cuperus and P.Boschius, *AASS Aug.*, vol. III, col. 293–4. For Orcisus, see DCB, no. 172 and *Recueil de chartes et documents de Saint-Martin-des-Champs: monastère parisien*, ed. J. Depoin (Paris, 1912), no. 218.
[20] Artem no. 212, and *Cartulaire*, ed. d'Herbomez, no. 106.
[21] See H. Tiefenbach, 'Ein übersehener Textzeuge des Trierer Capitulare', *Rheinische Vierteljahrsblätter*, 39 (1975), 272–310, who considers the capitulary to relate to later donations, but on flimsy grounds.

that institutions centred on the public exercise of power in a Carolingian frame were still vigorous in this area in the tenth century. For example, we happen to know that somewhere near Toul, property was still being confiscated from horse-rustlers convicted 'by the judgement of the scabini' in the 940s, and that the Count of Troyes was still holding a *mallum* court to test freedom in the 970s.[22]

However, not everything about the events at Destry seems lifted from a Carolingian formulary. For example, the transaction took place at Destry, a fortified comital residence perhaps complete with chapel, which was undoubtedly the centre of an eponymous county referred to in a number of charters, just the kind of site conspicuously absent from Carolingian-period evidence.[23] No trace of this building survives, nor has any archaeological excavation been undertaken; still, in the early twentieth century, two local residents, Nicolas Barthélémy 'surnommé le Gros-Colas' and Christophe Humbert, enjoying a day out from the old people's home, happily recounted in the local brasserie legends about a ruined fortification, and an eighteenth-century antiquarian and a mid-nineteenth-century priest also wrote about Destry's ruined castle (admittedly, quite how much faith one should have in such reports is not clear).[24]

The Destry charters' invocation of Carolingian ideas could at first glance be interpreted as the deliberate appropriation of ninth-century traditions for tenth-century purposes. But that would presuppose a disjunction between the forms of authority represented by Destry castle and by the *mallum publicum*. If we consider the *mallum publicum* less as a Carolingian 'institution', and more as an indication of the formalisation of comital authority in the locality, as suggested in Part I, then the holding of a *mallum* at the count's court appears less like a diversion or disjuncture, and more like an accentuation of previous trends. It may be significant that concrete evidence for the *mallum* is in fact stronger in this region in the tenth than in the ninth century, if we set aside model documents in formularies, but include narrative sources.[25] This might indicate that the

---

[22] *Les origines de l'abbaye de Bouxières-aux-Dames au diocèse de Toul: reconstitution du chartrier et édition critique des chartes antérieures à 1200*, ed. R-H. Bautier (Nancy, 1987), nos. 14 and 38 (concerning the widow, Alda); *Miracula Benedicti*, ed. E. de Certain, *Les miracles de St Benoît* (Paris, 1858), bk VI, ch. 2, pp. 219–20. This part of the *Miracula* was written in the middle eleventh century, but the reference to a Count Robert dates the incident to the mid tenth century (Robert died in 967).

[23] For the material remains, see P. Flotte and M. Fuchs, eds., *La Moselle*, Cartes archéologiques de la Gaule 57 (Paris, 2004b), p. 394.

[24] See L. Maujean, 'Histoire de Destry et du pays Saulnois', *Mémoires de l'Académie de Metz* 93 (1913), 231–532.

[25] P. Barnwell, 'The early Frankish mallus: its nature, participants and practices', in A. Pantos and S. Semple, eds., *Assembly places and practices in Medieval Europe* (Dublin, 2004), pp. 233–46.

count's court was becoming steadily more formal both before and after the fragmentation of the Carolingian empire.

A parallel argument can be mounted, again necessarily from an angle, and again starting from the documentary material. By the ninth century, most, though not quite all of those producing charters in this region were monks. On certain occasions, these scribes gave themselves a title, that of *cancellarius*, which had been used by sixth- and seventh-century 'public' scribes; and intriguingly, they do not seem to have done so wholly at random. The archive of the monastery of Stavelot, to the north of Prüm, is particularly interesting in this regard. Virtually all the monastery's charters made outside it, at Huy and Namur, were drawn up by scribes who called themselves *cancellarii*. But more telling are the charters made at Stavelot itself, for in these cases, whether the scribe was termed *cancellarius* apparently varied not according to the scribe's own status, but according to whether a count was present, or was present in his capacity as count, rather than as the (lay) abbot.[26] Several scribes ceased to call themselves *cancellarius* when a duke or count was not involved: we can show this for the scribes Hugh,[27] Bernard,[28] Werenfrid,[29] Theobert,[30] and, more ambiguously, Ebroin.[31] A similar pattern emerges from St-Maximin and from Gorze's charters.[32] So, in the course of the late ninth and tenth centuries, there was a tendency for those drawing up records of meetings held by counts to give themselves the title of *cancellarius*, a title that apparently tells us something about the meeting, not

---

[26] The three charters of Gerard *cancellarius* all involved counts: on two occasions counts witnessed, on the third occasion, the duke and lay abbot Reginar strikingly did not refer to himself as abbot. Only one charter made at Stavelot which does not seem to have involved a count or duke was made by a *cancellarius*.

[27] Hugh made one charter as a *notarius* in 905 (*Recueil*, ed. Halkin, no. 49), but for the donation of Count Otbert called himself *cancellarius* just two years later (*Recueil*, ed. Halkin, no. 50).

[28] Bernard wrote two charters as *notarius* and scribe (*Recueil*, ed. Halkin, nos. 58 and 59), and a third, which involved a comital donation, as *cancellarius* (*Recueil*, ed. Halkin, no. 60).

[29] Werenfrid did exactly the same as Bernard (*Recueil*, ed. Halkin, nos. 66, 67, 68).

[30] Theobert drew up three charters (*Recueil*, ed. Halkin, nos. 80, 82 and 83): in only one of these (*Recueil*, ed. Halkin, no. 80) was he called *cancellarius*, the only one to refer explicitly to a count.

[31] Ebroin wrote three charters as *cancellarius*, in each of which a count or duke was explicitly mentioned (*Recueil*, ed. Halkin, nos. 72, 76 and 77); but in a fourth charter, in which a count was not explicitly involved, he wrote as *notarius* (*Recueil*, ed. Halkin, no. 75). In fact, the advocate was a count, but only in this charter is he not titled count.

[32] Gorze: where a tenth-century scribe calls himself *cancellarius*, it seems that the abbot was also the count, e.g. *Cartulaire*, ed. d'Herbomez, no. 91. The case of Wogo from St-Maximin illustrates the same point. Wogo wrote a charter, as *cancellarius*, in 923. Three years later, in 926, he made a charter without styling himself a *cancellarius*. Later that same year, he was once again a *cancellarius*, or rather *in vicem cancellarii* (*UBMR*, nos. 163, 165, 167). Perhaps something about the meetings explains the inconsistency. The first was held at Trier, rather than St-Maximin, and no abbot is mentioned. The second charter has a lay abbot as a witness, but he is styled *comes et abbas*, and the charter was made at St-Maximin: Wogo was not in the role of *cancellarius*. The third charter was also made in the monastery, but here Gilbert is styled simply count, and Wogo is a *cancellarius* once more.

the scribe. Like the *mallum publicum*, this could reflect a growing sense of ceremony at the count's court, with implications for how his authority was perceived – which would fit well with the development of a form of comital authority that was no longer determined by geographical conditions.

The inference to be drawn from all this material – archaeological, documentary, and hagiographical – is that the formalisation of aristocratic authority promoted by the Carolingians was not impeded by the political crisis in the decades around 900, but rather continued steadily.[33] In such an environment, as counts dominated the local political scene with greater ease and confidence, and as the region was increasingly oriented around their formal authority, one might well imagine that the royal court might seem less indispensable than had once been the case, supporting the hypothesis ventured in the previous chapter. The general trajectory moreover continued into the later eleventh century, though this is a topic which will be discussed again in Chapter 8.

LORDS AND LANDLORDS IN THE LONG TENTH CENTURY

Arguments for an intensification of formalised comital authority over the tenth century only address one particular register of social change. Most of the elite were not after all counts, and for the practical concerns of most people living between Marne and Moselle, questions of the nature of comital authority would seldom have loomed large. If social relations were changing enough to alter the structures of authority which appear so strongly embedded in the ninth century, we need to try to develop a perspective which takes us a little closer to the ground. The key relation here, and one too often treated in separation from questions of politics, is that between lords and those who worked the land.

As a preliminary point, it should be stressed that these relations were not always hostile, and that a study of these relations does not equate to an exhaustive study of the tenth-century countryside. Even if some examples of autonomous village collective action from the tenth century seem better rooted in clerical fantasy than reality, later evidence alone would suggest that not everyone in the countryside had been totally embroiled in aristocratic networks, even if all must have been touched by them.[34] These networks were not necessarily always predatory. One charter from St-Vanne, for example, describes how a former landlord who had

---

[33] Cf. for a similar point Fouracre, 'Conflict, power and legitimation', p. 22.

[34] *Historia Mosomensis*, ed. and tr. M. Bur, *Chronique ou livre de fondation du Monastère de Mouzon* (Paris, 1989), on Gruyères, pp. 148–9. Cf. the celebrated St-Mihiel charter, *Chronique et chartes*, ed. Lesort, no. 33, showing independent freeholders struggling in the 1030s.

taken the monastic habit offered strings-free patronage to a former tenant of his, probably in the later tenth century.[35] It is precisely the existence of patronage relations that helps explain why the peasantry was sometimes targeted during aristocratic rivalry.[36] Nevertheless, a significant proportion of the countryside was engaged in relations of various kinds with a dominant elite, and given what was discussed in Chapter 2, this relationship would seem to have set a determining tone.

Historians have offered widely varying assessments of that relationship in the tenth century, and the direction in which it was travelling – an uncertainty that reflects the patchiness of the evidence, as well as historians' own preoccupations. Most of those working within the Feudal Revolution framework have tended to see the period as one in which aristocratic dominance was maintained and strengthened, when prowling aristocrats liquidated freeholdings and demolished legal distinctions to their own advantage.[37] Others have reacted against this, stressing instead a diversity that defies tidy generalisation, noting that the addition of new forms of exploitation did not necessarily replace those which came before, and further questioning whether the non-economic constraints visible in later sources were genuinely absent from the earlier period.[38]

To these approaches could be added a third, venerable though now rather neglected: that of Perrin, who argued that the tenth century, in Lotharingia in particular, was a period of accelerating fragmentation of estates, leading to a breakdown in the key relationship of tenured land to demesne land, which accordingly saw a steep reduction in the latter's extent.[39] The near-collapse of bipartite estate management meant that there was less need to produce instruments of estate management like polyptychs, though lists do survive from Remiremont and Mettlach.[40] Perrin considered this a crisis not so much for the peasantry, nor indeed really for the lords, but for the estate managers, who were rescued in the

[35] 'Urkunden', ed. Bloch, no. 34.
[36] For a sample of Heribert II's ravaging around Rheims, see *HRE*, bk IV, ch. 26, p. 418.
[37] P. Bonnassie, 'Les paysans du royaume franc au temps d'Hugues Capet et de Robert le Pieux', in M. Parisse, ed., *Le roi de France et son royaume autour de l'an mil* (Paris, 1992), pp. 117–30; cf. R. I. Moore, *First European revolution*, pp. 44–9. Duby himself was in fact ambivalent in his *The early growth of the European economy: warriors and peasants from the seventh to the twelfth century*, tr. H. Clarke (London, 1974).
[38] Barthélemy, 'Le servage et ses rites', in *La mutation*, pp. 93–171; J.-P. Devroey, 'Seigneurs et paysans au coeur de l'ancien empire carolingien de part et d'autre de l'an mil: les seigneuries de saint Rémi de Reims (ix–xi s.)' in P. Bonnassie and P. Toubert, eds., *Hommes et sociétés dans l'Europe de l'an mil* (Toulouse, 2004), pp. 253–71.
[39] Ch.-E. Perrin, *Recherches sur la seigneurie rurale en Lorraine d'après les plus anciens censiers* (Paris, 1935), pp. 626–59.
[40] See Desportes and Dolbeau, 'Découverte', contra Devroey's arguments for tenth-century amendations to St-Rémi's polyptych.

eleventh century only by the generalised application of non-economic forms of constraint, a phenomenon which will be considered in the next chapter.

These formulations are to some degree mutually exclusive. Either aristocrats were drawing more people into greater dependence in the long tenth century, or they were not, or there was a transformation operating within the manorial estate itself which cannot be expressed in quantitative terms. Establishing which approach is most accurate is not something that can be done from narrative sources. That is not because these provide no evidence: tenth-century hagiographical sources, like the Life of St Victor (of Montiéramey) which describes resentful ploughmen stealing grain, or the miracle collection from St-Maximin of Trier with its grim descriptions of aristocratic violence, are highly suggestive.[41] So, too, are the throw-away justifications of Bishop Adalbero of Laon – born and educated in Lotharingia – for the natural unpleasantness of life for those who worked the land, written around the year 1000.[42] But though they support readings of intensifying disorder of the kind promoted by Bisson, the problem is that these kinds of anecdotal texts can easily be paralleled with ninth- and eleventh-century miracle collections and other texts.

Other kinds of evidence are equally frustrating, suggestive without being conclusive. Archaeology, and particularly the archaeology of field systems, has much potential to shed light on the kinds of change happening in the tenth century, but as yet, at least, that potential has not been realised.[43] There are some estate surveys that are either entirely tenth-century, like the Remiremont 'polyptych' and two fragments from St-Maximin, or that have tenth-century elements, like the *Güterrolle* of Mettlach and the polyptych of St-Rémi; but not only are these list-like texts intrinsically difficult to interpret, they also pose formidable editorial challenges through the often complicated nature of their preservation. The observation that *donare* verbs, found in Carolingian polyptychs and perhaps representing an attempt to evoke an air of reciprocity between

[41] *Vita Victoris* (BHL 8583), ed. H. Moretus, 'Catalogus codicum hagiographicorum latinorum bibliothecae scholae medicinae Montepessulanensis', *Analecta Bollandiana* 34–5 (1915–16), pp. 276–89, at pp. 281–2; *Miracula Maximini*, ed. G. Henschius, D. Papebrochius, F. Baertius and C. Ianningus, *AASS Maii*, vol. VII (Antwerp, 1688), cols. 28, 29.

[42] Adalbero of Laon, *Poeta*, ed. and tr. C. Carozzi, *Poème au roi Robert/Adalbéron de Laon* (Paris, 1979) 'Hoc genus afflictum nil possidet absque dolore … Servorum lacrimae gemitus non terminus ullus', p. 22.

[43] Though see Theuws, 'Landed property'. A useful review of material up to 2004, pointing to its inconclusivity, is Y. Morimoto, 'Aperçu critique des recherches: vers une synthèse équilibrée (1993–2004)', in T. Morimoto, *Etudes sur l'économie rurale du haut moyen âge: historiographie, régime domanial, polyptyques carolingiens* (Brussels, 2008). On field systems, see M. Watteaux, 'Archéogéographie de l'habitat et du parcellaire au haut Moyen Age' in J. Guillaume and E. Peytremann, eds., *L'Austrasie: sociétés, économies, territoires, christianisation* (Nancy, 2008), pp. 109–20.

peasants and lords, dry up in these later texts is suggestive, but in itself insufficient to support far-reaching conclusions.[44]

As a consequence, if we want to understand what was happening at the lower social levels in the tenth century, even if only to formulate hypotheses that can be tested against more abundant later evidence, it is once again to charters that we have to turn, and particularly to Upper Lotharingian charters, since rather fewer have been preserved from the region of Champagne. These texts show no sign of the dramatic changes in diplomatics such as the explosion of *notitiae* in the west of France, texts which have proven so fruitful (and controversial) in the hands of recent historians like Barthélemy and Lesmesle.[45] There are occasional signs of monasteries expanding their networks of dependants via judicious use of *precaria*, but these are so scattered that they cannot be taken as representative.[46] Nevertheless, two observations can be made that do perhaps cast some light on tenth-century conditions, and more to the point, tenth-century dynamics.

Morville-sur-Nied

We can approach the first of these by considering an estate at Morville, as it happens an estate granted by Count Regimbald to St-Arnulf of Metz in one of the two charters discussed above.[47] Ten years after that donation, the inhabitants of the village came and asked the abbot to commit to the same conditions and demands as Regimbald had himself demanded from them. The abbot 'thought about it for a long time', but although it seemed initially not to be in the monastery's interest, he and the monks eventually judged it a not unworthy (*indignum*) request, and agreed. The resulting document was something like a polyptych extract, detailing which dues were liable and when, with the difference that, according to the charter, the initiative had come not from the managers, but the managed.

The Morville charter has long been seen as exceptional, comparable only to the franchise charters, privileges granted to the inhabitants of estates that began to be issued two centuries later, which are discussed in

---

[44] Kuchenbuch, '*Porcus*'.
[45] D. Barthélemy, *La société dans le comté de Vendôme*, especially pp. 30–2; B. Lemesle, *Conflits et justice au Moyen Age: normes, loi et résolution des conflits en Anjou aux xı^e et xıı^e siècles* (Paris, 2008).
[46] For example, *UBMR* no. 186, involving marriage restrictions.
[47] *Histoire de Metz*, ed. N. Tabouillot, 3 vols. (Metz, 1775), vol. ııı, preuves, pp. 71–3; cf. Artem no. 212. The precise identification of Morville is not wholly settled. W. Haubrichs, 'Gelenkte Siedlung des frühen Mittelalters im Seillegau. Zwei Urkunden des Metzer Klosters St. Arnulf und die lothringische Toponymie', *Zeitschrift für die Geschichte der Saargegend* 30 (1982), 7–39 and others prefer Morville-sur-Seille, while Bautier in *Les origines de l'abbaye de Bouxières-aux-Dames* (p. 24, n. 1) and others prefer Morville-sur-Nied.

Chapter 7. Though there is no reason to presume that the charter is anything other than genuine, it may be tempting to write it off as an anomaly, perhaps representing some quirk of the location, particularly as only fifty years later, the Morville inhabitants received still another unusual charter that granted its inhabitants rights to marry freely.[48] Yet not only would it not be methodologically sound to discount evidence simply because it fails to fit orthodoxies, when looked at in context, the Morville charter is not quite so unusual as it seems.

Another charter deals with land that was, as it happens, apparently donated by Count Regimbald in his other Destry charter, with Gorze as the recipient.[49] In 984, in a charter regulating the *census* of the serfs at the village of Bruoch, and as part of a surge of charters in the 980s dealing with the lower echelons of Gorze's dependants, Abbot John of Gorze set down what the peasants were to do, in the process revealing that the land had originally been 'fiscal' land, acquired by Regimbald.[50] As at Morville, the peasants at Bruoch were concerned to retain the same customs as they had always had, and Abbot John agreed that it was *indignum* to burden them with more obligations now than in the past.[51] These had apparently not been set down in writing before, so John had to ask them what they had performed, having first firmly warned them not to lie. If the St-Arnulf charter resembles a franchise, the Gorze one is more akin to a *Weistum*, a typically German document generally associated with the later Middle Ages, in which the inhabitants of a community formally declared their law.

Four other tenth-century charters from the region provide further comparative context. In one, the Archbishop of Trier confirmed *c.*970 the rights of the peasants at Wasserbillig (or possibly Welshbillig) to inherit their land.[52] In another, the abbot of St-Martin Metz established in 960 the dues owed by an estate which had apparently been unforthcoming.[53] A third example comes from Stavelot in 932, where in response to their request, the peasants on an estate at Xhoris were given rather lower duties,

---

[48] Artem no. 220 (1031) though this could be for Morville-sur-Seille rather than Morville-sur-Nied.

[49] The property is not mentioned in Regimbald's 957 charter, but it might have been implicitly included, though the possibility of a further, now lost, donation cannot be entirely ruled out.

[50] *Cartulaire*, ed. d'Herbomez, no. 116. A. Wagner, *Gorze au 11ᵉ siècle: contribution à l'histoire du monachisme bénédictin dans l'Empire* (Nancy, 1996) assumes at pp. 76–7 that the text has been revised in the course of complex textual alterations, but I am not yet convinced.

[51] *Cartulaire*, ed. d'Herbomez, no. 116, 'indignum nimis judicavimus nostro tempore majori eos quam antea gravari servitio'.

[52] *UBMR* vol. I, no. 230, and *Urkunden*, ed. Wampach no. 184. The document survives in the original. See J. Dahlhaus, M. Koch, and T. Kölzer, 'Die "Rebellen" von Wasserbillig: eine diplomatische Nachlesen', in S. Happ and H. Nonn, eds., *Vielfalt der Geschichte* (Berlin, 2004), pp. 109–25.

[53] *Histoire*, ed. Calmet, vol. II, col. 203, also in *Recueil*, ed. Halkin, no. 78 at 960. It seems to have entered the Stavelot archives as part of an exchange in 1089 (*Recueil*, ed. Halkin, no. 122).

obliged only to do one day's work a week for the monastery.[54] Finally, a similar charter was drawn up at Remiremont, also reducing on request the dues owed by tenants.[55]

Though the textual transmission of some of these charters is complicated, together they provide each other with some sort of mutual guarantee. And while six charters is rather a small dossier on which to base wide-ranging conclusions, they are really just the most dramatic examples of a noticeable growth in the documentation of interest in the dues owed by peasants to those who controlled the land. Charters recording various land transactions also began in the tenth century to note the *census* owed by those working the land, typically one or two pence a year.[56] This marks a clear break with precedent. Ninth-century charters, including all those contained in formulary collections, had frequently discussed the dues owed by those being granted the temporary control of land, who agreed to pay small amounts in recognition of the lender's ultimate rights; but none of them made any reference to what was paid by those working on it.

Obviously, these texts are not a transparent window onto the tenth-century countryside. They are representations, made by powerful institutions, for their own purposes, and for that reason partial and incomplete. However, the range of institutions involved, and the absence of ninth-century parallels, suggests that this shift in diplomatic does represent something new. In the first place, the preparedness of institutions to commit what was owed to them in writing, as part of a negotiation with the agricultural communities that they controlled, might imply that a certain equilibrium had been reached, after the secular growth in exactions to which ninth-century evidence attests. Secondly, and more significantly, is the way they document attempts to exercise precision in the context of landownership, as opposed to estate management. After all, for institutions to attempt to record their revenues, or to manage them, was in itself no novelty: that was what the polyptychs of Prüm, St-Rémi and Montier-en-Der had been for. What was essentially new was to associate these kinds of negotiations with the practice of landholding, to record them as charters, as part of the documentary records of an institution. Taking place at the same time as rhetorics of gift and countergift began to recede from these relations, this shift implies a significant

---

[54] *Recueil*, ed. Halkin, no. 59 (*c*.932).

[55] Edited in *Histoire*, ed. Calmet, vol. II, col. 183, and *Studien zur Äbtissinnenreihe von Remiremont*, ed. E. Hlawitschka (Saarbrücken, 1963), no. 94.

[56] Examples include *Cartulaire*, ed. d'Herbomez, no. 109; *Cartulaire de Bouxières*, ed. R.-H. Bautier, no. 32 (966); *Chronique et chartes*, ed. Lesort, no. 27; *Rheinisches Urkundenbuch, Ältere Urkunden bis 1100*, ed. E. Wisplinghoff (Düsseldorf, 1972–94), vol. II, nos. 179 (Gerresheim, 905), 206 (St-Florin, Koblenz, *c*.970) and 321 (St-Ursula, 927); *UBMR* no. 186 (Prüm, 948).

development in the conception of landownership.[57] However, all this is arguably just a part of a more general tenth-century phenomenon from the region, the 'decline' of the Carolingian formulary.

The transformation of the Carolingian formulary

Setting aside isolated examples, significant eighth- and ninth-century archives survive from the institutions of St-Maximin, Gorze, St-Arnulf, Montier-en-Der, Prüm and St-Mihiel; and just outside the region in question, St-Bénigne of Dijon, Werden, St-Cassius of Bonn and Stavelot. All these centres made charters in the eighth and ninth century in styles which recall those of formularies, and some of these even produced their own small-scale formulary collections.[58] However, from the mid tenth century, charters begin to drift somewhat from this stylised form.[59] As already mentioned, this region did not see the dramatic rise of the notitia, or notice visible in archives from the Loire valley. The process was, rather, gradual and erratic, as wholly Carolingian-styled charters were intermittently produced, together with charters which were less rigidly bound by convention. The changes could be subtle and the question of at which point a charter ceased to be 'formulaic' is subjective.[60] Yet though the transformation was one of stages, the cumulative change is nonetheless unmistakable from the late tenth century.

The slow transition can be exemplified using Gorze's archive. The first witness list combining secular and ecclesiastical figures, in a break from earlier practice, dates from 945 (n. 100). This is also the first donation made out to the altar of Gorze, and the first use of *servus* as opposed to *mancipia*. The final traditionally formulated *precaria* charter was produced in 946, and the past tense slipped into a charter in 959. Texts that resemble notices were made in 973 (n. 111), and strong narrative elements gain in prominence from 977 onwards (e.g. nos. 114, 115 and 119). From 974, abbots began routinely to issue charters in their own names, which had been rare before this date, and the

[57] Though gift-giving never totally died away, however: Kuchenbuch, '*Porcus*', and see also 'Güterroller', ed. Müller, p. 117, for details about a *convivium* at Valmünster arranged by the *dominus*.

[58] Formulary production: St-Maximin produced two in the early tenth century, for *precaria* grants and donations, in *MGH Formulae*, pp. 548–9, with similarities to some extant St-Maximin charters. Formula-like material was also produced at Metz and St-Mihiel: *MGH Formulae*, pp. 544, 549.

[59] See O. Guyotjeannin, '*Penuria scriptorum*. Le mythe de l'anarchie documentaire dans la France du Nord (x^e–première moitié du xie siècle)', *BEC* 155 (1997), 11–44.

[60] St-Maximin in 943 (*Urkunden*, ed. Wampach, no. 156) seems to be breaking away, by 993 the charters of donation are often phrased in the past (*Urkunden*, ed. Wampach, no. 208) and by the early eleventh century, charters have a narrative turn: *Urkunden*, ed. Wampach, no. 248. But Trier used a Marculfian turn of phrase in the 960s, as did St-Bertin.

traditional formulation of exchange documents was entirely abandoned by 1006 (n. 122), having been last fully used in 967 (n. 110).

The traditional approach was to see this phenomenon more or less in terms of technical decline, perhaps linked to post-Carolingian monastic decadence, even though at Gorze the complete abandonment of conventional phrasing took place only after the famous monastic reform.[61] More recent work has, however, thrown the assumptions behind such an interpretation into doubt.[62] In particular, a recent and powerful line of argument has been advanced that works on two levels. In the first place, it suggests that the change which took place was simply an index of changing levels of monastic education, so that more experimentation in charters simply reflected greater literary ambition, if not competence, amongst the scribes, and so perhaps is to be related to monastic reform, rather than decadence. In the second place, it posits that the most important aspect of the formulaic nature of ninth-century charters is that they misrepresented reality, so that the breakdown of the *formulae* allowed scribes better to describe what was 'really' going on.

Though these arguments seem superficially attractive, one needs to tread very carefully, for two reasons. While it is true that ninth-century charters were formulaic, to argue thence that this demonstrates thereby the irrelevance of their terms and phrasing to the material situation would be over-simplistic.[63] Not only would such an argument neglect instances where we can see that phrasing was adapted to suit particular cases, for example in terms of pertinence clauses, it would also neglect the importance of the formula in shaping social reality as well as recording it. The manuscripts containing formularies for the composition of charters, nearly all of which are Carolingian in date, were not born of administrative narrow-mindedness. Rather, these were manuscripts with a powerful ideological momentum of their own, projecting a vision of the world rightly ordered, which is presumably why the royal court took an interest in them. As we have seen, Carolingian charters were likewise highly charged 'performance' texts, designed to contribute to the maintenance and transfer of social domination, which is precisely why they were composed with such care.[64]

Secondly, there is an empirical problem. The shift away from Carolingian *formulae* is substantially earlier than the adoption of a new

[61] On which point see Nightingale, *Monasteries*, who argues on the basis of a few charters in the 930s and 940s for a continuity in the scriptorium and thus a streak of continuity with the pre-reform community.

[62] Barthélemy, *La mutation*, pp. 29–56, builds on earlier work.

[63] For a similar argument, see Innes, *State*, p. 111, and pp. 117–18.

[64] See H. Keller, 'Zu den Siegeln der Karolinger und Ottonen. Urkunden als 'Hoheitszeichen' des Königs mit seinen Getreuen', *FMS* 32 (1998), 400–41.

terminology that, according to the argument in question, supposedly revealed more accurately the true state of affairs. Roughly half a century separates the uncoupling from old styles and the adoption of more flexible ones from the emergence of a new vocabulary of property rights. As will be further discussed in Chapter 6, this hiatus increases the likelihood that these words described, if not radically new practices, certainly radically new ways of thinking about these practices. It also casts doubt on how far the abandonment of the formula can be put down simply to greater realism, let alone greater creativity, at least without doing gross injustice to the cultural energies of the vigorous ninth-century establishments responsible, we should not forget, for a huge range of stunning artefacts and texts.

With these objections in mind, it is clear that we need to develop a new interpretation to account for the slide away from Carolingian-style diplomatic formulations. Carolingian charters were not 'pure formula', since efforts were made to ensure they reflected the specificities of the particular grants they recorded; but the consistent and generally impressive use of a formulaic way of writing them perhaps reflects the way in which these texts were themselves attempts to mould reality, to make reality charter-shaped, with all the resonances that entailed. Pointing to discrepancies between text and reality is justifiable, but only if the ideological work done by the text is not thereby neglected.[65] For example, if Hincmar of Rheims drafted some charters based on texts by Gregory the Great, as he claimed he did, this does not show that the charters are useless as evidence, it shows us something of the authority and meaning charters were supposed to bear.[66] Perhaps, then, the Carolingian formula was abandoned when these efforts to alter reality were successful, when social relations had actually been moulded to fit the charters. In other words, when charters gained in straightforward descriptive power, that was because there was no longer a need to comply with certain norms, within certain agreed frameworks. The disappearance of the *formula* would be a sign of consolidation, as formulaic scaffolding was no longer needed to provide support for a particular way of viewing the world.

Put together with the evidence provided by growing interest in clarifying the dues associated with property ownership evidenced in the charters discussed above, it could be argued that the change in the formulation of charter writing indicates the beginning of a profound change in how

[65] For an analogous point about the role of written documents in shaping practices of property, see R. Congost, 'Property rights and historical analysis', *Past and Present* 181 (2003), 73–106, particularly pp. 95–6.
[66] *HRE*, bk III, ch. 27, pp. 350–1.

property rights were conceptualised in practice, with obvious implications for relations between those who worked the land, and those who, in an increasingly straightforward and obvious way, owned it. Whereas Chapter 3 tried to suggest that property ownership is not necessarily the best way of conceptualising Carolingian relations of production, even though that was clearly the aspiration of those who made formal records of it, it would seem to be rather more appropriate by the end of the tenth century.

RITUAL AND SOCIETY IN THE TENTH CENTURY

The previous two parts of this chapter have argued that in the tenth century, comital power became conceptually and practically better defined, and that patterns of domination in the countryside were consolidated. Both these developments could help account for the marginalisation of the king and the royal court. As domination became better locally anchored both as office and as property, one might expect the politics of the centre to have lost something of their urgency.

The final section of this chapter aims to complement these arguments, but also to develop them. It complements them by moving away from the predominantly charter-based evidence so far made use of. Charters are an excellent and vitally important source of evidence for the early medieval historian, but any single genre, even (or especially) those produced under certain conditions and clearly intended to have a practical bearing, inevitably offers only one perspective. To remedy this narrowness of focus, we turn now to a liturgical manual from Metz, material associated with Lotharingian monastic reform, and two historical records produced at Rheims. These texts are linked through their provenance, for all were produced in the area of our interest in the tenth century. But what also connects them is a common theme, one implicit in the arguments set out above. To the extent that changes in the nature of comital authority and in the local patterns of domination are dimly visible, they consisted of shifts in communication, as authority of various kinds was expressed in different ways. What follows uses a kind of triangulation, or collage, to suggest that analogous changes in communicative process can be detected in a far wider range of sources than charters alone.

The Liber de divinis officiis

We begin with a text which used – erroneously – to be attributed to Alcuin and that survives in a number of tenth- and eleventh-century manuscripts, often as the main or only content. Several of these manuscripts come from around Metz and the earliest, now forming folios 2–27 of Paris BnF lat. 9421, from tenth-century Echternach.[67] A succinct guide to various liturgical matters, generally thought to have been compiled in or around Metz or perhaps Trier in the early tenth century, the *Liber de divinis officiis* explains key dates in the church's calendar, and provides summaries of ecclesiastical hierarchies and duties, and short expositions on the mass and creed. What work has been done on the treatise has focused on identifying its sources, from which it becomes clear that the work is largely a compilation of a wide range of material, put together in a new way.[68] This kind of work is, of course, important, but the discussion of hypothetical stemmata and lost common sources should not distract us from the value of the actual surviving manuscripts.

The *De divinis officiis* is of interest from several points of view, providing evidence for excessively enthusiastic godparents, apocalyptic anxieties and a recurrent fascination with Rome. With its neat explanations for basic questions – why Christmas is celebrated, why Christ was crucified rather than stoned, why priests' sandals do not have laces – one can imagine it would have proven useful to those engaged in pastoral care, or those teaching them. Two elements are, however, particularly relevant here. The first is its extended description of the liturgy of penance. The *De divinis officiis* contains a penitential *ordo* that, amongst many other things, provides a great wealth of orchestration. It describes, or rather enjoins, with loving detail a whole range of gestures to be undertaken by both priest and penitent, including weeping and sighing, prostration, standing up and sitting down, as well as giving a short pre-scripted confession, before instructing both to enter church and continue with further prayers.[69] The second is the insistence that during the mass, the consecratory prayers to be said over the bread and wine, beginning with the *Te igitur*, must be recited by the priest silently, so that those attending

---

[67] *Clavis Scriptorum Latinorum medii aevi: territoire français, 735–987, Clavis Scriptorum Latinorum medii aevi: Auctores Galliae*, 2 vols. (Turnhout, 1994), vol. II, pp. 133–4, lists the manuscripts with all or part of this text, and provides the attribution of the work itself to Metz. For a detailed description of the Echternach manuscript, on which what follows largely depends, see F. Avril and C. Rabel, *Manuscrits enluminés d'origine germanique* (Paris, 1995), p. 14.

[68] *Liber de divinis officiis*, PL, vol. CI, cols. 1173–1286. J.-P. Bouhot, 'Les sources de l'*Expositio missae* de Rémi d'Auxerre', *Revue des études augustiniennes* 26 (1980), 118–69, suggests that the *De divinis officiis* was itself a re-edited version of an earlier compilation and that merely the structure, based on Amalarius of Trier, was new. The manuscripts of this compilation are, however, all later than the earliest manuscripts of the *De divinis officiis*, and Bouhot's arguments, not entirely convincing on this point, seem intended chiefly to bolster his claim that part of the text should be attributed to Remigius of Auxerre. Given Remigius's connections with Rheims, these arguments are in any case immaterial for my particular purpose here.

[69] Ch. 13 in the PL edition (based on Duchesne's edition, which is often inaccurate: a new edition is desirable); folios 4r-6r in Paris BnF. Lat. 9421.

the mass are unable to hear the words being said. The stated rationale is a double one. Were these words to be said aloud, they would be learned and then used inappropriately: this would not only cheapen them, it could call down God's vengeance, as was reported once to have happened to some shepherds.[70]

Both of these developments sit squarely in Carolingian traditions, yet modified them, too, in telling ways. An adapted version of the penitential *ordo* can also be found in later tenth- and eleventh-century manuscripts in the group collectively labelled as the Romano-German Pontifical. There, the interview between priest and penitent is followed by an elaborate (and implicitly episcopal) mass, involving the public imposition of a hairshirt upon, and ceremonial exclusion of, the penitent, drawing on a text for public penance used by Regino of Prüm in his handbook.[71] That has led to the suggestion that the encounter between priest and penitent that preceded the mass was equally intended to be staged publicly, perhaps just outside the church – and that this might explain its quite unusual attention to gesture.[72] However, while this is plausible for these manuscripts, the earliest manuscript witness to the *ordo* that I am aware of, the so-called Pontifical of Poitiers from (as it happens) early tenth-century Rheims, introduces it as an *ordo* for how penance can be done 'publice vel specialiter', which suggests that it could have been used in various circumstances.[73] Judged on its own terms, there is no reason to presume that the compiler of the *De divinis*, whose version of the text seems earlier than that in the Romano-German Pontifical and is not followed by an elaborate episcopal mass, necessarily had a public audience in mind when he wrote the text; in other words, the staging was not for the benefit of onlookers, but for the participants.[74] In fact, instructions for the actual performance of penance had been steadily growing in elaboration since they first began to circulate around 800, so the penitential *ordo* in the *De divinis* simply represents a further evolution of that trend.[75] An important mechanism of individualisation, and a moment of

---

[70] Paris lat. 9421, f. 19v: 'Unde fertur quod antequam haec consuetudo inolevisset cum pastores ea decantarent in agro divinitus sunt percussi' (ch. 40 in the *PL* edition).

[71] Regino, *Libri duo*, bk 1, ch. 295.

[72] S. Hamilton, *The practice of penance* (London, 2001), pp. 108–17, particularly pp. 115–17.

[73] A. Martini, *Il cosiddetto Pontificale di Poitiers: (Paris, Bibliothèque de l'Arsenal, cod. 227)* (Rome, 1979): p. 54* for the date of these particular folios ('inizio del X secolo' on palaeographical grounds), p. 12 for the text. See also N. Rasmussen, *Les pontificaux du haut moyen age: gènese du livre de l'évêque* (Louvain, 1998), pp. 423.

[74] As Hamilton, *Practice*, points out (pp. 113–14), the pontifical contains a reference to 'vices mentioned above' at p. 15 and again at p. 17, which in fact have not been; in the version of the *ordo* in the *De divinis*, however, there has been a long discussion of the eight deadly sins. The confession and the mass are separated in Paris lat. 9421 by a simple rubric, not reproduced in the edition.

[75] A helpful discussion of the development of these ninth-century *ordines* is provided in R. Kottje, 'Bußpraxis und Bußritus', *Settimane* 33 (1987), 369–95.

self-realisation as a Christian, as the sinner came to terms with his or her wayward human nature, was framed as essentially a ritual, with an increasingly prescribed routine recommended.[76]

As for the move to the silent recitation of the consecratory prayers, this too has earlier roots. The earliest Carolingian mass commentaries, such as the *Dominus vobiscum* and *Primus in ordine*, make no reference to it all. Mid-ninth century ones, such as Florus of Lyons's *De actione missarum*, Amalarius of Trier's *Liber Officialis* and the *Introitus missae* and *Quotiens contra se*, do state or imply that the canon of the mass was recited inaudibly, but without putting the same emphasis on the matter as does the *De divinis*.[77] These earlier commentaries had explained the silence as reflecting the need for intimate prayer with God, or by analogy with Christ's example. In the model presented by the manuscripts of the *De divinis officiis*, the silence had an altered function, moving from one designed to assist personal prayer to a kind of protection from the awesome power of God. The effect was surely to lend the mass, that central moment in Christian practice, an even more charged atmosphere, changing the canon of the mass into a secret in the sociological sense, and leaving the faithful to sit in silence after their role in the formal greeting that marked the beginning of the service. Here again, the *De divinis* was probably not itself radically innovative, but continuing to develop trends already underway in late Carolingian Francia.[78]

For both phenomena, then, the manuscripts of the *De divinis* represent both consolidation and further development, an intensification of the Carolingian preoccupation with defining and communicating the symbolic already discussed in Chapter 3. In both instances, we see a shift in the already heavily formalised moments of interaction with the holy, and with holy power, accentuating still further the ritualised nature of encounters which took place through Frankish society, reaching down to the very bottom of the social order as well as embracing those at the top. We should be careful not to infer that this made them less meaningful to

---

[76] Compare, for example, the Halitgar and Bede/Egbert penitentials, which lack this level of staging: Schmitz, *Die Bußbücher und das kanonische Bußverfahren* (Düsseldorf 1898), pp. 290–91, and pp. 680–1. A text very similar to the *De divinis*'s *ordo* is also found in late tenth-century Fulda manuscripts: see Hamilton, *Practice*, pp. 138–41.

[77] Cf. Jungmann, *Mass*, vol. II, pp. 104–6, and R. Suntrup, *Die Bedeutung der liturgischen Gebärden und Bewegungen in lateinischen und deutschen Auslegungen des 9. bis 13. Jahrhunderts* (Munich, 1978), pp. 457–64.

[78] The mass commentary uniquely preserved in Troyes BM 804 and edited in Bouhot, 'Les sources', pp. 140–51, offers a parallel interpretation of the reason for silence (p. 151), including a reference to the punishment of shepherds. This manuscript is usually dated to the mid ninth century, yet the allusion to shepherds is probably a reference to a passage in John Moschus's *Spiritual meadow* (see H. Chadwick, 'John Moschus and his friend Sophronius the Sophist', *Journal of Theological Studies* 25 (1974), 41–74), a text translated into Latin only at the end of the ninth century. Whatever their precise date, these mass commentaries certainly represent an elaboration of earlier ninth-century ones (see n. 77, above).

those engaged in them. Quite the reverse could be the case.[79] What matters, rather, is that already liturgical occasions familiar to most people were, so to speak, further liturgised. It seems likely that Pseudo-Alcuin was not the composer but the compiler of these texts, but in a sense that is beside the point: the manuscripts written in the tenth and early eleventh centuries demonstrate an interest in them, and probably played a role in disseminating them, though the state of the current edition makes that role difficult to quantify. Obviously it is impossible to say from these manuscripts what the 'practical' impact was, a problem that has long vexed studies of penitential practice. Yet it would be a peculiar starting-point to assume that changes in texts bore no relation to the people who wrote them, and for whom they were written.

Lotharingian monastic reform

Abbot John of Gorze, who served for a while as a priest in the countryside before taking the monastic vocation, might perhaps have been familiar with the *De Divinis Officiis*. He was certainly familiar with some of the charter evidence discussed above, since he was responsible for one of them. But John was also the subject of a saint's Life written by another abbot, himself responsible for another of those charters. This text, the *Vita Iohannis Gorziensis*, is the most informative account we have for the Lotharingian monastic reform of the tenth century, a reform that has grown to increasing prominence over the past few decades as a counterpart to Cluniac-inspired monasticism.[80]

The text is also well known, though amongst a largely different audience, for its tantalisingly incomplete account of John's visit on behalf of Emperor Otto I to the Caliphate of al-Andalus in the 960s, which included a lengthy stay in Cordoba. The author of the Life, Abbot John of St-Arnulf (Metz), had not himself been present, and even though he claims that his text was based on John's personal reminiscences, we obviously cannot treat the text as an accurate portrayal of the embassy, still less of the Caliphate of the time.[81] What we can use it for, however, are the attitudes of the Lotharingian monk who wrote it, and to some

[79] Cf. Cramer, *Baptism*, pp. 217–20, and Asad, *Genealogies of religion*, particularly pp. 55–79 and pp. 125–67.
[80] K. Hallinger, *Gorze-Kluny: studien zu den monastischen Lebensformen u. Gegensätzen im Hochmittelalter* (Rome, 1951), though he seeks to put a much wider range of material to work, too. For the Life, see M. Parisse, *La vie de Jean, abbé de Gorze* (Paris, 1999).
[81] M. Parisse, 'Une ambassade à Cordoue. La Vita de Jean, abbé de Gorze, vers 987', in *Autour de Gerbert d'Aurillac, le pape de l'an mil: album de documents commentés* (Paris, 1996), pp. 37–42, with references.

extent of the monks who were his sources. One of its most striking elements is the focus on ceremonial, particularly in the narration of John's meeting with the caliph. The latter is presented as surrounded by elaborate customs and random rules, which John studiously ignores, refusing to wash or change his clothes. A climax comes in a reported conversion between John and the caliph, in which they discuss Emperor Otto I. The caliph suggests that the emperor makes little use of ceremony compared with his own court, instead sharing his power, an assessment with which John readily agrees. But there is an implicit difference in their evaluation of this fact, resting in the way that John 'sees through' the caliph's court ceremony. In the terms of Philippe Buc, the Cordoban court is identified as 'bad ritual': shallow, misleading and empty.[82]

To an extent, this is simply standard orientalising material. Yet there is probably a more specific context here too, which helps explain why John of St-Arnulf included these details in his text (and, arguably, why John of Gorze was sent to Cordoba by the Ottonian court). The novelty of the tenth-century monastic reform movement is often played down in current scholarship, treated as at most an intensification of liturgical practice and a return to more demanding codes of behaviour, perhaps as linked to a new interest in group formation but in general more safely understood as a rhetorical position, and moreover a rhetoric often closely linked to political machinations of various kinds.[83] However, it can be argued that the monastic reform movement in general and the Lotharingian form in particular did have one identifiable characteristic, one which comes across very clearly in the *Vita Iohannis*, namely its fascination with ritual.

Reforming institutions associated with Lotharingian reform produced a number of texts known as monastic customaries, detailing the ceremonial lives of monks to an extent not recorded previously, though to be sure drawing on Carolingian precedent.[84] One of these, known to modern historians as the *Redactio sancti Emmerammi*, promised that those monks who followed its instructions about 'absolutely everything' would be 'quiet in mind' in this life and would achieve salvation in the next, before embarking on a remarkable description of the minutiae of communal life, ranging from the difference between the ringing of the bells between Nocturn and Vespers, and the question of what is to be carried in festive processions, or of precisely how communion wafers are to be baked, to the

---

[82] *Vita Iohannis*, pp. 156–60; cf. Buc, *Dangers*.

[83] Nightingale, *Monasteries*; Hlawitschka, 'Herzog Giselbert'.

[84] Cf. J. Wollasch, 'Reformmönchtum und Schriftlichkeit', *FMS* 26 (1992), 274–86. The essential editorial work was co-ordinated by Hallinger; for an update, see L. Donnat, 'Vie et coutume monastique dans la Vita de Jean de Gorze', in M. Parisse and G. Oexle, eds., *L'abbaye de Gorze au X siècle* (Nancy, 1993), pp. 159–82.

orchestration of blood-letting and the chapter meeting, the latter including basic stage directions.[85] Another text, known as the *Redactio Fuldensis-Trevirensis*, which had a very similar content, though differently arranged, explicitly offered its readers the customs of Trier and Gorze, setting itself up as a complement to the oral instructions of the famous Lotharingian reforming monk Sandrat of St-Maximin.[86] The novelty here was not so much the use of the written word (monks were hardly unfamiliar with it, after all), but the attempt to provide guidance for collective interaction for almost every part of the day. Put together (it seems) slightly before equivalent manuals were produced in Cluny, whose earliest custumaries focused almost exclusively on the liturgy in a strict sense, these texts effectively liturgised the entirety of collective monastic life.

It is, of course, extremely difficult to get an external perspective on what the Lotharingian tenth-century monastic reform was like, since most accounts were written by those committed to it – but it is interesting to note that one of its leading figures, Sandrat, was considered by his enemies to be preoccupied with a showy kind of ceremonial display. The image of him throwing himself on the ground amidst floods of tears and insincere groans which the eleventh-century historian and monk of St-Gall Ekkehard gave is surely manufactured, but still points to a salient aspect of the monastic reform, here in Lotharingia as elsewhere.[87] Of course, Carolingian monastic reforms had also been concerned with an intensified ritualisation of monastic life (not least the chapter meetings discussed earlier).[88] What was novel about the Lotharingian reform was simply the way it carried these concerns about questions of authenticity and performance, including in non-liturgical settings, to new heights.

The view from Rheims

A third text I want to consider is an account of the Council of St-Basle of June 991, whose main business was the deposition of Archbishop Arnulf of Rheims, the nephew of Carolingian Charles of Lorraine, whose claims to the west Frankish throne had been passed over in favour of Hugh Capet,

---

[85] *Redactio sancti Emmerammi*, ed. M. Weneger and C. Elvert, *Corpus Consuetudinum Monasticarum*, vol. vii:iii (Siegburg, 1984), pp. 187–256: 'consuetudines de omnibus omnino rebus', p. 193. Bells, p. 196; processions, p. 208; wafers, p. 213; blood-letting, p. 215; chapter meeting, pp. 251–2.

[86] Ibid., pp. 264, 273.

[87] Ekkehard of St-Gallen, *Casus sancti Galli*, ed. and tr. H. Haefele, *St. Galler Klostergeschichte* (Darmstadt, 1980), pp. 137–45. On Sandrat's visit to St-Gall, see W. Jezieski, '"Paranoia sangallensis". A microstudy in the etiquette of monastic persecution', *FMS* 42 (2008), 147–68.

[88] On Carolingian monastic ritualisation, see M. Mattingly, 'The *Memoriale Qualiter*. An eighth-century monastic customary', *American Benedictine Review*, 60 (2009), 62–75.

but who had launched a struggle against Hugh in the years that followed 987. The author of the text was probably also the master of ceremonies, Gerbert (later Pope Sylvester II), who was appointed as Arnulf's successor immediately after the council.[89] Gerbert was working with very unpromising material. Arnulf's deposition was seen by some contemporaries as nakedly political, part of Hugh Capet's attempt definitively to remove the Carolingian family from power, and even in the account given by Gerbert, the charges against Arnulf seem trumped-up.[90] The major element, Arnulf's complicity in Charles of Lorraine's seizure of Rheims in 989, rested on the testimony of a priest who was himself defrocked in the course of proceedings. That accusation was buttressed by other even less convincing arguments, for example the claim that Arnulf's excommunication of those pillaging Rheims's land had failed to give due weight to protecting church buildings. Arnulf conspicuously did not publicly admit his complicity with his uncle, and it is really hardly surprising that papal pressure saw him returned to his see just a few years later, at which point Gerbert left to join the imperial court.

Nevertheless, Gerbert did his best with the material at his disposal. He gives great emphasis to dramatic elements in proceedings, turning weaknesses in the case into strengths. Particular attention is given to the central problem, the fact that Arnulf at no point admitted that he had indeed connived with Charles in the assault on Rheims. Arnulf's lack of a confession is made into an inability to speak: he is depicted stuttering, unable to string a sentence together, when placed in full view of the kings.[91] The confession is instead said to have taken place off-stage, in the crypt at St-Basle, with a choreographical backdrop provided by the waves of different clerics who arrived to hear it. What they heard is not recorded, only hinted at, suggesting that he had confessed to further dark secrets that it was not necessary for everyone else to know. Gerbert also addresses the problem squarely, describing a layman's frustrated outburst at the lack of a public confession, and the way his complaint was slapped down. Not only is the inevitable ensuing deposition itself described, with plenty of ceremonial prostration and weeping, Gerbert even includes the preceding

---

[89] For the context, G. Giordanengo, 'Le concile de Saint-Basle: actes conciliaires rédigés par Gerbert', in *Autour de Gerbert*, pp. 134–41, with references; see also Glenn, *Politics*, pp. 98–109, who also stresses the constructed nature of Gerbert's account. G. Koziol, *Begging pardon and favor: ritual and political order in early medieval France* (Ithaca, 1992), draws attention to the ceremonial aspects, pp. 1–4, as part of his important book on supplication, though with less emphasis on the text itself. Lot, *Hugues*, pp. 31–81, provides a detailed guide to the text.

[90] The *Historia senonensis Francorum*, ed. G. Pertz, *MGH SS*, vol. IX (Hanover, 1851), pp. 364–9, was especially critical: p. 368. Gerbert's letters written in the name of Arnulf of Rheims also suggest that Arnulf was not quite so straightforwardly a partisan of Charles as he was made out to be.

[91] *MGH Concilia* vol. VI, p. 447.

discussions about how it was to be done – Arnulf's vestments were not to be ripped, but rather gently removed, with the observation that the removal of his pallium did not imply any insult to the Pope.[92] Just as important are the ceremonial events that Gerbert does not describe, but frequently draws attention to: in Gerbert's version of the Council of St-Basle, it is the oaths that Arnulf swore to the king that prove his wickedness, and Gerbert devotes great attention to these oaths, in written and other forms, throughout his account.

Gerbert's account is modelled on Carolingian synodal protocols, themselves novel in the way they provided a narrative framework in considerable detail for the synods. It goes a step further, however. In an extraordinary preface, Gerbert candidly admits that his account has taken liberties with the actual unfolding of events: it is, he says, a work of interpretation of the synod. Sometimes that interpretation takes the form of translation; sometimes it requires the rephrasing of speech; sometimes, however, it uses that speech in order to investigate what is hidden, and bring into the open the consequences.[93] It comes, therefore, as little surprise that the account is modelled on synodal *ordines*, and that long extracts from canon law have been neatly spliced into the proceedings, sometimes placed in participants' mouths (there is a remarkable amount of direct speech).[94] Gerbert is not, in other words, even pretending to be giving an exact account of what actually happened at the synod – his account of St-Basle is more like a play, a knowingly staged production which revealed certain truths precisely by and through its staging.

Gerbert was, of course, an exceptional figure, and one might think that not too much weight can be put on the way he chose to represent the events at St-Basle, were it not that it receives further contextualisation from another, even more important text from tenth-century Rheims. Richer of Rheims, a monk of St-Rémi, wrote his *Historiae* around 996, dedicating them to Archbishop Gerbert. Dealing with Francia from around 888, Richer's text has often been dismissed as idiosyncratic.[95] He based his account heavily on the Annals of Flodoard, becoming altogether more uncertain of his material when Flodoard's Annals ran out in 966, and very little in Richer that is not also in Flodoard can be treated as sound

[92] *MGH Concilia* vol. VI, pp. 443–5.
[93] *MGH Concilia* vol. VI, p. 392. Glenn, *Richer*, provides a translation, pp. 105–6. F. Lot, *Études sur le règne de Hugues Capet et la fin du xe siècle* (Paris, 1903) also drew attention to this, pp. 33–4.
[94] For the modelling on the *ordines*, see *MGH Concilia* vol. VI, p. 395. It is hardly a coincidence that tenth-century Rheims saw attention devoted to the compilation of new *ordines* for the holding of church councils, e.g. Rheims MS 340. For a description, see Rasmussen, *Les pontificaux*, pp. 346–70.
[95] Hoffmann's edition offers a sound Introduction, pp. 1–8. For more detail, see Glenn, *Politics*, particularly pp. 4–8.

evidence for the unfolding of political events. However, as historians have recently emphasised, that does not mean that Richer's text is without its significance. Though much excellent recent work has gone into establishing the writing process, since Richer's autograph copy itself survives complete with erasures and revisions, the way in which he moulds his sources to create the stories he tells bears further attention in this context.[96]

Richer was clearly as bewildered by Flodoard's Annals as are many modern readers, because Flodoard carefully and systematically avoided offering explanation for the events he described, merely recording them as they happened, in a detail which defies the discernment of pattern. Unlike modern historians, though, Richer had no reservations about expanding on Flodoard's account, to try to make it make some sort of historical sense. This required the imaginative reconstruction of individuals' motivations, which in turn required the imaginative reconstruction of events which could have prompted those motivations. Like Gerbert's account of St-Basle, Richer's text is overtly a work of interpretation, rendered in a quite intriguing way.

It is unlikely, for example, that Duke William Longsword's assassination in 942 was brought about by the resentment of King Henry I of East Francia (d.936) at being asked to stand up during an audience with Charles the Simple (deposed in 923), to make room on the couch for the plain-speaking, quick-thinking Norman duke; but it matters that this Rémois monk thought this must, or might, have been the cause underpinning Flodoard's dry recitation of events.[97] In fact, the major set-pieces of Richer are all crystalline in this way, encapsulating themes and conflicts in carefully drawn, hyper-real vignettes: a young king athletically jumping onto his horse without assistance to general applause, a castellan offered a choice between reward and punishment as represented by gold and iron rings, a count struck down by sudden death whilst dressed in all his finery, haranguing his men with arms stretched out, a duke at bedtime surrounded by his retinue, several vigorously rubbing his bare feet, and so on.[98] If these sorts of descriptions dry up in the later part of his work, it is only because Richer's concern shifts to properly liturgical events, including the Council of St-Basle, discussed above, for which he depends largely on Gerbert's version.[99] It seems that for Richer, the Frankish political elite moved in a crystalline, brittle world, dominated by signs of transparent

---

[96] Glenn, *Politics*, is superbly attuned to how Richer's surviving manuscript can be used to inform our understanding of the text itself: see especially 128–65. Glenn also comments extensively on Richer's reworking of Flodoard, though with a slightly different approach to that sketched out here: see pp. 176–214.

[97] Richer, *Historiae*, bk II, ch. 30, pp. 119–21. Cf. Flodoard, *Annales*, s. a. 943.

[98] Richer, *Historiae*, bk II ch. 4, p. 100; II, ch. 11, pp. 105–6; II, ch. 37, p. 125; III, ch. 88, p. 218.

[99] Though not slavishly: see Glenn, *Richer*, pp. 279–84.

and overwhelming legibility, and where politics was all about the struggle for an increasingly consistent sign.[100]

It might seem tempting to dismiss Richer's dissatisfaction with the deliberately thin, dry history of Flodoard in favour of something far more elaborated as simply the idiosyncrasy of an over-imaginative monk. But Richer, in correspondence with Abbo of Fleury amongst others, was far from a marginal figure; and it would be better to see his chronicle as revealing the historical perspective of the monastic community of which he was part. In any case, this heavily ritualised aspect of Richer's work is far from unparalleled by his contemporaries, even apart from Gerbert. Thietmar of Merseburg's chronicle, with its accounts of dropped crowns breaking bids for power, stolen staffs causing a loss of a material *honor* and great attention to the minutiae of gestures, shows signs of similar concerns.[101] The *History of the Normans*, written by Dudo of Saint-Quentin, perhaps educated at Rheims, has similar characteristics too.[102] Arguably, these are trends already visible in much earlier literature, what has been described in Auerbachian terms as the rhetoric of the scene.[103] The difference is that in these texts, the narrative does not merely progress by means of scenes; rather, these scenes are ascribed a real, positive meaning in themselves. The difference between sign and signified, so troublesome for Carolingian politics, was beginning to dissolve, at least in the historical imagination.

CONCLUSION: 'SYMBOLIC IMPOVERISHMENT'

If the tenth century between Marne and Moselle remains a problematic period, this is not so much a result of the lack of evidence as the lack of any clear overarching narrative or framework in which to place the abundant but fragmentary material. However, that fragmentation can be turned to our advantage, and taken as an invitation to compare different kinds of evidence, and to gain thereby a variety of perspectives. Using the full breadth of available evidence from the region, from archaeology to liturgy, this chapter has identified changes in the expression of local

---

[100] Cf. Koziol, *Begging*, pp. 115–21 for parallel interpretation; his emphasis is on the royal aspect of these rituals.

[101] Thietmar, *Chronicon*, bk II, ch. 23, p. 66 (dropped crown) and bk V, ch. 21, p. 245 (stolen staff: one of the earlier secular investiture examples).

[102] Cf. H. Kamp, 'Die Macht der Zeichen und Gesten. Öffentliches Verhalten bei Dudo von Saint-Quentin', in G. Althoff, ed., *Formen und Funktionen öffentlicher Kommunikation im Mittelalter* (Stuttgart, 2001), pp. 125–55, on Dudo's rituals; he draws attention to similarities in Richer and Thietmar, p. 155.

[103] J. Pizarro, A rhetoric of the scene: dramatic narrative in the early Middle Ages (Toronto, 1989), pp. 8–15.

landholding, in the constitution of comital power, and in certain representations of social relations.

It is the proposal of this chapter that all these characteristics can be seen as different aspects of a general process, one that could be inelegantly described as 'symbolic impoverishment', through which social meaning became relatively less polyvalent and fluid and relatively more legible and fixed, across a whole range of fields, from the practice of penance to the nature of comital authority. In this perspective, a process of 'symbolic impoverishment', working in terms of authoritative definition rather than contextual framing, began to take hold, gradually, in the decades around, and particularly after, 900. The way in which a count's authority was conceived broke free from contextualisation through the apparatus of the Carolingian court: the specific characteristics of comital power became defined in their own terms, hence the appearance of *comitatus* in charters and other material. The breakdown of the Carolingian formula, far from merely unmasking change, must be seen as another aspect of that change, again a liberation from the semantic contextualisation provided by the relatively uniform diplomatic of the ninth century. In a linked change, domination over the peasantry began to find articulation without requiring the crutches of Carolingian formularies, winning independent expression in a series of charters which point towards later franchise agreements. Finally, corroboratory material is provided by the various sources discussed in the third section, all of which shared a common concern with defining and articulating the symbolic in ever more precise, self-conscious and unambivalent ways. All these developments support the idea that the collapse of royal authority in this region in the tenth century was more likely to be a consequence than a cause of the localisation of power, as the court's role as the clearing house of social meaning, if that is not too grand a phrase, became increasingly irrelevant. The power of an elite no longer needed to be celebrated at the centre to be effective locally: something in the fabric of society was changing.

Admittedly this argument is suggestive, rather than demonstrative, and provisional, rather than definitive. However, it has the merit of connecting jigsaw pieces with one another in a way which better follows the grain of the evidence, and in bringing together in historical analysis various kinds of text concerning people of various statuses, reflecting the reality of social interactions of the time which did not respect modern scholarly specialisation. It also helps connect the period with both what came before and what came after in specific ways, instead of merely taking sides in the debate about which side of the line between Carolingian and central medieval to place the tenth century. If this argument holds, that question really makes no sense, since the tenth century is best understood as part of the development from one to the other. The crystallisation of social power which begins to be visible in this period is merely a continuation of processes initiated by the Carolingians, as discussed in Part I. This does not merely rehearse the central historiographical problem of the tenth century, that of always being interpreted in terms of another period. On the contrary, it restores to the period in question a proper dynamic: one whose very novelty was itself in continuity with earlier processes. Whether this provisional interpretation holds water, however, depends on the more abundant sources from the later eleventh century and after, with which Part III is concerned.

PART III

The exercise of authority through property rights, c.1030–c.1130

The previous two parts of this book were devoted to Carolingian and immediately post-Carolingian society between Marne and Moselle, up to around the early eleventh century. This part of the book extends the analysis from that point into the early twelfth century, using the increasing bulk of evidence to trace, in finer detail, the developments glimpsed in material from the earlier period. Chapter 6 deals chiefly with the emergence of a wholly new vocabulary of demands placed by lords upon their lower-status dependants, while Chapter 7 turns to a new vocabulary, and new concepts, for articulating hierarchies amongst the elite. Finally, Chapter 8 considers the varying historical development of the lands east and west of the Meuse in a comparative perspective, with particular reference to the emergence of units of political domination which integrated, to varying degrees, the regions in question.

Chapter 6

THE BANALITY OF POWER

With all charters and decrees, one should not stop at the superficiality of the letter, but inquire into the meaning, the intention of the writer.

Hugo Metellus, *Epistolae*.[1]

In the history of the monastery of Saint-Trond, now a town in modern Belgium, that he wrote around 1114, Abbot Rudolf recalled a journey he had made to Metz in 1107.[2] He had joined up with an armed group moving south, and he later remembered, and graphically described, the devastation wrought by the soldiers as they travelled through southern Lotharingia to Verdun. These armed men were commanded by dukes and counts, and this was no invading force, but that hardly mattered to those they encountered. Men in the agricultural communities along their route fled to the woods, and the women and children who were left tried desperately to persuade Rudolf to stay with them, in the hope that the presence of a monk might offer some kind of protection against looting, and worse. In their main camp, the soldiers constructed temporary shelters from material literally torn from peasants' buildings. The impression is of an entirely antagonistic relationship between those who fought and those who laboured, with those who prayed unable to do anything other than observe and in this instance, record.

Its descriptive force makes Rudolf's account a good way to begin thinking about the evolving relationships of power in the Lotharingian and *champenois* countryside. It reminds us that much did not change in the period in question. Violence by passing bands of armed men was a constant feature of medieval Europe, and the disruption caused by armies

---

[1] Hugo Metellus, *Epistolae*, in *Sacrae antiquitatis monumenta: historica, dogmatica, diplomatica* ed. C. Hugo (Étival, 1725), vol. II, p. 388.

[2] Rudolf, *Gesta abbatum Trudonensium*, ed. R. Köpke, *MGH SS*, vol. X (Hanover, 1852), pp. 213–448, at pp. 265–6. See also H-W. Goetz, *Geschichtsschreibung und Geschichtsbewußtsein im hohen Mittelalter* (Berlin, 2008), which gives essential background to the text.

even in peaceful transit was nothing new.[3] It also reminds us that when we evaluate our texts, we are examining the traces of real people, and real suffering (though of course that does not mean that Rudolf's account was anything other than intricately constructed). However, Rudolf's text is less sure as a guide to the less dramatic, more everyday, and for that reason more systemic exercise of power.[4] To glean a clearer sense of modalities of the relations between those who dominated and those who were dominated, and above all how they changed – for if the threat of armed thugs hardly changed from century to century, the way that social hierarchies were maintained and reproduced proved more susceptible to alteration – we need to turn once again to more mundane kinds of evidence.

THE RISE OF BANNAL POWER

From the second third of the eleventh century, the number of charters recording transactions of various kinds in this region begins inexorably to rise. The steady increase continued throughout the rest of the period in question, and in fact jumped to a new level in the middle of the twelfth century, as documents began to flood out from Cistercian and Premonstratensian institutions, matched by the invigorated output of episcopal *scriptoria*. This expansion in the written record allows historians to make increasingly secure reconstructions of monastic and family activities and connections, and of the day-to-day conflict of interests that the politics of any period involves.

Charters and the countryside

These charters, combined with the estate documents of the period such as the surveys compiled by the canons of Chaumousey near Toul, the nuns of St-Marie of Metz and, a little later, the monks of St-Maximin of Trier, can also be read for what they can tell us about changes in the organisation of the countryside.[5] The potential significance of such changes hardly needs emphasis. There is admittedly impressive evidence from this period for the growth of inter-regional and even international trade, and for the growth of towns, building on earlier movements towards urbanisation, that this trade fostered, of which the best examples in this region are Metz

---

[3] An example approximately a century earlier is provided by the *Chronicon S. Michaelis*, p. 28.

[4] Cf. A. Mbembe, 'The banality of power and the aesthetics of vulgarity in the postcolony', *Public Culture* 4 (1992), 1–30, from which I draw the chapter's title; it deals with the obscene and grotesque, which this chapter does not, but also with ideas of fetish and government as a system of signs.

[5] These estate surveys (and others) are extensively discussed in Perrin, *Recherches*, though note that in some cases more recent editions of the texts he discusses are now available.

and Troyes.[6] Yet the economy of this region, and of Western Europe as a whole, was in this period, and arguably for much longer, driven by agricultural production, so alterations in the organisation of that production mattered tremendously.[7]

Two conspicuous shifts documented within these sources are the disappearance of the Carolingian *mansus*, replaced by smaller units known as *quartarii*, and the commutation of labour services into cash payments. The former probably reflects the sustained demographic expansion that had begun well before the year 1000; the latter, either the reduction of the demesne or the increased use of waged labour to work it, measures explicitly recorded in documents from Marmoutier (Alsace), St-Rémi and Stavelot.[8] Yet quite how these particular textual changes correlated to material and physical conditions is not clear. Excavation reports from the region show a broad continuity of settlement patterns between the seventh century and the twelfth, and it may be that even field patterns saw no radical change in this period, either.[9] Moreover, we do not know the extent to which agricultural obligations had in practice been redeemed by cash in the ninth century, since the polyptychs on which our understanding relies offer an administrative template, not an accounting record.

It could therefore be argued from a nominalist perspective that these documentary changes are more apparent than real, reflecting nothing more drastic than the collapse of Carolingian practices of estate description, rather than the collapse of the Carolingian bipartite estate. However, our documents register another shift that is perhaps more amenable to comparative

---

[6] In general, see A. Verhulst, *The rise of cities in north-west Europe* (Cambridge, 1999). On Metz, see J. Schneider, *La ville de Metz aux XIIIe et XIVe siècles* (Nancy, 1950).

[7] For pottery, always a sensitive index to trade, see M. Georges-Leroy, 'La production céramique médiévale en Lorraine: état de la recherche archéologique', in N. Meyer-Rodrigues and M. Bur, eds., *Les arts du feu, Actes du 127e congrès des sociétés historiques et scientifiques, Nancy, 15–20 avril 2002* (2009), pp. 163–91, who concludes that non-local exchange was low-level until the twelfth century; M. Lenoble, 'La ceramique médiévale dans le départment de l'Aube', in *Mémoire de Champagne*, vol. 1 (Langres, 2000) pp. 137–59, agrees. In general, see S. Epstein, *Economic and social history of later medieval Europe* (Cambridge, 2009).

[8] Marmoutier (Alsace): *Les constitutions des campagnes de l'Alsace au moyen-âge: recueil de documents inédits*, ed. C. Hanauer (Paris, 1864) (reforms undertaken by an abbot from Gorze), p. 51; St-Rémi: AD de la Marne, 56 H 1029 (Cartulaire B), f. 90; *Recueil*, ed. Halkin, no. 144 (1126). For examples of cash-based manorial services, see 'Urkunden', ed. Bloch, Appendix 1, pp. 123–30.

[9] J.-M. Yante and A.-M. Bultot-Verleysen, eds., *Autour du 'village': établissements humains, finages et communautés rurales entre Seine et Rhin (IVe–XIIIe siècles)* (Louvain, 2010). See W. Rösener, *Grundherrschaft im Wandel: Untersuchungen zur Entwicklung geistlicher Grundherrschaften im südwestdeutschen Raum vom 9. bis 14. Jahrhundert* (Göttingen, 1991) on the end of the bipartite estate from a German perspective. On field systems, see J-L. Abbé, 'Le paysage peut-il être lu à rebours? Le paysage agraire médiéval et la méthode régressive', in B. Cursente and M. Mousnier, eds., *Les territoires du médiéviste* (Rennes, 2005), pp. 383–99, who suggests that there was no revolution in France to match that suggested for Anglo-Saxon England. For 'openfield', see J. M. Blaising, 'Les structures du openfield en pays thionvillois', *Les Cahiers Lorrains* 1 (2000), 19–28.

analysis, and that, interpreted sensitively, can yield great insight into the forces conditioning or re-conditioning agricultural production. For, over the course of the eleventh century, the charters drawn up between Marne and Moselle recording the transfer of lands increasingly add a new clause, to specify that the land in question was granted 'with *bannum*' (*cum banno*) or, more rarely, without it.[10]

Pinpointing the appearance of this in the evidence is relatively straight-forward. There are charters from this region dated to before 1000 that make use of this terminology, for example from St-Rémi, Gorze, Trier, Mouzon and St-Vanne. These are all, without exception, either certainly forged or highly suspect.[11] The first use of these terms in genuinely contemporary material would appear, therefore, to be an entry in the *Liber memorialis* of Remiremont, dated by the editors to the early eleventh century, and a 1038 charter from St-Vanne and a reference from Mouzon, from roughly the same period.[12] As these locations suggest, and contrary to what might have been expected in view of most understandings of Feudal Revolution – on which more later – the evidence from the east of the region is slightly earlier than from the west, though in view of the early material from the Ile-de-France, this could simply be a product of uneven preservation of sources.

Whatever the date of its emergence, the clause really makes its mark in the archives from the 1060s onwards, and from the early twelfth century it is routinely mentioned, particularly in the archives of the older Benedictine houses. For the most part, these texts were 'private' charters, but royal and imperial charters from this region fit more or less the same pattern, once we have filtered out the mere expression of royal power (*banno nostro*). When interpolations and forgeries can be given an approximate date, they are clustered around the later eleventh and first half of the twelfth centuries.[13]

What we might call bannal terminology grew increasingly wide-ranging in the course of the late eleventh and early twelfth centuries.

---

[10] J.-L. Fray, 'Recherches sur la seigneurie banale au XIIe siècle d'après le vocabulaire des actes des évêques de Metz (1050–1210)', *Publications de la section historique de l'Institut GD de Luxembourg* (1986), 75–101, for references. M.-J. Gasse-Grandjean, 'Le mot bannus dans les actes originaux du Haut Moyen Age', *Pays de Remiremont* 15 (2001), 44–60, is short and stays close to the material.

[11] St-Rémi, ascribed to 989, in *Recueil*, ed. Demouy, vol. I, pp. 31–2 (no number). Metz: *Histoire*, ed. Calmet, vol. II, col. 185; cf. col. 221. Verdun: 'Urkunden', ed. Bloch, no. 11b. Trier: *UBMR* no. 7a, dated to 706. Gorze: *Cartulaire*, ed. d'Herbomez, no. 11, dated to 765.

[12] Remiremont: *Liber memorialis of Remiremont*, ed. E. Hlawitschka and others, *MGH Libri memoriales*, vol. I, 2 vols. (Munich, 1981), f. 47r, v: 'Lainfridus … dedit … VII mansos … et bannum'. St-Vanne: 'Urkunden', ed. Bloch, no. 36. Mouzon: *Historia Mosomensis*, bk II, ch. 4, p. 165 (the editor dates it to the earlier eleventh century).

[13] On Hugh of Flavigny's tampering with *bannum* charters (e.g., *Chronicon*, p. 363), see P. Healy, *The chronicle of Hugh of Flavigny: reform and the investiture contest in the late-eleventh century* (Aldershot, 2006), pp. 86–8.

Mills and ovens, in the course of transfer, or sometimes as the subject of disputes, were specified as being *bannalis*, which is usually interpreted as meaning that their use was compulsory.[14] These facilities and the revenues they raised, known generally as *banalités*, are attested again on both sides of the Meuse before, and sometimes well before, 1130, though here the weight of early evidence has shifted to the west. Examples are recorded in documents from Rosnay, St-Dizier and Veuxhaules in the south, Epernay and Rheims in the west, Deuilly and Beuvillers in the east, and St-Prix, Longpont and Chateau-Porcien in the north.[15] Even processions to particular churches were described as bannal, though the phenomenon is very difficult to date; and the term was also occasionally applied to the people subject to various compulsory requirements, who were labelled as *bannales*.[16] Bannal terminology also began to take a pronounced spatial sense, too, giving rise to the *bannleuga*, meaning a zone with particular judicial significance, from which comes modern French *banlieu*.[17]

Historiographical perspectives

Given its prominence in contemporary records, it would be surprising if this terminological evolution had not been noted before, and indeed the foregoing really only confirms that the time-scale set out by Genicot in a seminal article on the significance and timing of the emergence of '*droits banaux*' in the region around Liège, similar to that established by Fossier for Picardy, applies to the region between Marne and

---

[14] *Recueil des actes des comtes de Pontieu 1026–1279*, ed. C. Brunel (Paris, 1930), no. 8 and *Recueil des chartes de Saint Germain des Pres: des origines au début du XIIe siècle*, ed. R. Poupardin (Paris, 1909), no. 103, spell out this element of compulsion.

[15] Rosnay: Artem no. 189 (1045). St-Dizier: AD de la Haute-Marne, 7 H 2 (second cartulary of Montier-en-Der), f. 36v-37r. Veuxhaules: *Cartulaires de l'abbaye de Molesme, ancien diocèse de Langres, 916–1250: recueil de documents sur le nord de la Bourgogne et le midi de la Champagne*, ed. J. Laurent (Paris 1911), vol. I, no. 100. Epernay: *Epernay et l'abbaye Saint-Martin de ce ville*, ed. A. Nicaise (Châlons, 1869), no. 7 (1130, but a confirmation). Rheims: *Papsturkunden in Frankreich Neue Folge, I. Band. Champagne und Lothringen*, ed. H. Meinert (Berlin, 1933), no. 18. Deuilly: *Histoire*, ed. Calmet, vol. II, col. 271. Beuvillers (Xarné): Paris, BnF nouv. acq. lat. 1608, f. 17v. Chateau-Porcien: *Chartes de l'abbaye de Saint-Hubert en Ardenne*, ed. G. Kurth (Brussels, 1903), no. 57 (1087). Longpont: *Cartulaire du Prieuré de Notre-Dame de Longpont de l'ordre de Cluny*, no editor given (Lyon, 1879), no. 45 (1098). St-Prix: *Mémoires pour servir à l'histoire écclesiastique, civile, et militaire de la province du Vermandois*, ed. L. Colliette, 3 vols. (Cambrai, 1771–3), vol. I, p. 687 (1047).

[16] *Urkunden*, ed. Wampach no. 385 (1120s). For *Bannpflicht*, see most recently S. Tada, 'The creation of a religious centre: Christianisation in the diocese of Liège in the Carolingian period', *Journal of Ecclesiastical History* 54 (2003), 220–1. HRE, bk III, ch. 8, p. 204, seems to mention something very similar *c.*950: it is voluntary to the extent that the *villa* which decided not to go was struck with poor harvests. However, Bishop Theoderic of Verdun introduced such a procession at Verdun only in 1074 (Gregory VII, *Registrum*, ed. E. Caspar, *MGH Epistolae Selectae* 2 (Berlin, 1920), bk I, no. 81), so perhaps these processions should not always be pushed back into the ninth century.

[17] E.g. *Metropolis*, ed. Marlot, vol. II, col. 214 (*c.*1100).

Moselle too.[18] However, if the timing of what is often termed as the rise of bannal lordship (*seigneurie banale* or, though less common, *Bannherrschaft*), is generally undisputed, the same cannot be said for its interpretation. What, actually, does *bannum* mean in these eleventh- and twelfth-century charters? There are, broadly speaking, two current interpretations.

The first, and older, is that the appearance in these charters of *bannum*, an old Frankish word, marks a devolution of regalian rights.[19] Since the word appears in ninth-century texts usually only in association with the king, historians, especially those working within Francophone traditions, have argued that it signified a particular mood or capacity of command that was a royal prerogative in the Carolingian period and that subsequently passed down to lower levels, thereby strengthening the hands of the locally dominant, and perhaps, in the view of Perrin already mentioned in Chapter 5, helping to compensate for a disintegrating estate organisation.[20] This transfer created 'a new form of economic exploitation based not on ownership of the land but on the domination of people', a form of lordship that G. Duby memorably described as 'a kind of legitimised and organised pillage'.[21] As Susan Reynolds points out, it is usually assumed that this transfer from kings to aristocrats happened either by grant (of immunity) or by the usurpation of governmental authority.[22] For historians like Duby, this is the process at the heart of the Feudal Revolution.

However, a number of problems are evident with this line of explanation. Crucially, it does little to account for the gap of well over a century between the fading away of intense Carolingian-style royal power, discussed in Chapter 4, and the actual emergence of bannal terminology. It also implies a failure of royal power more dramatic than actually occurred, and, still more fundamentally, the zero-sum conception of power on which this approach is predicated is problematic: it makes the articulation of social relationships resemble forms familiar to modern historians, inclined to concentrate on delegation, and to classify the

---

[18] L. Genicot, 'Les premières mentions de droits banaux dans la région de Liège', *Académie Royale de Belgique, bulletin de la classe des lettres et des sciences morales et politiques*, 5ᵉ série, 54 (1968a), 56–65, at p. 62; Fossier, *La terre*, vol. II, pp. 560–4.

[19] On the history of the word, see A. de Sousa-Costa, *Studien zu volkssprachigen Wörtern in karolingischen Kapitularien* (Göttingen, 1993), pp. 52–89.

[20] Perrin, *Recherches* (see p. 149 n. 39 above).

[21] Devroey, 'Seigneurs', p. 255: 'une nouvelle forme d'exploitation économique fondée non pas sur la propriété du sol mais sur la domination des personnes' (citing Bloch). Cf. also Duby, *Early growth*, p. 176.

[22] Reynolds, *Fiefs*, p. 61: 'When lay lords in the aftermath of the Carolingian empire began to acquire independent jurisdiction over free men and their supposedly full property it seems at first to have been by the usurpation of what had been governmental authority rather than by the formal grant to them of "immunities".'

exercise of power as either legitimate or not, foreclosing on more sophisticated possibilities.[23]

In view of these difficulties, it is perhaps unsurprising that an alternative
interpretation now holds sway. Just as the word, and the transformation of
lordship it is deemed to represent, is conceptually pivotal to most accounts
which emphasise systematic post-Carolingian change *à la* Duby, it is marginalised by those who emphasise continuity, for whom *seigneurie banale* is quite
simply chimerical. Richard Barton, for example, fiercely attacked the notion
that eleventh-century lordship might have been 'qualitatively different . . .
because of its essentially private, and hence illegitimate nature, than the older,
Carolingian model of lordship'.[24] In making this assault, he is in good
company. Traditional German historiography, with its focus on
Grundherrschaft, has always been readier to see early medieval control of landed
property as inherently involving far-reaching and autonomous political
powers, which is clearly congruent with this alternative view.[25] Historians
pursuing this line of argument have played down the significance of the
word's emergence in documentary material as merely the product of more
flexible practices of charter redaction. Scribes, so goes the argument, felt more
at liberty to describe what happened in ways better approximating reality, so
the appearance of *bannum* simply reflects a more realistic charter diplomatic,
which was moreover put to the service of a reformed monasticism keen to
assert its rights over its secular neighbours.[26]

These revisionists further argue that the lordship which bannal vocabulary designates was already a central concept in the Carolingian period, and
there was no significant change in its nature, merely an intensification.[27]
Indeed, it is as a further development along these lines that many historians
now suppose that the constraints indicated by bannal terminology had, in
practice, already existed in the Carolingian period.[28] Though the hints
to this effect in polyptychs are, simply by nature of the genre, hard to
pin down, the supposition might to an extent seem perfectly plausible: as
Part I has indicated, there was no lack of coercion in the Carolingian

[23] Cf. Patzold, *Episcopus*, pp. 37–45. [24] Barton, *Lordship*, pp. 2–3.
[25] Though for a critique of *Grundherrschaft*, see Kuchenbuch, 'Abschied'.
[26] Barthélemy, *Vendôme*, pp. 62–3 ; Guyotjeannin, 'Penuria'.
[27] For example E. Boshof, *Das Erzstift Trier und seine Stellung zu Königtum und Papsttum im ausgehenden 10. Jahrhundert: der Pontifikat des Theoderich* (Cologne, 1972): 'eine Intensivierung der Herrschaft des Grundherrn, eine räumlich und rechtliche Erweiterung seiner Anspruche und Befugnisse', p. 125.
[28] A point reiterated in Devroey, 'Seigneurs': 'la nouveauté de certains droits ou revenues commes les redevances militaires, la garde ou les cadeaux apportés aux assemblées judiciaires est sans doute en partie au moins un artifice documentaire', p. 269: in other words, they were not part of the polyptychs' concern. Barton, *Lordship*, takes this further, arguing that '*vicaria*, tolls, the ban, military service, tallage, and so forth . . . were ancient components of traditional rural lordship', p. 143. See, however, Champion, *Moulins*, for a contrary position, pp. 84–5.

countryside.[29] We can indeed safely assume 'a loose and unsystematic package of judicial, financial and the occasional labour obligations' was involved in aristocratic property-holding of the early Middle Ages.[30] And insofar as we can see inside village communities in the mid eleventh century, they seem fairly similar to those of the ninth century. For example, the Lotharingian 'One-Ox' (*Unibos*), a story about the comic adventures of a poor farmer which can be dated to approximately this period, reveals a local community predictably oriented around structures of aristocratic control, with peasants at the mercy of the lord's officials, and with only their native cunning to defend themselves and improve their lot. As in the ninth century, the actual lord of the settlement is surprisingly distant from the local reality.[31]

This 'continuist' point of view, denying that there was any structural difference between Carolingian estate-management and later lordship, and positing that the Carolingian manor was already a *seigneurie*, is now the dominant one.[32] Yet for all that it appears persuasive, it, too, suffers from nagging difficulties. Quite apart from the problem of timing which this approach resolves no better than the previous, the idea that *bannum* was a product of diplomatic revelation, not social revolution, raises quite serious methodological problems. It implies that historians can bypass their sources to access directly some hidden underlying reality, and it implies a distinction between concepts and words that surely fails to do justice to the complexities of this relation, much studied by historians elsewhere, for example in the field of conceptual history.[33] It does not entirely work at an empirical level, either. In fact, the imposition of 'customs' was not only something that churchmen accused secular men of, since sometimes churches themselves made these claims in the face of secular resistance.[34] References to these donations of bannal rights do not moreover make an appearance just in eleventh- and twelfth-century charters, they appear in contemporary

---

[29] The Prüm polyptych has a single, isolated reference to mainmorte: 'Si quis obierit, optimum quod habuerit, seniori datur' (*Prümer Urbar*, ed. Schwab, ch. 55 on Iversheim, p. 219). Caesarius's thirteenth-century gloss expanded this to all holdings. See Kuchenbuch, *Bäuerliche*, p. 173.

[30] Barton, *Lordship*, p. 73. On p. 123, he looks up 'exactio' in the index of Tessier's edition of the charters of Charles the Bald, and concludes: 'Practice similar to that ascribed to the post-millennial transformation had thus undoubtedly been occurring much earlier than 1000.' Cf. references to 'unjust customs' in the Council of Beauvais of 845 (*MGH Capit.* vol. II, p. 388).

[31] *Unibos*, ed. T. Klein, 'Versus de Unibove', *Studi medievali* 32 (1991), 843–86.

[32] Cf. Bruand, 'La villa carolingienne'; though see the recent critique of Sassier, 'Gesta', in *Auctoritas*.

[33] R. Koselleck is the most influential proponent of so-called *Begriffgeschichte*: see his *The practice of conceptual history* (Stanford, 2002). See p. 79, n. 2 for Richter, *History*.

[34] An excellent example is *DPhilip*. no. 159, for Compiègne.

narrative sources too.[35] If the concept of *bannum* in this sense merely better revealed already-existing conditions, what had prevented earlier narratives, presumably unconstrained by the conventions of diplomatic, from articulating it or some equivalent?

There is also a second, still more fundamental, problem with the proposition that the emergence of bannal terminology was predominantly produced by greater diplomatic freedom of expression. It is true that there are few signs of resistance to the kinds of claims labelled as bannal by those over whom they were exercised, or at least that these were not perceptibly more intense than resistance to domination had been in earlier periods.[36] But that does not mean that these bannal rights were uncontested by others who exercised rival authority in a particular area. In fact, on certain occasions, the rights or claims described with bannal terminology became the substance of conflict and debate. Such disputes cannot be paralleled in Carolingian evidence, and this suggests that there was a change in content as well as form. The best way of showing this, and also of getting a sense of what *bannum* might have meant, is to turn to three case studies. These all come from the first half of the twelfth century, when the evidence becomes denser, but still can perhaps be trusted to shed some light on somewhat earlier conditions.

Arguing over bannum: *three case studies*

The first example is a charter of 1130 that records a dispute between the monastery of St-Rémi and the cathedral of Rheims.[37] St-Rémi's abbot,

---

[35] E.g. *Chronicon sancti Huberti Andaginensis ('Cantatorium')*, ed. L. Bethmann and W. Wattenbach, *MGH SS*, vol. VII (Hanover, 1848), pp. 565–630 (written around 1100), e.g. p. 572 and 582; *Gesta episcoporum Virdunensium*, p. 45 (mid eleventh century); *Historia Mosomensis*, bk I, ch. 4, p. 165 (early eleventh century); and Laurentius, *Gesta*, p. 495 (mid twelfth century). It may conversely be noted here that some of the Carolingian charters to which Barton, *Lordship*, makes appeal are not of unimpeachable authority: for example, the charter of Charles the Bald, to which he refers on p. 132, n. 91, survives only in an early modern transcription of a lost cartulary, and its editor drew attention to the 'caractère anormal de certains expressions', including that to which Barton refers. Others, cited on p. 132, n. 92, do not support his interpretation. For example, *DCB* no. 130 indeed mentions *exactiones* – but the exaction in question is a royal one, the obligation to help maintain the royal palace at Aachen; while in *DCB* no. 170, the king does not remove an exaction but in fact concedes it (a bridge toll, in fact), so the *exactio* here is not really 'problematic'.

[36] A dispute in 1067 at Viry possibly relates to new emphasis on bannal rights: see M. Zerner, 'Note sur la seigneurie banale: à propos de la révolte des serfs de Viry', in *Histoire et société, mélanges offerts à Georges Duby, vol. II, Le tenancier, le fidèle et le citoyen* (Aix-en-Provence, 1992), pp. 49–58. Cf. *UBMR* no. 332.

[37] The document is edited only in *Veterum scriptorum et monumentorum historicorum, dogmaticorum, moralium; amplissima collectio*, ed. E. Martène and U. Durand (Paris, 1724–33), vol. II, col. 625–6, on the basis of a manuscript now in Arras (Arras Médiathèque MS 964). The date of the manuscript (s. XIII^in) excludes the possibility of early modern forgery.

Odo, claimed exclusive control of certain rights on behalf of the monastery over the village of Vrilly.[38] The Archbishop of Rheims, Rainald II, commissioned an enquiry, interrogating the elderly archiepiscopal officers (*ministeriales*) who had been alive in the time of Archbishop Rainald I. They helpfully confirmed that the rights in question had always been exercised by the archbishop. Indeed, in the *placitum* which followed, they argued that this had been the case for 300 years, seeking to prove this point by bringing out a recent (now lost) charter of Pope Calixtus II. Interesting for its combination of oral testimony with written charters, it is the rights in question that make the Vrilly charter important for our purposes. No one disputed that St-Rémi owned the land of the village. What was at stake was something else: the question of who owned the village's *bannum* ('cuius deberet esse bannus ille').[39]

A second example, from just east of the Meuse, offers both clarification and complication of the issues raised by the Vrilly charter. An agreement in 1142 was brokered by Matthew, the young Duke of Upper Lotharingia, to settle a dispute between the two institutions of St-Mihiel and St-Pierre-aux-Nonnains.[40] Two brothers had at some uncertain date, but probably in the early twelfth century, left property to St-Mihiel, consisting of whatever land (*terra*) they had at the village of Vandières. Their relatives, however, contested that donation. The issue was taken to St-Pierre-aux-Nonnain's court in Metz, and the court judged that St-Mihiel might indeed take the 'investiture of the legacy', but on condition that the 'customs' were respected with regard to the *bannum* of Vandières. However, a little later the agents of Vandières, representing St-Pierre, tried to seize the land. The duke resolved the issue in his own court. He judged that St-Mihiel had satisfactorily fulfilled its obligations regarding the 'customs of the land and of the *bannum*', and was not to be further molested by the *possessor* of Vandières.

The key to understanding this rather complicated dispute is to appreciate that there were two different levels of rights in Vandières. St-Pierre claimed an overarching control over the village, a control confusingly labelled as both the *fundus* and the *bannum*. Equivalent to the right disputed between Rheims and St-Rémi in the instance above, this control gave it the right to administer justice in Vandières, hence the appeal to its court, and hence the

---

[38] The charter is not mentioned in J. F. Lemarignier, ed., *Gallia monastica* (Paris, 1974); however the village in question is almost certainly Vrilly (Marne), close to Rheims.

[39] Not least as shown by a row of charters: see Lemarignier, ed., *Gallia monastica*, p. 59, for a list of St-Rémi's charters confirming its rights at Vrilly, before and after 1130.

[40] *Chronique et chartes*, ed. Lesort, no. 89. A. Gillen, *Saint-Mihiel im hohen und späten Mittelalter: Studien zu Abtei, Stadt und Landesherrschaft im Westen des Reiches* (Trier, 2003) mentions St-Mihiel's lands here at p. 179, n. 41 but does not discuss the dispute.

appearance of its agents there. Meanwhile St-Mihiel claimed the right to own the land that had been given to it. So long as it paid what was owed from that land to whoever controlled the *bannum*, that right was guaranteed by the structures of public control, in this case the duke. In other words, there was a distinction between the 'possessor' of Vandières, whose power was one of *bannum*, and the actual landowners, in this case either St-Mihiel or the donors' relatives, depending on one's point of view. The duke confirmed that judicial power over the village, that is the *bannum*, was separate from ownership of the land; these existed in parallel, and one might change hands without affecting the other. *Both* were equally forms of property, and – the real point of the judgement – holding the *bannum* over someone was not directly reducible to exercising active political dominance over them. St-Mihiel was not subordinated to St-Pierre-aux-Nonnains with respect to the village; each had their own property rights, of different sorts, which were to be mutually respected.

A third charter comes from the archives of the monastery of Gorze. Ostensibly recording a donation of Bishop Chrodegang in the eighth century, this charter describes Gorze's rights over four properties towards the Rhine, Petershain, Flamersheim, Isenburg and the unidentified *Dagolbesheim*. Particularly significant is its description of Flamersheim (Nordrhein-Westphalia). As well as giving details of mortmain, called here *herdocso*, Bishop Chrodegang is made to declare that 'since we gave [to Gorze] the *villa* with all the *bannum*, whosoever infringes this *bannum* … shall pay five shillings to the *curtis* and thirty pence to the advocate. If he does not want to pay, he shall be placed in custody'.[41] A glance at other eighth-century charters from Gorze and elsewhere make it obvious that the charter, which survived only in Gorze's cartulary, has been heavily interpolated. The aim of this interpolation was evidently not simply to guarantee Gorze's control over the lands in question, but to guarantee a certain kind of control. It would seem that the purpose of the fabrication was precisely to introduce these glaringly anachronistic comments about *bannum*. The date at which this took place cannot be deduced from the text, but the cartulary in which it was preserved (unfortunately destroyed in 1942), which dated to the twelfth century, at least provides a broad *terminus ante quem* for this textual alteration.

All these examples can be paralleled: from other charters we learn about the village at Evergnicourt (Aisne), where St-Hubert owned the *fundus*, but someone else the *bannum*, or about a dispute at St-Lumier (Marne),

---

[41] *Cartulaire*, ed. d'Herbomez, no. 11: 'Et quia villam cum toto banno tradimus, quicumque bannum fregerit … persolvat ad curtem V solidos et advocato xxx denarios; si persolvere noluerit, in cyppum mittatur'.

where St-Pierre-aux-Monts of Châlons's rights of ownership were uncontested, but where a certain Dudo claimed the right to impose 'certain exactions'.[42] What these three texts do particularly well, however, is reveal the poverty of approaches which insist on stressing the importance of charter diplomatic, because they prove that the change was not simply one of form. In other words, the institutions that produced them, located across the area between Marne and Moselle, were not just using a new terminology. Rather, that terminology, or better, what it represented, lay at the heart of the reasons for which these texts were put together. To put it slightly differently, the *bannum* in question was not just an addition to the charters, or a new way of phrasing an old idea, it was the very object of the disputes which the charters explicitly or tacitly recorded.

THE REIFICATION OF POLITICAL POWER

If arguments depicting the emergence of bannal terminology as the usurpation of royal authority and as a relatively inconsequential change in forms of charter redaction are both inadequate, as the above has attempted to demonstrate, we need to develop an alternative explanatory framework. Taking a step back, it is apparent that such a framework would have to engage with more than just bannal terminology narrowly defined, which was in truth just one part of a much broader development. It would have to take into consideration a whole raft of associated words that spring into the charters and other sources from, predictably enough, the middle eleventh century onwards, once forgeries have been filtered out.

Justice, constraint, customs and other synonyms

These terms included *centena, advocatio, districtus, consuetudo, vicecomitatus* and *justicia*. Doubtless the precise meanings of these individual words varied, and perhaps changed from specific text to text, at least in nuance. There are indications for regional preferences in terminology, too, which may have some significance. Lotharingian charters, for example, tended to use *bannum* more than did *champenois* ones, in which *justicia* and *consuetudo* were more common.[43] Yet though intriguing, differences of this kind are from one perspective unimportant. What matters is that all these terms,

---

[42] *Miracula Huberti*, bk II, col. 827 – undated but probably late eleventh century; AD Marne, H 646 (*c.* 1125). Another one would be *Chronicon S. Huberti*, ch. 16, p. 576, concerning exactions at Givet, which the *antiquiores et meliores* swore had been invented.

[43] Cf. Bur, *Formation*, pp. 332–40.

including here *bannum*, were labels for sets of rights, and specifically, rights pertaining to justice and jurisdiction, that could be, and were, distinguished from ownership of the land.

This is shown by disputes over them, in cases analogous to those discussed above about *bannum*, in which these words, and what they represented, formed the main subject of contestation, suggesting that we are not dealing with a purely textual issue, but rather one with quite practical implications. For example, one particularly interesting cache of texts concern the ownership of the *vicecomitatus* at the village of Trigny, near Rheims, from the mid twelfth century. The monastery of St-Thierry (Rheims) acquired the rights of *vicecomitatus* there, and carefully preserved the charters produced in the course of disputes between rival claimants, heirs, of varying statuses, of the original donors, from the 1140s through to the 1190s.[44] It is also shown by texts recording the transfer of similar rights, but not the land over which they were exercised.[45] We are, in other words, dealing with what are effectively synonyms (sometimes that is explicitly stated by our sources), used to label the kind of authority that permitted extractions of various sorts to be made – extractions such as talliage, a term that first appears in the documentation from the later eleventh century, and innumerable other 'customs'.[46]

As already suggested, it may be that the practices which *bannum* and these other words were used to describe or to justify were not in themselves new. It is likely that Carolingian lords had on occasion, or even frequently, capitalised on their status to extort surpluses from their neighbours and subordinates, as Chapter 2 showed, and without requiring usurped or delegated rights of royal *bannum*. This is really beside the point. What this vocabulary demonstrates is the emergence of a new perception of these practices and claims, a new conceptual field through which relations of domination could be articulated.[47] Age-old informal powers of more or less ad hoc coercion which had long existed in practice were now put on a formal footing, and became, moreover, the basis of power in the locality, without the need for any connection with the royal court.[48] In fact, what these texts document is how that aristocratic domination had itself become

---

[44] Some of these are preserved as the original, in AD Marne, H 113; the cartulary of St-Thierry (Rheims, Bibliothèque Municipale, MS 85) has the rest. The charters are enrolled in *Gallia monastica*.

[45] Molesme's acquisition of judicial rights at Grancey from the late eleventh century is a good example: *Cartulaires*, ed. Laurent, vol. i, nos. 15, 16, 68, 204, 206, 209 and 210; cf. vol. i, no. 121 for Stigny.

[46] Early customs: *Histoire*, ed. Calmet, vol. v, col. 181 (1132: St-Dié); *Metropolis*, ed. Marlot, vol. ii, col. 185 (1094); *Recueil*, ed. Demouy, vol. ii, no. 205 (1127 Vitry). Other customs include *hospitalitas* ('quam vulgo herbergariam vocant': *Cartulaires*, ed. Laurent, vol. i, no. 207). A classic case of *consuetudines* can be found in *Cartulaire*, ed. Pelicier, no. 30. *Rheinisches Urkundenbuch*, ed. Wisplinghoff, vol. ii, no. 288: 'iusticia, quae dicitur bann'.

[47] Cf. Lot, 'La vicaria et le vicarius', *Nouvelle Revue historique de droit français et étranger* 17 (1893), 281–301.

[48] Cf. Innes, *State*, p. 246.

an object of property. In the three charters discussed in detail above, and in dozens of others too, domination of a locality was discussed as if it were itself something that was owned: reified 'political' power. The game was no longer, if it had ever been, to turn property into power, it was now about turning power into property.

Arguments for continuity, that the *seigneurie banale* had in some sense 'always been there', clearly fail to do justice to this far-reaching transformation. However, we cannot simply fall back upon older explanatory schemata that identify the rise of bannal lordship either with the crisis of older practices of property, or as a response to that crisis. Both presuppose a rather eirenic view of Carolingian property which is hard to sustain. Chapter 2 argued that Carolingian property relations were not quite as uncontested and stable as they might seem, and that aristocratic estate-management was more akin to a church immunity, or a royal fisc, than to a single-layered exclusionary notion of property which springs to mind in the modern post-Smithian world. In fact, the Carolingian elite had neither *seigneurie foncière* nor *seigneurie banale*. They had diverse, context-dependent forms of local domination whose representation in the formulaic language of charters was not so much inaccurate as aspirational.

These new disputes over, and transactions in, jurisdiction are plausibly, then, not an assault on a pristine and hitherto untroubled practice of property ownership. Quite the reverse, they are part of the emergence of something far more like what we would recognise as property ownership.[49] The ownership of land was gradually differentiated from the exercise of a loosely conceived domination, meaning that both could be more readily treated as elements of transferable property – not straightforwardly transferable, of course, as countless disputes show, but nevertheless, transfers were now able to take place.[50] From the undifferentiated and rather diffuse social domination of the ninth century, there had emerged in the course of the eleventh century two overlapping, but nevertheless essentially distinct, property regimes: ownership of land and ownership of judicial rights over that land, the latter not confined to those holding formal office.[51] The emergence of terminologies of bannal

---

[49] Cf. Congost, 'Property rights'; compare also the interesting comments of B. van Bavel, *Markets and manors: economy and society in the Low Countries, 500–1600* (Oxford, 2010), pp. 51–2 and p. 166.

[50] On the difficulties of transferring land, see S. White, *Custom, kinship and gifts to the saints: the laudatio parentum in western France, 1050–1150* (London, 1988); and for an example of one allodial transfer being challenged by two successive generations, see *Metropolis*, ed. Marlot, vol. II, col. 228 (1102).

[51] Land might be donated *cum vicecomitatu* or even *cum comitatu* by people who were not themselves counts or viscounts: e.g., *Historia Mosomensis, Appendix*, no. 3; Rheims, 'cum vicecomitatu et banno' (Artem no. 1903, 1119); Chamouille ('Cartulaire de Saint-Vincent de Laon', ed. R. Poupardin, *Mémoires de la Société de l'Histoire de Paris et de l'Ile-de-France* 29 (1902), 173–267, no. 26, c.1140).

lordship show that something approximating to our idea of *seigneurie banale* began to develop simultaneously with something more like *seigneurie foncière*, like the granges associated with Cistercian foundations, representing a far more homogenised 'ownership' of tracts of land.[52] One could be, and sometimes was, converted into the other, but nevertheless, a distinction could be made.[53]

This sharper conception of social domination that the emergence of bannal rights represents can be seen, with hindsight, to have been foreshadowed in some of the texts discussed in the previous chapter, as charters became increasingly concerned with the dues that landownership entailed. Later, of course, these rights themselves would undergo almost endlessly proliferating subdivision, into variants of high and low justice familiar to historians of the central and later Middle Ages, and evident in both franchises and *Weistümer*, documents representing two different ways in which these rights were acknowledged and confirmed. We will turn to differences in how these rights were distributed in Chapter 8. But in spite of the bewildering complexities and subtleties involved, and a few important differences too, this was largely variation on a common theme.[54] The franchises that spread so widely in the later twelfth century in this region, adumbrated by texts from the early twelfth, and the *Weistümer*, whose earliest examples are in fact Lotharingian, certainly represent different patterns of domination, but they all fundamentally depend on the conception of judicial powers as rights which could be transferred or retained, like any other item of property.[55]

The establishment of local lordship

Associated with this crystallisation of elite domination, and its conversion into exchangeable units, is the emergence of a new set of relations at the very local level. One aspect of this is what might be called the micro-management of settlement patterns. Villages as such, as human communities, had – in spite of rather forced interpretations to the contrary – clearly existed in the ninth century. The Carolingian monk Ratramnus of Corbie had even considered living in villages to be a defining mark of what it was to

[52] Cf. I. Alfonso, 'Cistercians and feudalism', *Past and Present* 133 (1990), 3–30.
[53] *Histoire*, ed. Tabouillot, vol. III (1075), preuves, pp. 97–8, for St-Arnulf.
[54] On the franchises, see the essays collected in M. Bourin and M. Martinez Sopeña, eds., *Pour une anthropologie du prélèvement seigneurial dans les campagnes de l'Occident médiéval (XIe–XIVe siècles): réalités et représentations* (Paris, 2004), particularly those by Cursente, Beck and Morsel.
[55] Specifically, the advocacy regulations at Echternach in the 1090s. In general, see J. Morsel, 'Le prélèvement seigneurial est-il soluble dans les Weistümer? Appréhensions franconiennes (1200–1400)', in Bourin and Martinez Sopeña, eds., *Pour une anthropologie . . . :realités*, pp. 155–210.

be human.[56] But if anyone was thought to have created villages in the ninth century, it was saints, and there is no specific evidence from this region for lords building, constructing or moving settlements.[57] By contrast, from the late eleventh century, precisely that specific evidence is available; indeed, it may be that this sort of intervention played a role in the shift in settlement patterns in the twelfth century mentioned above.[58]

Another, and more everyday, aspect of the same shift is the far greater visibility of flourishing, locally rooted elites: a kind of gentry. People at this level of society, at the edges of the elite, have hardly been discussed hitherto in this book, for the good reason that before the eleventh century, they are scarcely visible except as retinues of the high-level aristocracy.[59] Doubtless the retainers (often called *milites*) of Carolingian and tenth-century bishops and lords had had local bases; and doubtless too, there had been families of free landowners who had avoided absorption into patronage relations, who had maintained a reasonable degree of prosperity, and who had not culti-vated their own fields, though this was exactly the level of society that kings were concerned was under pressure in the ninth century.[60] This kind of precarious, de facto local prestige that characterised the people who took their place at the top of local witness lists was put on a new footing as bannal rights emerged, for these rights could be owned by anyone.

It is therefore not really a surprise that it is in around 1100 that lords of individual villages, or of clusters of villages, begin to appear, albeit indis-tinctly, in the sources of this region.[61] In other words, this was not simply a question of knights moving out of castle garrisons, or of ministerials escaping the courts of their lords (*Seigneurialisierung*). It is also, in fact primarily, a product of better defined and by that token more easily delegated or transferred 'micro-dominance'.[62] Whilst rural settlements

---

[56] Cited by P. Depreux, *Les sociétés occidentales du milieu du VIe à la fin du IXe siècle* (Rennes, 2002), pp. 15–16. Ratramnus uses the word *villae*, but here it is difficult to translate it other than as 'villages'.

[57] For example, *HRE*, bk 1, ch. 20, p. 108, on St Remigius's establishment of a new settlement: 'incolasque de vicina episcopii villa nomine Berna dudum sibi a Francis [note the plural] data in eas transferens ibidem manere disposuit'.

[58] For example, the 1063 charter of Theobald I Count of Champagne (III of Blois), ed. in d'Arbois de Jubainville, *Histoire des ducs et des comtes de Champagne*, 6 vols. (Paris, 1859), vol. 1, p. 487, concerning a new village intriguingly called *villa Caroli* (Charleville); cf. *Histoire de l'abbaye et du village d'Hautvillers*, ed. J. Manceaux (Épernay, 1880), pp. 391 for Villeneuve (1126).

[59] Cf. L. Feller, 'Les hiérarchies'.   [60] Le Jan, '*Pauperes*'.

[61] Their fortified residences, often moated (so-called *maisons forts*) are visible from the thirteenth century: see C. Coulson, 'Castellation in the county of Champagne in the thirteenth century', *Château-Gaillard*, 9–10 (1982), 347–64. They are mentioned in the *L'ancien coutumier de Champagne*, ed. P. Portejoie (Poitiers, 1956), e.g. at pp. 142–3.

[62] C. Higounet, *La grange de Vaulerent: structure et exploitation d'un terroir cistercien de la plaine de France* (Paris, 1965); Morsel, 'Prélèvement'. For a concrete case-study, see J. Coudert, 'L'évêque de Metz et ses paysans: l'exemple du ban de Rémilly vers 1300 d'après le rapport des droits', *Les cahiers lorrains* 84 (2002), 313–38.

had doubtless always had more pre-eminent figures – the families responsible for building the local churches discussed in Chapter 1 – it was only from the late eleventh century that this pre-eminence was translated into something more substantial, making these figures into veritable lords, irrespective of pre-existing landownership claims.[63]

Key evidence in the early phase is the use of 'surnames' (more properly, toponyms) in documentary and other kinds of evidence, and it is no coincidence that this takes place at roughly the same time as the new terminologies of domination take root.[64] These figures were consolidating local networks of domination secure enough to earn them toponyms, which in turn permit their family histories to be traced forward into the twelfth century and beyond.[65] In a generation or two, these lords would also begin to be entitled *domini*, an appellation that increasingly separated them from those they commanded.[66] It was on the generosity of this minor elite, not new in itself but disposing of newly clarified rights, that the wealth of Cistercian monasteries, such as Preuilly, St-Benoit-aux-Woevre, Orval and in fact Citeaux itself, was based. The negotiations that established institutions were required to have with these new brokers are recorded with perfect clarity in a number of texts, such as Abbot Suger of St-Denis's *De Administratione*, sections of which concern land in the Champagne region.[67]

Of course there were differences between areas in the West Frankish kingdom and those in the *Reich*, differences which ought not to be overlooked, and which go beyond mere terminological preference. These will be examined in closer detail in the final chapter, but for the moment it can

---

[63] M. Parisse, *Noblesse et chevalerie en Lorraine médiévale – les familles nobles du 11ᵉ au 13ᵉ siècles* (Nancy, 1982), pp. 45–82: see particularly pp. 50–63.

[64] Surnames appear from the mid eleventh century onwards: for example, Artem no. 70 (Rheims, 1103), Artem no. 333 (Metz, 1065), and 'Güterroller', ed. Müller, p. 129 (Mettlach, 1095). There are occasional earlier references, but those prior to 1000 are *ipso facto* suspicious. Narrative sources corroborate a late eleventh-century focus (e.g., the *Translatio et miracula sancti Clementis* (ed. J. Dieterich, *MGH SS*, vol. xxx:ii (Hanover, 1934), p. 908, where a man possessed by a spirit calls on Albert of Briey and Widric of Waleicourt, both known from other sources.

[65] As done by T. Evergates, *Feudal society in the bailliage of Troyes under the counts of Champagne 1152–1284* (London 1976), in a detailed appendix, pp. 155–211: about half a dozen Champenois families can be traced in this way: most fell into the orbit of the Count of Champagne and saw their family properties become castellanies. A comparable list of Trier region surnames and families is provided by J. Bast, *Die Ministerialität des Erzstifts Trier*, Trierisches Archiv Erganzungsheft 17 (Trier 1918) (mostly from *c.*1100); cf. also J. Florange, *Histoire des seigneurs et comtes de Sierk* (Paris, 1895).

[66] The earliest examples of *domini* titles I have found come from the *Liber memorialis* of Remiremont, e.g. f. 26v, VI, from around the late eleventh or early twelfth century. For the names, see R. le Jan, 'Entre maîtres et dépendants: réflexions sur la famille paysanne en Lotharingie, aux Xᵉ et XIᵉ siècles', in E. Mornet, ed., *Campagnes médiévales. L'homme et son espace: études offertes à Robert Fossier* (Paris, 1995), pp. 277–96.

[67] Suger, *De administratione*, in F. Gasparri, ed. and tr., *Oeuvres – Suger*, 2 vols. (Paris, 1996), vol. i, p. 104, on Mareuil.

be noted that the rights labelled with bannal terminology seem to have been more concentrated towards the higher echelons of society east of the Meuse, and to have dispersed more widely to the west. Yet this is primarily a question of different distributions of the same thing, a quantitative, not a qualitative change. If this has not been properly recognised, that is partly because of the historiographical legacies of different traditions of scholarship: the traditional assumption in French scholarship that *seigneurie foncière* can be taken for granted in the early Middle Ages, and the blunt instrument of *Grundherrschaft* in German scholarship, which makes it impossible to analyse the kinds of change discussed above. On both sides of the Meuse, domination was henceforth primarily a matter of owning rights over people, whether this was termed *bannum* or not; and, perhaps more to the point, irrespective of the formal possession of the land itself. Even if these rights were not alienated, they were still very carefully listed.[68]

MATERIAL CONSEQUENCES

The rise of *bannum* was not actually a shift from power over land to power over people. One can see why that interpretation might seem appealing, but at bottom, control over 'land' is always, and intrinsically, power over people. Rather, instead of using the idiom of landed property as the primary means, alongside court-based ideas of office, of expressing durable rights over people – the socio-economic pre-eminence of agriculture naturally lending itself to this use – people in the eleventh century separated out a new layer. Now, property was fabricated directly out of social relations, anchored not in Roman-inspired notions of owning land, but in characteristically medieval ideas of jurisdiction. Social hierarchies were so fixed, so classified, so stable and so self-evidently real, that they were treated as if they actually were separate from the people who made them. Social relations were disembedded, becoming, consciously, the subject of exchanges and interactions: society began to perform operations on itself.

These kinds of changes may appear abstract. Even in cases where rights of *bannum* or *justitia* were being contested, it might seem that we are merely observing arguments over words. Yet it is in fact easy to identify eminently concrete consequences of the new social and political regime. For example, a mid-twelfth-century charter from Gorze recorded what happened when villagers decided to build their own ovens in spite of the monastery's claim to own a bannal oven, in other words one which had a local monopoly. An inquiry was held, and the outcome was both predictable and down-to-earth:

---

[68] St-Quirin evidence (1137): *Constitutions*, ed. Hanauer, pp. 90–2.

'Since many of the men of St-Gorgon confessed that they had unjustly built their own ovens in this village, these very builders destroyed them, in our presence, as justice demanded.'[69] Other similar examples could be given, for instance from St-Martin-des-Champs, showing how real mills and ovens really were demolished in the name of bannal power.[70] In addition to this kind of keyhole approach, there are two perspectives that offer the opportunity to grasp something more of the systematic nature of the changes at stake.

Encastellation

The first of these is to turn our attention to the most visible manifestation of the new order, the castle. Dates are difficult to establish with precision, thanks in part to difficulty in dating pottery, usually the surest diagnostic, from the post-Carolingian period.[71] Setting aside the fortifications used in the struggles of the late ninth and early tenth centuries, few of which can be shown to have been residential and most of which were used in relation to court-centred politics, a number of castles in this region can be tentatively dated to the later tenth or earlier eleventh century, associated with the consolidation of political authority discussed in Chapter 5. However, the surge in castle construction seems really to date from the mid eleventh century, as the lands on both sides of the Meuse were covered by a castellated network, whose well-studied density steadily increased into and beyond the twelfth century, in association with the consolidation of political authority at still lower levels, as discussed above.[72] The political impact can be registered by the growing interest taken in castles by local bishops.[73] By the year 1100, any lordship with any pretension to importance needed to control more than one: hence the Count of Bar held

---

[69] *Cartulaire*, ed. d'Herbomez, no. 183, dated 1152x1156. 'Et quoniam plerique de hominibus s' Gorgonii in predicta villa furnos proprios iniuste construxisse confessi sunt, ipsi edificatores in presentia nostra, dicante iuditio, eos destruxerunt'. No. 185, from the 1160s, makes further specific reference to the 'furnes bannales'.

[70] St-Martin: *Recueil*, ed. Depoin, no. 175 (1120).   [71] Böhme, 'Burgen der Salierzeit', p. 8.

[72] Useful catalogues are provided by E. Beck, 'Hochmittelalterliche Burganlagen in Trierer Land', *Trierer Zeitschrift* 69/70 (2006–7), 233–96; Böhme, 'Burgen'; M. Bur, *Vestiges d'habitat seigneurial fortifié*, vols. I to IV; and J. Metzler and J. Zimmer, 'Zum Burgenbau in Luxemburg in vorsalischer und salischer Zeit', in Böhme, ed., *Burgen*, vol. I, pp. 311–36. Already in the mid eleventh century, Anselm of St-Rémi's *Historia dedicationis* talks about the political situation in France as being dominated by castles (p. 218).

[73] Poppo was the first Archbishop of Trier (1016–47) to launch anti-castle campaigns (*Gesta episcoporum Treverorum*, pp. 172–3, around the same time as Bishop Adalbero II of Metz (*Vita Adalberonis* II, p. 665). Archbishops of Rheims had begun similar campaigns around sixty years previously (*Historia Mosomensis*, p. 153, setting aside the civil wars reported by Flodoard). For Bishop Udo of Toul's campaigns against castles, see G. Bönnen, *Die Bischofsstadt Toul und ihr Umland während des hohen und späten Mittelalters* (Trier, 1995), pp. 51–2. The account of Bishop Stephen of Metz (1120–63) in the *Gesta episcoporum Mettensium (continuatio)*, ed. G. Waitz, *MGH SS*, vol. X (Hanover, 1852), pp. 531–51, lists no fewer than nineteen castles, pp. 544–5.

Amance, Briey and Mousson, in addition to his comital residence. Even relatively small-scale lords controlled a family castle, many of which are archaeologically detectable: examples from the early twelfth century could include the lords (*Edelherren*) of Kerpen in the Saarland, of Chappes near Troyes, of Tincry near Metz, or of Autry near Rheims.[74]

Though there was doubtless an element of an arms race to their proliferation, it has long been recognised that these fortifications were not straightforwardly defensive in function. As a bishop of Châlons lamented in the 1030s, they were being built 'for the depredation of the people, and for the overthrow of the church, not its protection'.[75] Contemporaries regarded these buildings, and particularly the more impressive ones, with a mixture of horror and awe.[76] Yet though these castles took a quite different form – for example, built on mottes – they were not self-evidently the product of new technologies: up until the twelfth century, there was very little in these constructions which would have been beyond Carolingian technical capacities. Rather, the emergence of castles as central to the political scene, and the definite increase in the scale of their construction, reflected a social and political dynamic not a technological one, though there were undoubtedly consequences for the development of skills and trade.[77] Increasingly it was the territories defined by these castles that organised social activity – indeed, it is this political role, not the technical details of construction, that distinguishes these castles from earlier fortifications in the region.[78]

The structural shift in politics in reaction to castles, and the reified political power they promoted and represented is marked by the moment when local bishops began to mount concerted campaigns against them, and when forgeries were made to strengthen churches' hands, both from the later eleventh century, though in the long term the only practical form of rivalry proved to be imitation.[79] It is not a coincidence that the kind of coalescences of authority represented by Odo II and Godfrey the Bearded

---

[74] Kerpen: E. Beck, 'Hochmittelalterliche Burgenlagen'; Böhme, 'Burgen'. Chappes: see Bur, *Vestiges d'habitat seigneurial fortifié*, vol. IV, pp. 39–41. Tincry: G. Giuliato, 'Les premiers châteaux dans le pays du sel en Lorraine (Xᵉ–XIIᵉ siècle)', *Château Gaillard* 16 (1992), 215–32. Autry: Bur, *Vestiges d'habitat seigneurial fortifié*, vol. I, pp. 21–3. Pierrepont: Bur, *Vestiges d'habitat seigneurial fortifié*, vol. II, pp. 97–9.

[75] *Cartulaire*, ed. Pelicier, no. 28.

[76] E.g. Alberic, *Chronicon*, on the castle of the counts of Are, p. 828.

[77] *La France romane au temps des premiers capétiens (987–1152)* (Paris, 2005), shows in exquisite detail the proliferation of skills in a range of areas in eleventh-century France: see below, p. 217, n. 81, for some of this handiwork.

[78] The Oriculus material is edited in F. Dolbeau, 'Un vol de reliques dans le diocèse de Reims au milieu du XIᵉ siècle', *Revue bénédictine* 91 (1981), 172–84. For earlier fortifications: *UBMR* nos. 158 and 166.

[79] For the lack of connection with settlement, see M. Bur, 'Châteaux et peuplement dans le nord et l'est de la France au Moyen Âge', in M. Bur, *Châteaux et peuplements en Europe occidentale* (Auch, 1980), pp. 75–92. Forgery: e.g. *UBMR* no. 9.

discussed in Chapter 4 were not precisely replicated in the next generation: the kind of political agglomerations these figures had created could
not be made in a castled society without the use of quite different
mechanisms.

To an extent, castles attest to the supersession of Carolingian modes of
political control. For example, the way in which a number of castles, such as
Warcq, Bray, Ramerupt and Lay acquired relics in the course of the tenth
century points to an effort to create new poles of legitimate authority that
deliberately set them apart from preceding formations.[80] The shift here was
not, however, one from a society based on kinship to one based on space, as
has recently been suggested, for Carolingian Europe had never been as
dominated by kinship as that model implies.[81] Rather, this spatialisation
reflected a more tightly understood notion of domination. In other words,
we need to see these castles as themselves the nodes of bannal power,
reflecting the new territorialisation which bannality, based on quite specific
rights over specific places, implied. After all, as far as can be seen – and
admittedly the evidence here is suggestive rather than conclusive – these
centres of the new economy were built upon the profits largely of judicial
rights, not landed property.

A superb illustration is provided by the uniquely well-documented
circumstances surrounding the construction of a castle by Hugh of
Montfélix at Vanault, land in Champagne owned by the Lotharingian
monastery of Gorze, around 1120. After a protracted dispute, which even
saw a largely fruitless appeal to the Pope, Gorze ended up keeping only
the rents of its estates alone, losing the jurisdictional revenues to Hugh.[82]
Other lords are recorded as having done much the same: for example,
Wido of Möeslains's castle on Montier-en-Der's lands at St-Dizier both
represented and catalysed the emergence of his *seigneurie*, at almost exactly
the same time as Hugh's.[83] These lordships had nothing to do with the
ownership of land. That does not mean they were necessarily short-lived,
however. Hugh's *seigneurie* had been constructed out of thin air, perhaps
in relation to comital interventions in the area, but it proved remarkably

---

[80] Cf. Chapter 5.
[81] J. Morsel, *L'aristocratie médiévale: la domination sociale en Occident (v^c–xv^c siècle)* (Paris, 2004),
   particularly at pp. 108–9; cf. H. Tanner, *Families, friends, and allies: Boulogne and politics in northern
   France and England, c.879–1160* (Leiden, 2004), for an exactly inverted argument.
[82] *Cartulaire*, ed. d'Herbomez, nos. 153 and 155. See also: M. Bur, 'Les possessions de Gorze en
   Champagne', in *Saint Chrodegang: communications présentées au Colloque tenu à Metz à l'occasion du
   douzietme centenaire de sa mort* (Metz, 1967), pp. 169–82; A. Renoux, 'Les mutations morphologiques et fonctionnelles de la basse-cour du chateau des comtes de Champagne à Montfélix (x^c–xiii^c
   siecle)', *Château-Gaillard* 21 (2004), 259–70.
[83] AD Haute Marne, 7 H 2, f. 35v–36r.

durable, as a bundle of higher-level rights, lasting well into the thirteenth century.

Relative revenues: the case of Mandray

Of course, not all lords were castellans, and we should be careful not to let castles alone, for all their significance, determine our understanding. A second approach, therefore, to gauging the concrete impact of the emergence of bannal lordship is to attempt to estimate something of the value of these new rights, particularly in comparison with the revenues deriving from straightforward landownership. In other words, the charters may mention rights of justice and various judicial customs; but how much were these really worth?

The importance of this question is obvious, but answering it is notoriously difficult.[84] A number of documents give the value of particular bannal rights, but that does not allow us to work out the value relative to the income generated from owning the land, which is the only way to ascertain its true significance. One or two promising texts that do account for both streams of revenue are on closer inspection difficult to put to direct use. For example, an account in the polyptych of Mettlach that is probably late tenth- or early eleventh-century lists the revenues owed to the advocate as well as those taken by the monastery from the estate of Roden (Saarland). However, quite apart from problems in dating the text, its calculations are given in kind, and working out the relative value of 176 eggs compared with a night's hay for a horse is an exercise fraught with peril.[85] For the most part, one has to wait until the later Middle Ages at the earliest to be able to compare local court records with estate records, and thereby to work out relative value.[86]

However, there is a unique and remarkable text from this region that does allow us to estimate relative values: a list of revenues from the holdings of St-Dié. It was attributed by its first (and to my knowledge only) editor, Christophe Pfister, to the late tenth or early eleventh century, but a more authoritative dating was provided by the doyen of Lorraine rural economic history, Charles-Edmond Perrin, who assigned it to the eleventh century, and probably to the middle or later part of that

---

[84] Cf. Duby, *Early Growth*, pp. 227–9.
[85] 'Güterrolle', ed. Müller, pp. 123–4. For the estate, which has an interesting history, see T. Raach, *Kloster Mettlach/Saar und sein Grundbesitz: Untersuchungen zur Frühgeschichte und zur Grundherrschaft der ehemaligen Benediktinerabtei im Mittalalter* (Mainz, 1974), pp. 113–18, with n. 95 on p. 115 discussing the advocate passage. *UBMR*, no. 287, is a similar case.
[86] Duby, *Rural economy*; cf. Feller, *Paysans*, pp. 156–8; C. Wickham, 'Defining the seigneurie since the war', in Bourin and Martinez Sopeña, eds., *Pour une anthropologie ... :realités*, pp. 19–35.

period.[87] Sadly, the list's unique manuscript was destroyed along with the Saint-Dié's municipal archive in 1944, which perhaps explains the lack of attention to it over the past few decades.[88]

Incomplete on a number of levels – it neglects, for example, to inform us of the physical size of the estates it describes – the St-Dié list's importance rests in the fact that, rather startlingly, it discusses revenues from the *placitum*, in other words judicial dues, alongside the *census terrae* and other miscellaneous dues that clearly derive from landownership. Of the half a dozen estates listed, the most detailed description is that for the estate at Mandray, detailed enough to allow us to perform comparative calculations of value.[89] From the aggregate 'ground rent', or *census terrae*, at Mandray, St-Dié received 100 shillings. To this was added commuted labour dues of 103 shillings, and 6 shillings for the use of woodland, making a total yearly revenue of 203 shillings arising from ownership of the land. In comparison, annual *placitum* payments at Mandray were 42 shillings, and an *extractus* payment, enigmatic but clearly associated with the *placitum* and plausibly identified as talliage, was 60. In addition, 6 shillings were owed for *taberna* payments, which probably derived from another bannal right.

Two further payments are difficult to categorise. Thirty-two shillings were owed for the *opificalis rei*, a due that has attracted hypotheses but not definitive explanation and 28 shillings *de summis*, which may be the income from churches in, and also perhaps around, Mandray. The precise balance between income from the land and income from jurisdiction over it depends, therefore, on what these revenues represented, and this is unfortunately impossible to determine. Further, one of the peculiarities of the St-Dié survey is that it only included fixed revenues and explicitly excluded variable income. There might, for example, have been additional ad hoc labour redemptions, but it is likely that the revenue raised from fines would have considerably outweighed these. Nevertheless, even without taking these incalculable dues into account, it is apparent that the jurisdictional control of this particular property was probably around half as valuable as owning it outright, in other words representing at least a third of the value of an estate, with the additional advantage that it might well have been easier to increase the revenues from jurisdiction than those from landownership. No wonder, then, that these bannal rights attracted so much attention.

[87] Perrin, *Recherches*, pp. 316–17; C. Pfister, 'Les revenues de la collegiale de Saint-Dié au xe siècle', *Annales de l'Est* 2 (1888), 515–17 and 3 (1889), 407.

[88] Personal communication with the archivist at St-Dié, 2010.

[89] Perrin, *Recherches*, offers a schematic breakdown on p. 320.

CONCLUSION

Contrary to Duby's imagination, or at least to how historians have interpreted Duby, the Carolingian *villa* might well have been glued together by 'lordship' rather than clear-cut property law; but that does not mean that it can be treated analytically as the same as later formations. If, that is, Carolingian peasants were subject to extortion and exaction beyond the payment of rent (if rent is even the right word), the key point is that these were still the immediate product of (profoundly unequal) social relations, to which objective classifications, particularly legal status, contributed without dominating. By contrast, in the late eleventh century, lords everywhere were busily working out whether they had the right to do this or not. From this point of view, *bannum*, as social power made manifest, was simply the most radical expression of a shift towards impersonal lordship.

From this perspective, we could say that the concept of property, as we understand it, was penetrating deeper into the roots of social interaction, which produced a differentiation of social authority. Constraining power was now a thing in itself: petrified social power, which could be passed on, not as office, but more plainly as property, a critically important development. It could incidentally be argued that equivalent processes of differentiation were taking place at approximately the same time within the church, whose bundling up of individual parish church revenues as *altaria* ought perhaps to be connected to the developments described here, instead of being segregated away in the arcana of Gratianic canon law.[90]

It is not clear that this differentiation amounted to a change in the means of production in the Marxist sense of the phrase. Indeed, these developments did not even necessarily change the 'balance of power', let alone the physical organisation of villages or field patterns. They merely signified a new means of collectively thinking about social relations. It might be supposed that the development was likely to be to the disadvantage of the lowest and the highest levels. The lowest were more deprived of a certain freedom of manoeuvre, and any system which formalised such disadvantageous relations was therefore likely to work against them. Later medieval evidence would suggest that sometimes, however, it was the rural community itself which benefited from this precipitation of rights. The *Weistümer* from the Moselle region, for instance, seem to demonstrate villages with a quite remarkable degree of autonomy, with many, if not

---

[90] See, though from a different perspective, Wood, *Proprietary church*, pp. 821–4; on the Lotharingian perspective, see W. Petke, 'Von der klösterlichen Eigenkirche zur Inkorporation in Lothringen und Nordfrankreich im 11. und 12. Jahrhundert', *Revue d'histoire ecclésiastique* 87 (1992), 34–72. Altar donations appear from the mid eleventh century: e.g. Artem no. 24.

most, rural communities collectively retaining, at least to a degree, elements of the higher levels of jurisdiction.[91] Nevertheless, the new system probably increased the efficiency of production, which is to say in this period, exploitation: a kind of bottom-up control was after all likely to be better suited to extracting resources from a relatively decentralised society, with knock-on effects on possibilities for exchange and economic growth in general terms.[92] Changes in organisation can, after all, be just as powerful an influence on patterns of production and trade as technological innovation, to the extent that these can even be separated.[93]

That these particular articulations are not to be found in Carolingian sources does not imply that they were without any connection to Carolingian processes. To explain the transition from one to the other, we do not need to take refuge in vague ideas of breakdown just because the process is hard to explain. Collapse and renewal are part of the modern myths of the Middle Ages. What lies behind this shift is far more complicated, and interesting, than a question of collapse. As Goffart noted already in 1966, though the point has seldom been developed, the earliest systematic thinking about property since the Roman period was in fact in the ninth century.[94] This was specifically in church circles, but historians have learned not to try to introduce radical distinctions between the church and the secular world. Pseudo-Isidore's definition of church property, shared by many other clerics (all from aristocratic families), points, portentously, to attempts to draw lines round things and to define. More broadly, the Carolingian rulers were fascinated by the exercise of power, sought to give it much closer definition and imposed new possibilities of categorisation upon it. Exactly this seeking to pin down a formerly nebulous series of unequal relations into something more concrete, a system, was the first step in the process towards a reified system.

It was surely from this concern to define, if not actually create, 'property', that the roots of bannal lordship grew. As with Schroedinger's cat, the act of inspecting social relations described in Chapter 3 in fact altered them – and

[91] M. Nikolay-Panter, *Entstehung und Entwicklung der Landgemeinde im Trierer Raum* (Bonn, 1976), pp. 78–89 and pp. 104–10. Cf. also *Recueil*, ed. Halkin, no. 142. A selection of these texts is now available in a recent edition, *Les rapports de droit de la Mosellane romane (XIIIᵉ-début du XVIIᵉ siècle)*, ed. J. Coudert (Paris, 2008).
[92] For an exploration of these issues, see M. Innes, 'Framing the Carolingian economy', *Journal of Agrarian Change* 9 (2009), 42–58.
[93] For the argument that they simply cannot, see Latour, *Reassembling*, pp. 63–86. On technology, see G. Comet, 'Technology and agricultural expansion in the Middle Ages: the example of France north of the Loire', in G. Astill and J. Langdon, eds., *Medieval farming and technology: the impact of agricultural change in Northwest Europe* (London, 1977), pp. 11–39, arguing against dramatic changes.
[94] W. Goffart, *The Le Mans forgeries* (Cambridge, Mass., 1966), aroused controversy over the evidence, but oddly little over his bold interpretation of Carolingian ideas of church property.

the dynamic continued past the end of the dynasty itself. Of course this was not a smooth process, at least as far as it was socially manifested: as I have said, the emergence of bannal lordship indicates a substantive change in concept and, though this is harder to see, the organisation of practice. However, it remained congruent with Carolingian processes. Perhaps the main reason why this connection between Carolingian reform and later processes of differentiation has not been proposed before is because the historiography, particularly of the later period, is so deeply soaked in ideas of the Carolingian failure, that continuities in Carolingian practice beyond 900, beyond the weak notion of 'legacy', have simply not been considered as a possibility.

However, there is a problem which has not yet been addressed. If the links with Carolingian dynamics, set out as continuing to unfold in the tenth century, are convincing, then what lay behind the relatively sudden step-change in the middle third of the eleventh century? One explanation may simply be that Carolingian-initiated processes of the definition of social power took time to work through, which would explain, too, why the same process seems to be happening at slightly different times across Western Europe. But a more satisfying answer would be to contextualise this development in the exercise of social domination with changes in the articulation of social relations operating at a different level, which were taking place at approximately the same time. That is the task of the next chapter.

Chapter 7

FIEFS, HOMAGE AND
THE 'INVESTITURE QUARREL'

The ring and staff mean something different,

They signify something else, which my text will now explain.

Hugo Metellus, *Certamen.*[1]

INTRODUCTION

The previous chapter discussed changes in the expression and form of relations between dominant and dominated in the lands between Marne and Moselle from the mid eleventh century into the early and mid twelfth. This chapter suggests that the shifts identified and discussed there can be paralleled and contextualised by changes affecting the articulation of relations within the elite itself, taking place at approximately the same time. These arguments concern issues traditionally associated with feudalism, and this chapter thereby enters a field made controversial by the work of Susan Reynolds, the impact of whose devastatingly well-aimed book, *Fiefs and vassals*, continues to reverberate well over a decade after publication.[2]

In her book, Reynolds treated the concept of feudalism as a shorthand for a particular social system based on the conditional allocation of land (fiefs) in exchange for military service (vassalage), a relationship thought to structure the entire social formation. She argued that the concept was unhelpful, partly because of historiographical confusion over the details of what it signified, but mostly because its essential assumptions were simply inaccurate. She suggested that, right across the period from the eighth to the twelfth centuries, most aristocrats would have considered that they owned their land as fully as possible; that there was no 'system' of differentiated landed property rights

---

[1] Hugo Metellus, *Certamen papae et regis*, ed. E. Dümmler, *MGH Libelli de lite* vol. III, pp. 714–19: 'anulus et baculus aliud signare videntur / Significant aliud, quod iam mea scripta loquentur', p. 715.
[2] Reynolds, *Fiefs*.

before academic lawyers made their presence felt, which north of the Alps was not before the late twelfth century at the earliest; and that the notion of feudalism surreptitiously filters out other crucial aspects of medieval society, notably concerning communities and so-called horizontal bonds. All these arguments related to fiefs; the other major component of feudalism, vassalage, she dismissed as barely worth discussing in view of what she considered wholly inadequate evidence. Reynolds's book was timely, superbly argued and deeply troubling for medieval historians, but only recently has the process of direct engagement with the kernel of her work begun.[3] As well as contextualising arguments presented in the previous chapter, this chapter attempts, on the basis primarily of material from Marne and Moselle, to contribute to this engagement.

FIEFS AND DEPENDENT PROPERTY

As just mentioned, Reynolds thought the idea of fiefs the strongest part of the concept of feudalism, understood in a non-Marxist sense, and devoted her energies to stripping away the accumulated historiographical residues that had built up around the topic. The result was, however, not always quite as clear-cut as might have been expected, due partly to the problems with the evidence, but partly, too, to the assumptions that Reynolds herself brought to that evidence, though it should of course be noted that these assumptions have the merit of being carefully, if not always consistently, signalled. It is perhaps as well, then, to start from first principles, and from the later eleventh century.

It was around then that the word fief (*feodum* or variants) makes its first appearances in charters, and to an extent also narrative sources, in this region – around the same time or a little later, then, as the emergence of bannal terminology. The earliest evidence comes from the Champagne region, where the term emerged in the 1080s, though it only becomes common after 1100.[4] Parts of Lotharingia were not far behind. The term was used in charters from Gorze and St-Mihiel in the 1090s, and it appears

[3] R. Abels, 'The historiography of a construct: 'feudalism' and the medieval historian, *History Compass* 7 (2009), 1008–31 offers a English-language summary. Two relevant conference proceedings have recently been published, including J. Dendorfer and R. Deutinger, eds., *Das Lehnswesen im Hochmittelalter: Forschungskonstrukte, Quellenbefunde, Deutungsrelevanz* (Ostfildern, 2010) and S. Bagge, M. Gelting and T. Lindkvist, eds., *Feudalism: new landscapes of debate* (Turnhout, 2011). On the latter, see the online review by E. A. R. Brown in *The Medieval Review* 12.06.10, available at http://hdl.handle.net/2022/14548.

[4] E.g. Ventelay donation, Artem no. 48, though the addition to the Rheims polyptych 'Haec sunt feoda ...' (ed. Desportes and Dolbeau, 'Découverte', p. 589), is probably two decades older. Bur, *Formation*, cites one reference from 1076, p. 394. Robert of Rheims, who wrote his *Historia Iherosolimitana* based on the *Gesta Francorum* c.1106, seems to have avoided this new vocabulary.

in Trier, and in southern Lotharingia, around the 1130s, once flagrant forgeries have been excluded.[5] This kind of pattern is sometimes put down to the slow spread of 'French influence'. While such interpretation is impossible to rule out, it is not enough to talk airily of some French *Vorsprung* as if political developments were ethnically pre-determined, and it is equally possible that it reflects how underlying changes worked themselves out in different places at different speeds.[6] In the course of the twelfth century, the term became normalised. By 1144, Trier arch-bishops promised not to alienate things *in feodum*, as did bishops in Toul, or in Toul clerics' imagination, in the early twelfth century, while dukes described lands as being held '*feodaliter*'.[7] Of course, one should not get too fixated on particular words. Land might frequently be described as a *casamentum*, for example, another essentially new word with a slightly lower profile, whose meaning seems to have been similar.[8] Still, 'fief' serves to denote the phenomenon well enough.

So much, then, is clear: what is less so is what, if anything, this develop-ment indicates. In support of her overarching argument, Reynolds proposed that in general the term 'fief' was simply an innocuous re-labelling of aristocratic property rights. These rights, she suggested, were largely unchanged from the Carolingian period onwards, if not still earlier, because aristocrats always held their land in 'full property', or as close to it as contemporary conditions allowed. Much like the arguments advanced for changes in the management of the means of production discussed in the previous chapter, the terminological shifts in intra-elite relations are thereby construed as only, or primarily, terminological.

However, as in other contexts, this approach runs into a number of difficulties. Firstly, a point that has been made before should be made again here, that this terminological change was not restricted to any single genre of text – it appears in poetry as well as charters – so we should be instinctively

[5] For instance, *Cartulaire*, ed. d'Herbomez, no. 140 and *Chronique et chartes*, ed. Lesort, no. 49. In the Trier region, the first charter to mention *feoda* dates from 1008 (*UBMR*, no. 287), but has probably been interpolated. A charter purporting to come from 1030 that has the Archbishop of Trier regulating the dues owed to a certain Luof de Numage, 'qui advocatiam predicte curie … in feodo a me tenebat' (*UBMR* no. 302) is also certainly interpolated. The 1135 agreement over St-Maximin is the first to talk about fiefs (*UBMR* no. 483), followed by more charters from the 1140s.
[6] Reynolds, *Fiefs*, p. 429.
[7] Hugo Metellus, *Certamen*, p. 716. 'Dat presul feodum per virgam pontificalem.' *Feodum* was a word used plentifully in Caesarius of Heisterbach's thirteenth-century commentary on the Prüm polyptych ('que aliis in locis appelantur vulgariter lehn', ch. 24). 'Feodaliter': E. Duvernoy, *Le duc de Lorraine, Mathieu (1139–1176)* (Paris, 1904), Catalogue, no. 60 (*c.*1130 – the foundation of St-Marie-aux-Bois).
[8] 'ego vero, de cuius casamento erat, eandem donationem laudavi', in *Recueil des chartes de l'abbaye de Clairvaux au XII siècle*, ed. J. Waquet (Troyes 1982), no. 11 (1143). Cf. *Les Seigneurs de Nesle en Picardie*, ed. W. Newman, 2 vols. (Philadelphia, 1971), vol. II, nos. 5, 6, 8, describing the county of Soissons as a *casamentum* 'moving' from the bishop.

wary of any arguments based on ideas of the 'revelation' of pre-existing circumstances due to liberated documentary practice. More fundamentally, though, it is far from clear that elite property rights under the Carolingians and in the twelfth century *were* more or less the same. Property may be a common-sense concept for modern historians but, as Reynolds herself pointed out, ideas of property have historically varied, and so have practices, particularly when the property in question consists of stretches of inhabited and cultivated land on which a number of competing claims can be laid by a variety of people of different social status. Indeed, in the light of the evidence discussed in the previous chapter, it is surely inherently implausible that practices and concepts of aristocratic landholding remained broadly the same between the ninth and eleventh century.

It is certainly true that in Carolingian Francia, some elite claims to control land were more secure than others, and that a distinction was made between inherited claims, often termed *allodia*, and acquired claims, usually termed *beneficia*. The latter were commonly acquired through royal favour in some form, though, very rarely, we can see counts distributing land too.[9] Carolingian kings were capable of confiscating both kinds of land, but that speaks to their power, not to the invalidity of the distinction. This distinction seems similar to that between fief (or sometimes 'benefice') and allod found in later texts.[10] In that pairing, fief denoted a more precarious or dependent property relation, whereas allod tended to mean property held more absolutely, without or with few obligations. The division is not always posed quite so starkly – there were no dictionaries to define these words, so naturally we should expect variation – but the general distinction that the pairing made is nonetheless pervasive, and sometimes expressed very clearly indeed.[11]

However, on closer inspection, and in spite of superficial similarities (sometimes *beneficium* and fief were treated as synonymous, or nearly so), the pairing of allod/benefice was in fact not at all the same as that of allod/fief.[12] As Reynolds observes, there is no reason to believe that all twelfth-century fiefs had been distributed by a lord, whereas this does seem to have been the working assumption made about Carolingian benefices.[13] In

---

[9] E.g. *Monuments historiques*, ed. J. Tardif (Paris, 1866), no. 170 (859), though from outside our region.

[10] E.g. *Recueil*, ed. Demouy, vol. II, no. 119 (dating from 1100), detailing a donation of a *beneficium*, confirmed by the archbishop from whom the donor held it, and a donation of an *alodium*, confirmed by the donor's family.

[11] Alberic of Troisfontaines, *Chronica*, p. 784; Hugo Metellus, *Certamen*, distinguishes clearly between fiefs and other kinds of donation: p. 719: 'Rex Constantinus sua regia non feodavit / Sed neque Silvestrum secum guerrare rogavit.' Cf. Artem no. 73 and Artem no. 104.

[12] *Les seigneurs*, ed. Newman, no. 1: 'beneficium, quod nos laica lingua dicimus feodum'.

[13] For one example from many, Council of Soissons (853), ch. 5: *missi* are to check who gave out *beneficia* (*MGH Concilia*, vol. III, p. 287).

other words, whereas the status of land described as benefice in the ninth
century usually connected the obligations owed to the origins of the
property, that was not quite so clear for fiefs. That word expressed instead
the dependence in some way of that land, irrespective of how the holder
(or owner) had acquired it. In fact, in the course of the twelfth century,
there are increasingly explicit accounts detailing what later medieval
lawyers would call a 'reprise en fief', that is, the formal change in status
of land from allod to fief.[14] By the 1140s, a verb 'to feudalise' had been
coined at Remiremont to describe this act.[15]

In such cases, it is hard to argue anything other than that aristocrats
thereby surrendered some element of their landholding, recognising that
controlling the land entailed obligations to a superior (often but not
necessarily military), in return for some kind of political reward or under
some kind of political pressure. If it meant nothing at all, or had been an
obvious corollary of lordship, such transfers would not have taken place in
this way.[16] The potential meaning of such actions are revealed by the
abundant evidence for the limited but not negligible consequences that
precariousness of tenure might entail, in the shape of dozens of charters in
which lower echelons of the aristocracy sought permission from their
lords prior to alienating lands to ecclesiastical institutions, or else asked for
confirmations after the fact. Again, this is unprecedented in the
Carolingian period, when allods were generally granted without any
permission being sought, and benefices were generally not transferred at
all. The issue here is not therefore simply one of terminology, which
might have been affected by the increasingly ecclesiastical connotations of
'benefice', but of the nature of the rights involved.[17]

Reynolds was perfectly aware of this difference, but characterised it as
representing the extension of political control, rather than a change in

[14] On *reprises en fief* in Champagne, see Evergates, *Feudal society ... Troyes*, p. 131 (using early-thirteenth-century evidence). A good Lotharingian example is provided by the agreement over the castle of Sayn in 1152, handed over to Trier and taken back 'in feodum': *UBMR* no. 571.
[15] *Feodizare*, in *Studien*, ed. Hlawitschka, no. 6 (p. 147). Cf., however, *feodare* in *Cartulary*, ed. Bouchard, no. 121, regarding a donation by Odo IV in 1090, and in Hugo Metellus, p. 717 ('regia quae dantur non ecclesie feodantur').
[16] Military service: *UBMR* no. 382. Cf. *De Oorkonden der graven von Vlaanderen (Juli 1128–September 1191)*, ed. T. de Hemptinne and A. Verhulst (Brussels, 1988), no. 18 (St-Amand), 1132 (issued by the son of Duke Theoderic II of Upper Lotharingia), concerning *servitium* arising from a *feodum* but not an *allodium* (a 'reprise en fief').
[17] Fouracre, 'Beneficium', has recently promoted this interpretation of fief as a response to the change in the implications of *beneficium*, itself part of ecclesiastical reform. This is a point worth developing; yet the implication that *feoda* were therefore not different from what had been called *beneficia* seems odd. It is surely unlikely that changes in the church's 'discursive field' would not have had repercussions on the secular. Cf. n. 83, p. 81, where a distinction between registers ('quod vulgo dicitur') is described as an equivalence.

property rights. Permission was simply being requested from the effective rulers of the territory in question as a matter of pragmatism, nothing more. As she puts it, 'it is surely likely that eleventh-century counts were asked to give their consent to gifts not – or not only – because they were lords ... in the sense of the later law of fiefs, but because they were regarded as the effective rulers of their counties'.[18] Perhaps the issue cannot be dismissed so easily. First of all, for all that pragmatism was doubtless an important element in this as every development, there is also evidence for a kind of systematisation that implies that something more like a rule was being established. If references to 'feudal law' remain hard to decipher, there are other hints that *feodum* was taking on a technical meaning – for example, when altars are described as being held 'as though through a fief'.[19] Moreover, there survive a number of charters that confirm donations of fiefs already made explicitly on the grounds that such permission was necessary.[20] Other charters were apparently written simply to grant a blanket permission for an institution to acquire fiefs from subordinates; and sometimes it was even phrased as a general law, that 'no one is allowed to give all his fief away in alms without the license or permission of him from whom he holds it'.[21] Sometimes, charters were even forged to provide this kind of permission, particularly revealing given the propensity of forgeries to express contemporary priorities.[22]

More importantly, the notion that this represents merely an extension of political control, not a change in landholding, depends on an a priori distinction between rights over land and governmental rights that Reynolds is elsewhere justifiably reluctant to make.[23] We cannot read these charters and maintain that property remained the same and that it was merely government that had changed, because changes in government affect practices of property. It would surely be better to suggest the evidence implies that political or social dependence increasingly carried the possibility, and perhaps expectation, of tenurial dependence, marking a difference from the Carolingian period. There are signs, moreover, that

---

[18] Reynolds, *Fiefs*, p. 147–8, and cf. p. 163.

[19] *Cartulaire de l'abbaye de Saint-Corneille de Compiègne*, ed. E. Morel (Montdidier, 1904), no. 36 (1115), 'tamquam per feodum'.

[20] E.g. 'iure feodali' in *Recueil*, ed. Bautier, and *DLVI*, no. 79 for Châlons, and a similar phrase in Hugo Metellus, *Certamen*, 'feodali conditione', p. 718. For the charters, see Artem nos. 48, 73, 97, 231, 251, 4901 and 4958; there are many more surviving in cartularies.

[21] *Le Prieuré de Saint-Leu d'Esserent: Cartulaire*, ed. E. Müller (Pontoise, 1901), no. 21, from 1119: 'verum quia nulli totum suum feodum in elemosina dare licet sine licentia eius aut permissione a quo ipsum tenet'.

[22] Favier, J., 'La fabrication d'un faux à Saint-Maur-des-Fossés vers la fin du XIᵉ siècle', *BEC* 119 (1961), 233–41.

[23] E.g. Reynolds, *Fiefs*, p. 374.

the reverse also obtained, that, as Sigibert of Gembloux argued with reference to the church, tenurial dependence carried with it the implication of political subordination.[24]

Finally, we also need to recognise that more complicated 'hierarchies of tenure' become apparent in the late eleventh and twelfth centuries, again marking a distinction from Carolingian Francia, where there is no evidence for anything more than a single layer of formally delegated rights over land. A number of late-eleventh- and twelfth-century charters explicitly describe chains of dependent holding with the person actually in possession of the land holding it from someone else, who in turn held it from a third party, often a count, from whom the land was said to 'move', or from whom it was 'held'.[25] For example, Jacob of Germigny's donation to St-Nicaise of Rheims in 1121 explained that he held it from Count Hugh of Troyes, but in the charter of confirmation issued by the Archbishop of Rheims, it turned out that someone else held some of the property in *feodum* from Jacob.[26] This tenurial ladder could lead to surprisingly complex transactions, in which the permission of all parties concerned was required, and often accompanied, at least in our texts, by elaborate rituals, whereby tokens of a gift would be formally handed up the tenurial ladder before being passed to the recipient.[27] If we deconstruct this to indicate merely that the count held authority over all concerned, then indeed this reveals nothing significant. After all, patronage relations were hardly a novelty of the twelfth century, and patrons had presumably always had some informal influence over the alienation of their clients' resources. Yet to reduce these sources to really being about something other than what they say does not do them full justice. The point, analogous to that made in the previous chapter, is that only now did these patronage, or governmental, relations receive some kind of formal articulation in landed property terms.

---

[24] And specifically concerning *regalia*; cf. K. Kroeschell, 'Lehnrecht und Verfassung im deutschen Hochmittelalter', *Forum historiae iuris* 2 (1998), 1–41.

[25] *Histoire et cartulaire des Templiers à Provins*, ed. V. Carrières (Paris, 1919), no. 81 ('a quo totum movebat') and no. 20 ('quod de me tenebat'). Cf. the use of the verb *descendere* in *Cartulaire*, ed. Morel, no. 39.

[26] *Cartulaire de Saint-Nicaise de Reims*, ed. J. Cosse-Durlin (Paris, 1991), nos. 44 and 45. Another example, from further east, is given in *Chartes des Cisterciens de Saint-Benoît-en-Woëvre des origines à 1300*, ed. J. Denaix (Verdun, 1959), n. 2: Thecelinus donated some land in the 1130s to the new Cistercian foundation with the permission of Bovo and Agnes 'from whom he held the land *in feodo*'; they in turn sought permission from Nicholas, who requested permission from Gobert.

[27] E.g. in Soissons 1122: 'Analyse du Cartulaire de St-Pierre de Chézy', ed. E. de Barthélemy, *Mémoires de la société académique des sciences, arts … de Saint-Quentin* 1 (1876–8), 241–308, no. 17); cf. *Chartes et documents de l'abbaye cistercienne de Preuilly*, ed. A. Catel (Montereau, 1927), no. 1.

In summary, then, a number of changes can be observed in patterns of aristocratic landholding. The origin of the land became merely one factor amongst others in the determination of that land's status; the fief-holder's rights were somewhere between the Carolingian benefice-holder and allod-holder, explicitly reflecting political relations; and hierarchies of tenure began to emerge. Surely the neatest explanation is to suggest that patronage was increasingly built explicitly into claims over land. Only now, from the later eleventh century, was informal influence refashioned to create a distinctive kind of property right which could be layered, in theory without limits, without losing definition. It is to describe this new situation that the term fief was called upon, probably precisely because it avoided the ambivalences of the older *beneficium*, whose ecclesiastical connotations were growing in strength.[28] Viewed from this perspective, the apparent growth in messiness, as political power was more clearly imbricated in transactions over land, really points to an increase in precision, not the blurring of boundaries.[29]

HOMAGE

The parallels with the findings of the previous chapter are noteworthy: we have seen an increase in formality and sharper definitions of social relations. However, the arguments above are perhaps suggestive rather than conclusive, and anyway the traditional historiographical interpretation of fiefs, prior to the challenge posed by Reynolds, rested on their relationship with vassalage, or personal dependence of some kind. It is apparent, therefore, that we need to address the question of vassalage. In point of fact, the word *vassalus* is quite rare in eleventh- and twelfth-century sources from this region, where it is merely one of a range of words used to describe dependants, such as *meus homo, mei barones* and so forth.[30] A better entry to the issue is provided instead by a different word, which appears, in a variety of kinds of texts from the region under investigation, around the same time as fiefs, give or take a decade: homage (*hominium* or *homagium*).[31]

---

[28] Cf. Fouracre, '*Beneficium*'.

[29] Cf. R. Deutinger, 'Seit wann gibt es die Mehrfachvasallität?', *Zeitschrift der Savigny-Stiftung für Rechtsgeschichte, Germanistische Abteilung* 119 (2002), 78–105, though there is room for debate over his interpretation of the 892 charter at the article's heart.

[30] Barons: *Histoire*, ed. Carriére, no. 93 (1127); Balderic, *Gesta Alberonis*, p. 248.

[31] Clarius, *Chronicon*, ed. and tr. R.-H. Bautier, *Chronique de Saint-Pierre-le-Vif de Sens, dite de Clarius* (Paris, 1979), p. 144, describing an agreement around 1104; Hugh of Flavigny, *Chronicon*, p. 433 (and many more times in his notes from Flavigny), Laurentius, *Gesta*, p. 504. Count Henry of Champagne performed homage to the Archbishop of Rheims in 1154, the same year that he observed that his successors would hold the homage of the counts of Roucy (*Recueil des actes d'Henri le Libéral, comte de Champagne, 1152–1181*, ed. M. Bur (Paris, 2009), nos. 48 and 51). The term appears in a number of charters, too: e.g. from Toul (1107), Rheims (s. XII, concerning *c.*1100: in *Recueil*, ed. Demouy, vol. II, no. 106), Rethel (1117: *Metropolis*, ed. Marlot, vol. II, col. 258),

In ways which must now be familiar, the bulk of scholarship has played down the significance of this relatively clear terminological development in one of two ways. As a concept, homage was deeply embedded in the modern imagination of the Middle Ages, as one of those rituals which historians liked to think revealed something of the essence of medieval society;[32] and for that reason historians happily used to talk, and sometimes still do, of people doing homage in earlier periods, before the specific term itself was coined or used.[33] Contemporary authors did much the same thing. A letter written around 1125 by a clerical community near Verdun, for example, described how ninety years previously, Count Odo II had burned the Lotharingian castle of Commercy because its inhabitant had refused to do him homage (*hominium*).[34] The implicit argument in these cases is that the concepts and practices represented by late-eleventh- and twelfth-century material had always existed.[35] That has allowed Galbert of Bruges's celebrated description of the homage done to William Clito of Normandy, at this point Count of Flanders, though soon to be replaced by Theoderic 'of Alsace' (in fact from Upper Lotharingia), to be considered a model casting light on a practice generalised across both time and space.[36]

Newer research has tended to lead in the opposite direction, doubting that these words bore the precision of meaning even in the twelfth century that historians have attributed to them.[37] However, as we have seen

Bouillon (1127: *Metropolis*, ed. Marlot, vol. II, col. 294), Soissons (1140: *Les seigneurs*, ed. Newman, no. 6), Toul (1138: *Histoire*, ed. Calmet, vol. V, col. 303) and Orbais (*c.*1080: 'Histoire de l'abbaye d'Orbais', ed. N. Dubout, *Revue de Champagne et de Brie* 14 (1883), 142–3).

[32] J. Le Goff, 'The symbolic rituals of vassalage', in *Time, work, and culture in the Middle Ages*, trans. by Arthur Goldhammer (Chicago, 1980), pp. 237–87, is the standard text on medieval homage, which presents all the classic case-studies from the eighth century onwards.

[33] For example, the comment of Arbois de Jubainville on 1037: 'aucun texte précis n'établit ce refus d'hommage, mais c'est une hypothèse qui semble très naturelle et très logique', *Histoire*, vol. I, p. 357. Cf. H. Hoffmann, 'Grafschaften in Bischofshand', *Deutsches Archiv* 46 (1990), 375–480, who wonders whether counts performed 'Mannschaft' to bishop or king. Even Depreux, 'Politics of gesture', treats it as unproblematic for the Carolingian period.

[34] Edited in *Acta Sanctorum Ordinis S. Benedicti*, ed. J. Mabillon, 9 vols. (Paris, 1688–1701), vol. VI, pp. 536–7. The account is also mentioned in Hugh of Flavigny, *Chronicon*, pp. 374–5, though without the homage: and also in the *Vita Richardi*, (BHL 7220), ed. W. Wattenbach, *MGH SS*, vol. XI (Hanover, 1854), pp. 280–9, at p. 286. Later, the Bishop of Metz passed Commercy over to Duke Theoderic II (*c.*1070).

[35] This is also the argument of Le Goff, 'Symbolic', p. 240.

[36] For example, E. Hallam and J. Everard, *Capetian France, 987–1328* (Harlow, 2001), pp. 19–20, following Ganshof.

[37] See Reynolds, *Fiefs*, pp. 261–3, 269–71; J. Dendorfer, 'Das Wormser Konkordat – ein Schritt auf dem Weg zur Feudalisierung der Reichsverfassung?', in J. Dendorfer and R. Deutinger, eds., *Das Lehnswesen im Hochmittelalter*, pp. 299–328, and P. Depreux, 'Lehnsrechtliche Symbolhandlungen. Handgang und Investitur im Bericht Galberts von Brügge zur Anerkennung Wilhelm Clitos als Graf von Flandern', in J. Dendorfer and R. Deutinger, eds., *Das Lehnswesen im Hochmittelalter* (Ostfildern, 2010), pp. 387–400.

before, this revisionism risks in effect merely confirming a key part of the interpretation it ostensibly challenges. Whereas the older tradition happily made use of twelfth-century categories to classify medieval society at large, the newer works to empty these categories – but in order, again, to classify medieval society at large. The organising concepts are now no longer legalistic, but instead reflect a kind of soft-focus anthropology revolving around ideas of negotiation and continuity. But the effect of flattening historical change is the same and both attempt to see 'through' words to get at real history, methodologically a rather hazardous enterprise, as suggested in the previous chapter. It is indeed easy to propose that the appearance of words alone cannot indicate a substantial change in how people interacted with each other, still less bear the weight of interpretation which the traditional notion of feudalism entails. When, however, we pay close attention to these texts, what distinguishes them is not just the terminology, it is – again as with the material discussed in the previous chapter – the underlying conceptions. If we concentrate on the concepts which the words are expressing, then in fact it is clear that some process was indeed at work.[38]

A few examples will prove the point. For instance, the letter of St-Vanne just cited portrayed the refusal to do homage as the cause of war: however anachronistic it is for the early eleventh century, it must be taken seriously as a source for the early twelfth, and as it happens there is Verdun evidence from the early twelfth century suggesting that a failure to do homage could indeed have severe consequences.[39] Another example is provided by Balderic's *Gesta Alberonis*, a mid-twelfth-century text from Trier, according to which Count Henry of Luxembourg was dissuaded from a surprise attack on the Archbishop of Trier because he had not *formally* renounced his subordination to him, and though here the word homage is not in fact used, the underlying concept seems related.[40] Texts produced in this region about the First Crusade offer further evidence. Robert of Rheims was perhaps unfamiliar with the word 'homage' in his *Historia Iherosolimitana* (written around 1106), providing a gloss for it the first time he uses it; but he nevertheless keeps the distinction already made in the *Gesta Francorum*, his source text, between the homage done by most of the crusading leaders to the Byzantine emperor at Constantinople, and the oath eventually sworn by a reluctant Count

---

[38] *Begriffsgeschichte*-inspired approaches might be helpful here in unravelling the knots caused by too great a concentration by much recent scholarship on wording alone: see p. 180 n. 33 above.

[39] 'Pratiques féodales en Verdunois au XIIe siècle', ed. M. Parisse, *Lotharingia* 2 (1990), 289–95, no. 4.

[40] Balderic, *Gesta Alberonis*, p. 253: 'magnam ipsi et perpetuam infamiam, is quid tale contra dominum suum commiteret, antequam domino suo reunciasset'.

Raymond of St–Gilles, who explicitly refused to do homage.[41] Guibert of Nogent, whose *Dei Gesta per Francos* was probably written a few years later, not only strengthens the contrast between the homage sworn by most crusaders and the mere oath taken by Raymond, but also includes, later in the work, a didactic tale about a Frankish knight who made a pact with the devil, but was ultimately saved precisely because he refused to do homage, in spite of the devil's repeated insistence.[42] Finally, another illustrative case is provided by the dispute, admittedly a little outside our main area of interest, between the Duke of Burgundy and the Bishop of Langres, heard by King Louis VII in 1153. A key argument revolved around the duke's decision to renounce his homage, and indeed whether the duke had earlier come to the bishop's court because of homage, or because of friendship.[43]

This list of examples could easily be extended.[44] Whether these accounts are reliable evidence for events in the imperial capital, particular causes of war, Count Henry's decision not to press home his advantage, or the real cause of tension between duke and bishop is not the issue here. It is more profitable to understand these texts as revealing the suppositions of the chroniclers. Read like that, these texts suggest that the concept of homage was common currency in Lotharingia and Champagne by at least the middle twelfth century, and, more to the point, that even if the meaning of this word or concept might not have been clear enough to satisfy a lawyer, it was clear enough for everyday purposes. Often it was related to the holding of assets from the person in question, but not always; so insofar as homage is usually historiographically associated with vassalage, itself inextricably connected with landholding, the hesitation of Reynolds and others is entirely justified. There is no trace of anything like the modern concept of vassalage in the sources from between Marne and Moselle before around 1140. However, what the available evidence does suggest is that homage was a convenient label for a ceremony instituting a specially binding relationship between

[41] Robert of Rheims, *Historia Iherosolimitana*, PL 155, cols. 669–758, bk II, ch. 3. For a recent re-evaluation of these oaths, and the distinction between homage and fidelity, see J. Shepard, 'When Greek meets Greek: Alexius Comnenus and Bohemond in 1097–98', *Byzantine and modern Greek studies* 12 (1998), 185–277, suggesting that collation of the Latin sources 'shows clearly that not only an oath of fealty (*fidelitas*) but also the performance of homage was required of the princes', p. 231, and notes that Anna Comnena even talks later of what is clearly liege homage, 'lizion anthropon': ibid., p. 237.

[42] Guibert of Nogent, *Dei gesta per Francos*, ed. R. Huygens, CCCM, vol. CXXVIIA (Turnhout, 1996), bk III, pp. 143–4, for Raymond, and bk VII, pp. 323–7, for the unnamed knight.

[43] *Cartulaire du chapitre cathédral de Langres*, ed. H. Flammarion (Turnhout, 2004), no. 114. Another example is perhaps provided by the 1101 agreement between Count Robert of Flanders and King Henry I of England: see E. Oksanen, *Flanders and the Anglo-Norman world (1066–1216)* (Cambridge, 2013), ch. 2.

[44] E.g. J. F. Lemarignier, *Recherches sur l'hommage en marche et les frontières féodales* (Lille, 1945); *Recueil*, ed. Demouy, vol. II, no. 106.

aristocrats of different rank, in a way which went beyond a mere oath.[45] It was becoming an increasingly context-free relation, in the sense that it carried a set of implications with little or less variation according to who was concerned. It is hard to come up with any other explanation for why, for example, Suger of St-Denis suggested that kings were not supposed to do homage to anyone else.[46] No one had ever specified that Carolingian kings should not swear a particular kind of oath. A reasonable inference is therefore that increasing attention was being paid to the formal aspects of relations between lords, and that a semi-technical term was emerging to express one of these aspects. This term encapsulated a kind of patronage with relatively more defined implications, in ways quite distinct from the aristocratic interactions described in Chapter 2.

This might appear to be placing a great deal of explanatory weight on the appearance of a new word. It therefore bears reiterating that we should not be too preoccupied with terminological innovation, which is only a guide, and nothing more, to more important conceptual developments. There are, for example, a number of agreements which clearly echo homage agreements, but do not use the word. In any case, it should be noted that *hominium* was, as with the language of *bannum*, merely one of an associated network of terms emerging in the late eleventh century. Another was *ligius*, translated usually as liege, to express the priority of one particular bond of subordination over others, which was not so much a response to the so-called problem of multiple vassalage, but a new attempt, as in other spheres, at precision.[47] The region west of the Meuse is a particularly interesting place to study this development, because inspection of the manuscript Rheims Bibliothèque Municipale MS 15 suggests that a charter about liege homage it preserves may be a contemporary copy inserted into the manuscript, not a later transcription written after the volume was compiled, which could make it the earliest datable reference to the phenomenon (1055).[48]

---

[45] I therefore entirely agree with the argument of Dendorfer, 'Das Wormser Konkordat', that homage was a 'verengende Umdeutung' (p. 327) of commendation, though disagreeing with the implication that this means it was not 'feudal'.

[46] M. Ryan, 'Oath of fealty and the lawyers', in J. Canning and O.-G. Oexle, eds., *Politische Ideen im Mittelalter, Theorie und Wirklichkeit der Macht* (1999), pp. 209–26, at p. 213; Suger, *De administratione*, p. 66. Cf. J. Miethke, 'Rituelle Symbolik und Rechtswissenschaft im Kampf zwischen Kaiser und Papst. Friedrich Barbarossa und der Konflikt um die Bedeutung von Ritualen', in F. Felten and others, eds., *Ein gefüllter Willkomm. Festschrift für Knut Schulz zum 65. Geburtstag* (Aachen 2002), pp. 91–125.

[47] Cf. Hallam and Everard, *Capetian France*, p. 21.

[48] Rheims, Bibliothèque Municipale, lat. 15, f. 2v. Codicological examination shows the folio was not originally part of the manuscript, whose composition is complex: see the *Catalogue général* for Rheims (*Catalogue général des manuscrits des bibliothèques publiques de France*, vol. xxxviii, ed. H. Loriquet (Paris, 1904), though note its error in placing the oath on f. 3). For accounts of the Rheims oath, see W. Kienast, 'Lehnrecht und Staatsgewalt im Mittelalter', *Historische Zeitschrift* 158

It may be, too, that the sphere of gesture offers some confirmation that a new stage had been reached in how these relations were articulated. Galbert of Bruges's classic description of homage apparently focused on a quite specific gesture, that one of hands pressed together familiar from modern Western Christian postures of prayer. Admittedly, the Latin words he used, *manibus iunctis*, could simply mean 'holding hands', and the tendency of historians to denote anything involving hands with the technical term *inmixtio manuum* (a phrase which does not seem to be attested in the early period) is very unhelpful, at least before the twelfth century.[49] As Reynolds has remarked, people do a lot of things with their hands.[50] Yet there is some reason to think that a particular, almost technical manual gesture of formal submission, that Galbert and compilers of later manuscripts of the *Sachsenspiegel* or the *Libri Feudorum* would have recognised, and one distinct from earlier practices, was spreading in the eleventh and twelfth centuries.[51] Not only is there a greater emphasis on the particular hand gesture as initiating a relationship of obedience in a number of texts, ranging from Albert of Aachen's *Historia Ierosolimitana* (*c.*1130) to the Hérival statutes written near Toul in the early twelfth century by a notoriously rigorous reformed canonical community; but the 'younger prayer gesture' (kneeling with hands placed together, effectively the same posture as that associated with homage) itself only emerges for the first time in the eleventh and twelfth centuries, for example apparently appearing on coins made in Trier and Metz.[52] It is usually thought that this

---

(1938), 3–51, at 28; A. Becker, 'Urban II und die deutsche Kirche', in J. Fleckenstein, ed., *Investiturstreit und Reichsverfassung* (Sigmaringen, 1973), pp. 241–75. Ostensibly earlier references from elsewhere in France (e.g. Vendôme) are in later cartularies and may be interpolated.

[49] For an earlier and exemplarily non-feudal use of 'manibus iunctis', see Bede, *Ecclesiastical history*, ed. and tr. B. Colgrave and R. Mynors (Oxford, 1969), p. 372. Le Goff, 'Symbolic', draws on Ganshof to assume that the term *inmixtio manuum* denotes 'homage' which is thus pushed back into the ninth century (pp. 241–2), but this seems unwarranted. The phrase would appear to be one taken from later medieval law or liturgy; I have not come across it in any pre-1100 text.

[50] A hand gesture of some kind is, for example, referred to in the *Ordo Romanus I* (extant in a number of ninth-century manuscripts), p. 67.

[51] Cf. Poly and Bournazel, *Feudalism*, p. 51, who suggest that the Carolingian handshake ('*paumée*') should be distinguished from the more elaborate rituals of subordination expressed by homage. By the thirteenth century, it had become standard practice for homage to be performed kneeling: see S. Weinfurter, 'Lehnswesen, Treueid und Vertrauen. Grundlagen der neuen Ordnung im hohen Mittelalter', in J. Dendorfer and R. Deutinger, eds., *Das Lehnswesen*, pp. 443–62; see also R. Schmidt-Wiegand, 'Gebärdensprache im mittelalterlichen Recht', *FMS* 16 (1982), 363–79.

[52] Albert of Aachen, *Historia Ierosolimitana*, for example at bk II, ch. 16, p. 86; *Vetera Hyreevallis statuta*, in *Sacrae antiquitatis monumenta: historica, dogmatica, diplomatica*, ed. C. Hugo, 2 vols. (Etival, 1725), vol. I, pp. 135–44, at p. 138. The coin evidence has to my knowledge been neglected: see B. Kluge, *Deutsche Münzgeschichte von der späten Karolingerzeit bis zum Ende der Salier* (Sigmaringen, 1991), n. 351, and Flon, *Histoire*, p. 183. The Trier coins are catalogued in R. Weiller, *Die Münzen von Trier, 6 Jahrhundert-1307* (Düsseldorf, 2008), pp. 398–402 (nos. 110–12). On the 'modern prayer' gesture, see R. Trexler, 'Legitimating prayer gestures in the twelfth century. The de penitentia of Peter the Chanter', *History and Anthropology*, 1 (1984), 97–126; Schmitt, *Raison*, pp. 295–300.

particular postural attitude, indicating a reverent submission to God, was borrowed from secular practice, and that the feudal gesture 'leaked' into the liturgy, but the reverse may well be more likely.[53] Either way, there is quite a striking correlation in timing between this change and the development of new terminologies of submission.

In summary, and contrary to some of the classic interpretations, the evidence from before 1150 does not consistently support a direct connection between fiefs and homage, the root of conventional ideas of vassalage.[54] In that sense, Reynolds's critique of those ideas is fully justified. That is not to say, however, that there is no connection whatsoever to be made between fiefs and homage. Both indicate a far more formalised set of relations, a sharper conceptual grasp of 'lordship' and its implications, a clearer way of articulating the degree and form of honourable dependence. They should in other words be considered parallel developments, not serial ones.

Unlike *bannum*, there is not at first glance, however, a great deal of evidence for the concrete effects that these new conceptualisations had. There are some indications that fiefs really were confiscated, and, as we have seen, that homage or its absence could be of practical importance, but it must be admitted that such instances are relatively rare.[55] If the systematic differentiation of the late-twelfth-century *Feoda Campanie*, the Count of Champagne's massive list of dependent landholding, between liege homage and 'plain' homage certainly suggests that these distinctions had some practical effect on organisation, it is hard to glean, despite this register's size, precisely what implications were entailed.[56] Admittedly, thirteenth-century material is more forthcoming.[57] There is even explicit

[53] J. Berlioz, 'La raison des gestes: pourquoi on prie à genoux'; cf. Jungmann, *Mass*, who suggested it was a trace of 'germanischer Kultur', vol. I, p. 77, n. 17.

[54] Though there are occasional suggestions: e.g. Artem no. 75: 'unde hominium'.

[55] Cf. 'Pratiques', ed. Parisse; cf. also K-H. Spiess, *Das Lehnswesen in Deutschland im hohen und späten Mittelalter* (Idstein, 2002), pp. 22–35. An interesting example is afforded by Thierry Count of Flanders (son of Theoderic II, Duke of Upper Lotharingia)'s attempt at Trier in 1152 to add the *dignitas Cameraca* (perhaps to be understood as the county of Cambrai) to his fiefs, having done homage to the emperor and with the support of his nephew Matthew of Upper Lotharingia – in other words, an argument about feudal tenure; but the account, by Lambert of Wattrelos, was written *c.*1170 and so is perhaps a little late. Lambert of Wattrelos, *Annales Cameracenses*, ed. G. Pertz, *MGH SS*, vol. XVI (Leipzig, 1925), pp. 510–54, at pp. 523–4.

[56] *Feoda Campanie*, in *Documents relatifs au comté de Champagne et de Brie: 1172–1361*, ed. A. Longnon, 3 vols. (Paris, 1901–14), vol. I, pp. 1–74. On the distinction in the *Feoda Campanie*, see J. Benton, 'Written records and the development of systematic feudal relations', in J. Benton and T. Bisson, eds., *Culture, power and personality in medieval France* (London, 1991), pp. 275–90. On the *Feoda Campanie* in general, see T. Evergates, *The aristocracy in the county of Champagne 1100–1300* (Philadelphia, 2007), pp. 17–20.

[57] T. Evergates, *Feudal society in medieval France: documents from the county of Champagne* (Philadelpha, 1993), translates and edits a number of thirteenth-century documents in which homage is often prominent: see, for example, pp. 4–5.

engagement with the rules governing these practices in the shape of the *Coutumier de Champagne*, a description of customary law similar to those that appeared elsewhere in thirteenth-century Europe.[58] Yet though suggestive, this material is rather late to help us elucidate the significance of a shift in the late eleventh century. There is perhaps one earlier, well-known example of a shift from practices of loose commendation to a far stricter and more 'constitutive' bond with more precise tenurial implications, which created documented tension and disputes, but this, the Norman Conquest, is too far from this region to be more than alluded to (and its interpretation is anyway deeply contested).[59] It is for this reason that we need to turn to the 'Investiture Quarrel', as represented in sources from between Marne and Moselle.

THE 'INVESTITURE QUARREL'

This might appear at first sight a move bordering on the eccentric. Not only does such a vast topic inspire trepidation, but that this body of evidence could shed much light on the questions in hand may seem unlikely. After all, the entire thrust of recent scholarship over the past two decades has been to complicate previous narratives which centred squarely on the question of investiture of bishops by kings or emperors, hence the now obligatory inverted commas.[60] Instead, historians prefer to emphasise the sheer complexity of interwoven debates and disputes across Europe, dealing with any number of issues which escalated in ways which could never have been foreseen. Many of these debates were purely pragmatic contests over the distribution of power at various levels, local and imperial, not over its nature; others, particularly those relating to simony, are now argued to have roots deep in the tenth century, even while the associations of the Gregorian reforming papacy with tenth-century monastic ideals are often considered today as tenuous.[61] Much of

---

[58] *Coutumier de Champagne*, ed. Portejoie, pp. 158–9, concerning *fié* and *honmaige*.

[59] G. Garnett, *Conquered England: kingship, succession and tenure, 1066–1166* (Oxford, 2007). Interestingly, Anglo-Norman England also has some of the most insightful evidence for the investiture contest, which may not be a coincidence. See n. 67, below.

[60] S. Beulertz, *Das Verbot der Laieninvestitur im Investiturstreit* (Hanover, 1991), has full references to the recent literature. See also the thought-provoking M. Suchan, *Königsherrschaft im Streit: Konfliktaustragung in der Regierungszeit Heinrichs IV. zwischen Gewalt, Gespräch und Schriftlichkeit* (Stuttgart, 1997), though her stress on orality is questionable. M. Miller, 'The crisis in the Investiture Crisis narrative', *History Compass* 7 (2009), 1570–80, provides a useful, though brief, synthesis.

[61] J. Eldevik, 'Driving the chariot of the lord: Siegfried I of Mainz (1060–1084) and episcopal identity in an age of transition', in J. Ott and A. Trumbore Jones, eds., *The bishop reformed* (Aldershot, 2007), pp. 161–88, is an insightful analysis of one particular bishop, bringing out the complexities of the local situation. See his book, *Episcopal power and ecclesiastical reform in the German Empire: tithes, lordship and community, 950–1150* (Cambridge, 2012), which came out after this book went to press.

the eleventh-century debate, including, for example, the contribution by Wenric of Trier on behalf of the Bishop of Verdun, was primarily about whether the Pope could depose kings, mentioning the issue of investiture only in that broader context.[62]

Still, ideological principles articulated by concern over ceremony did become an important part of these disputes, in particular in the early twelfth century under the reign of Emperor Henry V (d.1125). One aspect of this concerns homage.[63] Attention had been paid to the oaths that bishops swore to kings in the initial stages of the dispute, but only in a quite general sense. For example, Gebhard of Salzburg's letter to Bishop Herman of Metz (*c*.1080) explicitly pitted oaths sworn to kings against those bishops swore on their ordination, arguing for the priority of the latter over the former.[64] Pope Urban II in 1095, according to some versions of the Clermont decree, at any rate, had prohibited bishops from performing 'liege fidelity' (*ligiam fidelitatem*), implicitly as opposed to some other kind of fidelity but without being more specific.[65] However, another late-eleventh-century source (the Chronicle of St-Bénigne) depicts an archbishop-elect, Halinard of Lyons, controversially refusing to swear a particular kind of oath to the king, as opposed to a promise of fidelity, which he was happy to provide.[66] By the early twelfth century, the issue was increasingly clearly focused specifically on homage, understood in a more technical sense. In England, an agreement brokered in 1107 saw kings abandoning investiture in exchange for keeping homage (*hominium*), and several of Pope Paschal II's letters addressed the issue directly.[67] The Lotharingian chronicler Hugh of Flavigny also discussed homage, trying to use Pseudo-Isidorian texts to demonstrate that bishops should not perform it, and it proved a major sticking point in

---

[62] Wenrich, *Epistola*, ed. K. Francke, *MGH Libelli de lite* vol. 1 (Hanover, 1891), pp. 284–99, at p. 297. On Trier's pro-imperial literary productions, and much else besides, see Erkens, *Trierer Kirchenprovinz*, p. 127.

[63] Cf. Hyams, 'Homage and feudalism: a judicious separation', in N. Fryde, P. Monnet and O.-G. Oexle, eds., *Die Gegenwart des Feudalismus* (Göttingen, 2002), pp. 13–50, who also stresses the importance of the Investiture Controversy in creating the institution of homage, though he confusingly proceeds to look for its pre-Investiture roots.

[64] *MGH Libelli* vol. 1, pp. 273–8 (with interesting comparison to secular oaths, p. 275). See in general S. Weinfurter, 'Lehnswesen'.

[65] *The councils of Urban II*, ed. R. Somerville (Amsterdam, 1972): p. 78 (from northern French group of manuscripts).

[66] Halinard refused even to pretend to swear it: 'Tantumdem est si simulavero ac si fecerim': *Chronicon Benigni*, col. 844; he agrees however to a verbal promise, 'verbo et promissis'.

[67] Eadmer, *Historia novorum in Anglia*, ed. M. Rule, Rolls Series 81 (London, 1884), p. 186. Paschal II changed his mind, since in a letter in 1102 to Anselm he had firmly forbidden homage (*hominium*). A now-lost manuscript from Igny (Marne) stated that the Council of Poitiers (1100), presided over by Paschal, banned homage: see Beulertz, *Verbot*, p. 15.

the negotiations between Archbishop Bruno of Trier and Pope Paschal II at Châlons in 1107, at least according to our mid-twelfth-century source.[68]

All this evidence seems to support the hints in the more straightforwardly secular evidence discussed above that homage and its related concepts had a relatively and increasingly clear meaning, and that it was becoming a semi-technical term – it is quite likely that the debates had helped sharpen the concept.[69] Yet still more important for shedding light on the questions of formalisation is the issue of investiture itself, which also took on increasing prominence from the early twelfth century.[70] The confirmation by a king or other 'secular' figure of the appointment of a bishop to his see was a moment that raised a number of difficulties. One aspect of these was the nature of episcopal property, since twelfth-century kings and emperors claimed to be using the ceremony of investiture to validate the transfer of property to the new incumbent. The debate accordingly explicitly brought into question the issue of how far episcopal lands could be assimilated to fiefs held from the king.[71] Perhaps this was an issue of fresh concern because of the new ideas of the firebrand Pope Gregory VII and his circle; but the coincidence with the spread of this categorisation elsewhere, discussed above, suggests an alternative inference: we do not have to assume, after all, that all changes in thinking came from Rome.[72] Whatever the case, the central contest came to revolve around the symbolic moment of investiture itself, and in particular the way in which it was performed, rather than its implications for the status of property.

The earliest evidence for emphasis on what would, by the twelfth century, be at the heart of the matter, comes from the pen of a Lotharingian, albeit one writing abroad, in the shape of Humbert of Moyenmoutier's 'Three Books against the Simoniacs' (*c.*1060).[73] Humbert, who enjoyed a distinguished

---

[68] Hugh of Flavigny, *Chronicon*, pp. 433–4, who in fact used Pseudo-Isidore to make his argument. For the negotiations at Châlons, including references to *hominium*, see Suger, *Vita Ludovici*, ch. 10, p. 58. On the importance of oaths, see Weinfurter, 'Lehnswesen'.

[69] Cf. for a hint in this direction Hyams, 'Homage and feudalism', p. 15.

[70] Twelfth-century writers tended to categorise the disputes as having been partly or largely about investiture: e.g., Alberic of Troisfontaines, *Chronica*, p. 805; Balderic, *Gesta Alberonis*, p. 243; *Chronicon Mauriniacensis*, PL CLXXX, col. 143; Hugh of Flavigny, *Chronicon*, pp. 342, 411–12; Laurentius, *Gesta*, p. 495. See S. Weinfurter, 'Investitur und Gnade. Überlegungen zur gratialen Herrschaftsordnung im Mittelalter', in *Investitur- und Krönungsrituale. Herrschaftseinsetzungen im kulturellen Vergleich* (2005), pp. 105–23, for a good summary.

[71] For a contrary view, see Dendorfer, 'Das Wormser Konkordat'; Hugo Metellus, however, makes the connection, 'Perdere pontifices nulla possunt ratione / quae data sunt illis feodali conditione', *Certamen*, p. 718.

[72] For a parallel argument, concentrating on canon law, see C. Rolker, *Canon law and the letters of Ivo of Chartres* (Cambridge, 2010), pp. 290–303.

[73] On Humbert, see the Introduction in *Libelli de lite*, and J. Gilchrist, 'Cardinal Humbert of Silva Candida, the canon law and ecclesiastical reform in the eleventh century', *Zeitschrift der Savigny Stiftung für Rechtsgeschichte, Kanonistische Abteilung* 58 (1972), 338–49. He dates *Adversus Simoniacos* to around 1058.

career in the train of Bishop Bruno of Toul, later Pope Leo IX, had some
fascinating things to say about the nature of property, drawing on Eriugena to
distinguish use from plain ownership in ways which seem oddly to prefigure
the distinction discussed in the previous chapter between rights of ownership
and rights of jurisdiction. It is, however, his comments on the objects of
investiture themselves that are more pressing for present purposes. For, in the
course of his attempt to show that any interference of laymen in church affairs
was a kind of simony and thus a heresy, he argued vehemently that the
liturgical interpretation of the ring and the staff set out by Isidore of Seville in
the seventh century was their *only* valid reading. As a result, their use in any
context necessarily implied pastoral power, and he deduced that kings were
being blasphemous in bestowing them at investiture.[74] It could be suggested
that Humbert's treatises, written in Italy, cannot be treated as properly
Lotharingian evidence. However, it ought to be noted that Humbert's
work was mostly based on sources certainly available in Lotharingia, such as
Hincmar of Rheims, the letters of Pope Nicholas I and John Scotus Eriugena,
perhaps reflecting something of Humbert's long education at Moyenmoutier
and Toul; and also that Humbert kept his Lotharingian links alive.[75]

In any case, Humbert's concerns were explicitly shared, albeit later, by
other texts connected to our area. The *Privilegium Maius*, for instance, a
text plausibly compiled in Trier in the early twelfth century, concentrates on the question of investiture, as does (as its name suggests) the *De
investitura episcoporum*, probably by Sigibert of Gembloux, which has the
distinction of being the first source written in the empire to talk of
'homage' and was perhaps consulted by Bruno, Archbishop of Trier.[76]
Investiture was the main issue at the Mouzon negotiations between
Henry V and Paschal II in 1119, according to Hesso, (probably) a

---

[74] Humbert, *Adversus Simoniacos Libri tres*, ed. E. Dümmler, *MGH Libelli de lite*, vol. 1 (Hanover, 1891),
pp. 95–293, 'Quicumque ergo his duobus aliquem initiant, procul dubio omnem pastoralem
auctoritatem hoc praesumendo sibi vindicant', p. 205.

[75] The arguments in H. Hoesch, *Die kanonischen Quellen im Werk Humberts von Moyenmoutier. Ein
Beitrag zur Geschichte der vorgregorianischen Reform* (Cologne, 1970), that Pseudo-Isidore was not
available in Upper Lotharingia are unconvincing. Moyenmoutier's library was greatly
improved in the late tenth century, according to the *Liber de successoribus S. Hildulfi in
Mediano monasterio*, ed. G. Waitz, *MGH SS*, vol. IV (Hanover, 1841), pp. 86–92, at p. 91.
Richer of Senones, *Gesta*, mentions one of Humbert's return trips, perhaps in the late 1050s (bk
II, ch. 19, p. 280). Humbert's letters are preserved in Bern, Burgerbibliothek Cod. 292, an
eleventh-century manuscript from St-Arnulf Metz, which also contains an early copy of the
Vita Leonis.

[76] See C. Märtl, *Die fälschen Investiturprivilegien* (Hanover, 1986), for a discussion of the provenance of
the *Privilegium Maius*, 84–9, with an edition of the text at pp. 179–205. The single extant manuscript is Trier Stadtbibliothek, 1081/29 (s. XII), which also contains Ivo of Chartres's celebrated
letter about investiture. For Sigibert's *De investitura episcoporum*, see 'Der Traktat "De investitura
episcoporum" von 1109', ed. J. Krimm-Beumann, *Deutsches Archiv* 33 (1977), 37–83.

canon of Strasbourg, and the cause of their ultimate breakdown.[77] More obscure accounts can also be useful in helping us understand the arguments of the time. For example, around 1140, a Toul cleric named Hugo Metellus all but rewrote Humbert's arguments in verse, in a poem in which the Pope and the king argue with each other as to the significance of the ring and staff. The king declares that they signify that the *regalia* can only be given to bishops; the Pope counters that they have only a liturgical meaning and so the king cannot hand them over.[78] The same manuscript which contains this work of Hugo, an early twelfth-century collection from Trier, also preserves a poem written around the same time by another Toul cleric, the otherwise obscure Hunald of Toul, proposing along similar lines certain ineradicable meanings for the objects in question, though also expressing frustration with the terms of debate.[79]

Some participants in this debate, including, perhaps most famously, Ivo of Chartres in a widely circulated letter, challenged this narrowing of meaning, arguing that it did not matter in what way or with what tokens investiture was performed. Yet these contributors failed to convince.[80] It is significant that it is from the late eleventh century that episcopal staffs began to take on a standardised form, that of a shepherd's crook; and that bishops of Langres, Meaux, Metz, Verdun and Trier all began to put curved staffs on their coins from the middle eleventh century, too.[81] The episcopal staff was increasingly a closely defined, relatively standardised, and prominent symbol of episcopal power.

These developments must be contextualised in two ways. In the first place, the stress put on the liturgical function of the passing over of these objects to the bishop-elect reflects the greater importance attributed to them since the ninth century, and needs therefore to be put in a longer historical context. Though Carolingian authors like Hincmar had dutifully copied out Isidore's ideas, in which the ring was a sign of the bishop's

[77] Hesso, *Relatio*.
[78] Hugo Metellus, *Certamen*, pp. 715–16. For the dating of the text, see p. 712.
[79] Hunald of Toul, *Carmen de anulo et baculo*: 'Papa docet, quia sunt duo mistica signa sacrorum / anulus et baculus, dos sacra pontificum', p. 721. Frustration: 'Pro nichilo pugnant rex et apostolicus', p. 722. The single manuscript is Brussels, Bibliothèque Royale, 10615–729. For the date, see p. 720.
[80] Cf. B. Bedos-Rezak, 'From ego to imago: mediation and agency in medieval France', *Haskins Society Journal* 14 (2003), 151–73; e.g. *De investitura episcoporum*: 'nil enim refert, sive vero, sive precepto, sive baculo', p. 77.
[81] T. Vogtherr, 'Bischofsstäbe und Abtsstäbe im frühen und hohen Mittelalter', in *Kleidung und Repräsentation in Antike und Mittelalter* (Munich, 2005), pp. 83–90; Focke, 'Szeptre'. For crosiers on coins, see F. Poey d'Avant, *Monnaies féodales de France* (Paris, 1858): Plate 135, no. 11 (Langres), Plate 139, no. 14 (Meaux); Kluge, *Deutsche Münzgeschichte*, no. 345 (Trier); Flon, *Histoire*, p. 194 (Metz) and p. 317 (Verdun). For some (superbly crafted) examples of surviving crosiers, see *La France romane*, for instance n. 81, a 'French' staff c.1100; cf. the 'Tau' abbatial staff, n. 84.

secret wisdom, the notion that the bishop could be thought to be married to his church gained ground in the ninth century, and a reinterpretation of, and greater emphasis upon, the bishop's ring, construed as a wedding ring, followed logically early in the tenth century.[82] Concurrent with this development, however, was another. Kings can be proven to have invested bishops with staffs only since the late ninth century, and with rings only from the eleventh.[83] Indeed, one may wonder whether the emergence of a legend about the staff of St Peter, the famous *Petrusstaab*, which spread in Lotharingia from the later tenth century, might be connected with this growth in attention to what had been a relatively low-profile token.[84] Humbert's treatise, and later texts working in the same vein, therefore seem to have been intended, in part, to assert the ineradicably liturgical signification of the ring and staff at the moment of ordination. The issue spread beyond bishops, too, and came to bear also on the question of abbatial appointments. At St-Mihiel, elaborate mechanisms were devised to ensure that the abbot did not receive his staff of office from any layman, but instead picked it up from the altar, as also attested in ducal dealings with its priory at Châtenois and probably at Springiersbach, near Trier.[85] We know that Abbot Walo of St-Arnulf was asked to return the staff by which the Archbishop of Rheims, Manasses, had invested him as abbot of St-Rémi.[86]

To point out this wave of increasingly sustained interest in the symbolic, which had begun in the late ninth century but reached a crescendo around the year 1100, is not, of course, to explain it. We need not view lay

---

[82] Hincmar, *Epistolae*, col. 188; for marriage to the church see, for instance, Pseudo-Isidore, *Decretales*, 1, Pseudo-Calixtus, p. 139. Bishops' rings surprised Greek commentators in the eleventh century: see T. Kolbaba, *The Byzantine lists: errors of the Latins* (Urbana, 2000), pp. 22, 53. See in general V. Labhart, *Zur Rechtssymbolik des Bischofsrings* (Cologne, 1963), especially pp. 24–36. The rings of archbishops Poppo of Trier (d.1047) and Gervaise of Rheims (d.1067) survive to this day. Bishop Gauzlin (d.962) of Toul's ring also survives, though as part of the relic collection of the saint.

[83] P. Depreux, '"Investitura per anulum et baculum". Ring und Stab als Zeichen der Investitur bis zum Investiturstreit', in J. Jarnut and M. Wemhoff, eds., *Vom Umbruch zur Erneuerung? Das 11. und beginnende 12. Jahrhundert* (Munich, 2006), pp. 169–95. It may be noted that kings themselves had been invested with ring and staff only from the late ninth century, too, to judge from the surviving *ordines*: see Jackson, *Ordines*, Ordo XIII (as p. 97, n. 67 above), which appears to be the first to give these objects.

[84] It may be noted that the *Gesta episcoporum Virdunensium*, written in the mid eleventh century, stresses how a bishop of Verdun who resigned his post was careful to return the *baculum* (p. 47), symptomatic, perhaps, of a greater interest in the token on the author's part.

[85] For Châtenois, see *Cartulaires*, ed. Laurent, no. 127. For St-Mihiel (itself linked to St-Vanne, according to Hugh of Flavigny, *Chronicon*, p. 499) see *Chronique et chartes*, ed. Lesort, no. 65, referring back to the late eleventh century. For Springiersbach, see *Consuetudines canonicorum regularum Springirsbacenses-Rodenses*, ch. 286, p. 153. Cf. Münster (Notre-Dame Luxembourg, in *Urkunden*, ed. Wampach, no. 385).

[86] Walo of St-Arnulf, *Epistolae*, ed. B. Schütte, *Die Briefe des Abtes Walo von St Arnulf von Metz*, MGH Studien und Texte 10 (Hanover, 1995), p. 62.

investiture as a long-unchecked abuse which threatened to lead to the
patrimonialisation of church assets; but nor can one quite share Hagen
Keller's subtle argument that the issue lies in the way individual parts of
the ritual were, from the late eleventh century, increasingly dissected and
separated out. After all, this had already been done by commentators like
Amalarius of Trier from the ninth century.[87] In fact, it seems counter-
intuitive to argue that the cause was anything other than an increasing
importance of the symbol, together with an increased concern for its
precise significance and efficacy, in ways which may shed light on relations
outside the church, too.[88] The problem was surely that the non-liturgical
moment of lay investiture, whether performed by a king or a count, was
assuming such constitutive importance that it was beginning to appear
rather liturgical. To put that differently, these rituals were increasingly not
about showing, they were about doing, and it was this which provoked
such disquiet. For a king to pass over a staff really made the recipient into a
bishop. It was this shift in the solidity of its meaning which produced a
counter-attack, to maintain the liturgical integrity of the ordination which
used just these symbols. This is why Humbert felt it necessary to draw
boundaries already around 1060: the traditional difference between secular rituals which worked on consensus and liturgical rituals which worked
on compliance, was increasingly challenged, and he was determined to
re-instil it.[89]

   It follows that Humbert's treatise and similar texts reflected a change not
simply in liturgical knowledge, but, we might infer, also in perceptions of
non-liturgical symbolic practice.[90] I would suggest, therefore, that we
could read the early twelfth-century debates about homage and investiture, which the earlier, vaguer arguments came eventually to be centred
upon, as the church defensively marking itself off from a world which was
becoming increasingly similar to it at a semiotic level, an attempt to
maintain the church's interpretative sovereignty (*Deutungshoheit*). It was
not just a matter of inspired popes and their legal collections; rather, the

[87] H. Keller, 'Die Investitur: ein Beitrag zur Problem der "Staatssymbolik" im Hochmittelalter', *FMS* 27 (1993), 51–86.
[88] Cf. Depreux, 'Investitura', arguing for investiture as a sign 'das eindeutig darstellte, dass im Unterschied zu den Ämtern, für die fortan das Erbrecht galt, der König bei der Bischofsernennung die Vollmacht hatte', p. 193 and P. Buc, 'The monster and the critics: a ritual reply', *EME* 15 (2007), 441–52, pp. 451–2.
[89] For the distinction, see I. Krause, *Konflikt und Ritual im Herrschaftsbereich der frühen Capetinger: Untersuchungen zur Darstellung und Funktion symbolischen Verhaltens* (Münster, 2006), pp. 24–5. Cf. along similar lines, distinguishing symbolism from association, Mitchell, *Colonising Egypt*, pp. 60–2 and 172–4.
[90] Humbert, *Libri tres*, bk III, ch. 6, pp. 205–6. The crooked staff signifies the invitation and the threat of pastoral care, the seal ring indicates the secret knowledge of God.

church was responding to new circumstances.[91] Some historians have described the consequence of that marking-off as the loss of ritual for the Emperor; but on the contrary, such was the importance of this symbolic gesture to kings that in the enforced absence of ring and staff, another symbol, the sceptre, was drafted in to complete the ceremony by which a bishop was acknowledged as an actor in the secular court.[92] Whereas ninth- and tenth-century accounts do not lay stress on the importance of the king handing out some symbol, it seemed by the twelfth century entirely indispensable.

The two-fold relevance of the 'Investiture Quarrel' to the argument of this chapter should now be apparent. Firstly, the debates over homage and the ceremony of investiture that appeared in its course offer context for the appearance of homage in different circumstances, as discussed in the previous sections, showing a new attention to ceremonies, and a new and urgent interest in their effectiveness, in other words in the transparency and rigidity of relations amongst the elite, from the late eleventh and early twelfth centuries. The debates around the relation between bishops and emperor in this sense acts as the canary in the mine for less well-documented changes, less well-documented perhaps because they provoked less opposition, since they were not imposing themselves on an already semi-defined set of symbolic practices. It is likely that these debates further sharpened distinctions, for example between homage and other kinds of oaths, that were already in the process of differentiation.

Secondly, though, it also demonstrates that these changes in conceptualisation had real-life consequences. Notwithstanding the much-needed widening of the parameters of study of the 'Investiture Quarrel', which bishop had performed what gesture to whom mattered, even as bishops tried to bridge the rival parties.[93] Bishop Theoderic of Verdun's reconciliation with the papacy explicitly concentrated on the ring and staff, and something similar was done by Archbishop Bruno of Trier in 1106.[94] Though homage was a contributory issue, the meeting at Châlons between Henry V's representatives, led by Bruno of Trier, and the Pope faltered explicitly over the question of investiture by ring

---

[91] Rolker, *Ivo* is an excellent reminder that arguments centring on the role of the papacy in inspiring a new legal renaissance, championed by Harold Berman, are potentially rather misleading.

[92] For example, Laurentius, *Gesta*, notes that Lothar III was in 1131 careful to give Albero, Bishop of Verdun, a sceptre as a token of office, p. 508. Comparable texts: Balderic, *Gesta Alberonis*, p. 251, and Hugo Metellus, *Carmen* p. 716, in which the pope suggests 'Per sceptrum regni donentur regia sane.' See in general K. Leyser, 'Ritual, ceremony and gesture: Ottonian Germany', in Leyser, *Communications and power*. The sceptre had been associated with kings since at least the ninth century, e.g. Ermold the Black, *In honorem*, p. 36.

[93] Erkens, *Trierer Kirchenprovinz*: e.g. the case of Richard of Verdun, pp. 210–17.

[94] For Bishop Theoderic, see Hugh of Flavigny, *Chronicon*, p. 459. Bruno of Trier: *Gesta Trevorum*, p. 192.

and staff.[95] The evidence from the bishoprics to the west is perhaps more equivocal, as here the conflict centred more directly on the extent and form of papal primacy, perhaps simply for pragmatic reasons.[96] Yet Pope Paschal II's most vehement anti-investiture decrees were issued in Champagne, at the Council of Troyes in 1107, and further debates about it took place in Rheims in 1119, so it should not seem surprising that Bishop Henry of Soissons went to Rome to seek pardon for royal investiture in 1088, and that Ivo of Chartres felt compelled to plead with the Pope in 1109 to confirm the compromise he had brokered between Louis VI and the new Archbishop of Rheims, Radulf, which seems to have involved some kind of investiture.[97]

TOWARDS A 'SECULAR LITURGY'?

The traditional model of feudalism used the term to denote a form of political organisation characterised by a lack of central authority that took shape in the wake of the collapse of the Carolingian state, paradoxically thought to be Carolingian in origin yet simultaneously associated with strong post-Carolingian states, and underpinned by the almost mystical notion of a union between fief and vassalage through the ritual of homage. For Reynolds, as we have seen, the concept of feudalism was simply unhelpful, unfairly prospering at the expense of attention to the communal aspects of the Middle Ages (solidarities of proximity, common interest and so on). Historians have trodden warily in the wake of her much-needed critique, and none (or few) would now use feudalism in quite the way that Ganshof and others did.

However, centralisation and decentralisation are not the only conceivable changes in socio-political structure, and in acknowledging that the old models put too much stress on the power of the link between fief and vassal, we do not have to accept that those historians were so totally enthralled to early modern constitutional speculation as to have invented their theories from whole cloth. Leaving to one side the question of how

---

[95] Suger, *Vita Ludovici*, p. 58.

[96] For example, see Gregory VII, *Registrum*, bk II, no. 56 about Roger of Châlons – the issue is simply one of obedience. Cf. J. Williams, 'Archbishop Manasses I of Rheims and Pope Gregory VII', *American Historical Review* 54 (1949), 804–24.

[97] Troyes 1107: *The early councils of Pope Paschal II, 1100–1110*, ed. U.-R. Blumenthal (Toronto, 1978), pp. 90–1; Rheims 1119: Hesso, *Relatio*, p. 27. Henry of Soissons: *Liber Pontificalis*, ed. L. Duchesne, 2 vols. (Paris, 1886–92), vol. II, p. 293, 'quia a rege francorum Philippo investituram acceperat'; cf. *Collectio Britannica*, ed. Brett, no. 32 (which also contains a version of the text concerning Henry of Soissons). Ivo of Chartres: *Epistolae*, no. 190, col. 196–7. The precise nature of the compromise is left vague, but it seems to have been some kind of investiture: 'per manum et sacramentum'. On the fizzling out, see Becker, *Studien*, pp. 111–37, and A. Fliche, *La réforme grégorienne* (Louvain, 1924–37).

far the issues discussed above affected community relations, which lies beyond the scope of this book, we should self-evidently not dissolve medieval society, which was deeply hierarchical, in an acid bath of pragmatic neighbourliness.[98] This chapter has sought an alternative approach to the phenomenon. Instead of tracking how feudalism worked for or against a state, and without denying the importance of communities, it has argued that relations amongst the elite became mediated through signs, practices and concepts that imbued these relations with ever clearer and less ambivalent content, often but not always or necessarily related to landholding.

In this way, it has been argued that the de facto dependence of most aristocratic landed property rights, implicated as they always had been in client/patron networks, found newly explicit designation (and to some extent greater security, since explicit terms work both ways) through being called fiefs, and were thereby more clearly distinguished from those increasingly rare property claims which could be considered as less dependent on patronage. From this classification, there flowed the possibility of further ones, such as extended hierarchies of tenure, and all the subtleties explored and exploited in later medieval texts such as the *Coutumier de Champagne*. The relationship that modern historians have been pleased to call vassalage also came under closer scrutiny, as the initiatory ceremony took on greater constitutive importance in defining of what that relationship consisted. Perhaps that ceremony did not always take place, but it became an icon for perceptions of how elites related to each other. Finally, I have suggested that the 'Investiture Quarrel', particularly in its later phases, should not be thought of as simply emerging from the devout, determined piety of reformers, but as part of a renegotiation of meaning as non-liturgical practices threatened to rival those imbued with formal authority by theology and long-standing doctrine; and that it therefore tells us at least as much about the world, and emergent practices like homage or fiefs, as it does about the reformers who sought a different kind of change.

What brings these superficially diverse developments together is their combination of communication and constitution, ways in which form was increasingly able to define, unambivalently, content. To put it differently, it is not decentralisation, the privileging of the land-fidelity nexus, or any of the other standard glosses on feudalism that distinguishes the early to mid twelfth and later centuries from previous centuries in sociopolitical terms. It is rather the enhanced precision of ways of thinking

---

[98] Cf. Wickham, *Courts*, p. 308.

about social relations, with a pronounced, and associated, tendency to reify them. At a certain point, these relations had become in a sense codified – not yet literally, but that would soon come too – across Western Europe. That increased precision was not a reaction to an earlier 'simple inability to construct theoretical norms of behaviour'. Quite the reverse, it was a continuation of certain approaches towards categorising elite interactions.[99] What we see in Lotharingian and Champenois sources, as in fact elsewhere, too, is an increasing abstraction of certain social relations, measuring them against particular, relatively codified models of what ought to take place. This made possible far more elaborated and durable networks of non-royal authority.

Homage, investiture and fiefs were in this sense merely the most prominent part of a whole network of changes, which had ramifications elsewhere, too. For example, the king's hands became the focus of attention to an unprecedented degree in quite a separate sphere, as charters decreeing that the advocates of important monasteries had to receive the office of ecclesiastical advocacy from the king in person (the so-called *Bannleihe*).[100] This development, which seems to parallel that of church investiture, may be most famously associated with Hirsau in Swabia, but it is first attested beyond there in Lotharingia, in (for example) charters written in the late eleventh or early twelfth century at Remiremont, St-Maximin, Moyenmoutier and Prüm.[101] Similarly, young men had doubtless undergone some sort of ceremony on their coming of age for centuries, but it is only from the late eleventh century that this began to evolve into the ceremony of dubbing, which changed their status almost like an ordination ritual.[102] No wonder that 'knights' were from the twelfth century increasingly viewed as an alternative *ordo* to clerics, and even perhaps a rival one, as hinted by the satirical 'Council of Remiremont' poem, written around Toul in the middle

[99] For the quote, G. Althoff, *Friends, family and followers: political and social bonds in early medieval Europe* (Cambridge, 2004).

[100] R. Scheying, *Eide, Amtsgewalt und Bannleihe: eine Untersuchung zur Bannleihe im hohen und späten Mittelalter* (Cologne, 1960), p. 207.

[101] Remiremont: *Chartes de l'abbaye de Remiremont des origines à 1231*, ed. J. Bridot (Turnhout, 1997), no. 44 (cf. the forged no. 3). St-Maximin: *DHIII*, no. 372. See T. Kölzer, *Studien zu den Urkundenfälschungen des Klosters St. Maximin vor Trier: (10.-12. Jahrhundert)* (Sigmaringen, 1989), 295–8, with further references to the 'Bannleihe'. Moyenmoutier: *Histoire*, ed. Calmet, vol. II, col. 71. Prüm: *DHIV* no. 476 (c.1102). Cf. also the famous St-Rémi dispute in 1149, ed. *MGH Constitutiones*, vol. I, no. 127.

[102] On Frankish precedent, see R. le Jan, 'Frankish giving of arms and rituals of power: continuity and change in the Carolingian period', in F. Theuws and J. Nelson, eds., *Rituals of power: from late antiquity to the early middle ages* (Leiden, 2000), pp. 377–99. In general, see Barthélemy, *Mutation*, pp. 255–70, with references to the older literature. A useful path of enquiry is opened up by G. Noiriel, 'La chevalerie dans la Geste des Lorrains', *Annales de l'Est* 3 (1976), 167–96, noting (p. 171) the importance of dubbing in the earliest (mid-twelfth-century) versions of this *chanson de geste*.

twelfth century, which pits the two against each other.[103] A new vocabulary was developed, too, to express the breaking of the kind of relationship that homage had cemented, with the emergence of descriptions of *diffidatio* or *exfestucatio*; and we could compare with this elaborations based on the word *vassalus*, or new ritualised forms of defiance, like the throwing of the gauntlet.[104] As with homage, historians have sometimes availed themselves of these terms to describe aspects of pre-twelfth-century history ('rear-vassals' and so forth), but this regressive approach is fraught with risk.[105] They were, however, fully in place by the time of a celebrated papal bull of 1179 for Rheims, when many 'feudal terms' were not only used but apparently used with some effect.[106]

More abstractly, we might even be tempted to bring in the debates surrounding the Eucharist, which also dealt with questions of symbolic efficacy, the lossless instantiation and transmission of meaning, or, to put it differently, with a change in the nature of representation – an issue which we know attracted attention from people living in this area.[107] The evidence of the manuscripts suggests that contemporaries sometimes associated the issues of the Eucharist debate and the 'Investiture Quarrel' – for example, Brussels, Bibliothèque Royale 5576–5604 (s. XII), compiled in this region, contains material on both the Eucharist and on investiture.[108] Another parallel issue would be the way in which secular elites began from the middle eleventh century to make increased use of seals, an appeal to a technology of reproduction that has been intriguingly interpreted as

---

[103] M. Parisse, 'Le concile de Remiremont: poème satirique du XIIᵉ siècle', in *Pays de Remiremont* 4 (1981), 10–15.

[104] On *diffidatio*, see *Gesta episcoporum Cameracensium, continuatio*, ed. G. H. Bethmann, *MGH SS*, vol. VII (Stuttgart, 1846), ch. 21, p. 496. On *exfestucatio*, see M. Bloch, 'Les formes de la rupture de l'hommage dans l'ancien droit féodal', in M. Bloch, ed., *Melanges historiques*, vol. I (Paris, 1963), pp. 189–208, who provides examples from the twelfth century onwards, with some extra examples added by Krause, *Konflikt*, p. 203, n. 966. On the gauntlet, see again Krause, *Konflikt*, p. 61, n. 257. The earliest example of rear-fiefs I am aware of is in a charter for Coulommiers in 1132, which mentions *minores fevales*, which are held by Theobald's *fevales* in turn (*Documents inédits tirés des collections manuscrites de la Bibliothèque royale*, ed. M. Champollion-Figeac (Paris, 1841), no. 8).

[105] E.g. Dhondt, *Études*, p. 8 (and cf. p. 142). A. Laret-Kayser, *Entre Bar et Luxembourg: le comté de Chiny des origines à 1300* (Brussels, 1986) cites Dhondt on p. 48 to show that Porcien, Omont-Rethel and Warcq 'relevaient de l'Eglise de Reims' *c.*1000, yet there is no explicit evidence for this.

[106] In 1187 the Count of Rethel refused to attack the Count of Champagne because of the agreement: see Bur *Formation*, p. 413.

[107] E.g. Paulinus of Metz's letter to Berengar, in *Thesaurus novus anecdotorum*, ed. E. Martène and U. Durand, 5 vols. (Paris, 1717), vol. I, col. 196.

[108] It contains Wenric of Trier's *Epistola* and Ivo of Chartres's celebrated letter, as well as Berengarian material: it is analysed in J. van der Gheyn, *Catalogue des manuscrits de la Bibliothèque Royale de Belgique*, vol. I (Brussels, 1901), pp. 194–9. Cf. Rheims, Bibliothèque Municipale, MS 15, whose oath (mentioned above) is in the company of a 'reform' canon law collection on simony; Paris BnF. 8922 also has material on Berengar and investiture, and Brussels 10615 (see n. 79 above) contains Lanfranc's letter to Berengar in the same quire as the Hunald and Hugo texts.

expressing a new rigour in concepts of aristocratic authority, though it should be noted that bishops had been doing this since the tenth century.[109] It may be the case, as Johannes Fried has argued, that the early eleventh century was beset by anxieties about the ambiguity and equivocity of signs; nevertheless by the late eleventh century, Althoff's vision of a ritualised world begins to have some purchase on the world – not because conflicts could be magically settled by careful *Inszenierung* (that 'black box' of ritual) or because this was a static society, but because it was one increasingly, though never totally, characterised by a kind of secular liturgy.[110]

From this perspective, *seigneurie banale*, as explored in Chapter 6, and the kinds of relations this chapter has dealt with can indeed be seen as two sides of the same coin. The sense in which both these sets of social relations were now deemed as verbally definable and manipulable, defined by ritual and property rights – the former a means of clarifying social relations, the latter in a sense its consequence – maps well onto how historians like Marc Bloch conceived of the period's essential unity.[111] It is true that these elite inter-actions were not quite as fully rendered as those relating to the non-elite, but the reasons for this are fairly self-evident. One need merely think of the celebrated outrage of one of Robert Curthose's vassals when his homage was transferred to see what impeded an entirely logical extension.[112] Fiefs were important, but Reynolds is certainly right to argue that they did not alone determine social process, and, as Chapter 4 showed, kings were still important in this region. Yet fiefs can stand for a rather broader conception of that social process, alongside homage, and for that matter, *bannum*: all were not only new ways of describing the relations between people at different levels, they expressed new forms of those relations, distinct from, though causally related to, early medieval kinds of social order.

CONCLUSION

Arguments in some ways analogous to those made above appear in Reynolds' *Fiefs and Vassals*, which includes a discussion of the importance

---

[109] B. Bedos-Rezak, 'From ego to imago'. On earlier episcopal seals, see T. Diederich, 'Sancta Colonia - Sancta Coloniensis Religio. Zur "Botschaft" der Bleibullen Erzbischof Pilgrims von Köln (1021–1036)', *Rheinische Vierteljahrsblätter* 75 (2011), 1–49.

[110] J. Fried, 'Ritual und Vernunft – Traum und Pendel des Thietmar von Merseburg', in L. Gall, ed., *Das Jahrtausend im Spiegel der Jahrhundertwenden* (Berlin 1999), pp. 15–63. Cf. W. Pohl, 'Staat und Herrschaft im Frühmittelalter: Überlegungen zum Forschungsstand', in Airlie, Pohl and Reimitz, eds., *Staat*, pp. 9–38, on Althoff's sublimated *Verfassungsgeschichte*-approach. On ritual as black box, see Pössel, 'Magic'.

[111] M. Bloch, *Feudal society*, tr. L. Manyon (London, 1961).

[112] Orderic Vitalis, *Historia ecclesiastica*, ed. and tr. M. Chibnall, *The ecclesiastical history of Orderic Vitalis*, 6 vols. (Oxford, 1990), II, ch. 10 (vol. VI, p. 58).

of greater precision in expressing and communicating social hierarchies. Reynolds, however, ultimately considered that such precision could only be the product of professional lawyers, which logically rules out any signs of such a system before such lawyers are attested at work, which is usually thought to be the twelfth century.[113] Whereas Ganshof thought that Carolingian practices of putting land at the disposal of its warriors were the seed from which feudalism grew, for Reynolds 'feudalism', insofar as it existed at all, was very much a product of the long twelfth century, not of the 'warrior society' that preceded it.[114]

In the argument about lawyers, however, one senses the influence of the functionalist anthropology which has brought so much vitality to historians of the early Middle Ages, but which has caused more problems for those of the central. These twelfth-century lawyers effectively function as the equivalent of the colonial officials and experts descending on previously untouched indigenous societies, reworking its very fabric like a *deus ex machina*. However, quite apart from a definite chronological disjuncture (professional lawyers in Reynolds's sense cannot be identified in the region studied here before the thirteenth century), there is a more profound methodological problem.[115] Functionalist models, devised to bracket off the colonial state in order to get at the 'authentic' underlying practice, are unsuitable for studying the interactions between indigenous society and a reifying elite. This is partly because these models are intrinsically ill-equipped to deal with formality, but also because they tend to occlude the ways in which societies can transform themselves without requiring that *deus ex machina* of colonial occupation, which was after all itself the product (and cause) of quite particular historical circumstances.[116]

More broadly, it could be suggested that the presupposition here that 'law' is something alien, new and modern in the twelfth century, a distinctively rational process by which problems are solved and fresh problems created, is problematic both in its presuppositions about earlier

[113] Cf. her arguments in 'The emergence of professional law in the long twelfth century', *Law and History Review* 21 (2003), 347–66. The argument has been adopted in Dendorfer and Deutinger, *Lehnswesen*, p. 23 and pp. 469–470, and developed, too, by Hyams, 'Homage and feudalism'. C. Radding, *The origins of medieval jurisprudence: Pavia and Bologna, 850–1100* (New Haven, 1988), puts the emergence of professional lawyers rather earlier, but in an Italian context; professional law in Champagne is associated with the 'Jours de Troyes', from the mid thirteenth century.
[114] For the phrase, see her *mise-à-jour* of her argument in 'Fiefs and vassals after twelve years', in Bagge, Gelting and Lindkvist, eds., *Feudalism: new landscapes of debate*, pp. 15–26, at p. 16.
[115] The *Summa 'Elegantius in iure divino' seu Colonensis*, ed. G. Fransen and S. Kuttner, 2 vols. (New York, 1969–78), a commentary on Gratian, perhaps written by Bertram of Metz in the late twelfth century, may be the earliest 'professional' canon law from the region, though there is much here that Regino would have been familiar with.
[116] Asad, *Anthropology*.

practice and in its image of modern law, which provides, tacitly or otherwise, the benchmark for evaluation. Many recent studies of modern law suggest that its self-definition should not be taken at face-value.[117] Indeed, with its combination of arcane knowledge, special experts and counter-intuitive rule, it could be read as nothing other than a particularly efficacious form of ritual practice, in which classifications, once established, have instant and indelible effect, from conviction to contract.

Even if that is to take the argument too far, we should certainly not assume that we can juxtapose a period of ritual law and a period of rational law, and so safely not worry about whence the latter emerged. With these points in mind, all the changes described above and in the previous chapter seem very much in line with the ninth-century dynamic laid out in Chapter 3, however far removed in their specifics. This was a dynamic of increasing formality and definability of social relations, which proceeded at a level subjacent to the flow of politics, even though, as we shall see, that flow conditioned the details of how this process worked itself out. Rituals like homage do not reveal an unchanging medieval essence; it is not clear anyway that there was an essence to be revealed. What they do show is a process at work, a parallel, perhaps, to that process which Giles Constable labelled in the field of theology as the moving apart of *signum* and *res*.[118] In the place of the loose, informal practices which appear to have dominated this field of social relations in the ninth and early tenth century, we have homage and fiefs: on the one hand essentially the same thing, on the other, a world apart. This was a society passing from symbol to sign, well before the arrival of the professional lawyer, a role that was just as plausibly enabled by changes of this kind as much as being responsible for fostering them.[119] To treat this process as juridification would be to place the cart before the horse.

---

[117] Amongst many possible references, see P. Fitzpatrick, *The mythology of modern law* (London, 1992) and R. Cotterrell, *The sociology of law: an introduction* (Oxford, 1984).

[118] G. Constable, 'The ceremonies and symbolism of entering religious life and taking the monastic habit, from the fourth to the twelfth century', *Settimane* 33 (1987), 771–834.

[119] On the distinction between symbol and sign, see Krause, *Konflikt*, pp. 19–22. Cf. S. Fish, *Is there a text in this class? The authority of interpretative communities* (Cambridge, Mass., 1980), particularly pp. 338–55.

Chapter 8

UPPER LOTHARINGIA AND CHAMPAGNE
AROUND 1100: UNITY AND DIVERSITY

Up till this point, the sources from the lands either side of the River Meuse, the regions eventually known as Champagne and Upper Lotharingia, have been treated together to produce a composite picture, and as a basis for drawing out generalisations about the whole area between Marne and Moselle. This chapter, however, takes a different perspective, paying closer attention to some regional specificities of the evidence, in order not only to move beyond these generalisations but also to demonstrate how social and political patterns, though evolving from a common basis, could nevertheless take quite different trajectories. Central to this point is the issue of ecclesiastical advocacy. Before we tackle it, however, it is necessary to begin by summarising the broad political landscape by around 1100, in the wake of the developments discussed in the previous two chapters.

THE NEW POLITICAL LANDSCAPE BETWEEN
MARNE AND MOSELLE

By the beginning of the twelfth century, the lands between Marne and Moselle were becoming defined by a new set of emergent political units, consolidating or dissolving the tentative tenth-century formations discussed in Chapter 5. Are, Arlon, Bar, Brienne, Chiny, Clermont, Dabo, Dammartin, Grandpré, Hochstaden, Laroche, Lutzelbourg, Luxembourg, Morsberg, Mousson, Ramerupt, Roucy, Rethel, Salm, Sayn and Vaudémont, to name but a selection of those that appear in documentation of various kinds from around this time, without including the steadily territorialising bishoprics: as Parisse has commented, listing these jurisdictions is like reading Prévert.[1] There is no single study of these as a phenomenon, and the history

---

[1] M. Parisse, 'Désintégration et regroupements territoriaux dans les principautés lotharingiennes du XIe au XIIIe siècle', in H. Heit, ed., *Zwischen Gallia und Germania, Frankreich und Deutschland. Konstanz und Wandel raumbestimmender Kräfte* (Trier, 1987), pp. 155–80.

of these political units is greatly complicated by the efforts of genealogists, medieval and modern, to push back their roots as far back as possible.[2] A tendency can nevertheless be noted for those in the west to appear a little earlier than those in the east, a point to which we will return.

Some of the territories that existed in the decades around 1100 would remain in existence for some time, while others would be fragmented and absorbed by their rivals. Whatever their fate, these lordships manifested and substantiated an increasingly coherent political authority, buttressed by all the formalism discussed in Chapter 7, and quite different from the form in which power was exercised in earlier periods. At their heart were the gatherings that were now routinely labelled as *curiae* in charters relating to the counts of, for example, Bar, Brienne, Dammartin and Roucy, and sometimes even to lesser lords like those of Chappes, quite apart from those referring to the courts of abbots, bishops and kings. This terminology is redolent of a new understanding of 'public' meetings which was far more clearly a reflection of the convenor's authority than of the traditional assemblies discussed in chapters 1 and 2.[3] These 'honour courts', as they are known in the scholarship where they have been most closely studied, were peopled with panels of judges and other followers, occasionally now called barons (*barones*), as well as by ranks of honorary domestic officials.[4] Seneschals and butlers are attested from the late eleventh century, and, before too long, chancellors appeared too, all of whom confirmed the dignity of what were intended to be replicas of the royal court.[5] These honour courts did not play simply an honorary role. A number of texts show them at work, for example arranging duels, deciding judgements, representing the formality at the heart of power, and setting out the particular variant of customs regulating intra-elite activity ('feudal custom') that applied in their locality.[6]

---

[2] Alberic of Troisfontaines is a particularly good example of this tendency, for example anachronistically locating the emergence of the counts of Rethel back into the early tenth century: *Chronica*, p. 765.

[3] Cf. Wickham, 'Public court practice'. On the *curia*, see L. Genicot, 'Le premier siècle de la *curia* de Hainaut', *Le Moyen Age* 53 (1947), 39–60. Bar: Artem no. 121; Brienne: *Cartulaires*, ed. Laurent, vol. 1, no. 80; Dammartin: *Le prieuré de Saint-Leu d'Esserent*, ed. Müller, no. 3; Roucy: *Cartulaire de Saint-Nicaise*, ed. Cosse-Durlin, no. 38. Chappes: *Cartulaires*, ed. Laurent, no. 248. For the *curia* of an abbot, Artem no. 276; for a bishop, Artem no. 770.

[4] *Barones*: e.g. Artem no. 869 (Molesme) and no. 257. On the honour courts, see D. Carpenter, 'The second century of feudalism', *Past and Present* 168 (2000), 30–71.

[5] E.g. a seneschal and a steward are attested for Duke Theoderic II: *Cartulaires*, ed. Laurent, no. 185 (1090) and Artem no. 713 (for Saint-Dié, 1114). Cf. E. Mason, 'Barons and their officials in the later eleventh century', *Anglo-Norman Studies* 13 (1990), 243–62.

[6] Records from St-Pierremont (Meurthe-et-Moselle) show the Count of Bar's court at work in the early twelfth century: Paris, BnF nouv. acq. lat. 1608, f. 15v, 16v, 17r, and 18v. For the *curia* and feudal law, see Parisse, 'Pratiques', no. 5, regulating a dispute 'juxta legem et consuetudinem quam Treverensis curia de feodis habere dinoscitur' (c.1160). On military service owed by those holding land, see *UBMR* no. 382 (1083). For a broader range of assistance, see *UBMR* no. 394 (1097).

It is a sign of how tightly defined these sets of domination were that around the late eleventh century we find for the first time systematic attempts to record in writing the entire content of a particular lordship, like the definition of the county of Toul ventured in the late eleventh century, or the territorial limits of the 'honour' of Bitche recorded in a letter from the mid twelfth century: quite different in nature from the conceptions of power suggested by Odo II's agreement with Châlons (above, p. 127).[7] Conceived in this way, these lordships were increasingly able to be transferred en bloc, or, conversely, formally split. The county of Porcien was sold off in the 1090s, and then later divided out of existence, while the county of Morsberg was transferred by marriage and the county of Are formally split in the mid twelfth century.[8] Along similar lines, the counties of Verdun and Soissons were explicitly given out in benefice by the bishops of these cities.[9] Smaller-scale lordships could now be written out on parchment, like the rights of *vicecomitatus* at Trigny, already mentioned in Chapter 6, or even be deliberately and consciously created, by hiving off bundles of rights, as Count Stephen of Blois is said to have done at Provins in 1101.[10] Notwithstanding the new coherence given by this territorial lordship, there was little qualitative difference between the rights these important lords enjoyed and those fragmented and recorded in scores of contemporary charters, whether labelled as *bannum*, *comitatus*, or *justitia*: the difference was primarily one of scale.

This helps explain why old distinctions between those holding formal comital office and those without became a little more blurred. Some aristocrats who had successfully built up *blocs* of lordships claimed the comital title, the so-called new 'allodial' counties of German scholarship that were in fact equally a feature of regions west of the Meuse too.[11] Others did not claim the comital title, or did so only intermittently, like the counts of Brixey or Reynel.[12] There were some lords of castles, or

---

[7] For Toul, see *Histoire*, ed. Picart, pr. 82, and Bönnen, *Toul*, pp. 55–73. For Bitche, see *Histoire*, ed. Calmet, vol. v, preuves, col. 340–1.

[8] Morsberg: *Monuments*, ed. Tardif, no. 397. Porcien: G. de Gostowski, 'Les émancipations seigneuriales dans le comté de Porcien aux xi–xiie siècles', *Revue Historique Ardennaise* 33 (1998), 13–96; see *Recueil*, ed. Demouy, vol. ii, no. 232 (1134). Are: U. Bader, *Geschichte der Grafen von Are bis zur Hochstadenschen Schenkung* (Bonn 1976), particularly pp. 141–80.

[9] Laurentius, *Gesta*, p. 498, p. 503; *Seigneurs*, ed. Newman, vol. ii, no. 6.

[10] On the grant at Provins, see K. LoPrete, *Adela of Blois, countess and lord (c.1067–1137)* (Dublin, 2007), pp. 109–11.

[11] The suggestion in N. Civel, *La fleur de France: les seigneurs d'Ile-de-France au xiie siècle* (Turnhout, 2006) at p. 152 that the emergent counties of Beaumont, Clermont, Dammartin and Meulan were established by the king is pure supposition: the parallels with allodial counties (e.g. Vianden) further east seem unavoidable.

[12] On Brixey, with a full list of relevant charters, see (despite its title) G. Poull, *Le château et les seigneurs de Bourlémont*, 2 vols. (Corbeil, 1962–4), vol. i. On Reynel, P. Lebel, 'Contribution à la recherche des origines de la ville et des seigneurs de Reynel', *Bulletin philologique et historique* (1936–7), 289–312.

groups of castles, with a concentration in the south between Marne and Meuse (for instance Clefmont, Joinville, Vignory) but also some further north (Commercy, Coucy, Florennes, Pierrefonds and Rumigny), who perhaps lacked the confidence to assert their place at the top table, yet who were clearly on a par in scale with minor counts like those of Breteuil, Vianden or Katzelnbogen.[13]

Though this set of developments was associated with important changes in family consciousness along the lines developed by Karl Schmid and others, they cannot be reduced down to it, and still less considered as produced by the triumph of some hereditary principle.[14] Carolingian counties had already passed down family lines, and anyway in this new world the place seems often to have been privileged over the family.[15] That is most clearly shown by bishoprics, for bishops, too, insofar as they had retained their position in this new political landscape, had done so only by transforming their authority to conform to the new framework. Indeed, some of the best evidence for the new political forms comes from bishoprics, particularly those east of the Meuse like Toul or Trier that received imperial grants formalising their position, for example in the form of entire counties, though there is evidence for similar situations to the west, too.[16] Their ordained status certainly distinguished them from the secular rivals, since their relatives could not inherit, and their patrimony was indivisible. But otherwise, they were building castles, holding courts and dealing in rights of jurisdiction, just like everyone else. It was only natural that from the later twelfth century, those bishops who controlled comital rights began to title themselves as both bishop and count.[17]

At the lower end of the spectrum, the countryside was populated by agrarian communities, subjected to exactions from their lords, just as they had been in the ninth century. However, there had been developments on two fronts since the ninth century. Firstly, as will be discussed briefly below, there are signs by the early twelfth century that other streams of

---

[13] For the south, see J. Lusse, 'Quelques types de bourgs castraux en Haute-Marne', in M. Bur, ed., *Les peuplements castraux dans les pays de l'Entre-Deux: Alsace, Bourgogne, Champagne, Franche-Comté, Lorraine, Luxembourg, Rhénanie-Palatinat, Sarre: aux origines du second réseau urbain* (Nancy, 1993), pp. 75–116. For northern Lotharingia, see M. Groten, 'Die Stunde der Burgherren. Zum Wandel adliger Lebensformen in den nördlichen Rheinlanden in der späten Stauferzeit', *Rheinische Vierteljahresblätter* 66 (2002), 74–110.

[14] Guenée, 'Les génealogies'. [15] Cf. Guerreau, 'Quelques caractères spécifiques'.

[16] Rheims had enjoyed the *comitatus* since at least the mid eleventh century: Jackson, *Ordines*, p. 232 (the manuscript though dates from *c.*1100, and may be connected with Archbishop Rodulf). In general, see Kaiser, *Bischofsherrschaft*, e.g. pp. 537–56 for Rheims and pp. 557–64 for Châlons.

[17] O. Guyotjeannin, *Episcopus et comes: affirmation et déclin de la seigneurie épiscopale au nord du royaume de France (Beauvais-Noyon, x^e–début xiiie siècle)* (Geneva, 1987), pp. 227–44; Hoffman, 'Grafschaften'. Cf. AD de la Marne, G 466 (1146), in which the bishop of Châlons claimed the *comitatus* of the city.

income were beginning to complement and even to rival revenues of rural origin, particularly control of trade within and between towns, though insofar as the meagre early twelfth-century evidence permits a judgement it would still seem in most cases to have played a lesser role. Secondly, these communities were now doubly subordinated. To their landlords, they owed dues for the continued possession of their lands which we could label rent, though eviction was rare and the dues paid not only in cash; and to their lords, who might or might not be the same person, they paid fines and other exactions levied in the name of jurisdiction. It should be stressed that not all of these communities were subordinated to the same degree, or in quite the same way (a point to be returned to below): the level of the dues varied greatly. Many had negotiated, or would later negotiate, arrangements with these lords, particularly over jurisdiction, and these negotiations could take very distinct forms, at a regional, and indeed local level. Still, it would be reasonable to assume that there were few settlements that escaped this double bond entirely, and that even exemptions, such as the famous franchises, attested to the strength of the overarching system.

UPPER LOTHARINGIA AND CHAMPAGNE COMPARED

These observations are specific enough to distinguish society in this region around the year 1100 from that in the ninth century, and to identify the salient driver of difference, centred on the formalisation of social relations at every level. Yet they are also general enough to apply equally to either side of the Meuse, and in that sense, they are deficient. Any historical analysis that does not allow for differentiation alongside identifying similarities can justifiably be accused of over-systematisation, because it is always necessary to see the room for manoeuvre, how people have made a difference and how divergences have come into being. The obvious, and as we shall see, largely justified, approach is to think comparatively about the lands on either side of the Meuse, that is the regions of Champagne and of Upper Lotharingia.

Historiographical divergence

Identifying the divergences within the territories between Marne and Moselle is, however, a complicated matter. In part, that is because of the different intellectual traditions involved. The main faultline lies naturally enough between Francophone and German scholarship, since Champagne and Lotharingia were located respectively in the kingdom of France and the Holy Roman Empire. Historians working in these traditions have approached the period in radically different ways, particularly since the development of the 'new constitutional history' in Germany from the 1930s that introduced specialised terminologies and assumptions that generally hampered comparison.[18] The risk is not just that similarities are obscured – though as has been shown in the previous two chapters, the similarities in the lands on either side of the Marne are quite striking; there is also the danger that real differences will not be appreciated, either.

The subsequent history of the region further muddies the waters, because later in the Middle Ages, the French-speaking areas around Verdun, Metz and Toul were acquired by the French king. As Upper Lotharingia transformed into modern French Lorraine, Trier and the lower Moselle valley became increasingly oriented to the Rhineland. This outcome was not just important for the later Middle Ages, it has shaped how the earlier period has been assessed, too. While virtually everything written on Champagne has been done within a Francophone framework (though not only by French historians), neighbouring Lotharingia is simultaneously treated as a duchy within the Holy Roman Empire, yet also, when convenient, as somewhat French.[19] Paradoxically, this too has made comparison harder, not easier, since one is faced with a 'moving target'.

These differences of approach, based around national traditions, have affected the history that is written of these regions – never systematically compared before – in various ways. Sometimes a national historical perspective is deployed quite consciously, for example in the construction of the national narratives of the kind that underpin all nation-states.[20] It is an easy, and in many ways reasonable, step for historians of France to see the eventual later incorporation of parts of Lotharingia into the French kingdom as little short of inevitable, reflecting innate connections that were there all along. It is with this in mind, one suspects, that historians have suggested the alignment of the political boundary with the 'civilisational' one between two languages, French and German, was a development with its own logic.[21] This is nevertheless an argument that needs to be treated with caution. It is certainly true that the language boundary became gradually clearer than it had been in the early Middle Ages, as pockets of Romance or Germanic were ironed out, and as village-level elites, groups perhaps more likely to be monolingual than their social superiors, became more influential. Yet even today, languages along frontiers tend to blur into

---

[18] Much of Reynolds, *Fiefs* is devoted to unpicking elements of these historiographical divergences.

[19] In an otherwise excellent article, Dendorfer, 'Das Wormser Konkordat' makes conspicuous use of this get-out clause, bracketing off developments in the west of the Empire as showing 'French' influence (e.g. pp. 310–11, 315, 321, 324).

[20] P. Geary, *The myth of nations: the medieval origins of Europe* (Princeton, 2003).

[21] Parisse, *Noblesse et chevalerie*, pp. 12–13, 298.

one another, and this was still more the case before the advent of linguistic policing undertaken by nation-states, and it is clear anyway that bilingualism was common.[22] In short, these distinctions should not be exaggerated.[23]

Sometimes, though, historiographical distinctions are generated less intentionally. A good example here is provided by the debate, or rather lack of it, over differing approaches to the retinues of powerful lords. Any historian of medieval France will be familiar with the extraordinary subtleties of argument devoted to defining knighthood and the relative position of knights to their inferiors and superiors.[24] Historians of Germany will be likewise familiar with the 'serf-knight', the ministerial (*ministerialis*).[25] The difference between these two figures has on occasion been elevated into another civilisational difference, between a society focused on nobility, and one oriented instead to freedom. This comparative interpretation is in itself a little shaky. After all, the rise of the ministerial could equally point to the lack of importance of legal status as to the reverse; ideas of freedom were as nuanced in Lotharingia as anywhere else, as shown by numerous people named *censuales* whose manumission 'freed' them to the control of churches.[26] Yet more to the point, it is largely unsupported by the evidence from the early twelfth century, which shows bishops and lords from either side of the Meuse accompanied by their *ministri* and *servientes*, with hardly a word about their legal status; it is not entirely clear that they were really considered to be unfree before the mid twelfth century.[27]

Finally, some differences have their origin in issues of evidence that have received historiographical amplification. A particularly good example of this concerns agricultural communities. Since the days of Perrin, if not before, historians have been aware that records detailing the legal relations between

[22] On the language boundary, see W. Haubrichs, 'Über die allmähliche Verfertigung von Sprachgrenzen. Das Beispiel der Kontaktzonen von Germania und Romania', in W. Haubrichs and and R. Schneider, eds., *Grenzen und Grenzregionen/Frontières et régions frontalières* (Saarbrücken, 1993), pp. 99–129. For examples of higher-level bilingualism, see Balderic's *Gesta Alberonis*, p. 257, and Suger, *Vita Ludovici*, p. 56. According to the *Vita Leonis*, p. 58, Leo IX (as Bishop of Toul) was used as an envoy by Konrad II, probably because of his French: cf. also Anselm of St-Rémi, *Historia*, p. 212.

[23] M. Parisse, *La noblesse Lorraine: XIe–XIIIe siècles*, 2 vols. (Lille, 1976), vol. I, pp. 392–4, draws some interesting maps showing marriage alliances and relating them to the language boundary, but these can be interpreted as proving that marriages continued to take place across the language boundary, such as it was, as much as the reverse.

[24] Barthélemy, *Mutation* contains an excellent summary of a uniquely tangled historiography, pp. 160–5.

[25] B. Arnold, *German knighthood, 1050–1300* (Oxford, 1985); T. Zotz, 'Die Formierung der Ministerialität', in S. Weinfurter, ed., *Die Salier und das Reich* (Sigmaringen, 1991), vol. III, pp. 3–50.

[26] G. Tellenbach, 'Servitus und libertas nach den Traditionen der Abtei Remiremont', *Saeculum* 21 (1970), 228–34.

[27] Bast, *Die Ministerialität*, is a good discussion but now somewhat dated, and his arguments for the unfree status of the earliest *ministeriales* are not wholly compelling. Still worth reading is Bloch, 'Ministerialité'. More recently, see Erkens, *Trierer Kirchenprovinz*, pp. 116–18.

lords and those who worked their estates generally came in two kinds, franchises and *Weistümer*.[28] The former, as already mentioned, took the form of a legal privilege from a lord to his dependants, conferring on them certain exemptions, and setting out their obligations. The latter took the form of the peasants' recognition of the lords' rights, as acknowledged in infrequent but regular meetings. The results are two very different kinds of records, suggesting that the communities concerned were quite different. Moreover, it is broadly true that the former was more common in France, the latter in the Empire. However, not only was there much overlap, the significance of this difference has hardly yet been researched. It is true that peasant communities would seem in parts of Lotharingia to have had more control over the performance of justice than was usually the case west of the Meuse, but the picture is too diversified to allow for easy generalisations.[29] It may be that differences in traditions of record-making have exaggerated difference.[30] More research is needed on what is often recalcitrant (and often very late) evidence, before definitive conclusions can be reached.

Duke Theoderic II and Count Hugh

If we set aside the historiographical differences that seem to be generated by national priorities, insufficiently critical appreciations of particular debates, and over-enthusiastic interpretations of ambiguous evidence, we are nevertheless left with one field in which a significant and indeed intensifying difference can be identified, and properly investigated; and that is in the sphere of political integration, that is to say in how the bearers of these agglomerated rights of jurisdiction related to one another. This is a delicate issue which can best be broached top-down, by looking at the principalities that made claims to dominate each region in question, namely the county of Champagne and the duchy of Upper Lotharingia. What follows will focus, to make a comparison more precise, on two contemporary figures, Count Hugh (1093–1124) and Duke Theoderic II (1073–1115), each of whom played an important role in the consolidation of the principalities which they ruled over a similar length of time (see figures 2 and 3 for genealogies).[31]

---

[28] Ch-E. Perrin, 'Chartes de franchise et rapports de droit en Lorraine', *Moyen Age* 52 (1946), 11–42.
[29] Nikolay-Panter, *Enstehung und Entwicklung*, p. 78 (as p. 197, n. 91 above). Cf., however, A. Girardot, *Le droit et la terre: le Verdunois à la fin du Moyen Age*, 2 vols. (Nancy, 1992), vol. I, pp. 367–91, for a discussion of variation within the region.
[30] Morsel, 'Le prélèvement seigneurial'.
[31] On Theoderic, see the dense but effective summary by W. Mohr, *Geschichte des Herzogtums Lothringen*, 3 vols. (Sarrebruck, 1978), vol. III, pp. 17–19, which can be supplemented by Barth, *Lotharingien*, pp. 32–6. I have discussed Hugh's charters in greater detail in 'Count Hugh of Troyes and the territorial principality in early twelfth-century Europe', *English Historical Review* 127 (2012), 523–48.

In the case of Upper Lotharingia, the most important point is also a simple one. The term 'duchy of Upper Lotharingia' implies that the entire region between Jura and Vosges, the entire province of Trier, was under the authority of a single duke. That was certainly not so by 1100. In fact, the principality ruled by the dukes in the later eleventh and early twelfth centuries in no sense stretched over southern Lotharingia, any more than there was really a duchy of Lower Lotharingia in the north, by this point equally nominal.[32] It can be debated whether actually it ever had, for the evidence that the early dukes, who had appeared in the south in the middle tenth century, had ever actually exerted an authority over a duchy is decidedly patchy, and its interpretation may have been influenced by now-superseded ideas of 'stem-duchies'.[33] Be that as it may, the southern duchy as it appeared after Emperor Henry III had defeated Duke Godfrey the Bearded and given his backing to a new family, as discussed in Chapter 4, was in practical terms confined to the south-east of the region.[34] It may be that the duke claimed some kind of nominal superiority elsewhere in southern Lotharingia, as suggested by the occasional use in charters of his *ducatus* as a dating reference, by ceremonial honours like the 'three banners' given in the thirteenth century to dukes on their appointment, or by token minting rights, yet none of these carried any practical implications.[35] The tendency of contemporaries like Lampert of Hersfeld to talk about the duke 'of the Moselle' was entirely justified.[36]

The reason for this is that the dukes exercised virtually no influence, let alone authority, over other developing political units, such as Luxembourg in the north and Bar in the west, to mention only the most important.[37] The southern Lotharingian bishops, too, had escaped whatever ducal authority there had ever been. Toul, where Theoderic II attended a relic translation in 1104, briefly had Theoderic's son Henry as its bishop in 1126.[38] However, even here the connections were not always close; meanwhile, the Archbishop of Trier held his own court, surrounded by his own

---

[32] M. Werner, 'Der Herzog von Lothringen in salischer Zeit', in *Die Salier und das Reich*, ed. S. Weinfurter (Sigmaringen, 1991), vol. I, pp. 367–473.

[33] Cf. Goetz, *'Dux' und 'Ducatus'*.

[34] The concentration of this family in the region probably dates back well into the eleventh century: even though Gerard, the grandfather of Theoderic II, had interests at Heimbach, it is interesting that the major source here, Alpert, talks of him as 'Gerardus Mosellensis'.

[35] Cf. Goetz, *'Dux' und 'Ducatus'*.

[36] Mohr, *Geschichte*, vol. III, pp. 8–9, and on Theoderic II, pp. 16–19. On the coins, see Flon, *Histoire*, pp. 268–71.

[37] M. Parisse, 'Les ducs et le duché de Lorraine au xiiᵉ siècle (1048–1206)', *Blätter für deutsche Landesgeschichte* 111 (1975), 86–102.

[38] *Translatio secunda Mansuetis*, ed. O. Holder-Egger, *MGH SS*, vol. xv:ii (Hanover, 1888), pp. 931–2, at p. 931.

mouvance of counts and other lords, such as those of Veldenz, Katzelnbogen and Sayn, and the situation in Metz was much the same.[39] Insofar as 'Upper Lotharingia', understood here as the region between Moselle and Meuse, Ardennes and Jura, existed as a practical reality in the twelfth century, it was as the province of Trier, whose energetic archbishops, particularly Albero, did their best to activate a latent metropolitan authority, not as the duchy under the control of a duke.[40]

This is not to say that the duke was entirely insignificant. Duke Theoderic II, for example, had a warlike reputation sufficient to win the release of a kidnapped bishop of Châlons who had been whisked away to a stronghold near Toul.[41] A loyal ally of the Emperor Henry IV, Theoderic attested dozens of the emperor's charters, and attempted (unsuccessfully) to act as a broker between him and Gregory VII in 1079.[42] Theoderic fought bravely on Henry's side in the Saxon wars, and was allegedly prevented from joining the First Crusade only by illness, according to later accounts.[43] He was also capable of determined efforts to expand. Not content with signing occasional charters in Trier, and indeed putting his name on coins based on Trier exemplars, Duke Theoderic II took advantage of an opportunity provided by the 'Investiture Quarrel' to attempt to take the city of Metz, claiming control over the monastery of St-Arnulf, and even calling himself in one charter 'duke of Metz'.[44] He even toyed with negotiating an Italian marriage alliance, and the two marriages he did contract show again a certain breadth of vision, connecting him to Saxony and Flanders.[45]

---

[39] R. Schieffer, 'Rheinische Zeugen in den Urkunden Friederich Barbarossas', in *Geschichtliche Landeskunde der Rheinlande. Regionale Befunde und raumübergreifende Perspektiven. Georg Droege zum Gedenken* (Cologne, 1994), pp. 104–30. Cf. J. Halbekann, *Die älteren Grafen von Sayn. Personen-, Verfassungs- und Besitzgeschichte eines rheinischen Grafengeschlechts 1139–1246/47* (Wiesbaden, 1997); O. Engels, 'Grundlinien der rheinischen Verfassungsgeschichte im 12. Jahrhundert', *Rheinische Vierteljahrsblätter* 39 (1975), 1–27.

[40] Balderic, *Gesta Adalberonis*, p. 252, gives some indications of this. Albero had interestingly held prebends at all three of Trier's suffragans prior to becoming Archbishop (p. 247). Cf., though, the negative comments of Hugo Metellus, *Epistolae*, col. 334.

[41] Lambert of Arras, *Epistolae*, ed. and tr. C. Giordanengo, *Le registre de Lambert, évêque d'Arras (1093–1115)* (Paris, 2007), no. 41, p. 195. On the *milites* of Theoderic, see *Recueil*, ed. Bruel, no. 3785.

[42] Gregory VII, *Registrum*, bk VI no. 22, rebuffing the suggestion.

[43] *Carmen de Bello Saxonico*, ed. O. Holder-Egger, *MGH SRG* vol. XVII (Berlin, 1889), p. 17; Lampert of Hersfeld, *Annales*, ed. O. Holder-Egger, *MGH SRG* vol. XXXVIII (Hanover, 1894), s. a. 1075, p. 234; Bonizo of Sutri, *Liber ad amicum*, *MGH Libelli* vol. I, pp. 606, 609. The crusading reference comes from eighteenth-century antiquaries, and Mohr, *Geschichte*, vol. III, wisely counsels caution (at n. 95) on accepting it at face value.

[44] Mohr, *Lotharingien*, vol. III, pp. 17–19; see *DHIV* no. 30. On the coins, see Flon, *Histoire*, pp. 268–71 and Weiller, *Münzen*, pp. 544–5 (no. 234: four of these coins are known, though unfortunately none is very clear).

[45] See Pope Gregory VII's letter, as n. 42 above. On the marriages that did take place, see E. Duvernoy, *Catalogue des actes des ducs de Lorraine de 1048 à 1139* (Nancy, 1915), pp. 151–5.

Nevertheless, in practice Duke Theoderic II was just one of several lords jostling for power in the region. His grip on Metz proved fragile as the bishop soon regained control (and Theoderic quickly came to terms with him), and most relevant charters show him embroiled in the immediate area around Toul and his ducal castles. Perhaps the most vivid evidence is provided by the chronicle written by Seher, Abbot of Chaumousey, a house of reformed canons near Toul, in the early twelfth century.[46] In this chronicle, Seher described how Duke Theoderic's *curia* made a judgement in Chaumousey's favour against some relatives of its founders, who were attempting to revoke an earlier donation. The *placitum* that Theoderic chaired was a formal one, peopled by men grandly termed '*principes terrae*' (though later just called *liberi*, free men), and Theoderic took a close interest in the matter, personally visiting the allod in question and speaking to the *familia* resident there. The transgressor, a *miles* named Joscelin, however, repeatedly refused to turn up, let alone comply with the judgement, in spite of a number of additional hearings, until the Bishop of Toul became involved. The canons eventually paid Joscelin off. In another Chaumousey charter, one of Theoderic's own *milites*, Walter of Balléville, is said to have sidestepped the duke's authority by simply avoiding the duke for two years, during which time he continued making his claims against the monastery: again, the Bishop of Toul's assistance was required to force Walter to come to court, though the resolution proved only temporary.[47]

We cannot deduce from this evidence that the duke was a uniquely incompetent or weak figure. His relation with Chaumousey was at times rather strained, so perhaps he was not putting his full effort into the affair.[48] Yet nearly all the evidence we have for Theoderic in Lotharingia shows him on the local stage. Far more typical than his excursion to Metz in the wings of Henry IV was his lobbying of the Bishop of Toul for a village under his control to be permitted to build its own church.[49] Maintaining a toe-hold in Metz through advocacy of the relatively small but prestigious churches of St-Martin and St-Pierre-aux-Dames, many of whose lands were bundled into the Premonstratensian foundation of St-Marie-aux-Bois (near Prény), Theoderic II clearly recognised that his power was territorially based or nothing. This is shown by the care which he took over his castles, founding priories at sites which he had inherited from his

---

[46] On Chaumousey, see Erkens, *Trierer*, p. 192.
[47] Seher of Chaumousey, *De primordiis Calmocensis monasterii*, ed. L. Duhamel, *Documents rares ou inédits de l'histoire des Vosges*, vol. II (Paris 1869), pp. 13–17, 49–52.
[48] For strained relations (because of Chaumousey's dispute with Remiremont), see Seher, *Chronicon*, p. 24.
[49] Mont-le-Vignole (1079), in *Capitularia regum Francorum*, ed. Baluze, Appendix, col. 153.

grandfather and father, such as Châtenois, Nancy and Neufchâteau, and setting up a new castle, despite heated opposition from Remiremont, at Arches (sur-Moselle), sparking a dispute which continued well into the 1130s.[50] When his son Duke Simon was (unusually) called upon to help in Verdun, he could be of little assistance.[51]

The situation west of the Meuse at around the same point in time was somewhat different, and increasingly so. Theoderic's contemporary, Count Hugh, was the grandson of Odo II discussed in Chapter 4, but the principality which he headed had little in common with his illustrious ancestor's. As was touched on in Chapter 4, the mid eleventh century had shaken the family's grip on power east of Paris, excluding them from around Rheims, an area in which they had exercised considerable influence into the early eleventh century, and confronting them with a challenge in the shape of Count Rodulf of Valois/Vermandois's territories, whose legacy came to nothing only because one of his sons died, and the other suffered a crisis of conscience and retreated to a monastery.[52] There was no formal office conferring claims to regional supremacy in anything like the form of the dukedom in southern Lotharingia, empty though this would seem to have been. Hugh's resources on his accession *c.*1093 consisted only of Troyes and, by inheritance, Bar-sur-Aube; he was very much the poor relation of his brother Stephen-Henry, whose rich domains extended from the Loire valley into Brie.[53] His network of castles, including places like Pringy, was no more developed than that of Theoderic II, in fact probably less so.[54]

Nevertheless, during a relatively short rule that encompassed a number of extended visits abroad, Count Hugh was able to forge an expansive political unit. This was partly an issue of connections. Hugh's almost fifty surviving charters show that he was in contact with over twenty-five different institutions, in the dioceses of Châlons, Rheims, Toul, Verdun, Troyes, Sens and Auxerre.[55] By contrast, only eight charters survive from

---

[50] Other important ducal castles at this time include Prény (which though first properly attested in 1130 might have been built by Theoderic II); and Sierck (first reliably mentioned in 1067). For Neufchâteau, see L. Douche, 'Actes de Pibo et de Ricuin évêques de Toul de 1069 a 1124', unpublished Mémoire de Maîtrise, Université de Nancy 2, 1985, no. 35. For Nancy, see Laurent, *Cartulaires*, vol. I, nos. 64 and 185. For Châtenois, see *Histoire*, ed. Calmet, vol. II (though cf. Laurent, *Cartulaires*). On Arches, the relevant charter is lost: see, however, for a probably reliable resumé *Histoire*, ed. Calmet, vol. II, col. 242. The castle was certainly built by 1123 (see *Chartes*, ed. Bridot, no. 50) and later legends attributed it to Theoderic, too. For subsequent dispute over the castle, see *Chartes*, ed. Bridot, no. 52.

[51] Laurentius, *Gesta* (concerning Simon, around 1130), p. 509.   [52] Bur, *Champagne*, pp. 211–17.

[53] As stressed by LoPrete, *Adela*, pp. 68–9.

[54] On Pringy, which Hugh may have built, see Bur, *Champagne*, p. 263.

[55] All of Hugh's charters, and indeed those of the other counts of Troyes, are now available in the massive pre-edition which M. Bur has placed online: *Chartes comtales pour la Champagne et la Brie (963–1151)*, http://halshs.archives-ouvertes.fr/halshs-00638840.

Duke Theoderic II, with only a handful more known now to be lost.[56] This was not because Duke Theoderic's court was less literate – we have, after all, some of the duke's own letters, and later accounts claimed that he had made a written will.[57] The dividing line seems to be that Hugh was simply involved with more institutions, across a wider area. In a sense, therefore, Hugh's rule was less territorialised than Theoderic's; correspondingly, it also had a much greater capacity for integration, proving highly successful at integrating rivals into its network and eventually swallowing them up altogether. Count Hugh consolidated his uncle's expansion southwards into the region of Auxerre, and a number of unpublished texts further show that Hugh consolidated his influence in Châlons with a series of strategic grants.[58] It was in fact Hugh, the first count routinely to take the title of Champagne (*Campanensis*), who really began the work of integrating the emerging castellan lords in the region – men who had successfully staked a claim in the kinds of developments discussed in Chapter 6 – into a cohesive system. There are indications that Hugh began to frame their castles as castellanies, administrative districts answering to the count: perhaps a subtle distinction to those living in the area, but ripe with potential for co-ordinating political authority.[59]

ARCHITECTURES OF POWER

Hugh's political momentum was sustained by his successor, Count Theobald (IV of Blois), and by Theobald's son, Count Henry the Liberal. These men were able to bring various figures in the north, around Rheims, into their *mouvance*, and thereby to create a principality of considerable size and wealth. Within two generations, the Champenois counts who succeeded to Hugh would be making lists of those formally subject to their authority, the famous *Feoda Campanie* mentioned in a previous chapter. From this perspective, and without prejudice to the question of the contribution made by the thirteenth-century *Interregnum* to the so-called German medieval *Sonderweg*, critical structural differences are indeed apparent from 1100 onwards in political organisation on either

---

[56] Duvernoy, *Catalogue*, provides a list of seven charters, alongside a number of letters, but was apparently unaware of another charter in Epinal, Bibliothèque multimedia intercommunale, MS 101, a copy of the cartulary-chronicle of Chaumousey, which is still not published. My thanks to Anne-Bénédicte Levollant for her help in acquiring a copy of this document, on which I plan further study.

[57] Duvernoy, *Catalogue*, nos. 24 and 37.

[58] E.g. for St-Pierre-aux-Monts: AD Marne H 737 (1114), H 653 (undated) and H 585 (undated).

[59] An indication in this direction is provided by the case of Vendeuvre; but perhaps Montfélix might be another instance: see West, 'Count Hugh'.

side of the Meuse. The key issue is therefore how the counts of Champagne were able gradually to create a regional hegemony in a way in which the dukes of Upper Lotharingia were not.

A whole array of factors could be brought into the analysis at this point. For example, we could point to the inability of the duke to secure control of a town, or to tap the profits of commerce; or to the relative freedom of Lotharingian 'prince-bishops', growing rich from the revenues of trade in their cities; or we could suggest that Count Hugh had inherited resources greater than they seemed. All these points are valid, but only take us so far. The bishops of Châlons and Rheims were hardly insignificant figures, for example, while the duke's connection to Toul was, if not quite as strong as the count's control of Troyes, still not inconsequential. Likewise, the counts of Troyes did not just tap the profits of commerce, they actively promoted it, perhaps from Hugh onwards.[60] It is true that the heartland of ducal power was something of an economic backwater, but with castles on the Moselle, there was the potential to develop.[61] Finally, if we look at Hugh's charters more closely, we see that his networks were based not on gifts of land, but on exemptions from the exercise of judicial power. As we have discussed in Chapter 4, men like Hugh were not powerful because they were rich; they were rich because they were powerful.

The point has also been made that we should be looking at things from the other way round: not at the failure of the duke to achieve a regional hegemony, but at the success of other local lords in resisting him. In this vein, Benjamin Arnold has pointed to the emergence of durable, viable principalities east of the Meuse as the sign of success, not failure, and ascribes that success to 'savage energy and forceful personality traits'.[62] Yet while the point is well-taken that exploring differences should not lead to teleologically inspired moral judgement, as an explanation this rather ducks the issue, unless we suppose that Hugh and his successors' rivals lacked energy and personality, which seems unlikely. If the difference does not reside in personal qualities, and whilst our comparison should avoid imposing anachronistic terms of reference, there is, however, one aspect of a kind of structural difference between the nature of principalities

---

[60] Pottery evidence for urban activity, in Georges-Leroy, 'La production céramique'. On the promotion of the fairs, see R. H. Bautier, 'Les principales étapes du développement des foires de Champagne', *Comptes-rendus des séances de l'Académie des Inscriptions et Belles-Lettres*, 96 (1952), 314–26; M. Bur, 'Remarques sur les plus anciens documents concernant les foires de Champagne', in Bur, *La Champagne médiévale*, pp. 463–84.

[61] On the lack of towns, see P. Racine, 'La Lorraine au haut Moyen Age. Structures économiques et relations sociales', in A. Heit, ed., *Zwischen Gallia und Germania, Frankreich und Deutschland. Konstanz und Wandel raumbestimmender Kräfte* (Trier, 1987), pp. 205–18, which has a good, succinct, summary, with further references.

[62] B. Arnold, *Princes and territories in medieval Germany* (Cambridge, 1991), p. 5.

that can be observed, one with a direct bearing on the differing political developments taking place in Champagne and Upper Lotharingia: ecclesiastical advocacy.

Ecclesiastical advocacy in Upper Lotharingia and Champagne

Around the mid eleventh century, there began a slow crescendo of complaints by churches, and particularly monasteries, about oppressive figures named ecclesiastical advocates. The criticism was expressed in a variety of sources (charters, letters and hagiography), and from all the regions of the Holy Roman Empire, and, as we will see, beyond it, too.[63] Not all advocates were oppressive, and indeed sometimes we can glimpse the advocate conscientiously at work, as evidence from St-Pierremont near Metz and perhaps also from Trier suggests – but the tone of the monastic evidence is in general unremittingly hostile.[64]

Traditionally, these complaints, and the negotiations that later ensued, have been seen as marking the transition from a Carolingian-style advocacy, discussed in Chapter 1, to a 'lordly' advocacy (*Beamtenvogtei* to *Herrenvogtei*), a transition itself put down to a supposed greater need for church protection. More recently, though, historians have despaired of the construct of the Carolingian state on which the contrast was predicated, to the point of arguing that there was essentially no difference between Carolingian advocacy and later forms of it, as both were really about *Herrschaft*.[65] Logical in its own terms, this argument however overplays (or rather misinterprets) the continuity between advocacy in the Carolingian sources and advocacy in the later period. Admittedly, the same word was used for the person in question, and it similarly carried connotations of legal protection. But we can hardly overlook the striking chronological rupture, with a clear century

---

[63] The literature on later ecclesiastical advocacy in the Empire is vast and intimidating. A good point of entry is M. Parisse, ed., *L'avouerie en Lotharingie*, Publications de la section historique de l'institut grand-ducal 98 (Luxembourg, 1984). A useful summary of the older German literature (notably Aubin, Brunner and Waas), which has still not been superseded, is set out in W. Dohrmann, *Die Vögte des Klosters St. Gallen in der Karolingerzeit* (Bochum, 1985), pp. 4–52; a similar survey is available in M. Clauss, *Die Untervogtei: Studien zur Stellvertretung in der Kirchenvogtei im Rahmen der deutschen Verfassungsgeschichte des 11. und 12. Jahrhunderts* (Siegburg, 2002).

[64] There are references to the episcopal advocate's court at Trier in the 1030s (*UBMR* nos. 305, 310, 320 and 325), but these seem more a variation on the archiepiscopal court. Unequivocal is an advocate's Christmas court in the 1130s, in the cartulary of St-Pierremont, Metz (Paris, BnF nouv. acq. lat. 1608) where an advocate judged whether some local inhabitants were obliged to attend his court, f. 18v: odd, since at its foundation all rights of advocacy had been abolished! For the cartulary, see the register produced by Mangin, *Cartulaire*, and the study of some charters – though not this one – by M. Parisse, 'Justice comtale dans la seigneurie de Briey', *Publications de la section historique de l'Institut (Royal) Grand-Ducal de Luxembourg*, 102 (1986), 113–27.

[65] Dohrmann, *Die Vögte*.

separating the two phenomena – for advocates retreat into obscurity between the later ninth and early eleventh centuries, for the most part mentioned only as witnesses.[66] Tenth-century lords of monasteries were, judging from available documentation, not these monasteries' advocates.[67] By the middle eleventh, though, they were.

We have a pretty good idea of what these new advocates were getting, because over the course of the late eleventh, but particularly the twelfth century, written agreements regulating the advocacy by means of defining the rights these advocates enjoyed over the monasteries' lands were drawn up.[68] Many of these charters pose formidable problems of dating, especially those texts that claim an earlier date but which were probably redacted during this period.[69] Nevertheless, we can be confident in estimating that there are perhaps around forty from southern Lotharingia, many quite lengthy texts, from the mid eleventh through to the mid twelfth century.[70] As an example, let us take the regulation of the rights of the advocate, Liethard, at Condé (Meuse), set out by Sophie Countess of Bar in 1091 in agreement with the monastery of St-Mihiel, which survives as an original charter.[71] It was agreed that the advocate would have no role in any matter that the abbot and his officers considered they could deal with themselves, but that if support were needed, the abbot would go to no one but the advocate. If the advocate was involved, he would have a third of the profits of justice. That justice could be done at his residence (*domus*) in certain circumstances, though duels were always to be held within the abbey's estates. The advocate was entitled to take four horses from Condé if he needed to accompany the Count of Bar in time of war, and was entitled to stay at Condé, with six followers, three times a year, at the abbey's expense, if on the count's business. Liethard

---

[66] Though St-Maximin has a rare inscription, too: see *Die Inschriften der Stadt Trier*, ed. R. Fuchs (Wiesbaden, 2006), pp. 74–6. For a similar point, see Parisse, *Noblesse Lorraine*, vol. I, p. 64.

[67] E.g., Reginar and Lobbes: *Gesta abbatum Lobiensium*, ed. G. Pertz, *MGH SS*, vol. IV (Hanover, 1841), pp. 52–74, at p. 68; cf. *Chronicon S. Mihaelis*, p. 11, on Frederick of Bar.

[68] E. Boshof, 'Untersuchungen zur Kirchenvogtei in Lothringen im 10 und 11 Jahrhundert', *Zeitschrift der Savigny Stiftung für Rechtsgeschichte (Kanonistische Abteilung)* 65 (1979), 55–119, refers to most of the earlier ones; Pergameni, *Avouerie* has a list of those concerning, anachronistically, Belgian institutions; F. Senn, *L'institution des Avoueries ecclésiastiques en France* (Paris, 1903), has an uncritical list of many French ones.

[69] Celebrated forgeries relating to this region include sets from St-Maximin, and more distantly, Brauweiler, but there are plenty of others: for example *Chartes*, ed. Bridot, no. 3, from Remiremont, purporting to be a seventh-century papal intervention in the advocacy of the convent, or *DCM* no. 261, for Prüm, in fact twelfth-century. There are also some interesting examples from St-Vanne (Verdun).

[70] Parisse, 'Les règlements d'avouerie en Lorraine au XIe siècle', in Parisse, ed., *L'avouerie*, pp. 159–73, lists seventeen dating from before 1100.

[71] Artem no. 117 (AD Meuse, 4 H 33).

was also entitled to receive bread, chickens, grain and some cash from surrounding estates, and could stay there twice a year. There is every reason to suspect that this charter is a reasonably accurate description of the advocacy at Condé, not least because the charter was subsequently twice re-issued, with almost identical wording.[72]

The advocacy of Condé is fairly representative, and there are several charters very like it: for example, that produced by the otherwise obscure monastery of Rettel (Moselle) in 1084.[73] Others were different. Several regulation charters dealt with a monastery as a whole, not with just a part of its holdings (for example St-Maximin in 1135), and elements present in other charters are absent in the Condé text.[74] For instance, some charters sought to exclude in total or in part certain groups of people, like monastic servants, from the advocate's purview.[75] As the charter's reference to the abbot's officers (provosts and *ministri*) suggests, monasteries made attempts to create their own networks of dependent officials, and other charters explicitly restricted the advocate's role in the appointment of these men, as a tactic to reduce his role still further.[76] By the middle of the twelfth century, monasteries were seeking to buy themselves out of advocacy altogether, or to reclassify the advocate as a mere 'defender' (showing how technical the term had become). However, by this point they had often lost much of their resources, and the title of 'defender' quickly took on a technical ring to it not unlike that of advocate.[77]

What makes these advocacies significant is that most of the Lotharingian principalities appear to have been largely powered by the resources afforded by the tapping of the jurisdictional rights of monastic networks. The way Luxembourg was built upon the resources of the monasteries of St-Maximin and Echternach is particularly well known.[78] However, many other

---

[72] In 1116 (Artem no. 121) and again in 1135 (*Chronique et chartes*, ed. Lesort, no. 79, AD Meuse 4 H 33, no. 37). The wording is very similar – but not quite identical. Further work may produce interesting results here. It may be noted in passing that documents in this archive show St-Mihiel managed to hold onto its rights at Condé, at least into the fifteenth century.

[73] The Rettel charter is edited in Parisse, 'Les règlements d'avouerie'.

[74] *UBMR*, vol. II, no. 483.

[75] For example, a charter apparently dating to 1058 for St-Clement Metz (Artem no. 2405).

[76] Appointment of *villici*: Hanauer, ed., *Constitutiones*, pp. 90–2 for St-Quirin; cf. *Rheinisches Urkundenbuch*, ed. Wisplinghoff, vol. I, no. 96, probably s. XII. Linck, *Wandel*, studies the rise of monastic officials across the twelfth century: his book can usefully be compared with R. Berkhofer, *Day of reckoning: power and accountability in medieval France* (Philadelphia, 2004), particularly pp. 130–51, who concentrates on northern French monasteries.

[77] Buying out: e.g. *The cartulary and charters of Notre-Dame of Homblières*, ed. T. Evergates (Cambridge, Mass., 1990), no. 32. Defender: see the Brogne charter, edited in *Actes des comtes de Namur de la première race, 946–1196*, ed. F. Rousseau (Brussels, 1937), no. 9 (1154).

[78] M. Margue, 'Remarques sur l'avouerie locale en Luxembourg', in M. Parisse, ed., *L'avouerie en Lotharingie*, pp. 201–14.

principalities in the region were similarly connected to one or two major institutions. Bar, Berg, Louvain, Salm, Sarrewerden, Vaudémont, Vianden – almost every single major territorial unit in Lotharingia, and quite a few of the insignificant ones, too, are considered with justification to be based on advocatial relations with ancient monasteries or with newly established ones.[79] The duchy of Upper Lotharingia fits very neatly into this picture. Duke Theoderic's control of a number of key institutions, articulated through ecclesiastical advocacy, was remarkably strong, persistent, and formally defined: Remiremont, St-Dié, Chaumousey, Moyenmoutier, St-Evre, St-Leo and an outlier in Metz in the form of St-Pierre-aux-Nonnains, for most of which we have surviving texts regulating the nature of ducal authority. In spite of occasional complaints and renegotiations, particularly concerning St-Dié and Remiremont, his successors Simon and Matthew kept their grip on these endowments.[80] So close was this relation between advocacy and principality from a late eleventh-century perspective that patronage of a monastery implied advocacy, and advocacy implied a principality. Hence the county of Luxembourg, for instance, which in fact emerged only in the later tenth century and took on firm contours only in the eleventh, could be confidently projected back into the ninth by twelfth-century writers on the assumption that the counts had patronised St-Maximin.[81]

As has been noted elsewhere, matters were quite different to the west.[82] Admittedly, some traces of ecclesiastical advocacy can be detected in the region of Champagne. For instance, Fleury had a generation-long conflict with advocates at its estate at *Tauriacus* near Troyes.[83] There are signs, too, of a more overarching kind of advocacy in this region. The family of Joinville were advocates of St-Urbain in the early twelfth century, according to unpublished charters.[84] Coucy and St-Rémi, Chauny and Notre-Dame of Paris, and indeed St-Maur des Fossés: the more one looks for these texts connecting aristocratic families with major monasteries, the more one can find in the east of France.[85] It is perhaps not surprising that Count Hugh of Champagne occasionally expressed his authority in terms of advocacy.[86] Nevertheless, a difference in emphasis is difficult to overlook. Counties like

---

[79] Parisse, *Noblesse Lorraine*, vol. I, pp. 81–106.   [80] See Mohr, *Lothringien*, vol. III, pp. 20–6.
[81] *MGH SS*, vol. XXII, p. 25.   [82] A general survey is provided by Bur, *Champagne*, pp. 343–89.
[83] *Miracula Benedicti*, bk III, ch. 13 (p. 159), bk VI, ch. 3 (pp. 221–3), both probably referring to early eleventh-century incidents. Cf. also *Miracula Benedicti*, bk VIII ch. 6 (pp. 282–9) for advocates further north.
[84] Unpublished charter of regulation from 1132: Paris, BnF, Coll. Moreau 55, 139.
[85] Additional examples would include St-Pierre-aux-Monts of Châlons (AD de la Marne H 646) and an unedited early modern French translation of a Nesle charter from 1126 (AD de l'Aube H 8 1, f. 1); cf. *Actes des évêques de Laon: des origines à 1151*, ed. A. Dufour-Malbezin (Paris, 2001), n. 18.
[86] For the monasteries of St-Basle, Molesme, Avenay and St-Paul (Verdun).

Rethel, Chateau-Porcien, Roucy, Brienne and Dampierre all certainly had links with monasteries, but these links seem to have been looser, and in general less important: these principalities were apparently more straightforwardly castle-based. Insofar as advocacy did exist west of the Meuse, it tended to be flabbier, and more liable to collapse into an undifferentiated sense of seigneurial control. For example, a charter from St-Nicaise of Rheims that can be dated to around 1130 describes an agreement over the advocacy of Houdilcourt, held by Heribert, then his widow's second husband, from the counts of Roucy. What is striking is not the formal revocation of the rights, it is that they are only uncertainly described as advocacy at all: 'advocacy, which is commonly called *voaria*'.[87] *Voaria*, a hapax, seems to be related to *vicaria*, one of the words discussed in Chapter 6 to describe a set of jurisdictional rights. What this charter shows is not just that advocacy was conceived as a jurisdictional right, for that is obvious; rather, it suggests that there was not really a clear-cut distinction between these various kinds of jurisdictional property.

The counts of Champagne fitted into this pattern. Rights over Rozay, a village dependent on the cathedral of Paris, that were understood as deriving from advocacy in 1020 (one of the very earliest examples) were by 1100 just another kind of *consuetudo*.[88] Another example is provided by an original charter issued for St-Rémi concerning its property at Alliancelles, issued in 1129.[89] A certain Manasses of Possesse held the advocacy of this village in fief ('tenebat in feodo') from Count Theobald (IV of Blois), but had pledged it to Andrew of Baudrémont for £40, whose agents, bent on recuperating the investment, the monastery found irksome. It was in Count Theobald's presence, before his *curia* at his castle of Vitry, that Andrew was persuaded to renounce his customs for the £40, and it was Theobald's judgement that Manasses should not reclaim the advocacy unless that money were repaid. Yet it is not only the monastery's buying-out of advocatial rights that is interesting – earlier than comparable examples east of the Meuse – but the fact that despite his evident authority over the monastery's affairs, Count Theobald himself is at no point called advocate.

Can we sense here a reluctance to have his authority defined in such sharp terms, or simply a less definite sense of what advocacy was? Whenever the counts, or those who wrote their charters, did use the term, it carried a slightly vaguer sense than seems to have been standard in Lotharingia.[90] For

---

[87] *Cartulaire de St-Nicaise*, ed. Cosse-Durlin, no. 38: 'advocationem, que vulgo voaria dicitur'.
[88] Cf. Artem no. 2070 with no. 2114/2190.
[89] The charter is (poorly) edited in *Histoire de la maison de Chastillon sur Marne*, ed. A. Duchesne (Paris, 1621), pr. 22; the original is AD Marne, Annexe de Reims, 56 H 102.
[90] Cf. Bur, *Champagne*, pp. 352–4. *Cartulaire*, ed. Morel, no. 39 is a particularly clear example.

example, while Count Hugh's advocacy over Avenay was acknowledged in one charter, it was considered in some way synonymous with *potestas*.[91] Even when the far more abundant charters of Hugh's successors are taken into account, the counts seem never to have made a great regulation charter to compare with those of the dukes, or the counts of Luxembourg. Instead, they cultivated the deliberately looser notion of *custodia*, or *garde*.[92] This concept could admittedly be found in parts of Lotharingia, but not to the same extent as in Champagne.[93] Ecclesiastical advocacy reflects, therefore, a kind of relationship common around the Moselle and further to the east, and far less so across the Meuse. It is not that there was no advocacy in Champagne, more that it was less intense there, less definite as an identifiably separate concept.

This relatively blurry distinction seems to have had clear-cut consequences. The dukes may have been firmly entrenched with their footholds in monasteries around the Vosges, but the corollary was that the duke faced rivals equally anchored in their own monastic rights. The counts of Bar, for example, controlled St-Mihiel as closely as the dukes controlled Remiremont. The counts of Luxembourg controlled St-Maximin in a similar fashion. They eventually did lose the advocacy of that monastery, but it took a major and sustained war, and imperial intervention, to evict them.[94] Indeed, the descendants of Theoderic II's own brother, Gerard, were able successfully to carve out a principality within the duchy itself, Vaudémont, based on the abbey of Belval whose foundation effectively guaranteed the long-term independence of the territory.[95] Integrating principalities of this kind into an umbrella-style lordship was, effectively, impossible.

The counts of Champagne were faced with a different situation, which offered different possibilities. The counts of Brienne, who appear in our records in the late tenth century, offer an excellent illustration. They seem to have developed a close relationship with the important monastery of Montier-en-Der from around 1000, in ways which remind the observer of advocacy.[96] They did not consistently articulate it in these terms, however,

---

[91] *Avenay*, ed. Paris, no. 5.   [92] For example, *Recueil*, ed. Bur, e.g. nos. 18, 54 and 474.

[93] More work is needed here: cf. T. Mayer, *Fürsten und Staat: Studien zur Verfassungsgeschichte des deutschen Mittelalters* (Weimar, 1950); Senn, *L'institution*; and also N. Didier, *La garde des églises au xiii siècle* (Paris, 1927), still the standard work despite its anachronistic concentration on *souveraineté* and its difficulties in separating advocacy from 'garde'. For efforts to create *custodia* in place of advocacy, see *Histoire*, ed. Picart, pr. 85 (for St-Leo, Toul).

[94] H. Büttner, 'Die Übergang der Abtei St. Maximin an das Erzstift Trier unter Erzbischof Albero von Montreuil', in S. Jenks, ed., *Festschrift Ludwig Petry* (Wiesbaden, 1968), pp. 65–77.

[95] See G. Giuliato, ed., Autour des comtes de Vaudémont: lieux, symboles et images d'un pouvoir princier au Moyen Âge (Nancy, 2011).

[96] Bur, 'L'abbaye de Montier-en-Der face aux princes et aux évêques (xie–xiie siècles)', in P. Corbet, ed., *Les Moines du Der*, (Langres, 2000), pp. 531–49.

247

and the counts of Champagne were able to insert themselves between the monastery and the Brienne counts in the latter half of the eleventh century.[97] The county of Brienne survived into the thirteenth century, but it became ever more closely caught up in the patronage circles of the county of Champagne, and its members increasingly sought opportunities abroad.[98] By 1125 at the latest, the counts of Champagne had positioned themselves as the highest-placed lay people with whom regional ecclesiastical institutions had formal relations, dominating a number of key monasteries: Montier-en-Der, Montiéramey, Compiègne and Orbais, for example.[99] In spite of this superiority, they were termed advocates only occasionally, and the word is conspicuous in its absence in a number of charters where one might expect to find it.

The causes of differentiation

This raises an obvious question: why was ecclesiastical advocacy different in these neighbouring regions? The question becomes only more pressing when its full dimensions are appreciated. There seems to have been a clear pattern in the importance of ecclesiastical advocacy in eleventh- and twelfth-century Europe north of the Alps, largely moving from west to east and without exactly reflecting political boundaries.[100] It is well known that the west of France, including Normandy, had nothing quite like ecclesiastical advocacy at all, while conversely its importance in the Empire is widely recognised. Areas in between can be thought of as a mixture, where advocacy was present, but less distinctly. Champagne is one example, Flanders another. Indeed, the county of Ponthieu in (royal) Flanders developed out of an explicitly advocatial relationship with the monastery of St-Riquier, according to a nearly contemporary text.[101]

---

[97] *Cartulary*, ed. Bouchard, nos. 34 and 41.

[98] Notably in the Holy Land: see G. Federenko, 'The crusading career of John of Brienne', *Nottingham Medieval Studies* 52 (2008), 43–79. More generally, see the still-indispensable 'Catalogue d'actes des comtes de Brienne, 950–1356', *BEC* 33 (1872), 141–86.

[99] The count gave Montiéramey to be reformed to St-Vanne: Laurentius, *Gesta*, p. 491. Count Theobald II was in charge of the advocate of Compiègne, but was not himself termed advocate: (*Cartulaire*, ed. Morel, nos. 39 and 52). Theobald I's charter with Orbais *c.*1090 covers the same ground as advocacy agreements, but the count is not called advocate: Dubout, 'Orbais'. In general, see Bur, *Champagne*, pp. 352–7.

[100] J. Yver, 'Autour de l'absence d'avouerie en Normandie. Notes sur le double thème du développement du pouvoir ducal et de l'application de la réforme grégorienne en Normandie', *Bulletin de la société des antiquaires de Normandie* 67 (1963–4), 189–283; for an Anglo-Norman perspective, see Brett, 'The English abbeys'.

[101] Hariulf, *Chronicon*, IV, ch. 12, pp. 204–5; ch. 21, pp. 229–30. See also *Cartulaire*, ed. Morel no. 16. For Flanders, see *Chartes de coutume en Picardie: XIᵉ- XIIᵉ siècle*, ed. R. Fossier (Paris, 1974), no. 2 (Corbie, *c.*1055).

Rather than an absolute division, then, between areas where power was to some degree structured around advocacy and areas where it was wholly absent, there was a shading-off. This shading-off in fact makes advocacy more interesting, not less, since it means that it can neither be considered an absolute peculiarity of the Empire, perhaps the product of imperial decree, nor merely a documentary illusion.

Previous generations of historians tended to associate the importance of ecclesiastical advocacy with 'Germanic' ideas of the proprietary church, and its absence with church reform, whether Cluniac, Gregorian, or Cistercian. The limitation of this approach is, however, very clear, not least thanks to the observation that it in fact was not a purely German or imperial phenomenon, as the case of Ponthieu shows. It is true that Cluniac monasteries in the west tended to avoid the term, and as far as possible, the relationships it implied. Yet Cluny's influence in Champagne was never very great, and in any case, Cluniac and Cluniac-inspired monasteries in the Holy Roman Empire made use of, and were used by, advocates just as much as non-Cluniac monasteries, with Hirsau in Swabia an exemplary demonstration.[102] Much the same could be said of Cistercian monasteries, in spite of a much-vaunted but fundamentally illusory Cistercian 'freedom from advocacy'.[103] As for notions that suggest a specifically Germanic concept of *Eigenkirchenrecht* found articulation in advocacy: there are arguments from ethnicity lurking here, of the kind that have been demolished elsewhere and that need to be explicitly ruled out. There is no reason to imagine that people had intrinsically different relationships with monasteries or other kinds of churches in the east simply because they spoke German.[104]

A final resolution of why ecclesiastical advocacy was so different in Champagne and Upper Lotharingia is not possible here, since that would require a full-scale study across the whole of tenth- and eleventh-century Western Europe. However, two possible factors deserve to be mentioned, if only as suggestions for future research.

The first relates to the endurance of Carolingian monastic institutions. Many of the Lotharingian principalities mentioned above were connected

---

[102] *DHIV* no. 280 (1075). In general, see H. Jakobs, *Die Hirsauer: ihre Ausbreitung und Rechtsstellung im Zeitalter des Investiturstreites* (Cologne, 1961), pp. 153–70.

[103] E.g. Himmerod: see C. Wilkes, *Die zisterzienserabtei Himmerode im 12 und 13 Jahrhundert* (Munster, 1924), pp. 93–8; see also A. Thiele, *Echternach und Himmerod. Beispiele benediktinischer und zisterziensischer Wirtschaftsführung im 12. und 13. Jahrhundert* (Stuttgart, 1964), pp. 74–9.

[104] Wood, *Proprietary*, whose book is in effect a fundamental re-evaluation of Stutz's ideas of *Eigenkirchenrecht*. These ideas percolated into much of the 'new constitutional history', too: A. Waas, *Vogtei und Bede in der deutschen Kaiserzeit*, 2 vols. (Berlin, 1919) is a good example of how advocacy was treated as intrinsically Germanic.

to old, well-established monastic communities, which had been greatly favoured by Carolingian rulers and elites: St-Mihiel, St-Maximin, Echternach, Remiremont and so on. The networks represented by these institutions were, as already suggested, what bound certain principalities together from the mid eleventh century onwards. Areas where old Carolingian monasteries had done less well, for whatever reason, did not see advocacy develop in the same way. Normandy is again the obvious example, where tenth-century disruption has been extensively discussed.[105] Yet the monasteries in the region of Champagne may have been in a way comparable. Nesle-la-Resposte, Avenay and St-Urbain were institutions in the dioceses of Troyes, Rheims and Châlons respectively that had been extremely favoured in the ninth century, and counted perhaps as amongst the richest in Francia.[106] They survived into the eleventh and twelfth centuries, but did apparently little more than that, and very little is known about them in the post-Carolingian period. Only one of them was able to provide the basis for independent advocacy (St-Urbain), and that on an apparently rather reduced scale.

The second relates to the importance of the imperial court in 'standardising' the concept of ecclesiastical advocacy. By the late eleventh century, emperors were paying attention to it, as the *Bannleihe* charters discussed in Chapter 7 make clear – charters which were not restricted to Lotharingia, though they were certainly prominent there. By the early twelfth, emperors were legislating about advocacy and subadvocacy, possibly to empire-wide effect.[107] It may well be that the greater coherence of advocacy in eastern Francia reflects the coherence of the Empire, in which clerics and aristocrats from different parts of the huge empire, from Bavaria to Lower Lotharingia, and amongst many other things, talked about advocacy.

If these suggestions prove to have any value, then the pattern of advocacy would in part be a reflection of how the politics of post-Carolingian Europe worked themselves out in broader terms. It is extremely difficult to say why monastic networks survived better in some regions than others, on account of obvious problems with sources. We should not, for example, neglect the way in which some institutions

---

[105] C. Potts, *Monastic revival and regional identity in early Normandy* (Woodbridge, 1997), pp. 15–32, who suggests that nearly half of Normandy's Carolingian monasteries vanished (p. 20). See also F. Lifshitz, *The Norman conquest of Pious Neustria* (Toronto, 1995), p. 124 on the fate of Fontanelles, and p. 180–1 on Fécamp.

[106] On Nesle, see Crété-Protin, *Église*, pp. 342–6. On difficulties faced by early institutions in Châlons (e.g. St-Memmius), see Benner, *Châlons*, pp. 62–9.

[107] For example, the *Sententia de iure advocatorum*, in *MGH Constitutiones*, vol. I, no. 75, pp. 126–7, dating to 1104. Advocates also appeared in later legislation, for example Frederic Barbarossa's *Constitutio de pace tenenda* from 1152: *MGH Constitutiones*, vol. I, no. 140, ch. 17, p. 198. For efforts to prohibit subadvocacy, on an empire-wide scale, see Clauss, *Untervogtei*, pp. 123–52.

constructed collective memories that were inherently more durable than others'. A divergence here between western and eastern Francia in this regard may be visible already in the ninth century, for example in the creation of cartularies (the first in this region was that of Prüm).[108] However, the problems faced by monastic communities in western Francia also seem likely to be connected to the greater political turbulence in that kingdom in the immediate post-Carolingian period. This turbulence was not the result of some primaeval anarchy, but was tied to struggles over the crown. Eastern Frankish kings faced rebellions, it is true, but the kingship in western Francia was bitterly disputed for generation after generation in the tenth century. Charles the Simple against Robert, Louis IV against Hugh the Great, Hugh Capet against Charles of Lorraine: these were wars whose impact was felt strongly east of Paris (Châlons, for instance, was burned twice, in 931 and 963). There was undeniably a dynastic component at work here, but we do not need to envisage a long-term Robertian 'plan'. Equally important were the repeated interventions on the part of the eastern kings which served to exacerbate instability. Ottonian emperors time and again lent support to whichever party appeared to be doing worse, and it is difficult to avoid the suspicion that this was in part a deliberate strategy.[109]

Since instability seems to have been bad for monastic communities, for their landholding and for their institutional consciousness (the two aspects were of course connected), it is perhaps to be expected that many formerly important monasteries fell on hard times in the western kingdom.[110] Conversely, while Upper Lotharingia was hardly a haven of peace and tranquillity, from 925 onwards it was a part (a peripheral part, it is true) of a more stable political unit, one relatively less riven by conflict at the centre. In view of this stability, it is hardly surprising either that political culture in the east was ostensibly more conservative. The fact that most people who mattered in the east were counts or dukes, the fact that the exercise of bannal rights by the lower echelons of the elite seems to have emerged late and hesitantly, simply shows how the formal structures of power kept their shape (though not their content) better in

---

[108] On different strategies of memorialisation see P. Geary, *Phantoms of remembrance: memory and oblivion at the end of the first millennium* (Princeton, 1994), particularly pp. 81–114. Western Frankish monasteries did not, for example, use cartularies until the eleventh century. It would be interesting to see whether connections could be made between institutional memory and later monastic advocacy. On Carolingian cartularies, see H. Hummer, 'The production and preservation of documents in Francia: the evidence of cartularies', in Brown, Costambeys, Innes and Kosto, eds., *Documentary culture.* For Prüm, see above, p. 115 n. 22.

[109] Leyser, 'Ottonian connection'.

[110] On the vulnerability of large-scale ecclesiastical estates to sustained political disruption, see I. Wood, 'Entrusting Western Europe to the Church', *TRHS*, forthcoming.

the east than the west. While it is true that ecclesiastical advocacy as such was not a Carolingian institution, the way that a semi-institutional nature was produced at least in part by a court-centred discourse, to the extent of inventing the notion of a 'subadvocate' (a notion entirely absent west of the Meuse), may be a reflection of this kind of political conservatism.[111] We do not need to invoke supposedly more archaic ideas of freedom as relentlessly espoused by historians such as Droege and others, simply a kingdom which cohered more than its neighbour to the west, even though the capillary forms of power exercised by the Carolingian rulers seem to have dried up.[112]

It is precisely because there seems to have been nothing innate about any of this that the final point which should be made concerns the role of contingency. The events of (and leading up to) 888 dealt Arnulf of East Francia a winning hand, shifting the centre of power markedly to the east; but Arnulf's leading position in late ninth-century Europe was not inevitable, it was the result of the political short-term. It was mostly because the last surviving adult Carolingian in the legitimate male line happened to have been one based in East Francia, Charles the Fat. Had Louis the Stammerer or his sons, kings in the west, lived longer and been active in the 880s, then things would have been very different.[113]

Yet I should like to finish with another element of chance: the battle of Soissons of 923, when King Charles the Simple succeeded in killing his rival, but somehow nevertheless lost the battle, and, discredited, fell into what proved a permanent and humiliating captivity a little later. Pitched battles were notoriously risky in the early Middle Ages, and there is no reason to suspect that Charles's defeat can be attributed to structural reasons. It was nevertheless this defeat, and Charles's ensuing imprisonment, that enabled Henry I to conquer Lotharingia in 925.[114] The acquisition of Lotharingia proved absolutely crucial for east Frankish kingship, just as it promised to transform Charles's own rule. Lotharingian forces accompanied the Ottonians in their military adventures to the south, making a contribution beautifully, and for once quantifiably, captured by the celebrated *Indiculus loricatorum*, the list of military retinues already discussed in Chapter 4. It was in no small part the acquisition of Lotharingia in around 925 that enabled the East Frankish kings to create and maintain a polity that was distinctly more cosmopolitan, and imperial, than the west, powering

---

[111] On subadvocates, conspicuously absent from the west, see Clauss, *Untervogtei*, pp. 281–7.

[112] G. Droege, *Landrecht und Lehnrecht im hohen Mittelalter* (Bonn, 1969).

[113] On Louis the Stammerer, see M. McCarthy, 'Louis the Stammerer', unpublished PhD thesis, Cambridge 2012.

[114] Flodoard, *Annales*, depicts Henry's campaigns, s. a. 923 and 925.

them through to Italy, and making sure their court remained attractive to aristocrats.[115]

The effects on the western Frankish kingdom were, however, equally important. Not only was the balance of power thrown in favour of aristocrats in the west of the kingdom, as discussed in Chapter 4, but it gave Ottonian rulers an interest in western Frankish politics, and a stake in keeping these kings embroiled in internal strife. The result was the perpetual crisis which endured until a resolution was reached in 987 (or 991, when Charles of Lorraine was captured) – significantly, during a period of minority rule in the east. In this light, the importance of advocacy is an index of historical developments that were themselves entirely unpredictable.

CONCLUSION

The differences discussed above, created, or at least promoted, by chance and the political short-term, were real ones that affected the distribution of power, and so changed the history of these regions. It mattered that ecclesiastical advocacy was a more clearly defined role in the eastern Frankish kingdom, since it seems to have promoted the endurance of independent principalities that resisted encroachment from their neighbours better than their counterparts further west. The historiographical divide between German-language concentration on advocacy, and Francophone attention to the *seigneurie*, maps onto a genuine difference, at least concerning west and east of the Meuse, in scale and distribution, and one with heavy consequences for future change. The play of possibilities that the framing of the new system of symbolic communication entailed was, as a result, very different in the west from that in the east. In the west it favoured the Count of Troyes, and in the east it constrained the Duke of Upper Lotharingia.[116]

Nevertheless, in discussing these differences, and in attempting to account for them, we should be careful not to lose sight of a crucial point. Though the distribution of power varied, its altered *nature* did not. Ecclesiastical advocacy was simply the banner term for bannal rights connected with church, and particularly monastic, lands: the co-ordinated, regulated conversion of the latent power of vast monastic networks into the newer, crystallised idiom of judicial authority, enabling a particular architecture of power to take shape.

---

[115] Cf. for this point E. Hlawitschka, *Lotharingien und das Reich an der Schwelle der deutschen Geschichte* (Stuttgart, 1968), pp. 3–5 and pp. 205–6; and from a different perspective, Giese, *Heinrich I*, pp. 88–9.

[116] Cf. Benton, 'Written records'; B. Diestelkamp, 'Lehnrecht und Lehnspolitik als Mittel des Territorialausbaus', *Rheinische Vierteljahresblätter* 63 (1999), 26–38.

Since it is reasonable to assume that what the advocates demanded from monastic assets, they demanded from their own too, advocacy charters could be seen as functionally equivalent to the lists of 'bad customs' compiled by monasteries further to the west, as Timothy Reuter suggested.[117]

In other words, judicial rights emerged from the undifferentiated authority of the ninth century everywhere; it was merely the means by which they did so that differed. East of the Meuse, the process took place in a more ordered way, managed by the kings and co-ordinated by the exploitation of intact ecclesiastical estates; in the west, with less co-ordination provided either by ecclesiastical estates or the royal court, there was greater fragmentation. The underlying development, however, was not so different as it might seem, since the same kinds of changes were taking place, whether against or through the system of government. In this way the comparison between the county of Champagne and the duchy of Upper Lotharingia demonstrates both the possibilities for differentiation, rich in consequences for the future, but also, and in fact above all, the essentially shared political and social culture, which reflected the legacy of Carolingian dynamics.

---

[117] T. Reuter, 'Forms of lordship in German historiography', in Bourin and Martinez Sopeña, eds., *Pour une anthropologie . . . :realités*, pp. 51–2.

CONCLUSION

Curieuse épithète, au demeurant, pour une 'révolution' qui ne crée pas les fiefs![1]

The broad focus of this book has been on the lands between the rivers Marne and Moselle, yet it makes no claims to be a regional history in a conventional sense. After all, this geographical space had no particular political or social unity at the book's point of departure of around 800, and in that sense was not a region at all, merely a portion of Francia; while at the book's close, it had become not one region but two, Champagne and Upper Lotharingia. Instead, this book's intention was to contribute to the debate about the Feudal Revolution by investigating a discrete body of material from a part of Western Europe over an extended period of time, in order to put any observable changes into a fuller historical framework. As set out in the Introduction, its overarching argument, based on that material, is three-fold: that radical change did take place in the way that communities were organised and power articulated in Carolingian and post-Carolingian Europe between around 800 and 1100, that this change should be perceived as linked to a process of formalisation of social relations, and that this process was in continuity with the general thrust of Carolingian reforms. This conclusion seeks to clarify these points, and to set them in their historiographical context.

BETWEEN THE 'LONG TWELFTH CENTURY' AND THE 'SETTLEMENT OF DISPUTES'

As the Introduction proposed, the model of Feudal Revolution devised by Duby and elaborated thereafter has run into trouble in the face of two distinct kinds of critique. On the one hand, some historians have stressed

[1] Barthélemy, *Mutation*, p. 224, n. 15.

255

on largely empirical grounds the importance of the twelfth century as medieval Europe's true transformational moment, while on the other, methodological doubts inspired by certain currents within anthropology and other social sciences have been raised about the very possibility of the kind of structural transformation that Duby envisaged. Though there is clearly much of value in these critiques, the debate has stalled because each suffers from its own intrinsic limitations.

The first approach, placing an emphasis on the importance of developments of the twelfth century, seems to offer a neat means of side-stepping the Feudal Revolution debate. Work along these lines commonly invokes a complex nexus of change operating in a long (or sometimes late) twelfth century, typically revolving around transformations in administration and economic growth. While the precise emphasis on the elements in the mixture varies widely, the arguments are nevertheless remarkably similar. For Susan Reynolds, it was the rise of bureaucracy and professional law that constituted the crucial caesura, though these themselves depended on 'much more profound changes in society – the growth of population, of economies and of supply of silver, coined and uncoined, and the spread of literacy and academic education'.[2] For Dominique Barthélemy, it is the economic transformation marked by the growth of urban communities from the twelfth century that forms the break.[3]

No historian could seriously contest that these and similar arguments reflect real phenomena. To be sure, the European population grew in the twelfth century, monetary supply expanded, towns boomed, and clerical schools flourished. The question is really whether we are justified at stopping there, or whether we should not perhaps inquire into the causes that underlay these trends. In both the spheres of writing and the economy, for example, there are signs that tendencies that become most visible in the twelfth century were in fact rooted in the Carolingian period. Arguments for a dramatic twelfth-century growth in literacy rates function only by ignoring Carolingian evidence; conversely, arguments for twelfth-century economic take-off are convincing only when they take on board the now-overwhelming arguments for the origins of that growth in the earlier period.[4] The twelfth century

---

[2] Reynolds, *Fiefs*, p. 482.   [3] Barthélemy, 'La mutation'.

[4] McKitterick, *Carolingians and written word*; see also A. Kosto, *Making agreements in medieval Catalonia: power, order, and the written word, 1000–1200* (Cambridge, 2001). Cf. B. Stock, *The implications of literacy: written language and models of interpretation in the eleventh and twelfth centuries* (Princeton, 1983), whose brilliant arguments are somewhat weakened by the assumption that Europe was largely an oral culture before 1000. For the economics, see M. McCormick, *Origins of the European economy: communications and commerce AD 300–900* (Cambridge, 2001) and from an entirely different angle, but from this point of view to quite the same effect, Wickham, *Framing*, e.g. pp. 802–5, 828.

certainly saw all kinds of innovations, but it should not, in these and other fields, be regarded as some kind of *tabula rasa*.

The methodological difficulties are just as far-reaching as these empirical ones. To begin with, one might suggest that the thrust of these arguments derives from Weberian-inspired analyses that identify bureaucracy and towns as driving forces of modernity. In locating their origin in the Middle Ages, these arguments bring their own challenge to periodisation, which is to be welcomed. Yet I would suggest that historians need to revisit wholesale the application of nineteenth-century sociological categories such as the charismatic and the bureaucratic, the oral and the written, the ritual and the legal and the personal and the institutional. As Matthew Innes noted a decade ago, Weberian-style dichotomies have impeded our understanding of the Carolingian reform, precisely because it cannot be pigeon-holed as administrative and thus evades certain kinds of conceptualisation.[5] More broadly, studies framed by these concepts often tacitly or inadvertently rehearse modernisation or proto-modernisation narratives even as they qualify them. Defining modernity, in nineteenth-century terms, was of overriding concern for Weber and others; but as historians become less certain about these scales of progress, and more alert to the role of the Middle Ages in underpinning them, it is opportune to reconsider the approaches that have smuggled them in. Weber's ideal-types tend naturally to encourage concentration on classification, not on dynamics. It would surely be more profitable to consider practices like bureaucracy and ritual, for example, not as opposed or incommensurate, but as variants within a fundamental unity, as differing means of managing meaning. Only from some such position will we be able to understand shifts between these variants, and not simply record, applaud or marvel at them.

It should further be noted that these analyses tend to explain change by appeal to one or more external factors, a black box acting as the hidden source of change. In this way, historical phenomena are insidiously classified as causes or (mediated) consequences. Few would deny that material factors such as the environment, the supply of coinage, or demographic circumstances are without traction on the ways in which human communities organise themselves.[6] Yet it is inadequate to explain change through economic growth, or demographic shifts, or environmental alteration, because these are part of the picture, not its frame. It has recently, for instance, been shown that (medieval) demographic growth can be a product of economic growth and not just its cause; and, while a rise in the population necessarily has an effect on the way in which social

---

[5] Innes, *State*, 4–12. [6] Latour, *Reassembling*, pp. 63–86 (as p. 6, n. 19 above).

domination is exercised, it can be argued that changes in the patterns of domination themselves promoted growth in the medieval economy, with demographic consequences.[7] Analogously, as already suggested in Chapter 7, while the advent of professional law clearly promoted the systematic use of the written word in government, it could also be posited that professional lawyers – in the sense not simply of legal experts, no novelty of the late twelfth century, but as influential social typologists – depend on consistent and persistent forms of categorisation, on clarity in the symbolic communication of unequal social relations. The implication is that we cannot see the kind of changes this book has discussed as necessarily secondary or superstructural to ones deemed more fundamental; we need, instead, to pay more attention to how different kinds of transformation were interrelated. There should be no black boxes in history, only more causal connections to be traced.

The second strand of critiques of the Feudal Revolution, that associated with ideas of the resolution of conflict, questions whether ideas of transformation are heuristically useful. Whereas influential arguments about the nature of post-Carolingian change once appealed to the processes by which conflicts were settled to prove that society underwent radical transformation around the year 1000, and the approach was still used to interrogate this question closely in the 1980s, most of those who still work in this conceptual framework ironically now tend to argue that the study of conflict resolution actually rules out precisely this kind of large-scale transformation in social relations. Looked at more closely, Carolingian and twelfth-century conflicts are revealed as not so very different after all, since, given enough detail, they can be reduced to interactions of interest and the strategic use of resources that included the very rules supposedly directing the course of action.

It could, however, be argued that all such a conclusion really demonstrates are the limits of conflict analysis as a key to understanding social change. The observation that to a certain extent all conflicts are really the same, no matter what the formal framework, was an important step in the deconstruction of an old-fashioned constitutional approach to medieval life, which assumed that without explicit, iron-clad rules guaranteed by a state or equivalent authority, society dissolved into chaos. Now, however, the approach tends only to impose a new kind of structuralism, this time implicit, along the lines that everywhere social relations are 'negotiated' through conflict in basically analogous ways. The risk of elevating conflict

---

[7] J. Langdon and J. Masschaele, 'Commercial activity and population growth in medieval England', *Past and Present* 190 (2006), 35–81. For the early Middle Ages, Wickham, *Framing*, pp. 547–50; see also Bavel, *Markets*, in general, though pp. 2–12 in particular.

settlement from an important element of analysis into a totalising approach to medieval society is that this is a role for which it is intrinsically ill-suited, as its very frame of reference, when developed along standard lines, tends to exclude the investigation of important historical questions, such as the role and function of the state, the shaping of agency, or for that matter the nuances of the cultures in which conflicts take place, all of which are effectively discounted. One can well understand why many historians, even those active in the field, are beginning to show dissatisfaction with some of the applications and implications of dispute resolution.[8]

REFRAMING THE FEUDAL REVOLUTION: THE CAROLINGIAN LEGACY

In spite of these problems, much of the argument of this book is in sympathy with elements of these revisionist evaluations of the Feudal Revolution. I cannot find convincing evidence for an upsurge in violence at any particular moment other than during moments of wide-scale warfare that were anyway fairly evenly distributed across the period, and usually linked to high politics rather than elemental social breakdown; and the notion that the Carolingians had created a public state that then crumpled in the face of private power is over-simplistic. These ideas are too closely linked to historians' concerns about the diminishing role of the modern state for comfort, almost the historiographical equivalent of the post-apocalyptic film. There was far more continuity than either of these approaches to post-Carolingian Europe assumes. Nevertheless, I have argued that society was organised in different ways in the lands between Marne and Moselle *c.*800 and *c.*1100, and that key to this difference was a far more formalised understanding of the nature of power, both as exercised over dependants and as distributed amongst the elite.

This observation has, of course, been advanced by historians before. The novelty of this book's argument is less about identifying the nature of the change, and more about proposing an alternative causality for it (though of course such a separation is in the end artificial).[9] For the most part, those historians who have addressed the issue directly have considered it a result of the failure of Carolingian rulership, whether because Carolingian inability 'to define the realities of local power' meant that when power became formalised it did so as property rather than as fiscal administration, or simply because there was a power vacuum to be filled.[10] This book, in contrast, proposes that this development be

---

[8] Cf. Lemesle, *Conflits*, pp. 7–12.   [9] Cf. Innes, *State*, p. 242.
[10] Innes, *State*, p. 222 and pp. 262–3; Wickham, 'Feudal Revolution', p. 207, Wickham, *Courts and conflict*, p. 19.

seen as the consummation of the Carolingian moment, one that under-pinned the subsequent changes in the location of authority as the exercise of power became increasingly locally rooted, making higher levels of co-ordination and governance less important. I have suggested that the Carolingians, by turning their attention to the nature of power itself, through their experiment in 'applied ecclesiology', laid the groundwork for politics to be played through power that was increasingly reified.[11] Expressing their hopes and aspirations for change in a language of politics infused with a liturgised theology, they shaped social practice into insti-tutionalised power, and it was simply an extension of this process which distilled that institutionalised power in certain circumstances – particularly over those of low status – into property relations: a form of domination whose efficiency may well be connected with the continued economic expansion of the central Middle Ages.[12]

That formalisation was in no way inevitable: it was one that reflected a particular social, cultural and political convergence. This is not so much, then, an attempt to impose teleology or determinism, but rather to point to a path-dependency that risks being overlooked if historians choose to look at the Carolingian period only in its 'own terms' without reference to what came later, and still more so if they ignore the Carolingian period altogether. The idea of path-dependency has little to offer those interested primarily in reconstructing thought-worlds and perceptions of contem-poraries, but a great deal to those seeking explanation for change. It was because of this formalisation that Western European society took on a trajectory shaped not primarily by office, nor land alone, but by jurisdic-tion. This shift, expressed by historians in different ways, has been described as the end of distinctively early medieval patterns of social organisation: if so, the jolt was a ninth-century one.[13] Put differently, if there was a radical difference between the ways in which Carolingian and early twelfth-century societies were organised in the regions between Marne and Moselle, this difference was not irrespective of, but rather precisely due to, continuity.

Of course, the way these processes played out varied. No one was simply acting from a Carolingian script, and Chapter 8 showed that in certain respects, the lands east and west of the Meuse were becoming more and

---

[11] For the phrase, see W. Ullmann, *Carolingian Renaissance*, p. 8.

[12] The economic stimulus produced by the construction of (stone) castles and churches in the post-Carolingian world is an example of how enhanced political control could be translated into economic intensification. See Bavel, *Markets*, for an analogous argument about economic develop-ment, though with a different take on the Carolingians; and p. 192 above.

[13] Cf. Innes, *State*, p. 250, a point developed again in Costambeys, Innes and MacLean, pp. 432–3, which places emphasis on the economic changes.

more different. Yet these were variations on a common post-Carolingian theme, which did not detract from a persistent underlying unity.

To what extent is it appropriate to think of all this as a Feudal Revolution? That question breaks down naturally into two parts: whether it is appropriate to talk of a revolution, and what precisely was feudal about it. The first issue should be given short shrift. For some historians speed and a clean break are the essence of any revolution, in which case my approach would exclude the word. For other historians, though, it is the depth of historical change that is significant – in which case its use seems legitimate in this context, analogous to how historians talk of the Industrial Revolution.[14] The changes evoked in this book may have been gradual and cumulative, but they were certainly transformational in their effect: little wonder that historians have borrowed from studies of the impact of colonialism to understand aspects of the problem.[15] Semantic or, even worse, etymological disputes about what is and what is not a revolution are simply beside the point, since the language of historians is a living one, not a pickled technical jargon.

The issue of 'feudal' is more complex: in what way could these changes be thought associated with feudalism? This obviously depends on what one means by that term. Chris Wickham has suggested that historians use the notion in broadly three ways: as the Marxian label for a society based on the coercive extraction of surplus from a dependent peasantry; as a Weberian ideal-type, notably Marc Bloch's description of a society characterised by a dependent peasantry, the absence of a wage economy, a warrior aristocracy and (stressed by more recent work) a dominant church; and finally, as the Ganshofian concept of feodo-vassalic relations.[16]

While Wickham went on to suggest that the diagnostic elements of these three approaches have nothing in common with one another – that the fief is not connected to the serf – I would venture that the previous chapters have suggested a historical connection between them, and have moreover connected them to the ninth century. It might be profitable in this context to reconsider Perry Anderson's definition of feudalism,

---

[14] See the book-length entry for the concept of 'Revolution' in *Geschichtliche Grundbegriffe: historisches Lexikon zur politisch-sozialen Sprache in Deutschland* (Stuttgart, 1972–97), vol. v, pp. 653–788, setting out at pp. 653–4 the two main modern senses of the word, labelling both short-term, often violent, political change and longer-term 'Strukturwandel', such as the Industrial Revolution.

[15] Cf. Mitchell, *Colonising Egypt*, p. ix, suggesting that colonising was not simply a matter of the presence of outsiders, but of 'the spread of a political order that inscribes in the social world a new conception of space, new forms of personhood, and a new means of manufacturing the experience of the real'.

[16] C. Wickham, 'Le forme del feudalismo', *Settimane* 47 (2000), 15–46. For the dominant church, see the arguments associated with Alain Guerreau, synthesised by J. Baschet, *La civilisation féodale: de l'an mil à la colonisation de l'Amérique* (Paris, 2004), notably pp. 223–337.

linking notions of the 'parcellisation of sovereignty' to the coercion over the peasantry, which seems to offer a characterisation of social relations that covers most (all?) of Latin Europe, and so has the merit of specificity.[17] The forms that that coercion took were, it seems to me at any rate, directly linked to the elaboration of those relations studied by Ganshof. From this perspective, the changes that have been discussed above have something to do with feudalism after all. I still find convincing the argument that, provided we remember they are historiographical tools and not in themselves historical realities, abstract terms of this kind are useful.[18] Historians who complain about the anachronism inherent to such terms might perhaps reflect on how far another label created by historians, that of the Middle Ages itself, shapes their research.

Does this mean that this book can be taken as supporting the notion of a 'Feudal Revolution'? I have some reservations on this point, because the Feudal Revolution debates have tended to polarise the issue, so that the term has become strongly associated with both an unhelpful dichotomy and a limited engagement with Carolingian evidence. It might seem better to abandon the term to find another, carrying less intellectual baggage. Yet insofar as I have argued that a social transformation, rooted in the ninth century, took place leading to a social formation that could conveniently (and for various reasons) be termed feudalism, it seems hard to set it aside, and perhaps an already elastic label ought to be stretched once again, if reframed in the way the preceding chapters have set out.

Arguments about terminology are, however, useful only insofar as they draw attention to the underlying issues, and not away from it. Whatever labels one prefers, my central point is that the impasse in which the Feudal Revolution debate finds itself can best be resolved by careful attention to the ninth century, with consequences for historical analysis which this book has attempted to outline. This continuity is the point that both critics and supporters of the Feudal Revolution have neglected or ignored, choosing to quarantine off Carolingian Francia safely into the 'warrior societies' of the early Middle Ages. This has found support in the implicit identification of a transformation in government and society with the fate of a particular dynasty and the extent of its territorial control. That would

[17] P. Anderson, *Passages from feudalism to antiquity* (London, 1974), pp. 147–53. Anderson's integration of political and economic forms have proven controversial amongst specialists; for a recent development of Anderson's ideas, however, see G. Comninel's stimulating 'English feudalism and the origins of capitalism', *Journal of Peasant Studies* 27 (2000), 1–53.
[18] Cf. L. Kuchenbuch, 'Feudalismus: Versuch über die Gebrauchsstrategien eines wissenspolitischen Reizworts in der Mediävistik', in N. Fryde, P. Monnet and O. Oexle, eds., *Gegenwart des feudalismus. Présence du féodalisme et présent de la féodalité. The presence of feudalism*, Veröffentlichungen des Max-Planck-Instituts für Geschichte 173 (Göttingen 2002), pp. 293–323.

doubtless have appealed to members of this dynasty, and finds support in the notoriously self-serving historiography produced directly or indirectly under that dynasty's patronage: yet that does not mean that it will do as historical analysis.

The foregoing argument may seem to be presenting the reader with another 'black box', bearing consequences but defying explanation: that inchoate group of associated tendencies conveniently labelled as the Carolingian reforms. I would prefer to suggest that it invites further research into this already well-discussed topic. Perhaps it was in part the problems of succeeding to the Merovingians and negotiating an ideological deficit, now so hard to grasp due to the Carolingian-sponsored programme of self-justification, that encouraged a dynasty and its collaborators to promote new forms of power; or perhaps it was something to do with their epoch-making integration of Italy with northern Europe, laying the latter open to influences from the south. These influences would certainly merit further investigation, since, though Italy has not been considered in the writing of this book, many of the phenomena discussed here may have first appeared there. Yet I would tentatively propose that a point already raised in Chapter 3 was more important. The Carolingian kings and emperors found themselves tasked with running an empire without any of the mechanisms by which empires are usually supported. In the absence of Roman-style means, though with a keen appreciation for things Roman, these rulers and their advisers, secular and tonsured, turned to the church, and not simply to its accumulated wealth, but to its epistemologies and forms of knowledge, to create a kind of decentralised centralisation, operating through a co-ordinated coalescence of interests: a liturgical kingship, reifying informal claims into rights, power into what became jurisdiction.

Under the Carolingians and thenceforth, Francia was no longer scrabbling about amidst the ruins of the Roman Empire, for its cohesion was rooted differently; nor can it properly be considered a warrior society in anything but a most reductive sense. Its efficacy and co-ordination of action depended neither on tax nor on brute force but on a sustained engagement with the nature of authority itself, a new kind of knowledge of power. The ruling family's monopoly on rule was eventually lost, but in the end this was a mere matter of dynastic accident. It seems more important that had the Carolingian project continued, it would have ended in a world dominated by power so formalised and well-defined that it could in some circumstances even be thought of as property, which is more or less exactly what happened.

BIBLIOGRAPHY

PRIMARY SOURCES

1. MANUSCRIPTS AND UNPUBLISHED CHARTERS CITED

AD de l'Aisne, MS 455 (cartulary of St-Crépin, Soissons, s. xvii)

AD de l'Aube, H 8 1 (cartulary of Nesle-la-Reposte, s. xvii)

AD de la Haute-Marne, 7 H 2 (second cartulary of Montier-en-Der, s. xii)

AD de la Marne, H 646 (St-Pierre-aux-Monts)

AD de la Marne, H 737 (St-Pierre-aux-Monts)

AD de la Marne, 56 H 1029 (Cartulary B of St-Rémi, s. xiii)

AD de la Marne, Annexe de Reims, 56 H 102 (Alliancelles)

Arras, Bibliothèque Municipale, MS lat. 964 (composite manuscript from St-Vaast, s. xii)

Bern, Burgerbibliothek, Cod. 292 (composite manuscript from St-Arnulf, s. xi)

Brussels, Bibliothèque Royale, MS 5576–5604 (theological manuscript from Gembloux, s. xii)

Brussels, Bibliothèque Royale, MS 10615–729 (composite manuscript from St-Eucharius, Trier, s. xii)

Laon Bibliothèque Municipale, MS 288 (priest's reader, s. ix)

London British Library Addit. 19725 (priest's handbook, s. ix)

Metz, Bibliothèque Municipale †MS 226 (composite manuscript from St-Arnulf, s. xi)

Munich, Bayerische Staatsbibliothek, Clm 3851 (composite manuscript, s. ix)

Munich, Bayerische Staatsbibliothek, Clm 14508, ff. 64–148 (priests' reader, s. ix – the preceding part of the manuscript is a later addition)

Oxford, Bodleian Library, Bodley Eng. Hist. c.242 (transcription of the St-Rémi polyptych, s. xvii)

Paris, Bibliothèque Nationale, Coll. Moreau 55

Paris, Bibliothèque Nationale, MS lat. 8922 (composite manuscript from Echternach, s. xi)

Paris, Bibliothèque Nationale, MS lat. 9421 (*De divinis officiis*, Echternach, s. xi)

Paris, Bibliothèque Nationale, MS lat. 9654 (legal collection, s. x)

Paris, Bibliothèque Nationale, MS lat. 13784 (homilary, s. xi)

Paris, Bibliothèque Nationale, nouv. acq., Lat. 1608 (cartulary of St-Pierremont, s. xiii)

Rheims, Bibliothèque Municipale, MS lat. 15 (composite manuscript from St-Rémi, s. xi/xii)

Rheims, Bibliothèque Municipale, MS lat. 85 (cartulary of St-Thierry, s. xiii)

Trier, Stadtbibliothek, Hs 1245 (Prüm chapter book, s. ix)

Troyes, Bibliothèque Municipale, MS. 1979

Vatican, Biblioteca apostolica Vaticana, Reg. lat. 1283 (composite manuscript)

Verdun, Bibliothèque Municipale 69 (penitential, perhaps Moselle region, s. ix^(ex))

Vienna Österreiche Nationalbibliothek, cod. 529

2. EDITIONS OF ROYAL DIPLOMATA

Recueil des actes de Charles II le Chauve, ed. G. Tessier, Chartes et diplômes relatifs à l'histoire de France 8–10, 3 vols. (Paris, 1943–55)

Recueil des actes de Charles III le Simple, ed. P. Lauer, Chartes et diplômes relatifs à l'histoire de France (Paris, 1940)

Recueil des actes de Louis II le Bègue, Louis III et Carloman II, rois de France 877–884, ed. F. Grat, Chartes et diplômes relatifs à l'histoire de France (Paris, 1978)

Recueil des actes de Louis VI, Roi de France (1108–1137), ed. J. Dufour, Chartes et diplômes relatifs à l'histoire de France, 4 vols. (Paris, 1992–4)

Recueil des actes de Philippe I^(er), Roi de France (1059–1108), ed. M. Prou, Chartes et diplômes relatifs à l'histoire de France (Paris 1908)

Recueil des actes de Robert I^(er) et de Raoul, rois de France: 922–936, ed. J. Dufour, Chartes et diplômes relatifs à l'histoire de France (Paris, 1978)

Regesta imperii. Die Regesten des Kaisserreichs under den Karolingern, 751–918, ed. J. F. Böhmer, revised by E. Mühlbacher with J. Lechner, 2nd edn (Innsbruck, 1908). See also online resources, below.

Die Urkunden Arnolfs, ed. P. Kehr, *MGH Diplomata regum Germaniae ex stirpe Karolinorum 3* (Berlin, 1940)

Die Urkunden Heinrichs IV, ed. D. von Gladiss, *MGH Diplomata regum et imperatorum Germaniae 6*, 3 vols. (1952–2001)

Die Urkunden Karls III, ed. P. Kehr, *MGH Diplomata regum Germaniae ex stirpe Karolinorum 2* (Berlin, 1937)

Die Urkunden Konrad I, Heinrich I und Otto I, ed. T. Sickel, *MGH Diplomata regum et imperatorum Germaniae 1* (Hanover, 1879–84)

Die Urkunden Lothars I und Lothars II, ed. T. Schieffer, *MGH Diplomata Karolinorum 3* (Munich, 1979)

Die Urkunden Ludwigs des Deutschen, Karlmanns und Ludwigs des Jüngeren, ed. P. Kehr, Diplomata regum Germaniae ex stirpe Karolinorum 1 (Berlin, 1934)

Die Urkunden der Merowinger, ed. T. Kölzer, *MGH Diplomata regum Francorum e stirpe merovingica* (Hanover, 2001)

Die Urkunden Otto des II. und Otto des III, ed. T. Sickel, *MGH Diplomata regum et imperatorum Germaniae 2* (Hanover 1893)

Die Urkunden Pippins, Karlmanns und Karls des Grossen, ed. E. Mühlbacher, *MGH Diplomata Karolinorum 1* (Hanover, 1906)

Die Urkunden Zwentibolds und Ludwigs des Kindes, ed. T. Schieffer, *MGH Diplomata regum Germaniae ex stirpe Karolinorum 4* (Berlin, 1960)

3. OTHER CHARTER EDITIONS

Actes des comtes de Namur de la première race, 946–1196, ed. F. Rousseau (Brussels, 1937)

Actes des évêques de Laon: des origines à 1151, ed. A. Dufour-Malbezin (Paris, 2001)

'Actes de Pibo et de Ricuin évêques de Toul de 1069 à 1124', ed. L. Douche, unpublished Mémoire de Maîtrise, Université de Nancy II, 1985

'Die älteren Urkunden des Klosters S. Vanne in Verdun', ed. H. Bloch, *Jahrbuch der Gesellschaft für Lothringische Geschichte und Altertüm* 10 (1898), 338–449 and 14 (1902), 48–150

'Analyse du cartulaire de St-Pierre de Chézy', ed. E. de Barthélemy, *Mémoires de la société académique des sciences, arts . . . de Saint-Quentin* 1 (1876–8), 241–308

'Die Benediktinerabtei St. Arnulf vor Metz in der ersten Hälfte des Mittelalters', ed. E. Müsebeck *Jahrbuch für lothringische Geschichte und Altertumskunde* 13 (1901), 164–244

Capitularia regum Francorum, ed. E. Baluze (Paris, 1677)

Cartulaire de l'abbaye de Gorze, Ms. 826 de la bibliothèque de Metz, ed. A. d'Herbomez, Mettensia II (Paris, 1898)

Cartulaire de l'abbaye de Montiéramey, ed. C. Lalore, Collection des principaux cartulaires du Diocèse de Troyes, vol. VII (Paris, 1890)

Cartulaire de l'abbaye de Saint-Corneille de Compiègne, ed. E. Morel (Montdidier, 1904)

Cartulaire de l'abbaye de St-Loup de Troyes, ed. C. Lalore, Collection des principaux cartulaires du Diocèse de Troyes, vol. I (Paris, 1878)

Cartulaire du chapitre cathédral de Langres, ed. H. Flammarion (Turnhout, 2004)

Cartulaire du chapitre de l'église cathédrale de Châlons-sur-Marne. Par le chantre Warin, ed. P. Pelicier (Paris, 1897)

Cartulaire de Chaumousey, no editor given, *Documents rares ou inedits de l'histoire des Vosges* vol. X (1891)

Cartulaire de l'Eglise Notre-Dame de Paris, ed. M. Guerard (Paris, 1850)

Cartulaire de Montier-la-Celle, ed. C. Lalore, Collection des principaux Cartulaires du Diocèse de Troyes, vol. VI (Paris, 1875)

Cartulaire du Prieuré de Notre-Dame de Longpont de l'ordre de Cluny, no editor given (Lyon, 1879)

Cartulaire de Saint-Nicaise de Reims, ed. J. Cosse-Durlin (Paris, 1991)

'Cartulaire de Saint-Vincent de Laon', ed. R. Poupardin, *Mémoires de la Société de l'Histoire de Paris et de l'Ile-de-France* 29 (1902), 173–267

Cartulaires de l'abbaye de Molesme, ancien diocèse de Langres, 916–1250: recueil de documents sur le nord de la Bourgogne et le midi de la Champagne, ed. J. Laurent, 2 vols. (Paris 1911)

The cartulary and charters of Notre-Dame of Homblières, ed. T. Evergates (Cambridge, Mass., 1990)

The cartulary of Montier-en-Der, 666–1129, ed. C. Bouchard (Toronto, 2005)

Catalogue des actes des ducs de Lorraine de 1048 à 1138 et de 1176 à 1220, ed. E. Duvernoy (Nancy, 1915)

Catalogue général des manuscrits des bibliothèques publiques de France, vol. XXXVIII ed. H. Loriquet (Paris, 1904)

Chartes de l'abbaye de Remiremont des origines à 1231, ed. J. Bridot (Turnhout, 1997)

Chartes de l'abbaye de Saint-Hubert en Ardenne, ed. G. Kurth (Brussels, 1903)

Chartes des Cisterciens de Saint-Benoît-en-Woëvre des origines à 1300, ed. J. Denaix (Verdun, 1959)

Chartes de coutume en Picardie: XIe–XIIe siècle, ed. R. Fossier (Paris, 1974)

Chartes et documents de l'abbaye cistercienne de Preuilly, ed. A. Catel (Montereau, 1927)

Bibliography

Chartes et documents de Saint-Bénigne de Dijon, prieurés et dépendances des origines à 1300, ed. G. Chevrier and M. Chaume, 2 vols. (Dijon 1943–86)

Chronique et chartes de l'abbaye de Saint Mihiel, ed. A. Lesort, Mettensia vol. VI (Paris, 1909)

Les constitutions des campagnes de l'Alsace au moyen-âge: recueil de documents inédits, ed. C. Hanauer (Paris, 1864)

'Documents carolingiens de l'abbaye de Montiéramey', ed. A. Giry, *Etudes d'histoire du moyen age dediées a G. Monod* (Paris, 1896), pp. 107–36

Documents inédits tirés des collections manuscrites de la Bibliothèque royale, ed. M. Champollion-Figeac (Paris, 1841)

Epernay et l'abbaye Saint-Martin de ce ville, ed. A. Nicaise (Châlons, 1869)

'Fragments du recueil perdu de formules franques dites "Formulae Pithoei"', ed. R. Poupardin, *BEC* 69 (1908), pp. 643–62

'Histoire de l'abbaye d'Orbais', ed. N. Dubout, *Revue de Champagne et de Brie* 14 (1883), 142–3

Histoire de l'abbaye et du village d'Hautvillers, ed. J. Manceaux (Épernay, 1880)

Histoire et cartulaire des Templiers à Provins, ed. V. Carrières (Paris, 1919)

Histoire ecclésiastique et politique de la ville et du diocèse de Toul, ed. B. Picart (Toul, 1707)

Histoire de Lorraine, ed. A. Calmet, 6 vols. (2nd edition: Nancy, 1745–57)

Histoire de la maison de Chastillon sur Marne, ed. A. Duchesne (Paris, 1621)

Histoire de Metz, ed. N. Tabouillot, 3 vols. (Metz, 1775)

Indiculus loricatorum, ed, L. Weiland. *MGH Constitutiones*, vol. I, no. 436, pp. 632–3

Mémoires pour servir à l'histoire écclesiastique, civile, et militaire de la province du Vermandois, ed. L. Colliette, 3 vols. (Cambrai, 1771–3)

Monuments historiques, ed. J. Tardif (Paris, 1866)

De Oorkonden der graven von Vlaanderen (Juli 1128–September 1191), ed. T. de Hemptinne and A. Verhulst (Brussels, 1988)

Les origines de l'abbaye de Bouxières-aux-Dames au diocèse de Toul: reconstitution du chartrier et édition critique des chartes antérieures à 1200, ed. R-H. Bautier (Nancy, 1987)

Papsturkunden in Frankreich Neue Folge, I. Band. Champagne und Lothringen, ed. H. Meinert (Berlin, 1933)

'Pratiques féodales en Verdunois au XIIe siècle', ed. M. Parisse, *Lotharingia* 2 (1990), 289–95

Le Prieuré de Saint-Leu d'Esserent: Cartulaire, ed. E. Müller (Pontoise, 1901)

Les rapports de droit de la Mosellane romane (XIIIe-début du XVIIe siècle), ed. J. Coudert (Paris, 2008)

'Recueil des actes des archevêques de Reims d'Arnoul à Renaud II (997–1139)', ed. P. Demouy, 2 vols., unpublished thesis, Université de Nancy II, 1982

Recueil des actes des comtes de Pontieu 1026–1279, ed. C. Brunel (Paris, 1930)

Recueil des actes d'Henri le Libéral, comte de Champagne, 1152–1181, ed. M. Bur (Paris, 2009)

Recueil des chartes de l'abbaye de Clairvaux au XII siècle, ed. J. Waquet (Troyes 1982)

Recueil des chartes de l'abbaye de Cluny, ed. A. Bruel, 6 vols. (Paris 1876–1903)

Recueil des chartes de l'abbaye de Stavelot-Malmedy, ed. J. Halkin. and C. G. Roland (Brussels, 1908)

Recueil de chartes et documents de Saint-Martin-des-Champs: monastère parisien, ed. J. Depoin (Paris, 1912)

Recueil des chartes de Saint Germain des Prés: des origines au début du XIIe siècle, ed. R. Poupardin (Paris, 1909)

Bibliography

Rheinisches Urkundenbuch: ältere Urkunden bis 1100, ed. E. Wisplinghoff, 2 vols. (Bonn, 1972)

Sacrae antiquitatis monumenta: historica, dogmatica, diplomatica, ed. C. Hugo, 2 vols. (Etival, 1725)

Les seigneurs de Nesle en Picardie, ed. W. Newman, 2 vols. (Philadelphia, 1971)

Le souvenir des Carolingiens à Metz au Moyen Âge: le petit cartulaire de Saint-Arnoul ed. M. Gaillard (Paris, 2006)

Studien zur Äbtissinnenreihe von Remiremont, ed. E. Hlawitschka (Saarbrücken, 1963)

Thesaurus novus anecdotorum, ed. E. Martène and U. Durand, 5 vols. (Paris, 1717)

Traditiones Wizenburgenses: d. Urkunden d. Klosters Weissenburg: 661–864, ed. K. Glöckner and A. Doll (Darmstadt, 1979)

Urkunden und Quellenbuch zur Geschichte der altluxemburgischen territorien ed. C. Wampach, vol. I (Luxembourg, 1935)

Urkundenbuch zur Geschichte der jetzt die Preussischen Regierungsbezirke Coblenz und Trier bildenden mittelrheinischen Territorien, vol. I, Von den ältesten Zeiten bis zum Jahre 1169, ed. H. Beyer (Koblenz, 1860)

Veterum scriptorum et monumentorum historicorum, dogmaticorum, moralium; amplissima collectio, ed. E. Martène and U. Durand (Paris, 1724–33)

4. POLYPTYCHS

Das Polyptichon von Montierender, ed. C.-D. Droste (Trier, 1988)

Das Polyptychon und die Notitia de Areis von Saint-Maur-des-Fossés, ed. D. Hägermann and A. Hedwig (Sigmaringen, 1990)

Le polyptyque et les listes de cens de l'abbaye de Saint-Remi de Reims (9ᵉ-11ᵉ siècle), ed. J.-P. Devroey (Rheims, 1984)

Das Prümer Urbar, ed. I. Schwab (Düsseldorf, 1983)

5. OTHER PRIMARY SOURCES (INCLUDING HAGIOGRAPHY, HISTORIES AND LETTERS)

Acta sanctorum ordinis S. Benedicti, ed. J. Mabillon, 9 vols. (Paris, 1688–1701)

Actus fundatorum Brunwilarensis monasterii, ed. G. Waitz, MGH SS, vol. XIV (1883), pp. 121–44

Adalard, *Consuetudines corbeienses*, ed. J. Semmler, *Corpus consuetudinum monasticarum*, vol. I (Siegburg, 1963), pp. 355–420

Adalbero of Laon, *Poeta*, ed. and tr. C. Carozzi, *Poème au roi Robert/Adalbéron de Laon* (Paris, 1979)

Adso of Montier-en-Der, *Epistola de ortu et tempore antichristo*, ed. D. Verhelst, *CCCM*, vol. XLV (Turnhout, 1976)

    Vita Bercharii (BHL 1178), ed. J. Vandermoere and J. Vanhecke, *AASS Oct.*, vol. I (Brussels, 1845), cols. 1010–30

Adventius of Metz (?), *Epistolae ad Divortium Lotharii II pertinentes*, ed. E. Dümmler, *MGH Epp.*, vol. VI (Berlin, 1925), pp. 207–40

Aimo, *De translatione SS. Martyrum Georgii monachi, Aurelii et Nathalie* (BHL 3409), ed. J. Sollerius, J. Pinius, G. Cuperus and P. Boschius, *AASS Jul.*, vol. VI (1729), pp. 459–69

Aimo, *Vita Abbonis*, ed. and tr. R.-H. Bautier and G. Labory, *L'abbaye de Fleury en l'an mil* (Paris, 2004)

Alberic of Troisfontaines, *Chronica*, ed. G. Pertz, *MGH SS*, vol. XXIII (Hanover, 1874), pp. 631–950

Albert of Aachen, *Historia Ierosolimitana*, ed. and tr. S. Edgington, *History of the journey to Jerusalem* (Oxford, 2007)

Alpert of Metz, *De diversitate Temporum*, ed. and tr. H. van Rijj and A. Sapir Abulafia, *Gebeurtenissen van deze tijd; Een fragment over bisschop Diederik I van Metz; De mirakelen van de heilige Walburg in Tiel* (Amsterdam, 1980)

Amalarius of Trier, *Liber officialis*, ed. J. M. Hanssens, *Amalarii episcopi opera*, Studi e testi 138–40, 3 vols. (Rome, 1948), vol. II, pp. 3–543

L'ancien coutumier de Champagne, ed. P. Portejoie (Poitiers, 1956)

Annales Altahenses maiores, ed. W. von Giesebrecht and E. von Oefele, *MGH SRG*, vol. IV (Hanover, 1891)

Annales Bertiniani, ed. F. Grat (Paris, 1964) and tr. J. Nelson, *The annals of St-Bertin* (Manchester, 1991)

Annales Fuldenses, ed. F. Kurze, *MGH SRG*, vol. VII (Hanover, 1891) and tr. T. Reuter, *The annals of Fulda* (Manchester, 1991)

Annales Quedlinburgenses, ed. M. Giese, *MGH SRG*, vol. LXXII (Hanover, 2004)

Annales sanctae Columbae, ed. G. Pertz, *MGH SS*, vol. I (Berlin, 1826), pp. 102–9

Annales Xantenses, ed. B. von Simson, *MGH SRG*, vol. XII (Hanover, 1909), pp. 7–33

Ansegis, *Capitularia*, ed. G. Schmitz, *Die Kapitulariensammlung des Ansegis, MGH Capitularia* (Hanover, 1996)

Anselm of St-Rémi, *Historia dedicationis Ecclesiae sancti Remigii*, ed. J. Hourlier, 'Histoire de la dédicace de Saint-Remy', *Travaux de l'académie nationale de Reims* 160 (1981), 181–297

Astronomer, *Vita Ludovici*, ed. E. Tremp, *MGH SRG*, vol. LXIV (Hanover, 1995)

Balderic, *Gesta Adalberonis archiepiscopi Treverensis*, ed. G. Waitz, *MGH SS*, vol. VIII (Hanover, 1848), pp. 243–60

Bede, *Ecclesiastical history*, ed. and tr. B. Colgrave and R. Mynors (Oxford, 1969)

Benedict Levita, *Capitularia*, ed. E. Baluze, *Capitularia regum Francorum*, 3 vols. (Paris, 1667), vol. I, col. 801–1232: see internet sources above

Bruno of Merseburg, *Liber de Bello Saxonico*, ed. W. Wattenbach, *MGH SRG*, vol. XV (Hanover, 1880)

Capitularia regum Francorum, ed. A. Boretius and V. Krause, *MGH Leges Sectio* III, 2 vols. (Hanover, 1897)

Carmen de Bello Saxonico, ed. O. Holder-Egger, *MGH SRG*, vol. XVII (Berlin, 1889), pp. 1–23

Charles the Bald, *Epistolae*, *PL*, vol. CXXIV, col 861–96

'Charte de Metz accompagnée de notes tironiennes', ed. J. Havet, *Bibliothèque de l'Ecole des Chartes* 49 (1888), 95–101

Chartes comtales pour la Champagne et la Brie (963–1151), ed. M. Bur, http://halshs. archives-ouvertes.fr/halshs-00638840

Christian 'of Stavelot', *Expositio super librum generationis*, ed. R. Huygens, *CCCM*, vol. CCXXIV (Turnhout, 2008)

Chronicon Mauriniacensis, *PL*, vol. CLXXX, col. 131–76

Chronicon S. Michaelis, ed. A. Lesort, *Chronique et Chartes de l'abbaye de Saint Mihiel*, A. Lesort, Mettensia vol. VI (Paris, 1909)

Chronicon sancti Benigni Divionensi, PL, vol. CLXII, col. 755–847

Chronicon sancti Huberti Andaginensis ('Cantatorium'), ed. L. Bethmann and W. Wattenbach, *MGH SS*, vol. VII (Hanover, 1848), pp. 565–630

Clarius, *Chronicon*, ed. and tr. R.-H. Bautier, *Chronique de Saint-Pierre-le-Vif de Sens, dite de Clarius* (Paris, 1979)

Concilia aevi Karolini [742–842], ed. A. Werminghoff, *MGH Concilia* 2, 2 vols. (Hanover, Leipzig, 1906–8)

Concilia aevi Karolini 843–859, ed. W. Hartmann, *MGH Concilia* 3 (Hanover, 1984)

Concilia aevi Karolini 860–874, ed. W. Hartmann, *MGH Concilia* 4 (Hanover, 1998)

Concilia aevi Saxonici 916–1001, ed. E.-D. Hehl, *MGH Concilia* 6 (Hanover, 1987–2007)

Consuetudines canonicorum regularium Springirsbacenses, ed. S. Weinfurter, *CCCM*, XLVIII (Turnhout 1978)

Il cosiddetto Pontificale di Poitiers: (Paris, Bibliothèque de l'Arsenal, cod. 227), ed. A. Martini (Rome, 1979)

The councils of Urban II, ed. R. Somerville (Amsterdam, 1972)

Dhuoda, *Liber manualis*, ed. and tr. M. Thiebaux (Cambridge, 1998)

Eadmer, *Historia novorum in Anglia*, ed. M. Rule, Rolls Series 81 (London, 1884)

The early councils of Pope Paschal II, 1100–1110, ed. U.-R. Blumenthal (Toronto, 1978)

Einhard, *Epistolae*, ed. K. Hampe, *MGH Epp.*, (Hanover, 1898–9), vol. V, pp. 109–45

Ekkehard of St-Gallen, *Casus sancti Galli*, ed. and tr. H. Haefele, *St. Galler Klostergeschichte* (Darmstadt, 1980)

Ermold, *Carmen in Honorem Ludovici*, ed. and tr. E. Faral, *Ermold le Noir* (Paris, 1964)

Feoda Campanie, in *Documents relatifs au comté de Champagne et de Brie: 1172–1361*, ed. A. Longnon, 3 vols. (Paris, 1901–14), vol. I, pp. 1–74

Flodoard of Rheims, *Annales*, ed. P. Lauer (Paris, 1905)

   Historia Remensis Ecclesiae, ed. M. Stratmann, *Die Geschichte der Reimser Kirche*, *MGH SS*, vol. XXXVI (Hanover, 1998)

Flodoardi Presbyteri ecclesiae remensis canonici historiarum eiusdem ecclesiæ libri IV, ed. J. Sirmond (Paris, 1644)

Folcuin, *Gesta abbatum Lobiensium*, ed. G. Pertz, *MGH SS*, vol. IV (Hanover, 1841), pp. 52–74

Formulae Merowingici et Karolini aevi, ed. K. Zeumer, *MGH Leges*, vol. V (Hanover, 1886)

Frothar of Toul, *Epistolae*, ed. and tr. M. Parisse, *La correspondance d'un évêque carolingien, Frothaire de Toul (ca 813–847), avec les lettres de Theuthilde, abbesse de Remiremont* (Paris, 1998)

Fulbert of Chartres, *Epistolae*, ed. and tr. F. Behrends, *The Letters and Poems of Fulbert of Chartres* (Oxford, 1976)

Gerbert of Rheims, *Epistolae*, ed. and tr. P. Riché and J.-P. Callu, *Correspondance*, 2 vols. (Paris, 1993)

Gervaise of Rheims, *Epistolae, PL*, vol. CXLIII, col. 1360–2

Geschichte der Grundherrschaft Echternach im Frühmittelalter, ed. C. Wampach (Luxembourg, 1930)

Gesta Dagoberti I regis Francorum, ed. B. Krusch, *MGH SRM* vol. II (Hanover, 1888), pp. 399–425

Gesta episcoporum Cameracensium, ed. G. H. Bethmann, *MGH SS*, vol. VII (Stuttgart, 1846), pp. 402–88

Gesta episcoporum Cameracensium continuatio, ed. G. H. Bethmann, *MGH SS*, vol. VII (Stuttgart, 1846), pp. 489–500

Gesta episcoporum Mettensium (continuatio), ed. G. Waitz, *MGH SS*, vol. X (Hanover, 1852), pp. 531–51

Gesta episcoporum Treverorum, ed. G. Waitz, *MGH SS*, vol. VIII (Hanover, 1848), pp. 111–74

Gesta episcoporum Treverorum continuato, ed. G. Waitz, *MGH SS*, vol. VIII (Hanover, 1848), pp. 175–200

Gesta episcoporum Tullensium, ed. G. Waitz, *MGH SS*, vol. VIII (Hanover, 1848), pp. 631–48

Gesta episcoporum Virdunensium, ed. G. Waitz, *MGH SS*, vol. IV (Hanover, 1841), pp. 38–45

Gregory VII, *Epistolae Vagantes*, ed. and tr. H. Cowdrey, *The 'Epistolae vagantes' of Pope Gregory VII* (Oxford 1972)

    Registrum, ed. E. Caspar, *MGH Epistolae Selectae*, vol. II (Berlin, 1920)

Guibert of Nogent, *Dei Gesta per Francos*, ed. R. Huygens, *CCCM* CXXVIIa (Turnhout, 1996)

Hariulf, *Chronicon centulense*, ed. F. Lot, *Chronique de l'abbaye de Saint-Riquier (ve siècle–1104)* (Paris, 1894)

Heiric of Auxerre, *Miracula S. Germani* (BHL 3462), *PL*, vol. CXXIV, col. 1207–1272

Helgaud of Fleury, *Epitoma vitae regis Rotberti*, ed. and tr. R.-H. Bautier, *Vie de Robert le Pieux* (Paris, 1965)

Hesso Scholasticus, *Relatio de concilio Remensi*, ed. W. Wattenbach, *MGH Libelli de lite* (Hanover, 1897), vol. III, pp. 21–8

Hincmar of Laon, *Epistolae*, ed. J. P. Migne, *PL*, vol. CXXIV, col. 979–1072

    Rotula Prolixa, ed. R. Schieffer, *Die Streitschriften Hinkmars von Reims und Hinkmars von Laon 869–871, MGH Concilia* (Hanover, 2003), 363–408

Hincmar of Rheims, *Ad Episcopos regni Admonitio Altera*, *PL*, vol. CXXV, col. 1007–17

    Ad Ludovicum Balbum, *PL*, vol. CXXV, col. 983–90

    Capitula I–V, ed. P. Brommer, R. Pokorny and M. Stratmann, *MGH Capitula episcoporum*, 4 vols. (Hanover/Berlin, 1984–2005), vol. II, pp. 1–90.

    De Cavendis vitiis et virtutibus exercendis, ed. D. Nachtman, *MGH* Quellen zur Geistesgeschichte des Mittelalters, vol. XVI (Munich 1998)

    De Coercendis militum rapinis, *PL*, vol. CXXV, col. 953–6

    Collectio de Ecclesiis et Capellis, *MGH Fontes iuris Germanici*, ed. M. Stratmann (Hanover 1990), vol. XIV

    Collectio de una et non trina deitate, *PL*, vol. CXXV, col. 473–618

    De divortio, ed. L. Böhringer, *De divortio Lotharii regis et Theutbergae regina, MGH Concilia Supplementum* (Hanover, 1992)

    Epistola Ad Ludovicum Germaniae, MGH Concilia vol. IV, pp. 408–27

    Epistolae, *PL*, vol. CXXVI, cols. 9–280A

    Expositiones, *PL*, vol. CXXV, col. 1035–70

    De fide Carolo servanda, *PL*, vol. CXXV, col. 961–84

    Libellus expostulationis, *MGH Concilia*, vol. IV, pp. 420–87

    MGH Epistolae, ed. E. Perels, *MGH Epp.*, vol. VIII (Berlin, 1939)

Bibliography

De Noviliaco, ed. H. Mordek, 'Ein exemplarischer Rechtsstreit: Hinkmar von Reims und das Landgut Neuilly-Saint-Front', *Zeitschrift der Savigny-Stiftung für Rechtsgeschichte. Kanonistische Abteilung* 83 (1997), 86–112

Opusculum in LV Capitulis, ed. R. Schieffer, *Die Streitschriften Hinkmars von Reims und Hinkmars von Laon 869–871, MGH Concilia* (Hanover, 2003), pp. 99–408

De ordine palatii, ed. T. Gross and R. Schieffer, *MGH Fontes* 3 (Hanover, 1980)

De presbiteris criminosis: ein Memorandum Erzbischof Hinkmars von Reims über straffällige Kleriker, ed. G. Schmitz, *MGH* Studien und Texte 34 (Hanover, 2004)

'Eine Übersehene Schrift', in 'Eine übersehene Schrift Hinkmars von Reims über Priestertum und Königtum', ed. R. Schieffer, *Deutsches Archiv* 37 (1981), 511–28

Historia Mosomensis, ed. and tr. M. Bur, *Chronique ou livre de fondation du Monastère de Mouzon* (Paris, 1989)

Historia senonensis Francorum, ed. G. Pertz, *MGH SS*, vol. IX (Hanover, 1851), pp. 364–9

Historia translationis Germani (BHL 3474–6), *AASS Maii*, vol. VI, ed. G. Henschenius (Antwerp, 1688), cols. 788–96

Historia translationis Helenae (BHL 3773), ed. J. Sollerius, J. Pinius, G. Cuperus and P. Boschius, *AASS Aug.*, vol. III (Antwerp 1737), col. 601–3

Hugh of Flavigny, *Chronicon*, ed. G. Pertz, *MGH SS*, vol. VIII (Hanover, 1848), pp. 280–503

Hugo Metellus, *Certamen papae et regis*, ed. E. Dümmler, *MGH Libelli de lite* vol. III (Hanover, 1897), pp. 714–719

Epistolae, in *Sacrae antiquitatis monumenta: historica, dogmatica, diplomatica*, ed. C. Hugo, 2 vols. (Étival, 1725), vol. II, pp. 312–412

Humbert of Moyenmoutier, *Adversus Simoniacos libri tres*, ed. E. Dümmler, *MGH Libelli de lite*, vol. I (Hanover, 1891), pp. 95–293

Hunald of Toul, *Carmen de anulo et baculo*, ed. H. Böhmer, *MGH Libelli de lite*, vol. III (Hanover, 1897), pp. 721–2

Die Inschriften der Stadt Trier, ed. R. Fuchs (Wiesbaden, 2006)

Jean de Bayon, *Chronicon mediani monasterii*, ed. J. Belhomme, *Historia mediani in monte Vosago monasterii* (Strasbourg, 1724), pp. 228–77

John the Deacon, *Vita Gregorii*, *PL*, vol. LXXV, col. 59–242

John of St-Arnulf, *Vita Iohannis Gorziensis* (BHL 4396), ed. and tr. M. Parisse, *La vie de Jean, abbé de Gorze* (Paris, 1999)

Jonas of Orléans, *De institutione laicali*, *PL*, vol. CVI, col. 121–278

Die Kapitulariensammlung Bischof Ghaerbalds, ed. W. Eckhardt (Göttingen, 1955)

Lambert of Arras, *Epistolae*, ed. and tr. C. Giordanengo, *Le registre de Lambert, évêque d'Arras (1093–1115)* (Paris, 2007)

Lambert of Wattrelos, *Annales Cameracenses*, ed. G. Pertz, *MGH SS*, vol. XVI (Leipzig, 1925), pp. 510–54

Lampert of Hersfeld, *Annales*, ed. O. Holder-Egger, *MGH SRG* vol. XXXVIII (Hanover, 1894)

Laurentius of Liège, *Gesta episcoporum Virdunensium*, ed. G. Waitz, *MGH SS*, vol. X (1852), pp. 486–530

Liber de divinis officiis, *PL*, vol. CI, cols. 1173–1286

Liber memorialis von Remiremont, ed. E. Hlawitschka, K. Schmid and G. Tellenbach, *MGH Libri memoriales*, 2 vols., vol. I, (Munich, 1981)

Liber Pontificalis, ed. L. Duchesne, 2 vols. (Paris, 1886–92)

Liber de successoribus S. Hildulfi in Mediano monasterio, ed. G. Waitz, *MGH SS*, vol. IV (Hanover, 1841), pp. 86–92

Lupus of Ferrières, *Epistolae*, ed. E. Dümmler, *MGH Epp.*, vol. VI (Berlin, 1925)

Vita Maximini (BHL 5824), ed. B. Krusch, *MGH SRM*, vol. III (Hanover, 1896), pp. 71–82

Mancio Bishop of Châlons, *Epistola*, *PL*, vol. CXXXI, col. 23 (*c*.900)

'Mandement inedit d'Adventius de Metz à l'occasion d'une incursion normande (mai–juin 867)', ed. D. Misonne, *Revue bénédictine* 93 (1983), 71–9

Metropolis Remensis historia, ed. G. Marlot, 2 vols. (Rheims, 1666)

'Die Mettlacher Güterrolle', ed. H. Müller, *Zeitschrift für die Geschichte der Saargegend* 15 (1965), 110–46

Miracula Benedicti, ed. E. de Certain, *Les miracles de St Benoît* (Paris, 1858)

Miracula Bertini (BHL 1291), ed. O. Holder-Egger, *MGH SS*, vol. XV:i (Hanover, 1887), pp. 516–22

Miracula Dionysii (BHL 2201-), ed. J. Mabillon, *Acta sanctorum ordinis sancti Benedicti* (Paris, 1672), vol. III:ii, pp. 358–423

Miracula Gisleni, ed. O. Holder-Egger, *MGH SS*, vol. XV:ii (Hanover, 1888), pp. 576–9

Miracula Gorgonii (BHL 3621), ed. G. Pertz, *MGH SS*, vol. IV (Hanover, 1841), pp. 238–47

Miracula Huberti (BHL 3996-), ed. C. de Smedt, G. van Hooff and J. de Backer, *AASS Nov.*, vol. I (Paris, 1887), col. 819–29

Miracula Maximini (BHL 5826), ed. G. Henschenius, D. Papebrochius, F. Baertius, and C. Ianningus., Mai,, vol. VII (Antwerp, 1688), col. 25–33

Miracula Remacli (BHL 7120-), ed. J. Pinius, J. Stiltingus, J. Limpenus and J. Veldius, *AASS Sept.*, vol. I, cols. 696–721

Miracula Richarii (BHL 7230), ed. G. Henschenius and D. Papebrochius, *AASS Apr.*, vol. III, cols. 447–57

Miracula Vedasti (BHL 8513), ed. J. Bolland and G. Henschius, *AASS Febr.*, vol. I (Antwerp, 1658), cols. 807–8

Miracula Vedasti auctore Haimini (BHL 8510), ed. J. Bolland and G. Henschius, *AASS Febr.*, vol. I (Antwerp, 1658) cols. 801–2

Muretach, *In Donati artem maiorem*, ed. L. Holtz, *CCCM*, vol. XL (Turnhout, 1977)

Narratio clericorum Remensium, ed. A. Werminghoff, *MGH Concilia*, vol. II:i (1908), pp. 809–10

'Neue Texte zur bischöflichen Reformgesetzgebung aus den Jahren 829/31. Vier Diözesansynoden Halitgars von Cambrai', ed. W. Hartmann, *Deutsches Archiv* 25 (1979), 368–94

Notker, *Gesta Karoli Magni*, ed. H. Haefele, *MGH SRG*, vol. XII (Berlin, 1959)

Odorannus of Sens, *Opera omnia*, ed. and tr. R.-H. Bautier and M. Gilles (Paris, 1972)

Orderic Vitalis, *Historia ecclesiastica*, ed. and tr. M. Chibnall, *The ecclesiastical history of Orderic Vitalis*, 6 vols. (Oxford, 1990)

Ordines de celebrando concilio, ed. H. Schneider, *MGH Leges* (Hanover, 1996)

Ordines coronationis Franciae, ed. R. Jackson, 2 vols. (Philadelphia, 1995)

Paschasius Radbertus, *Vita Walae, PL*, vol. cxx, col. 1557–650

Passio Luciani (BHL 5009), ed. J. Bolland, *AASS Jan.*, vol. I (Antwerp, 1664), cols. 461–6

Paul the Deacon, *Gesta episcoporum Mettensium*, ed. G. Pertz, *MGH SS*, vol. II (Hanover, 1829), pp. 260–8

Paulinus of Metz, *Epistola*, in *Thesaurus novus anecdotorum*, ed. E. Martène and U. Durand, vol. I (Paris, 1717), p. 196

Pseudo-Isidore, *Decretales*, ed. P. Hinschius, *Decretales Pseudo-Isidorianae et Capitula Angilramni* (Leipzig, 1863). See also internet resources.

Redactio sancti Emmerammi, ed. M. Weneger and C. Elvert, *Corpus Consuetudinum Monasticarum*, vol. VII:iii (Siegburg, 1984), pp. 187–256

Regino of Prüm, *Chronicon*, ed. F. Kurze, *MGH SRG*, vol. L (Hanover, 1890)
Libri duo de synodalibus causis, ed. and tr. W. Hartmann, *Das Sendhandbuch des Regino von Prüm* (Darmstadt, 2004)

Richer of St-Rémi, *Historiae*, ed. H. Hoffmann, *MGH SS*, vol. XXXVIII (Hanover, 2000)

Richer of Senones, *Gesta Senoniensis Ecclesiae*, ed. G. Waitz, *MGH SS*, vol. XXV (1880), pp. 249–348

Robert of Rheims, *Historia Iherosolimitana, PL*, vol. CLV, 669–758

Rodulf Glaber, *Historiae*, ed. and tr. J. France, *The five books of the histories* (Oxford, 1989)

Roger of Trier, *Capitula*, ed. P. Brommer, *MGH Capitula episcoporum*, vol. I (Hanover, 1984), pp. 57–70

Rothard of Soissons, *Libellus proclamationis*, *MGH Concilia*, vol. IV, pp. 182–6

Rudolf, *Gesta abbatum Trudonensium*, ed. R. Köpke, *MGH SS*, vol. X (Hanover, 1852), p. 213–448

Seher of Chaumousey, *De primordiis Calmocensis monasterii*, ed. L. Duhamel, *Documents rares ou inédits de l'histoire des Vosges*, vol. II (Paris 1869)

Die Sendgerichte in Deutschland, ed. A. Koeniger (Munich, 1907)

Smaragdus of St-Mihiel, *Expositio in regulam S. Benedicti*, ed. A. Spannagel, *Corpus Consuetudinum Monasticarum*, vol. VIII (Siegburg, 1978)
Liber in partibus Donati, ed. L. Lofstedt, *CCCM* vol. LXVIII (Turnhout, 1986)
Via regia, PL, vol. CII, col. 933–70

Suger of St-Denis, *De administratione*, in F. Gasparri, ed. and tr., *Oeuvres – Suger*, 2 vols. (Paris, 1996), vol. I, pp. 54–155
Vita Ludovici, ed. and tr. H. Waquet, *Vie de Louis VI le Gros* (Paris, 1964)

Summa 'Elegantius in iure divino' seu Coloniensis, ed. G. Fransen and S. Kuttner, 2 vols. (New York, 1969–78)

Thietmar of Merseburg, *Chronicon*, ed. R. Holtzmann, *MGH SRG N. S.* 9 (Berlin, 1935)

Thiofrid of Echternach, *Flores epytaphii sanctorum*, ed. M. Ferrari, *CCCM*, vol. CXXXIII (Turnhout, 1999)
Vita sancti Willibrordi (BHL 8940), ed. L. Weiland, *MGH SS*, vol. XXIII (Hanover, 1874), pp. 23–4

'Der Traktat "De investitura episcoporum" von 1109', ed. J. Krimm-Beumann, *Deutsches Archiv* 33 (1977), 37–83

Translatio Celsi (BHL 1720), ed. J. Bolland and G. Henschen, *AASS Febr.*, vol. III (Antwerp, 1658), pp. 396–400

Translatio et miracula sancti Clementis, ed. J. Dieterich, *MGH SS*, vol. XXX:ii (Hanover, 1934), pp. 893–908

Translatio Modoaldi (BHL 5985), ed. P. Jaffé, *MGH SS* vol. XII (Hanover 1856), pp. 289–310

Translatio SS. Chrysanthi et Dariae, ed. H. Floss, 'Romreise des Abtes Markward von Prüm und Übertragung der hl. Chrysanthus und Daria nach Münstereifel im Jahre 844', *Annalen des historischen Vereins für den Niederrhein* 20 (1869), 172–83

Translatio secunda Mansuetis, ed. O. Holder-Egger, *MGH SS*, vol. XV:ii (Hanover, 1888), pp. 931–2

Unibos, ed. T. Klein, 'Versus de Unibove', *Studi medievali* 32 (1991), pp. 843–86

Vetera Hyreevallis statuta, in *Sacrae antiquitatis monumenta: historica, dogmatica, diplomatica*, ed. C. Hugo, 2 vols. (Etival, 1725), vol. I, col. 135–44

Vita Adalberonis II (BHL), ed. G. Pertz, *MGH SS*, vol. IV (Hanover, 1841), pp. 658–72

Vita Amati (BHL 358), ed. B. Krüsch, *MGH SRM*, vol. V (Hanover, 1896), pp. 428–49

Vita Arnulfi Suessionensis (BHL 703), *PL*, vol. CLXXIV, col. 1375–1438

Vita Balsemii (BHL 904), ed. J. Sollerius, J. Pinius, G. Cuperus and P. Boschius, *AASS Aug.*, vol. III, col. 293–4

Vita Benedicti Anianensis, ed. G. Waitz, *MGH SS*, vol. XV:i. (Hanover, 1887), pp. 200–20

Vita Burchardi, ed. C. Bourel de la Roncière, *Vie de Bouchard le Venerable* (Paris, 1892)

Vita Elaphii (BHL 2441a), ed. H. Moretus, 'Catalogus Codicum Hagiographicum Latinorum Bibliothecae Scholae Medicinae in Universitate Montepessulanensi', *Analecta Bollandiana* 34–5 (1915–16), pp. 271–76

Vita Faronis (BHL 2825), ed. B. Krusch, *MGH SRM* vol. V (Hanover, 1896), pp. 171–203

Vita Frodoberti (BHL 3178), ed. M. Goullet, *Adsonis Dervensis opera hagiographica*, *CCCM* vol. CXCVIII (Turnhout, 2003), pp. 25–52

Vita Gerardi Tullensis (BHL 3431), ed. G. Waitz, *MGH SS*, vol. IV (Hanover, 1841), pp. 485–520

Vita Goaris (BHL 3566), ed. B. Krusch, *MGH SRM*, vol. IV (Hanover, 1902), pp. 402–23

Vita Leodegarii (BHL 4857), ed. G. Henschenius, D. Papebrochius, F. Baertius, and C. Janningus, *AASS Jun.*, vol. IV (Antwerp, 1707), 486–8

Vita Leonis (BHL 4818), ed. M. Parisse and tr. M. Goullet, *La vie du Pape Léon IX (Brunon, évêque de Toul)* (Paris, 2007)

Vita Magnerici (BHL 5149), ed. J. Sollerius, J. Pinius, G. Cuperus and P. Boschius, *AASS Jul.*, vol. VI, pp. 183–92

Vita Medardi (BHL 5866), ed. D. Papebroch, *AASS Jun.*, vol. II (Anvers 1698), cols. 82–6

Vita Memmii (BHL 5907), ed. J. Sollerius, J. Pinius, G. Cuperus and P. Boschius, *AASS Aug.*, vol. II (Antwerp, 1735)

Vita Modoaldi (BHL 5984), ed. G. Henschenius and D. Papebrochius, *AASS Maii*, vol. III (Antwerp, 1680), pp. 51–62

Vita Nivardi (BHL 6243), ed. W. Levison, *MGH SRM*, vol. V (Hanover, 1896), pp. 239–341

Bibliography

Vita Pauli (BHL 6600), ed. J. Mabillon, *AASS Feb.*, vol. II (Anvers, 1658), cols. 175–8

Vita Remigii (BHL 7152–64), ed. B. Krusch, *MGH SRM* vol. V (Hanover, 1896), pp. 239–341

Vita Richardi (BHL 7220), ed. W. Wattenbach, *MGH SS*, vol. XI (Hanover, 1854), pp. 280–9

Vita Rigoberti (BHL 7253), ed. W. Levison, *MGH SRM* vol. VII (Hanover, 1920), pp. 58–78

Vita Theodorici altera (BHL 8060), ed. J. Sollerius, *AASS Jul.*, vol. I, cols. 64–70

Vita Theoderici Mettensis (BHL 8055), ed. G. Pertz, *MGH SS*, vol. IV (1841), pp. 464–83

Vita Theodulfi (BHL 8098/9), ed. G. Henschenius and D. Papebrochius, *AASS Maii*, vol. I (Antwerp, 1680), cols. 96–9

Vita Vedasti (BHL 8506–8508), ed. B. Krüsch *MGH SRM*, vol. III (Hanover, 1896) pp. 414–27

Vita Victoris (BHL 8583), ed. H. Moretus, 'Catalogus codicum hagiographicorum latinorum bibliothecae scholae medicinae Montepessulanensis', *Analecta Bollandiana* 34–5 (1915–16), pp. 276–89

Walo of St-Arnulf, *Epistolae*, ed. B. Schütte, *Die Briefe des Abtes Walo von St Arnulf von Metz*, *MGH*, Studien und Texte 10 (Hanover, 1995)

Wandalbert of Prüm, *De mensium duodecim nominibus*, ed. E. Dümmler, *MGH poetae Latini aevi carolini*, vol. II (Berlin 1884), pp. 604–33

Miracula Goaris (BHL 3566–8), ed. O. Holder-Egger, *MGH SS*, vol. XV: i (Hanover, 1887), pp. 361–73

Wenric of Trier, *Epistola*, ed. K. Francke, *MGH Libelli de lite*, vol. I (Hanover, 1891), pp. 284–99

Wido of Bazoches, *Liber epistularum Guidonis de Basoches*, ed. H. Adolfsson (Stockholm, 1969)

INTERNET SOURCES

Benedict Levita, *Capitularia* www.benedictus.mgh.de

Chartes originales antérieures à 1121 conservées en France: www.cn-telma.fr/originaux/index/

INRAP (L'Institute national de recherches archéologiques) www.inrap.fr

Projekt pseudoisidor, www.pseudoisidor.mgh.de

Regesta imperii, http://regesten.regesta-imperii.de

SECONDARY WORKS

Abbé, J-L., 'Le paysage peut-il être lu à rebours? Le paysage agraire médiéval et la méthode régressive', in B. Cursente and M. Mousnier, eds., *Les territoires du médiéviste* (Rennes, 2005), pp. 383–99

Abels, R., 'The historiography of a construct: "feudalism" and the medieval historian', *History Compass* 7 (2009), 1008–31

Airlie, S., 'The aristocracy', in R. McKitterick, ed., *New Cambridge medieval history, vol. II AD 700–900* (Cambridge, 1995), pp. 43–50

Bibliography

'Bonds of power and bonds of association in the court circles of Louis the Pious', in P. Godman and R. Collins, eds., *Charlemagne's heir* (Oxford, 1990), pp. 191–204

Alfonso, I., 'Cistercians and feudalism', *Past and Present* 133 (1990), 3–30

Algazi, G., *Herrengewalt und Gewalt der Herren in späten Mittelalter. Herrschaft, Gegenseitigkeit und Sprachgebrauch* (Frankfurt, 1996)

Althoff, G., *Amicitia und pacta: Bündnis, Einung, Politik und Gebetsgedenken im beginnenden 10. Jahrhundert* (Hanover, 1992)

Family, friends and followers: political and social bonds in medieval Europe (Cambridge, 2004)

Die Macht der Rituale: Symbolik und Herrschaft im Mittelalter (Darmstadt, 2003)

Die Ottonen: Königsherrschaft ohne Staat (Stuttgart, 2000)

Anderson, P., *Passages from feudalism to antiquity* (London, 1974)

Angenendt, A., *Das Frühmittelalter: die abendländische Christenheit von 400 bis 900* (Stuttgart, 1990)

Anton, H., and Haverkamp, A., eds., *Trier im Mittelalter* (Trier, 1996)

Arbois de Jubainville, H., 'Catalogue d'actes des comtes de Brienne, 950–1356', *BEC* 33 (1872), 141–86

Histoire des ducs et des comtes de Champagne, 6 vols. (Paris, 1859)

'Les premiers seigneurs de Ramerupt', *BEC* 22 (1861), 440–58

Arnold, B., *German knighthood, 1050–1300* (Oxford, 1985)

Princes and territories in medieval Germany (Cambridge, 1991)

Asad, T., *Anthropology and the colonial encounter* (London, 1973)

Genealogies of religion: discipline and reasons of power in Christianity and Islam (Baltimore, 1993)

Atsma, H. and J. Vezin, *Les plus anciens documents originaux de l'abbaye de Cluny* (Turnhout, 1997).

Avril, F. and C. Rabel, *Manuscrits enluminés d'origine germanique* (Paris, 1995)

Bader, U., *Geschichte der Grafen von Are bis zur Hochstadenschen Schenkung* (Bonn 1976)

Bagge, S., Gelting, M. and Lindkvist, T., eds., *Feudalism: new landscapes of debate* (Turnhout, 2011)

Barbier, J., '"De minimis curat praetor": Hincmar, le polyptyque de Saint-Remi de Reims et les esclaves de Courtisols', in G. Constable and M. Rouche, eds., *Auctoritas: Mélanges offerts à Olivier Guillot* (Paris, 2006), pp. 267–79

'Rois et moines en Perthois pendant le haut Moyen Âge. À propos des origines et du temporel de Montiérender', in P. Corbet, J. Lusse and G. Viard, eds., *Les moines du Der (673–1790)* (Langres, 2000), pp. 45–81

Barnwell, P., 'The early Frankish mallus: its nature, participants and practices', in A. Pantos and S. Semple. eds., *Assembly places and practices in Medieval Europe* (Dublin, 2004), pp. 233–46

Barth, R., *Der Herzog in Lotharingien im 10 Jahrhundert* (Sigmaringen, 1990)

Barthélemy, D., 'La mutation de l'an 1100', *Journal de Savants* (2005), 3–28

La mutation de l'an mil, a-t-elle eu lieu?: servage et chevalerie dans la France des Xe et XIe siècles (Paris, 1997)

'Deux mutations du "féodalisme" (Point de vue)', in O. Bruand and D. Barthélemy, eds., *Les pouvoirs locaux dans la France du centre et de l'ouest (VIIIe–XIe siècles)* (Rennes, 2005), pp. 233–48

'La Renaissance du XIIe siécle n'aura pas lieu', *BEC* 154 (1996), 607–24

Bibliography

The serf, the knight, and the historian, tr. G. R. Edwards (Ithaca, 2009). This translation of Barthélemy's *La mutation de l'an mil* also includes some additional material.

La société dans le comté de Vendôme de l'an mil au XIVᵉ siècle (Paris 1993)

Bartlett, R., *Making of Europe: conquest, colonization and cultural change, 950–1350* (London, 1994)

Barton, R., *Lordship in the county of Maine c.890–1160* (Woodbridge, 2004)

Baschet, *La civilisation féodale: de l'an mil à la colonisation de l'Amérique* (Paris, 2004)

Bast, J., *Die Ministerialität des Erzstifts Trier*, Trierisches Archiv Erganzungsheft 17 (Trier 1918)

Bates, D., 'England and the "Feudal Revolution"', *Il Feudalesimo nell'alto medioevo, Settimane* 47 (2000), 611–46

Bauer, T., *Lotharingien als historischer Raum: Raumbildung und Raumbewusstsein im Mittelalter* (Cologne, 1997)

'Die mittelalterliche Gaue', *Geschichtlicher atlas der Rheinlande* IV/9, ed. Gesellschaft für Rheinische Geschichtskunde (Cologne, 2000)

Bautier, R.-H., 'Les principales étapes du développement des foires de Champagne', *Comptes-rendus des séances de l'Académie des Inscriptions et Belles-Lettres*, 96 (1952), 314–26

van Bavel, B., *Markets and manors: economy and society in the Low Countries, 500–1600* (Oxford, 2010)

Béague-Tahon, N., and Georges-Leroy, M., 'Deux habitats ruraux du Haut Moyen Age en Champagne crayeuse: Juvigny et Torcy le Petit', in C. Lorren and P. Périn, eds., *L'habitat rural du haut Moyen Age: France, Pays-Bas, Danemark et Grande Bretagne* (Rouen, 1995), pp. 175–83

Beck, E., 'Hochmittelalterliche Burganlagen in Trierer Land', *Trierer Zeitschrift* 69/70 (2006/7), 233–96

Becker, A., *Studien zum investiturproblem in Frankreich: Papsttum, Königtum und Episkopat im Zeitalter der gregorianischen Kirchenform (1049–1119)* (Saarbrücken, 1955)

'Urban II und die deutsche Kirche', in J. Fleckenstein, ed., *Investiturstreit und Reichsverfassung* (Sigmaringen, 1973)

Bedos-Rezak, B. M., 'From ego to imago: mediation and agency in medieval France', *Haskins Society Journal* 14 (2003), 151–73

Benner, S., *Châlons-en-Champagne: die Stadt, das Chorherrenstift Toussaint und das Umland bis zur Mitte des 14. Jahrhunderts* (Trier, 2005)

Benton, J., 'Written records and the development of systematic feudal relations', in J. Benton and T. Bisson, eds., *Culture, power and personality in medieval France* (London, 1991), pp. 275–90

Berkhofer, R., *Day of reckoning: power and accountability in medieval France* (Philadelphia, 2004)

Berlioz, J., 'La raison des gestes: pourquoi on prie à genoux', in *Moines et religieux au Moyen Age* (Paris, 1994), pp. 157–61

Bernhardt, J., *Itinerant kingship and royal monasteries in early medieval Germany, c.936–1075* (Cambridge, 1993)

Beuletz, S., *Das Verbot der Laieninvestitur im Investiturstreit* (Hanover, 1991)

Beumann, H., 'König Zwentibolds Kurswechsel im Jahre 898', *Rheinische Vierteljahrsblätter* 31 (1966/7), 17–41

Bibliography

Bienert, B., 'Zur frühmittelalterlichen Besiedlung Triers und des Trierer Landes', in H. Anton and A. Haverkamp, eds., *Trier im Mittelalter* (Trier, 1996), pp. 119–59

Bisson, T., *The crisis of the twelfth century: power, lordship, and the origins of European government* (Princeton, 2008)

'The Feudal Revolution', *Past and Present* 142 (1994), 6–42

'Medieval lordship', *Speculum* 70 (1995), 743–59

'La Terre et les hommes: a programme fulfilled?', *French History* 14 (2000), 322–34

Blaising, J.-M., 'Les structures du openfield en pays thionvillois', *Les Cahiers Lorrains* 1 (2000), 19–28

Bloch, Marc, *Feudal society*, tr. L. Manyon (London, 1961)

'Les formes de la rupture de l'hommage dans l'ancien droit féodal', in M. Bloch, ed., *Mélanges historiques*, 2 vols. (Paris, 1963), vol. 1, pp. 189–208

Bloch, Maurice, *Ritual, history and power: selected papers in anthropology* (London, 1989)

Böhme, H., ed., *Burgen der Salierzeit*, 2 vols. (Sigmaringen, 1991)

ed., 'Burgen der Salierzeit in Hessen, in Rheinland-Pfalz, und im Saarland', in H. Böhme, ed., *Burgen der Salierzeit*, vol. II, pp. 7–80

Bois, G., *La mutation de l'an mil: Lormand, village mâconais, de l'Antiquité au féodalisme* (Paris, 1989)

Bonnassie, P., *La Catalogne du milieu du xe à la fin du xie siècle* (Toulouse, 1975–6)

'Les paysans du royaume franc au temps d'Hugues Capet et de Robert le Pieux', in M. Parisse and X. Altet, eds., *Le roi de France et son royaume autour de l'an mil* (Paris, 1992), pp. 117–30

Bonnaud-Delamare, R., 'Les institutions de paix dans la province ecclésiastique de Reims au xie siècle', *Bulletin philologique et historique du Comité des travaux historiques et scientifiques* 10 (1957), 143–200

Bönnen, G., *Die Bischofsstadt Toul und ihr Umland während des hohen und späten Mittelalters* (Trier, 1995)

Boshof, E., *Das Erzstift Trier und seine Stellung zu Königtum und Papsttum im ausgehenden 10. Jahrhundert: der Pontifikat des Theoderich* (Cologne, 1972)

'Köln-Mainz-Trier – Die Auseinandersetzung um die Spitzenstellung der deutschen Episkopat in ottonisch-salianisch Zeit', *Jahrbuch des Kölnischen Geschichtsvereins* 49 (1978), 19–48

'Lothringen, Frankreich, und das Reich in der Regierungszeit Heinrichs III', *Rheinische Vierteljahrsblätter* 42 (1978), 63–127

'Untersuchungen zur Kirchenvogtei in Lothringen im 10 und 11 Jahrhundert', *Zeitschrift der Savigny stiftung für Rechtsgeschichte (Kanonistische Abteilung)* 65 (1979), 55–119

Bougard F. and Noyé, G., 'Archéologie médiévale et structures sociales: encore un effort', in D. Barthélemy, ed., *Liber largitorius: études d'histoire médiévale offertes à Pierre Toubert par ses élèves* (Geneva, 2003), pp. 331–46

Bouhot, J., 'Les sources de l'*Expositio missae* de Rémi d'Auxerre', *Revue des études augustiniennes* 26 (1980), 118–69

Bourin, M. and Martinez Sopeña, M., eds., *Pour une anthropologie du prélèvement seigneurial dans les campagnes de l'Occident médiéval (xie–xive siècles): réalités et représentations* (Paris, 2004)

Bowman, J., 'Do neo-Romans Curse? Law, land and ritual in the Midi (900–1100)', *Viator* 28 (1997), 1–32

Bradley, R. et al, 'Climate in medieval time', *Science* 17 (2003), 404–5

Brown, W., *Unjust seizure: conflict, interest and authority in an early medieval society* (Ithaca, 2001).

and Górecki, P., eds., *Conflict in medieval Europe* (Aldershot, 2003)

Bruand, O., 'La villa carolingienne: une seigneurie? Réflexions sur les cas des villas d'Hammelburg, Perrecy-les-Forges et Courçay', in D. Barthélemy, ed., *Liber largitorius: études d'histoire médiévale offertes à Pierre Toubert par ses élèves* (Geneva, 2003), pp. 349–73

Voyageurs et marchandises aux temps carolingiens: les réseaux de communication entre Loire et Meuse aux VIIIe et IXe siècles (Brussels, 2002)

Brühl, C.-R., *Deutschland – Frankreich: die Geburt zweier Völker* (Cologne, 1990)

Fodrum, gistum, servitium regis: studien zu den wirtschaftlichen Grundlagen des Königtums im Frankenreich und in den fränkischen Nachfolgestaaten Deutschland, Frankreich und Italien vom 6. bis zur Mitte des 14. Jahrhunderts (Cologne, 1968)

Palatium und Civitas: Studien zur Profantopographie spätantiker Civitates vom 3. bis 13. Jahrhundert, 2 vols. (Cologne, 1975)

Buc, P., *The dangers of ritual: between early medieval texts and social scientific theory* (Princeton, 2001)

'The monster and the critics: a ritual reply', *EME* 15 (2007), 441–52

Bullimore, K., 'Folcwin of Rankweil', *EME* 13 (2005), 43–77

Bullough, D., 'The Carolingian liturgical experience', *Studies in Church History* 35 (1999), 29–64

Bur, M., 'L'abbaye de Montier-en-Der face aux princes et aux évêques (XIe–XIIe siècles)', in P. Corbet, ed., *Les moines du Der (673–1790)* (Langres, 2000), pp. 531–49

'Adalbéron, archevêque de Reims, reconsidéré', in M. Parisse and X. Altet, eds., *Le roi de France et son royaume autour de l'an mil* (Paris, 1992), pp. 55–63

La Champagne médiévale: recueil d'articles (Langres, 2005)

'Châteaux et peuplement dans le Nord et l'Est de la France au Moyen Âge', in M. Bur, *Châteaux et peuplements en Europe occidentale* (Auch, 1980), pp. 75–92

La formation du comté de Champagne: v. 950–v. 1150 (Nancy, 1977)

'La frontière entre la Champagne et la Lorraine du milieu du Xe siècle à la fin du XIIe siècle', *Francia* 4 (1976), 237–54

Inventaire de sites archéologiques non monumentaux de Champagne. I: Vestiges d'habitat seigneurial fortifié des Ardennes et de la Vallée de l'Aisne (Rheims, 1980)

Inventaire de sites archéologiques non monumentaux de Champagne. II: Vestiges d'habitat seigneurial fortifié en Champagne méridionale (Rheims, 1997)

'Léon IX et la France (1026–1054)', in G. Bischoff and B. Tocks, eds., *Léon IX et son temps* (Turnhout, 2007), pp. 233–57

'Menre, speculum temporis', in E. Mornet, ed., *Campagnes médiévales. L'homme et son espace: études offertes à Robert Fossier* (Paris, 1995), pp. 135–43

'Les possessions de Gorze en Champagne', in *Saint Chrodegang: communications présentées au Colloque tenu à Metz à l'occasion du douzième centenaire de sa mort* (Metz, 1967), pp. 169–82

'Remarques sur les plus anciens documents concernant les foires de Champagne', in *La Champagne médiévale: recueil d'articles* (Langres, 2005), pp. 463–84

Büttner, H., 'Die Übergang der Abtei St. Maximin an das Erzstift Trier unter Erzbischof Albero von Montreuil', in S. Jenks, ed., *Festschrift Ludwig Petry* (Wiesbaden, 1968), pp. 65–77

Cardot, F., *L'espace et le pouvoir. Etude sur l'Austrasie mérovingienne* (Paris, 1987)

Carozzi, C., 'La vie de saint Dagobert de Stenay: histoire et hagiographie', *Revue Belge de Philologie et d'Histoire* 62 (1984), 225–58

Carpenter, D., 'The second century of feudalism', *Past and Present* 168 (2000), 30–71

Carte archéologique de la Gaule, various authors, 113 vols. (Paris, 1988–)

Chabot, G., *Géographie régionale de la France* (Paris, 1966)

Chadwick, H., 'John Moschus and his friend Sophronius the Sophist', *Journal of Theological Studies* 25 (1974), 41–74

Champion, E., *Moulins et meuniers carolingiens: dans les polyptyques entre Loire et Rhin* (Paris, 1996)

Chapelot, J., 'L'habitat rural du haut Moyen Age. Quelques reflexions à partir de ce que nous en font connaître les fouilles d'Ile-de-France', in J-M. Yante and A.-M. Bultot-Verleysen, eds., *Autour du 'village': établissements humains, finages et communautés rurales entre Seine et Rhin (IVe – XIIIe siècles)* (Louvain, 2010), pp. 85–140

Chossenot, R., ed., *La Marne*, Cartes archéologiques de la Gaule 51/1 (Paris 2004)

Civel, N., *La fleur de France: les seigneurs d'Ile-de-France au XIIe siècle* (Turnhout, 2006)

Clauss, M., *Die Untervogtei: Studien zur Stellvertretung in der Kirchenvogtei im Rahmen der deutschen Verfassungsgeschichte des 11. und 12. Jahrhunderts* (Siegburg, 2002)

Claussen, M., *The reform of the Frankish church: Chrodegang of Metz and the Regula canonicorum in the eighth century* (Cambridge, 2004)

Clavis Scriptorum Latinorum medii aevi: territoire français, 735–987, Clavis Scriptorum Latinorum medii aevi: Auctores Galliae, 2 vols., vol. II (Turnhout, 1994)

Comaroff, J. and Comaroff, J., *Of revelation and revolution*, 2 vols. (Chicago, 1991–7)

Comet, G., 'Technology and agricultural expansion in the Middle Ages: the example of France north of the Loire', in G. Astill and J. Langdon, eds., *Medieval farming and technology: the impact of agricultural change in Northwest Europe* (London, 1977), pp. 11–39

Congost, R., 'Property rights and historical analysis', *Past and Present* 181 (2003), 73–106

Constable, G., 'The ceremonies and symbolism of entering religious life and taking the monastic habit, from the fourth to the twelfth century', *Settimane* 33 (1987), 771–834

Contreni, J., *The cathedral school of Laon from 850 to 930: its manuscripts and masters* (Munich, 1978)

Corbet, P., ed., *Les moines du Der (673–1790)* (Langres, 2000)

Costambeys, M., *Power and patronage in the early medieval Italy: local society, Italian politics, and the abbey of Farfa, c. 700–900* (Cambridge, 2007)

and Innes, M. and MacLean, S., *The Carolingian world* (Cambridge, 2011)

Cotterrell, R., *The sociology of law: an introduction* (Oxford, 1984)

Coudert, J., 'L'évêque de Metz et ses paysans: l'exemple du ban de Rémilly vers 1300 d'après le rapport des droits', *Les cahiers lorrains* 84 (2002), 313–38

Coulson, C., 'Castellation in the county of Champagne in the thirteenth century', *Château-Gaillard* 9–10 (1982), 347–64

Cramer, P., *Baptism and change in the early Middle Ages, c. 200–c. 1150* (Cambridge, 1993)

Bibliography

Crété-Protin, I., *Église et vie chrétienne dans le diocèse de Troyes du 4 au 9 siècle* (Villeneuve-d'Ascq, 2002)

Crinon, P. and Lemant, J., 'Les deniers d'Otton III empereur et Arnoul archevêque de Reims (998–1021), émis pour la partie orientale du diocèse (Mouzon)', *Bulletin de la Société française de numismatique* 51 (1996), 166–71

Curta, F., 'Merovingian and Carolingian gift giving', *Speculum* 81 (2006), 671–99

Dahlhaus, J., Koch, M., and Kölzer, T., 'Die "Rebellen" von Wasserbillig: eine diplomatische Nachlesen', in S. Happ and H. Nonn, eds., *Vielfalt der Geschichte* (Berlin, 2004), pp. 109–25

Daux, V., C. Lecuyer, F. Adam, F. Martineau and F. Vimeux, 'Oxygen isotope composition of human teeth and the record of climate changes in France (Lorraine) during the last 1700 years', *Climactic Change* 70 (2005), 445–64

Davies, W., *Small worlds: the village community in early medieval Brittany* (Berkeley, 1988)
and Fouracre, P., eds., *The languages of gift in the early Middle Ages* (Cambridge, 2010)
eds., *Power and property in the early Middle Ages* (Cambridge, 1995)
eds., *The settlement of disputes in early medieval Europe* (Cambridge, 1986)

Davis, K., *Periodization and sovereignty: how ideas of feudalism and secularization govern the politics of time* (Philadelphia, 2008)

Delisle, L., *Littérature Latine et histoire du Moyen Age* (Paris, 1890)

Demade, J., 'The medieval countryside in German-language historiography since the 1930s', in I. Alfonso, ed., *The rural history of medieval European societies: trends and perspectives* (Turnhout, 2007), pp. 173–252

Demouy, P., *Genèse d'une cathédrale: les archevêques de Reims et leur église aux XI* et XII* siècles* (Rheims, 2005)

Dendorfer, J., 'Das Wormser Konkordat – ein Schritt auf dem Weg zur Feudalisierung der Reichsverfassung?', in J. Dendorfer and R. Deutinger, eds., *Das Lehnswesen im Hochmittelalter: Forschungskonstrukte, Quellenbefunde, Deutungsrelevanz* (Ostfildern, 2010) pp. 299–328
and Deutinger, R., eds., *Das Lehnswesen im Hochmittelalter: Forschungskonstrukte, Quellenbefunde, Deutungsrelevanz* (Ostfildern, 2010)

Denajar, L., ed., *L'Aube*, Cartes archéologiques de la Gaule 10 (Paris, 2005)

Depreux, P., 'Gestures and comportment at the Carolingian court: between practice and perception', *Past and Present* 203 (2009), 57–79
'"Investitura per anulum et baculum". Ring und Stab als Zeichen der Investitur bis zum Investiturstreit', in J. Jarnut and M. Wemhoff, eds., *Vom Umbruch zur Erneuerung? Das 11. und beginnende 12. Jahrhundert* (Munich, 2006), pp. 169–95
'Lehnsrechtliche Symbolhandlungen. Handgang und Investitur im Bericht Galberts von Brügge zur Anerkennung Wilhelm Clitos als Graf von Flandern', in J. Dendorfer and R. Deutinger, eds., *Das Lehnswesen im Hochmittelalter* (Ostfildern, 2010) pp. 387–400
Les sociétés occidentales du milieu du VI à la fin du IX* siècle* (Rennes, 2002)

Desporte, P., and Dolbeau, F., 'Découverte de nouveaux documents relatifs au polyptyque de Saint-Rémi de Reims. À propos d'une édition récente', *Revue du Nord* 270 (1986), 575–607

Deutinger, R., *Königsherrschaft im Ostfränkischen Reich: eine pragmatische Verfassungsgeschichte der späten Karolingerzeit* (Ostfildern, 2006)

'Seit wann gibt es die Mehrfachvasallität?', in *Zeitschrift der Savigny-Stiftung für Rechtsgeschichte, Germanistische Abteilung* 119 (2002), 78–105

Devisse, J., *Hincmar: archevêque de Reims, 845–882*, 3 vols. (Geneva, 1975–6)

Devroey, J-P., 'Communiquer et signifier entre seigneurs et paysans', *Settimane* 52 (2005), 121–54

Economie rurale et société dans l'Europe franque (vi^e–ixe siècles) (Paris, 2003)

Puissants et misérables: système social et monde paysan dans l'Europe des Francs (vi^e–ixe siècles) (Brussels, 2006)

'Seigneurs et paysans au coeur de l'ancien empire carolingien de part et d'autre de l'an mil: les seigneuries de saint Rémi de Reims (ix–xi s.)' in P. Bonnassie and P. Toubert, eds., *Hommes et sociétés dans l'Europe de l'an mil* (Toulouse, 2004), pp. 253–71

'La "villa Floriacus" et la présence de l'abbaye des Fossés en Rémois durant le Haut Moyen Âge', *Revue belge de Philologie et d'histoire* 82 (2004), 809–38

and N. Schroeder, 'Beyond royal estates and monasteries: landownership in the early medieval Ardennes', *EME* 20 (2012), 39–69

Dewolf, Y. and Pomerol, C., 'The Parisian basin', in E. Koster, ed., *The physical geography of Western Europe* (Oxford, 2005), pp. 251–66

Dhénin, M., 'Obole inédite de Lothaire (954–986) et Herbert II, comte de Troyes (967–983)', *Bulletin de la Société française de numismatique* 48 (1993), 473–4

Dhondt, J., *Études sur la naissance des principautés territoriales* (Bruges, 1948)

Didier, N., *La garde des églises au xiii siècle* (Paris, 1927)

Diederich, T., 'Sancta Colonia – Sancta Coloniensis Religio. Zur "Botschaft" der Bleibullen Erzbischof Pilgrims von Köln (1021–1036)', *Rheinische Vierteljahrsblätter* 75 (2011), 1–49

Diestelkamp, B., 'Lehnrecht und Lehnspolitik als Mittel des Territorialausbaus', *Rheinische Vierteljahrsblätter* 63 (1999), 26–38

de Dion, A., *Les seigneurs de Breteuil en Beauvaisais* (Paris, 1884)

Dohrmann, W., *Die Vögte des Klosters St. Gallen in der Karolingerzeit* (Bochum, 1985)

Dolbeau, F., 'Vie latine de Sainte Ame, composée au xie siècle par Etienne, abbé de Saint-Urbain', *Analecta bollandiana* 105 (1987), 25–63

'Un vol de reliques dans le diocèse de Reims au milieu du xie siècle', *Revue bénédictine* 91 (1981), 172–84

Donnat, L., 'Vie et coutume monastique dans la Vita de Jean de Gorze', in M. Parisse and G. Oexle, eds., *L'abbaye de Gorze au x siècle* (Nancy, 1993), pp. 159–82

Droege, G., *Landrecht und Lehnrecht im hohen Mittelalter* (Bonn, 1969)

'Pfalzgrafschaft, Grafschaften und allodiale Herrschaften zwischen Maas und Rhein in salisch-staufische Zeit', *Rheinische Vierteljahrsblätter* 26 (1961), 1–21

Duby, G., *The early growth of the European economy: warriors and peasants from the seventh to the twelfth century*, tr. H. Clarke (London, 1974)

La société aux xie et xiie siècles dans la région mâconnaise (Paris, 1953)

Dumas, F., 'La monnaie au xe siècle', *Settimane* 38 (1991), 565–609

Durliat, J., *Les finances publiques de Dioclétien aux Carolingiens (284–889)* (Sigmaringen, 1990)

Dutton, P., *The politics of dreaming in the Carolingian empire* (Lincoln Nebraska, 1994)

'Whispering secrets to a dark age', in P. Dutton, *Charlemagne's mustache, and other cultural clusters of a dark age* (New York, 2009), pp. 129–50

Duvernoy, E., *Catalogue des actes des ducs de Lorraine de 1048 à 1139* (Nancy, 1915)

Le duc de Lorraine, Mathieu (1139–1176) (Paris, 1904)

Dyer, C., 'Language of oppression: the vocabulary of rents and services in England', in M. Bourin and P. Martinez Sopeña, eds., *Pour une anthropologie du prélèvement seigneurial dans les campagnes médiévales, xie–xive siècles: Les mots, les temps, les lieux* (Paris, 2007), pp. 71–86

Ehlers, J., 'Carolingiens, Robertiens, Ottoniens: politique familiale ou relations franco-allemandes', in M. Parisse, ed., *Le roi de France et son royaume autour de l'an mil* (Paris, 1992), pp. 39–45

Die Entstehung des deutschen Reiches (Munich, 1994)

Eldevik, J., 'Driving the chariot of the lord: Siegfried I of Mainz (1060–1084) and episcopal identity in an age of transition', in J. Ott and A. Trumbore Jones, eds., *The bishop reformed* (Aldershot, 2007)

Episcopal power and ecclesiastical reform in the German Empire: tithes, lordship and community, 950–1150 (Cambridge, 2012)

Engels, O., 'Grundlinien der rheinischen Verfassungsgeschichte im 12. Jahrhundert', *Rheinische Vierteljahrsblätter* 39 (1975), 1–27

Epstein, S., *Economic and social history of later medieval Europe* (Cambridge, 2009)

Erhart, P. and Kleindinst, J., *Urkundenlandschaft Rätien* (Vienna, 2004)

Erkens, F-R., *Die Trierer Kirchenprovinz im Investiturstreit* (Cologne, 1987)

'Etude sur une charte privée redigée à Huy', ed. with facsimile by G. Despy, *Bulletin de la Commission Royale* (1960), 110–17.

Evergates, T., *The aristocracy in the county of Champagne 1100–1300* (Philadelphia, 2007)

Feudal society in the bailliage of Troyes under the counts of Champagne 1152–1284 (London 1976)

Feudal society in medieval France: documents from the county of Champagne (Philadelpha, 1993)

Ewig, E., 'Descriptio Franciae', in W. Braunfels, ed., *Karl der Grosse*, 5 vols. (Düsseldorf, 1967), vol. v, pp. 143–72

Fasolt, C., 'Hegel's ghost: Europe, the Reformation, and the Middle Ages', *Viator* 39 (2008), 345–86

Favier, J., 'La fabrication d'un faux à Saint-Maur-des-Fossés vers la fin du xie siècle', *BEC* 119 (1961), 233–41

Federenko, G., 'The crusading career of John of Brienne', *Nottingham Medieval Studies* 52 (2008), 43–79

Feller, L., 'Les hiérarchies dans le monde rural', in D. Iogna-Prat, F. Bougard and R. le Jan, eds., *Hiérarchie et stratification sociale dans l'Occident médiéval (400–1100)* (Turnhout, 2008), pp. 257–76

Paysans et seigneurs au Moyen Age: viiie–xve siècles (Paris, 2007)

Finck von Finckenstein, A., *Bischof und Reich: Untersuchungen zum Integrationsprozess des ottonisch-frühsalischen Reiches (919–1056)* (Sigmaringen, 1989)

Fish, S., *Is there a text in this class? The authority of interpretive communities* (Cambridge, Mass., 1980)

Fitzpatrick, P., *The Mythology of modern law* (London, 1992)

Fliche, A. *La réforme grégorienne* (Louvain, 1924–37)

Flon, D., *Histoire monétaire de la Lorraine et des Trois-Évêchés* (Nancy, 2002)

Florange, J. *Histoire des seigneurs et comtes de Sierk* (Paris, 1895)

Flotte, P. and Fuchs, M., eds., *La Moselle*, Cartes archéologiques de la Gaule 57 (Paris, 2004)

Fossier, R., *La terre et les hommes en Picardie jusqu'à la fin du* XIII*ᵉ siècle*, 2 vols. (Paris, 1968)
 L'enfance de l'Europe X–XII *siècles: aspects économiques et sociaux* (Paris, 1982)
Fouracre, P., 'Conflict, power and legitimation in Francia in the late seventh and early eighth centuries', in I. Alfonso, H. Kennedy and J. Escalona, eds., *Building legitimacy: political discourses and forms of legitimacy in medieval societies* (Leiden, 2004), pp. 3–26
 'The use of the term *beneficium* in Frankish sources: a society based on favours?', in W. Davies and P. Fouracre, eds., *The languages of gift in the early Middle Ages* (Cambridge, 2010), pp. 62–88
 La France romane au temps des premiers capétiens (987–1152) (Paris, 2005)
Fray, J.-L., 'Recherches sur la seigneurie banale au XII siècle d'après le vocabulaire des actes des évêques de Metz (1050–1210)', *Publications de la section historique de l'Institut GD de Luxembourg* (1986), 75–101
Fried, J., 'Elite und ideologie, oder die Nachfolgeordnung Karls des Grossen vom Jahre 813', in R. le Jan ed., *La royauté et les élites dans l'Europe carolingienne: début* IX*ᵉ siècle aux environs de 920* (Villeneuve, 1998), pp. 71–109
 'Ritual und Vernunft – Traum und Pendel des Thietmar von Merseburg', in L. Gall, ed., *Das Jahrtausend im Spiegel der Jahrhundertwenden* (Berlin 1999), pp. 15–63
Fuhrmann, H., *Einfluss und Verbreitung der pseudoisidorischen Fälschungen: von ihrem Auftauchen bis in die neuere Zeit*, 3 vols. (Stuttgart, 1972–4)
Ganshof, F.-L., *Feudalism*, tr. P. Grierson (London, 1952)
Ganz, D., 'The ideology of sharing', in W. Davies and P. Fouracre, eds., *Property and power in the early Middle Ages* (Cambridge, 1995), pp. 17–30
Garipzanov, I., *The symbolic language of authority in the Carolingian world (c.751–877)* (Leiden, 2008)
Garnett, G., *Conquered England: kingship, succession and tenure, 1066–1166* (Oxford, 2007)
Gasse-Grandjean, M.-J., 'Le mot bannus dans les actes originaux du Haut Moyen Age', *Pays de Remiremont* 15 (2001), 44–60
Gauthier, N., *Topographie chrétienne des cités de la Gaule: origines au milieu du* VIII*ᵉ siècle*, 8 vols. (Paris, 1986–)
Gautier, A., *Le Festin dans l'Angleterre anglo-saxonne* (Rennes, 2006)
Gautier, P., 'Note sur des diplômes carolingiens des archives de la Haute-Marne', *Le Moyen Age* 16 (1912), 77–89
Geary, P., *The myth of nations: the medieval origins of Europe* (Princeton, 2003)
 Phantoms of remembrance: memory and oblivion at the end of the first millennium (Princeton, 1994)
Genicot, L., 'Le premier siècle de la *curia* de Hainaut', *Le Moyen Age* 53 (1947), 39–60
 'Les premières mentions de droits banaux dans la région de Liège', *Académie Royale de Belgique, bulletin de la classe des lettres et des sciences morales et politiques*, 5ᵉ série, 54 (1968), 56–65
 'Les premières mentions de droits banaux dans la région de Liège', *Académie Royale de Belgique, Bulletin de la Classe des Lettres et des Sciences morales et politiques*, 5e série, 54 (1968), 56–65
Georges-Leroy, M., 'La production céramique médiévale en Lorraine: état de la recherche archéologique', in N. Meyer-Rodrigues and M. Bur, eds., *Les arts*

du feu, Actes du 127e congrès des sociétés historiques et scientifiques, Nancy, 15–20 avril 2002 (2009), pp. 163–91.

Geschichtliche Grundbegriffe: historisches Lexikon zur politisch-sozialen Sprache in Deutschland (Stuttgart, 1972–97)

van der Gheyn, J., *Catalogue des manuscrits de la Bibliothèque Royale de Belgique* (Brussels, 1901), vol. I

Giese, W., *Heinrich I.: Begründer der ottonischen Herrschaft* (Darmstadt, 2008)

Gilchrist, J., 'Cardinal Humbert of Silva Candida, the canon law and ecclesiastical reform in the eleventh century', *Zeitschrift der Savigny Stiftung für Rechtsgeschichte, Kanonistische Abteilung* 58 (1972), 338–49

Gillen, A., *Saint-Mihiel im hohen und späten Mittelalter: Studien zu Abtei, Stadt und Landesherrschaft im Westen des Reiches* (Trier, 2003)

Giordanengo, G., 'Le concile de Saint-Basle: actes conciliaires rédigés par Gerbert', in *Autour de Gerbert d'Aurillac, le pape de l'an mil: album de documents commentés* (Paris, 1996), pp. 134–41

Girardot, A., *Le droit et la terre: le Verdunois à la fin du Moyen Age, 2 vols.* (Nancy, 1992)

Giuliato, G., 'Le château, reflet de l'art défensif en Lorraine du xe au début du xiiie siècle', *Annales de l'Est* 53 (2003), 55–76

'Les premiers châteaux dans le pays du sel en Lorraine (x^e–xiie siècle)', *Château Gaillard* 16 (1992), 215–32

ed., *Autour des comtes de Vaudémont: lieux, symboles et images d'un pouvoir princier au Moyen Âge* (Nancy, 2011)

Glenn, J., *Politics and history in the tenth century: the work and world of Richer of Reims* (Cambridge, 2004)

Gockel, M., 'Kritische Bemerkungen zu einer Neuausgabe des Liber possessionum Wizenburgensis', *Hessisches Jahrbuch für Landesgeschichte* 39 (1989), 353–80

Goetz, H.-W., *'Dux' und 'ducatus': begriffs- und verfassungsgeschichtliche Untersuchungen zur Entstehung des sogenannten 'jüngeren' Stammesherzogtums an der Wende vom neunten zum zehnten Jahrhundert* (Bochum, 1977)

'Gesellschaftliche Neuformierungen um die zweite Jahrtausendwende? Zum Streit um die "mutation de l'an mil"', in A. Hubel and B. Schneidmüller, eds., *Aufbruch ins zweite Jahrtausend. Innovation und Kontinuität in der Mitte des Mittelalters*, Mittelalter-Forschungen 16 (Ostfildern 2004), pp. 31–50

Geschichtsschreibung und Geschichtsbewusstsein im hohen Mittelalter (Berlin, 1999)

'Herrschaft und Recht in der frühmittelalterlichen Grundherrschaft', *Historisches Jahrbuch* 104 (1984), 392–410

le Goff, J., 'The symbolic rituals of vassalage', in *Time, work, and culture in the Middle Ages*, trans. by Arthur Goldhammer (Chicago, 1980), pp. 237–87

Goffart, W., *The Le Mans forgeries* (Cambridge, Mass., 1966)

Goldberg, E., 'Popular revolt, dynastic politics, and aristocratic factionalism in the Early Middle Ages: the Saxon stellinga reconsidered', *Speculum* 70 (1995), 485–96

Goodman, J., 'History and anthropology', in M. Bentley, ed., *Companion to historiography* (London, 1997), pp. 783–804

de Gostowski, G., 'Les émancipations seigneuriales dans le comté de Porcien aux xie–xiie siècles', *Revue Historique Ardennaise* 33 (1998), 13–96

Groten, M., 'Die Stunde der Burgherren. Zum Wandel adliger Lebensformen in den nördlichen Rheinlanden in der späten Stauferzeit', *Rheinische Vierteljahrsblätter* 66 (2002), 74–110

Guenée, B., 'Les génealogies entre l'histoire et la politique: la fierté d'être Capétien en France au Moyen Âge', *Annales* 33 (1978), 450–77

Guerreau, A., 'Quelques caractères spécifiques de l'espace féodal européen', in N. Bulst, R. Descimon and A. Guerreau, eds., *L'état ou le roi. Les fondations de la modernité monarchique en France (XIVe–XVIIe siècles)* (Paris, 1996), pp. 85–101

Guillot, O., 'Formes, fondements et limites de l'organisation politique en France au xe siècle', *Settimane* 38 (1991), 57–116

Guyotjeannin, O., *Episcopus et comes: affirmation et déclin de la seigneurie épiscopale au nord du royaume de France (Beauvais-Noyon, x^e-début xiiie siècle)* (Geneva, 1987)

   'Les évêques dans l'entourage royal sous les premiers Capétiens', in M. Parisse, ed., *Le roi de France et son royaume autour de l'an mil* (Paris, 1992), pp. 91–8

   '*Penuria scriptorum.* Le mythe de l'anarchie documentaire dans la France du Nord (x^e-première moitié du xie siècle)', *BEC* 155 (1997), 11–44

   and Poulle, E., eds., *Autour de Gerbert d'Aurillac, le pape de l'an mil: album de documents commentés* (Paris, 1996)

Halbekann, J., *Die älteren Grafen von Sayn. Personen-, Verfassungs- und Besitzgeschichte eines rheinischen Grafengeschlechts 1139–1246/47* (Wiesbaden, 1997)

Hallam, E. and Everard, J., *Capetian France, 987–1328* (Harlow, 2001)

Hallinger, K., *Gorze-Kluny: studien zu den monastischen Lebensformen u. Gegensätzen im Hochmittelalter* (Rome, 1951)

Halsall, G., ed., *Violence and society in the early medieval West* (Woodbridge, 1998)

Hamilton, S., *The practice of penance* (London, 2001)

Hamm, G., ed., *La Meurthe-et-Moselle*, Cartes archéologiques de la Gaule 54 (Paris, 2004)

Hartmann, W., 'Die Capita incerta im Sendhandbuch Reginos von Prüm', in O. Münsch and T. Zotz, eds., *Scientia Veritatis. Festschrift für Hubert Mordek zum 65 Geburtstag* (Ostfildern, 2004), pp. 207–26

   'Zu Effektivität und Aktualität von Reginos Sendhandbuch', in W. Müller and M. Sommar, eds., *Medieval church law and the origins of the Western legal tradition* (Washington, DC, 2006), pp. 33–49

Haubrichs, W., 'Gelenkte Siedlung des frühen Mittelalters im Seillegau. Zwei Urkunden des Metzer Klosters St. Arnulf und die lothringische Toponymie', *Zeitschrift für die Geschichte der Saargegend* 30 (1982), 7–39

   Georgslied und Georgslegende im frühen Mittelalter: text und rekonstruktion (Königstein, 1979)

   'Über die allmähliche Verfertigung von Sprachgrenzen. Das Beispiel der Kontaktzonen von Germania und Romania', in W. Haubrichs and R. Schneider, eds., *Grenzen und Grenzregionen/Frontières et régions frontalières* (Saarbrücken, 1993), pp. 99–129

Healy, P., *The chronicle of Hugh of Flavigny: reform and the investiture contest in the late-eleventh century* (Aldershot, 2006)

Hen, Y. and Innes, M., eds., *Roman barbarians: the royal court and culture in the early medieval west* (Basingstoke, 2007)

Bibliography

The royal patronage of liturgy in Frankish Gaul to the death of Charles the Bald (London, 2001)

The uses of the past in early medieval Europe (Cambridge, 2000)

Henn, V., 'Zur Bedeutung von "mansus" im Prümer Urbar', in G. Droege, W. Frühwald and F. Pauly, eds., *Verführung zur Geschichte* (Trier 1973), pp. 35–45

Hernes, T., *Understanding organization as process: theory for a tangled world* (London, 2008)

Herrmann, H. W., ed., *Geschichtliche Landeskunde des Saarlandes: vom Faustkeil zum Fördertum* (Saarbrücken, 1960)

Higounet, C., *La grange de Vaulerent: structure et exploitation d'un terroir cistercien de la plaine de France* (Paris, 1965)

Hirschmann, F., *Verdun im hohen Mittelalter: eine lothringische Kathedralstadt und ihr Umland im Spiegel der geistlichen Institutionen,* 2 vols. (Trier, 1996)

Hlawitschka, E., *Die Anfänge des Hauses Habsburg-Lothringen: Genealogische Untersuchungen zur Geschichte Lothringens und des Reiches im 9, 10 und 11 Jahrhundert* (Saarbrücken, 1969)

'Herzog Giselbert von Lothringen und das Kloster Remiremont', *Zeitschrift für die Geschichte des Oberrheins* 108 (1960), 422–65

Lotharingien und das Reich an der Schwelle der deutschen Geschichte (Stuttgart, 1968)

Hoffmann, H., 'Grafschaften in Bischofshand', *Deutsches Archiv* 46 (1990), 375–480

Hughes, M., and Diaz, H., 'Was there a medieval warm period?', *Climactic Change* 26 (1994), 109–42

Hummer, H., *Politics and power in early medieval Europe: Alsace and the Frankish realm, 600–1000* (Cambridge, 2005)

'The production and preservation of documents in Francia: the evidence of cartularies', in W. Brown, M. Costambeys, M. Innes and A. Kosto, eds., *Documentary culture and the laity in the early Middle Ages* (Cambridge, 2012)

Hyams, P., 'Homage and feudalism: a judicious separation', in N. Fryde, P. Monnet and O.-G Oexle, eds., *Die Gegenwart des Feudalismus* (Göttingen, 2002), pp. 13–50

Innes, M., 'Economies and societies in early medieval Western Europe', in C. Lansing and E. English, eds., *A companion to the medieval world* (Oxford, 2009), pp. 9–35

'Framing the Carolingian economy', *Journal of Agrarian Change* 9 (2009), 42–58

'On the material culture of legal documents: charters and their preservation in the Cluny archive, ninth to eleventh centuries', in W. Brown, M. Costambeys, M. Innes and A. Kosto, eds., *Documentary culture and the laity in the Early Middle Ages* (Cambridge, 2012)

'Practices of property in the Carolingian empire', in J. Davies and M. McCormick, eds., *The long morning of medieval Europe: new directions in early medieval studies* (Aldershot, 2008), pp. 247–66

State and society in the early Middle Ages: the middle Rhine valley, 400–1000 (Cambridge, 2000)

Iogna-Prat, D., *La maison Dieu: une histoire monumentale de l'église au Moyen-âge (v. 800–v. 1200)* (Paris, 2006)

Irsigler, F., 'Mehring. Ein Prümer Winzerdorf um 900', in J-M. Duvosquel and E. Thoen, eds., *Peasants and townsmen in medieval Europe* (Weimar, 1995), pp. 65–86

Bibliography

Isphording, B., *Prüm: Studien zur Geschichte der Abtei von ihrer Gründung bis zum Tod Kaiser Lothars I. (721–855)* (Mainz, 2005)

Jakobs, H., *Die Hirsauer: ihre Ausbreitung und Rechtsstellung im Zeitalter des Investiturstreites* (Cologne, 1961)

le Jan, R., 'L'aristocratie Lotharingienne: structure interne et conscience politique', in H. W. Herrmann and R. Schneider, eds., *Lotharingia: Eine europäische Kernlandschaft um das Jahr 1000. Une région au centre de l'Europe autour de l'an mil* (Saarbrücken, 1995), pp. 71–88

'Entre maîtres et dependants: réflexions sur la famille paysanne en Lotharingie, aux xᵉ et xiᵉ siècles', in E. Mornet, ed., *Campagnes médiévales. L'homme et son espace: études offertes à Robert Fossier* (Paris, 1995), pp. 277–96

Famille et pouvoir dans le monde franc (vIIᵉ–xᵉ siècle): essai d'anthropologie sociale (Paris, 1995)

'Frankish giving of arms and rituals of power: continuity and change in the Carolingian period', in F. Theuws and J. Nelson, eds., *Rituals of power: from late antiquity to the early middle ages* (Leiden, 2000), pp. 377–99

'Justice royale et pratiques sociales dans le royaume franc au ixᵉ siècle', *Settimane* 44 (1997), 47–86

'Pauperes et paupertas dans l'occident carolingien aux ix et x siècles', *Revue du Nord* 50 (1968), 169–87

'Structures familiales et politiques au ixᵉ siècle: un groupe familial de l'aristocratie franque', *Revue Historique* 265 (1981), 289–333

Jezieski, W., '"Paranoia sangallensis". A micro-study in the etiquette of monastic persecution', *FMS* 42 (2008), 147–68

de Jong, M., 'Ecclesia and the early medieval polity', in S. Airlie, W. Pohl and H. Reimitz, eds., *Staat im frühen Mittelalter* (Vienna, 2006), pp. 113–32

The penitential state: authority and atonement in the age of Louis the Pious, 814–840 (Cambridge, 2009)

'What was public about public penance? Paenitentia publica and justice in the Carolingian world', *Settimane* 44 (1997), 863–904

Joyce, P., 'What is the social in social history?', *Past and Present* 206 (2010), 213–48

Jungmann, J., *The mass of the Roman rite*, tr. F. Brunner, 2 vols. (New York, 1951)

Kaiser, R., *Bischofsherrschaft zwischen Königtum und Fürstenmacht* (Bonn, 1981)

'Münzprivilegien und bischöflichen Münzpragung in Frankreich, Deutschland und Burgund im 9–12 Jahrhundert', *Vierteljahrschrift für Sozial- und Wirtschaftsgeschichte* 63 (1976), 289–339

Kamp, H., 'Die Macht der Zeichen und Gesten. Öffentliches Verhalten bei Dudo von Saint-Quentin', in G. Althoff, ed., *Formen und Funktionen öffentlicher Kommunikation im Mittelalter* (Stuttgart, 2001), pp. 125–55

Keefe, S., *Water and the word: baptism and the education of the clergy in the Carolingian empire*, 2 vols. (Notre Dame, 2002)

Keller, H., 'Die Investitur: ein Beitrag zur Problem der "Staatssymbolik" im Hochmittelalter', *FMS* 27 (1993), 51–86

'Zu den Siegeln der Karolinger und Ottonen. Urkunden als "Hoheitszeichen" des Königs mit seinen Getreuen', *FMS* 32 (1998), 400–41

Kershaw, P., 'Eberhard of Friuli, a Carolingian lay intellectual', in J. Nelson and P. Wormald, eds., *Lay intellectuals in the Carolingian world* (Cambridge, 2007), pp. 77–105

Keyser, R., 'La transformation de l'échange des dons pieux: Montier-la-Celle, Champagne, 1100–1350', *Revue historique* 628 (2003), 793–816

Kienast, W., 'Lehnrecht und Staatsgewalt im Mittelalter', *Historische Zeitschrift* 158 (1938), 3–51

Kirsch, T., *Spirits and letters: reading, writing and charisma in African Christianity* (New York, 2008)

Kluge, B., *Deutsche Münzgeschichte von der späten Karolingerzeit bis zum Ende der Salier* (Sigmaringen, 1991)

Kolbaba, T., *The Byzantine lists: errors of the Latins* (Urbana, 2000)

Kölzer, T., *Studien zu den Urkundenfälschungen des Klosters St. Maximin vor Trier: (10.-12. Jahrhundert)* (Sigmaringen, 1989)

Körntgen, L., 'Bußbuch und Bußpraxis in der zweiten Hälfte des 9. Jahrhunderts', in W. Hartmann, ed., *Recht und Gericht in Kirche und Welt um 900* (Munich, 2007), pp. 197–215

Koselleck, R., *The practice of conceptual history* (Stanford, 2002)

Kosto, A., *Making agreements in medieval Catalonia: power, order, and the written word, 1000–1200* (Cambridge, 2001)

Kottje, R., 'Bußpraxis und Bußritus', in *Segni e riti nella chiesa altomedievale occidentale, Settimane* 33 (1987), 369–95

Koziol, G., *Begging pardon and favor: ritual and political order in early medieval France* (Ithaca, 1992)

'Charles the Simple, Robert of Neustria, and the vexilla of Saint-Denis', *EME* 14 (2006), 385–6

Krause, I., *Konflikt und Ritual im Herrschaftsbereich der frühen Capetinger: Untersuchungen zur Darstellung und Funktion symbolischen Verhaltens* (Münster, 2006)

Kroeschell, K., 'Lehnrecht und Verfassung im deutschen Hochmittelalter', *Forum historiae iuris* 2 (1998), 1–41

Krönert, K., *L'exaltation de Trèves: écriture hagiographique et passé historique de la métropole mosellane, VIIIe–XIe siècle* (Ostfildern, 2010)

Kuchenbuch, L., 'Abschied von der "Grundherrschaft". Ein Prüfgang durch das ostfränkisch-deutsche Reich (950–1050)', *Zeitschrift der Savigny-Stiftung für Rechtsgeschichte. Germanistische Abteilung* 121 (2004), 1–99

Bäuerliche Gesellschaft und Klosterherrschaft im 9. Jahrhundert. Studien zur Sozialstruktur der Familia der Abtei Prüm (Wiesbaden, 1978)

'Feudalismus: Versuch über die Gebrauchsstrategien eines wissenspolitischen Reizworts in der Mediävistik', in N. Fryde, P. Monnet and O. Oexle, eds., *Gegenwart des Feudalismus. Présence du féodalisme et présent de la féodalité. The presence of feudalism*, Veröffentlichungen des Max-Planck-Instituts für Geschichte 173 (Göttingen 2002), pp. 293–323

'*Porcus donativus*: language use and gifting in seigniorial records between the eighth and the twelfth centuries', in G. Algazi, V. Groebner and B. Jussen, eds., *Negotiating the gift. Pre-modern figurations of exchange* (Göttingen, 2003), pp. 193–246

Labhart, V., *Zur Rechtssymbolik des Bischofsrings* (Cologne, 1963)

Langdon, J. and Masschaele, J., 'Commercial activity and population growth in medieval England', *Past and Present* 190 (2006), 35–81

Laret-Kayser, A., *Entre Bar et Luxembourg: le comté de Chiny des origines à 1300* (Brussels, 1986)

    and Dupont, C., 'A propos des comtés post-Carolingiens: les exemples d'Ivoix et de Bastogne', *Revue Belge de Philologie et d'Histoire* 57 (1979), 805–23

Latour, B., *Reassembling the social: an introduction to actor-network theory* (Oxford, 2005)

Law, V., 'The study of grammar', in R. McKitterick, ed., *Carolingian culture: emulation and innovation* (Cambridge, 1993), pp. 88–110

Lebel, P., 'Contribution à la recherche des origines de la ville et des seigneurs de Reynel', *Bulletin philologique et historique* (1936–7), 289–312

Lemarignier, J.-F., 'La Dislocation du "Pagus" et le problème des "Consuetudines" (x^e–xie siècles)', in *Mélanges Louis Halphen* (Paris, 1951), pp. 401–10

    Recherches sur l'hommage en marche et les frontières féodales (Lille, 1945)

    ed., *Gallia monastica* (Paris, 1974)

Lemesle, B., *Conflits et justice au Moyen Age: normes, loi et résolution des conflits en Anjou aux xie et xiie siècles* (Paris, 2008)

Lenoble, M., '*La céramique médiévale dans le départment de l'Aube*', in *Mémoire de Champagne* (Langres, 2000) vol. I, pp. 137–59

Lewald, U., 'Die Ezzonen. Das Schicksal eines rheinischen Fürstengeschlechts', *Rheinische Vierteljahrsblätter* 43 (1979), 120–68

Leyser, K., '987: the Ottonian connection', in *Communications and power in medieval Europe, vol. I. The Carolingian and Ottonian centuries*, ed. T. Reuter (London, 1994), pp. 165–79

    'Ritual, ceremony and gesture: Ottonian Germany', *Communications and Power, vol. I. The Carolingian and Ottonian centuries*, ed. T. Reuter (London, 1994), pp. 189–213

Lifshitz, F., *The name of the saint: the martyrology of Jerome and access to the sacred in Francia, 627–827* (Notre Dame, 2006)

    The Norman conquest of Pious Neustria (Toronto, 1995)

Linck, E., *Sozialer Wandel in klösterlichen Grundherrschaften des 11. bis 13. Jahrhunderts: Studien zu den familiae von Gembloux, Stablo-Malmedy und St. Trond* (Göttingen, 1979)

LoPrete, K., *Adela of Blois, Countess and Lord (c.1067–1137)* (Dublin, 2007)

Lot, F., *Études sur le règne de Hugues Capet et la fin du xe siècle* (Paris, 1903)

    'La vicaria et le vicarius', *Nouvelle Revue historique de droit français et étranger*, 17 (1893), 281–301

van der Lugt, M., 'Tradition and revision: the textual tradition of Hincmar of Rheims's Visio Bernoldi', *Bulletin du Cange* 52 (1994), 109–49

Lund, C. *Local politics and the dynamics of property in Africa* (New York, 2008)

Lusse, J., 'Marmoutier et Cluny en Champagne', *Etudes champenoises* 2 (1976), 27–44

    'La présence royale en Champagne au Haut Moyen Age', in G. Clause, S. Guilbert and M. Vaisse, eds., *La Champagne et ses administrations à travers le temps* (Paris, 1990), pp. 69–92

    'Quelques types de bourgs castraux en Haute-Marne', in M. Bur, ed., *Les peuplements castraux dans les pays de l'Entre-Deux: Alsace, Bourgogne, Champagne, Franche-Comté,*

Bibliography

Lorraine, Luxembourg, Rhénanie-Palatinat, Sarre: aux origines du second réseau urbain (Nancy, 1993), pp. 75–116

McCarthy, M., 'Louis the Stammerer', unpublished PhD thesis, Cambridge 2012

McCormick, M., *Eternal victory: triumphal rulership in late antiquity, Byzantium, and the early medieval West* (Cambridge, 1986)

    Origins of the European economy: communications and commerce A.D. 300–900 (Cambridge, 2001)

McKeon, P., *Hincmar of Laon and Carolingian politics* (Urbana, 1978)

McKitterick, R., *Carolingian culture: emulation and innovation* (Cambridge, 1993)

    The Carolingians and the written word (Cambridge, 1989)

    Charlemagne: the formation of a European identity (Cambridge, 2008)

    The Frankish kingdoms under the Carolingians, 751–987 (London, 1983)

    Perceptions of the past in the early Middle Ages (Notre Dame, 2006)

    ed., *The Frankish church and the Carolingian reforms* (London, 1977)

MacLean, S., 'The Carolingian response to the revolt of Boso, 879–887', *EME* 10 (2001), 21–48

    'Insinuation, censorship and the struggle for late Carolingian Lotharingia in Regino of Prüm's chronicle', *English Historical Review* 124 (2009), 1–28

    Kingship and politics in the late ninth century: Charles the Fat and the end of the Carolingian Empire (Cambridge, 2003)

    'Ritual, misunderstanding, and the contest for meaning: representations of the disrupted royal assembly at Frankfurt (873)', in B. Weiler and S. MacLean, eds., *Representations of power in medieval Germany* (Turnhout, 2006), pp. 97–120

Mann, M., 'Climate over the past two millennia', *Annual Review of Earth and Planetary Sciences* 35 (2007), 111–36

Margue, M., 'Remarques sur l'avouerie locale en Luxembourg', in M. Parisse, ed., *L'avouerie en Lotharingie*, Publications de la section historique de l'Institut grand-ducal 98 (Luxembourg, 1984), pp. 201–14

Martindale, J., 'The kingdom of Aquitaine and the dissolution of the Carolingian fisc', *Francia* 11 (1984), 131–91

Märtl, C., *Die fälschen Investiturprivilegien* (Hanover, 1986)

Mason, E., 'Barons and their officials in the later eleventh century', *Anglo-Norman Studies* 13 (1990), 243–62

Mattingly, M., 'The *Memoriale Qualiter*. An eighth-century monastic customary', *American Benedictine Review* 60 (2009), 62–75

Maujean, L., 'Histoire de Destry et du pays Saulnois', *Mémoires de l'Académie de Metz* 93 (1913), 231–532

Mayer, T., *Fürsten und Staat: Studien zur Verfassungsgeschichte des deutschen Mittelalters* (Weimar, 1950)

Mazel, F., ed., *L'espace du diocèse: Genèse d'un territoire dans l'Occident médiéval V^e–XIIIe siècle* (Rennes, 2008)

Mbembe, A., *On the postcolony* (Berkeley, 2001)

Mersiowsky, M., 'Regierungspraxis und Schriftlichkeit im Karolingerreich: Das Fallbeispiel der Mandate und Briefe', in R. Schieffer, ed., *Schriftkultur und Reichsverwaltung unter den Karolingern. Referate des Kolloquiums der Nordrhein-Westfälischen Akademie der Wissenschaften am 17. /18. Februar 1994 in Bonn* (Opladen, 1996), pp. 109–66

Metz, W., *Das karolingische Reichsgut: eine verfassungs- und verwaltungsgeschichtliche Untersuchung* (Berlin, 1960)

Metzler, J., and Zimmer, J., 'Zum Burgenbau in Luxemburg in vorsalischer und salischer Zeit', in Böhme, ed., *Burgen*, vol. i, pp. 311–36

Miethke, J., 'Rituelle Symbolik und Rechtswissenschaft im Kampf zwischen Kaiser und Papst. Friedrich Barbarossa und der Konflikt um die Bedeutung von Ritualen', in F. Felten and others, ed., *Ein gefüllter Willkomm. Festschrift für Knut Schulz zum 65. Geburtstag* (Aachen 2002), pp. 91–125

Miller, M., 'The crisis in the Investiture Crisis narrative', *History Compass* 7 (2009), 1570–80

'New religious movements and reform', in C. Lansing and E. English, ed., *A companion to the medieval world* (2010), pp. 211–30

Mitchell, T., *Colonising Egypt* (Cambridge, 1988)

Mohr, W., *Geschichte des Herzogtums Lothringen,* 3 vols. (Sarrebruck, 1978)

Moore, R. I., *The first European revolution, c.970–1215* (Oxford, 2000)

'The transformation of Europe as a Eurasian phenomenon', *Medieval Encounters* 10 (2004), 77–98.

Moore, S. F., *Law as process: an anthropological approach* (London, 1983)

Mordek, H., *Bibliotheca capitularium regum Francorum manuscripta: Überlieferung und Traditionszusammenhang der fränkischen Herrscherlasse* (Munich, 1995)

Moreland, J., 'Going native, becoming German', *postmedieval* 1 (2010), 142–9

Morimoto, Y., 'Aperçu critique des recherches: vers une synthèse équilibrée (1993–2004)', in T. Morimoto, *Etudes sur l'économie rurale du haut moyen âge: historiographie, régime domanial, polyptyques carolingiens* (Brussels, 2008), pp. 133–88

Morsel, J., *L'aristocratie médiévale: la domination sociale en Occident (v^e–xve siècle)* (Paris, 2004)

'Le prélèvement seigneurial est-il soluble dans les Weistümer? Appréhensions franconiennes (1200–1400)', in M. Bourin and M. Martinez Sopeña, eds., *Pour une anthropologie du prélèvement seigneurial dans les campagnes de l'Occident médiéval (xie–xive siècles): réalités et représentations paysannes*, pp. 155–210

Müller-Kehlen, H., *Die Ardennen im Frühmittelalter: Untersuchungen zum Königsgut in einem karolingischen Kernland* (Göttingen, 1973)

Müller-Mertens, E., *Reichsstruktur im Spiegel der Herrschaftspraxis Ottos des Grossen: mit historiographischen Prolegomena zur Frage Feudalstaat auf deutschem Boden, seit wann deutscher Feudalstaat?* (Berlin, 1980)

Nelson, J., 'The church's military service in the ninth century', *Studies in Church History* 20 (1983), 15–30

'Dispute settlement in Carolingian West Francia', in W. Davies and P. Fouracre, eds., *The settlement of disputes in early medieval Europe* (Cambridge, 1986), pp. 45–64

'England and the Continent ii: the Vikings and others, *TRHS* 13 (2003), 1–28

'England and the Continent iv: bodies and minds', *TRHS* 15 (2005), 1–27

'Ninth-century knighthood: the evidence of Nithard', in C. Harper-Bill, C. J. Holdsworth and Janet L. Nelson, eds., *Studies in medieval history presented to R. Allen Brown,* (Woodbridge, 1989), pp. 255–66.

'The wary widow', in W. Davies and P. Fouracre, eds., *Property and power in the early Middle Ages* (Cambridge, 1995), 54–82

Nightingale, J., *Monasteries and patrons in the Gorze reform: Lotharingia c.850–1000* (Oxford, 2001)

Nikolay-Panter, M., *Entstehung und Entwicklung der Landgemeinde im Trierer Raum* (Bonn, 1976)

Noiriel, G., 'La chevalerie dans la Geste des Lorrains', *Annales de l'Est* 3 (1976), 167–96

Nonn, U., 'Die Grafschaft Wallerfangen', *Jahrbuch für westdeutsche Landesgeschichte* 8 (1982), 1–12

Pagus und Comitatus in Niederlothringen (Bonn, 1983)

Oksanen, E., *Flanders and the Anglo-Norman World (1066–1216)* (Cambridge, 2013)

Oliver, L. *The body legal in barbarian law* (Toronto 2011)

Parisot, R., *Les origines de la Haute Lorraine et sa première maison ducale 959–1033* (Paris, 1909)

Parisse, M., 'Une ambassade à Cordoue. La Vita de Jean, abbé de Gorze, vers 987', in *Autour de Gerbert d'Aurillac, le pape de l'an mil: album de documents commentés* (Paris, 1996), pp. 37–42

'Le concile de Remiremont, poème satirique du xiie siècle', *Pays de Remiremont* 4 (1981), 10–15

'Désintégration et regroupements territoriaux dans les principautés lotharingiennes du xie au xiiie siècle', in H. Heit, ed., *Zwischen Gallia und Germania, Frankreich und Deutschland. Konstanz und Wandel raumbestimmender Kräfte* (Trier, 1987), pp. 155–80

'Les ducs et le duché de Lorraine au xiie siècle (1048–1206)', *Blätter für deutsche Landesgeschichte* 111 (1975), 86–102

'L'évêque d'Empire au xie siècle. L'exemple lorrain', in *Cahiers de civilisation médiévale* 27 (1984), 95–105

'In media Francia. St Mihiel, Salonnes et St. Denis', in *Media in Francia. Recueil de mélanges offert à Karl Ferdinand Werner à l'occasion de son 65e anniversaire par ses amis et collègues français* (Paris 1989) pp. 319–42

'Justice comtale dans la seigneurie de Briey', *Publications de la section historique de l'Institut (Royal) Grand-Ducal de Luxembourg* 102 (1986), 113–27

'Lotharingia', in Reuter, ed., *New Cambridge medieval history*, (Cambridge, 1999) vol. iii, pp. 310–27

Noblesse et chevalerie en lorraine médiévale – les familles nobles du 11e au 13e siècles (Nancy, 1982)

La noblesse Lorraine: XIe–XIIIe siècles, 2 vols. (Lille, 1976)

'Les règlements d'avouerie en Lorraine au xie siècle', in Parisse, ed., *L'avouerie* (Luxembourg, 1984), pp. 159–73

La vie de Jean, abbé de Gorze (Paris, 1999)

ed., *L'avouerie en Lotharingie,* Publications de la section historique de l'Institut grand-ducal 98 (Luxembourg, 1984)

ed., *La Maison d'Ardenne,* Publications de la section historique de l'Institut grand-ducal 95 (Luxembourg, 1981)

Patzold, S., *Episcopus: Wissen über Bischöfe im Frankenreich des späten 8. bis frühen 10. Jahrhunderts* (Ostfildern, 2008)

'"… inter pagensium nostrorum gladios vivimus". Zu den "Spielregeln" der Konfliktführung in Niederlothringen zur Zeit der Ottonen und frühen Salier', *Zeitschrift der Savigny-Stiftung für Rechtsgeschichte, Germanistische Abteilung* 118 (2001), 578–99

Perrin, Ch-E., 'Chartes de franchise et rapports de droit en Lorraine', *Moyen Age* 52 (1946), 11–42

    Recherches sur la seigneurie rurale en Lorraine d'après les plus anciens censiers (Paris, 1935)

Petke, W., 'Von der klösterlichen Eigenkirche zur Inkorporation in Lothringen und Nordfrankreich im 11. und 12. Jahrhundert', *Revue d'histoire ecclésiastique* 87 (1992), 34–72

Peytremann, E., *Archéologie de l'habitat rural dans le nord de la France du IVe au XIIe siècle*, 2 vols. (Saint-Germain-en-Laye, 2003)

Pfister, C., 'Les revenues de la collegiale de Saint-Dié au xe siècle', *Annales de l'Est* 2 (1888), 515–17, and 3 (1889), 407

Pitz, M., 'Der Frühbesitz der Abtei Prüm im lothringischen Salzgebiet. Philologisch-onomastische Überlegungen zu den Brevia 41–3 des Prümer Urbars', *Rheinische Vierteljahrsblätter* 70 (2006), 1–35

    Siedlungsnamen auf vilare (-weiler, -villers) zwischen Mosel, Hunsrück und Vogesen: Untersuchungen zu einem germanisch-romanisch Mischtypus der jüngeren Merowinger- und der Karolingerzeit, 2 vols. (Saarbrücken, 1997)

Pizarro, J., *A rhetoric of the scene: dramatic narrative in the early Middle Ages* (Toronto, 1989)

Poey d'Avant, F., *Monnaies féodales de Franc* (Paris, 1858)

Pohl, W., 'Staat und Herrschaft im Frühmittelalter: Überlegungen zum Forschungsstand', in S. Airlie, W. Pohl and H. Reimitz, eds., *Staat im frühen Mittelalter* (Vienna, 2006), pp. 9–38

    and Wieser, V., eds., *Der frühmittelalterliche Staat – Europäische Perspektiven* (Vienna, 2010)

Polfer, M., 'Spätantike und frühmittelalterliche Kirchenbauten der Kirchenprovinz Trier: einen Bestandaufnahme aus archäologischer Sicht', in *L'évangélisation des régions entre Meuse et Moselle et la fondation de l'abbaye d'Echternach (v^e-1x^e siècle)* (Luxembourg, 2000), pp. 37–92

Poly, J.-P, and Bournazel, E., *Les féodalités* (Paris, 1998)

    La mutation féodale: x^e–xII^e siècles (Paris, 1980), tr. C. Higgitt as: *The feudal transformation: 900–1200* (New York, 1991),

Pössel, C., 'The magic of early medieval ritual', *EME* 17 (2009), 111–25

    'Symbolic communication and the negotiation of power at Carolingian regnal assemblies, 814–840', unpublished PhD thesis, Cambridge 2004

Potts, C., *Monastic revival and regional identity in early Normandy* (Woodbridge, 1997)

Poull, G., *Le château et les seigneurs de Bourlémont*, 2 vols. (Corbeil, 1962–4)

    La maison ducale de Bar (Rupt, 1977)

Puhl, R., *Die Gaue und Grafschaften des frühen Mittelalters im Saar-Mosel-Raum: philologisch-onomastische Studien zur frühmittelalterlichen Raumorganisation anhand der Raumnamen und der mit ihnen spezifizierten Ortsnamen* (Saarbrücken, 1999)

Raach, T., *Kloster Mettlach / Saar und sein Grundbesitz: Untersuchungen zur Frühgeschichte und zur Grundherrschaft der ehemaligen Benediktinerabtei im Mittalalter* (Mainz, 1974)

Racine, P., 'La Lorraine au haut Moyen Age. Structures économiques et relations sociales', in A. Heit, ed., *Zwischen Gallia und Germania, Frankreich und Deutschland. Konstanz und Wandel raumbestimmender Kräfte* (Trier, 1987), pp. 205–18

Radding, C., *The origins of medieval jurisprudence: Pavia and Bologna, 850–1100* (New Haven, 1988)

Rasmussen, N., *Les pontificaux du haut moyen age: gènese du livre de l'évêque* (Louvain, 1998)

Renard, E., 'Genèse et manipulations d'un polyptyque carolingien: Montier-en-Der, IXe–XIe siècles', *Le Moyen Age* 110 (2004), 55–77

'Les *mancipia* carolingiens étaient-ils des esclaves?' in P. Corbet, ed., *Les moines du Der, 673–1790* (Langres, 2000), pp. 179–209

Renoux, A., 'Les mutations morphologiques et fonctionnelles de la basse-cour du chateau des comtes de Champagne à Montfélix (x^e–xiiie siècle)', *Château-Gaillard* 21 (2004), 259–70

Reuter, T., 'Assembly politics in Western Europe from the eighth century to the twelfth', in P. Linehan and J. Nelson, eds., *The medieval world* (London, 2001), pp. 432–50

'Forms of lordship in German historiography', in M. Bourin, ed., *Pour une anthropologie du prélèvement seigneurial dans les campagnes médiévales (xi–xiv siècles)* (Paris 2004), pp. 51–2

'Introduction: reading the tenth century', in T. Reuter, ed., *New Cambridge medieval history* (Cambridge, 1999), vol. III, pp. 1–26

'"Pastorale pedum ante pedes apostolici posuit": Dis- and reinvestiture in the era of the investiture contest', in R. Gameson and H. Leyser, eds., *Belief and culture in the Middle Ages* (Oxford, 2001), pp. 197–210

'Plunder and tribute in the Carolingian empire', *TRHS*, 5th ser. 35. (1985), 75–94

'*Velle sibi fieri in forma hac:* Symbolisches Handeln im Becketstreit', in G. Althoff, ed., *Formen und Funktionen offentlicher Kommunikation im Mittelalter* (Stuttgart, 2001), pp. 201–25

Reynolds, P., *Marriage in the Western Church: the Christianization of marriage during the patristic and early medieval periods* (Leiden, 1994)

Reynolds, S., 'The emergence of professional law in the long twelfth century', *Law and History Review* 21 (2003), 347–66

Fiefs and vassals: the medieval evidence reinterpreted (Oxford, 1994)

'Fiefs and vassals after twelve years', in S. Bagge, M. Gelting and T. Lindkvist, eds., *Feudalism: new landscapes of debate* (Turnhout, 2011), pp. 15–26

'Historiography of the medieval state', in M. Bentley, ed., *Companion to historiography* (London, 1997), pp. 117–38

van Rhijn, C., *Shepherds of the Lord: priests and episcopal statutes in the Carolingian period* (Turnhout, 2007)

Riches, T., 'The peace of God, the "weakness" of Robert the Pious and the struggle for the German throne, 1023–5', *EME* 18 (2010), 202–22

Richter, M., *The history of social and political concepts: a critical introduction* (New York, 1995)

Rio, A., *Legal practice and the written word in the early Middle Ages: Frankish formulae, c.500–1000* (Cambridge, 2009)

Rolker, C., *Canon law and the letters of Ivo of Chartres* (Cambridge, 2010)

Rösener, W., *Grundherrschaft im Wandel: Untersuchungen zur Entwicklung geistlicher Grundherrschaften im südwestdeutschen Raum vom 9. bis 14. Jahrhundert* (Göttingen, 1991)

Rosenwein, B., 'Francia and Polynesia: rethinking anthropological approaches', in G. Algazi, V. Groebner and B. Jussen, eds., *Negotiating the gift. Pre-modern figurations of exchange* (Göttingen, 2003), pp. 361–79

Ryan, M., 'Oath of fealty and the lawyers', in J. Canning and O.-G. Oexle, eds., *Politische Ideen im Mittelalter, Theorie und Wirklichkeit der Macht* (1999), pp. 209–26

Scheying, R., *Eide, Amtsgewalt und Bannleihe: eine Untersuchung zur Bannleihe im hohen und späten Mittelalter* (Cologne, 1960)

Schieffer, R., 'Rheinische Zeugen in den Urkunden Friederich Barbarossas', in *Geschichtliche Landeskunde der Rheinlande. Regionale Befunde und raumübergreifende Perspektiven. Georg Droege zum Gedenken* (Cologne, 1994), pp. 104–30

Schmid, K., 'Unerforschte Quellen aus quellenarmer Zeit: zur *amicitia* zwischen Heinrich I und dem westfränkisch König Robert im Jahre 923', *Francia* 12 (1984), 119–47

Schmidt-Wiegand, R., 'Gebärdensprache im mittelalterlichen Recht', *FMS* 16 (1982), 363–79

Schmitt, J. C., *La raison des gestes dans l'occident médiéval* (Paris, 1990)

Schmitz, H., *Die Bußbücher und das kanonische Bußverfahren* (Düsseldorf 1898)

Schneider, Jean, 'Recherches sur les confins de la Lorraine et de la Champagne: les origines de Vaucouleurs', *Comptes-rendus des séances de l'Académie des Inscriptions et Belles-Lettres* 105 (1961), 270–4

    La ville de Metz aux XIIIe et XIVe siècles (Nancy, 1950)

Schneider, Jens, *Auf der Suche nach dem verlorenen Reich: Lotharingien im 9. und 10. Jahrhundert* (Cologne, 2010)

Schneidmuller, B., 'Französische Lothringenpolitik im 10. Jahrhundert', *Jahrbuch für Westdeutsche Geschichte* 5 (1979), 1–32

    Karolingische Tradition und frühes französisches Königtum (Wiesbaden, 1979)

Schuurmans, C., 'Climate: mean state, variability, and change', in Koster, ed., *Physical Geography*, pp. 289–308

Schwager, H., *Graf Heribert II. von Soissons, Omois, Meaux, Madrie sowie Vermandois (900/06–943) und die Francia (Nord-Frankreich) in der 1. Hälfte des 10. Jahrhunderts* (Kallmunz, 1994)

Semmler, J., 'Mission und Pfarrorganisation in den rheinischen, mosel- und maasländischen Bistümern 5–10 Jahrhundert', *Settimane* 28 (1982), 813–88

    'Zehntgebot und Pfarrtermination in karolingischer Zeit', in H. Mordek, ed., *Aus Kirche und Reich* (1983), pp. 33–44

Senn, F., *L'institution des Avoueries ecclésiastiques en France* (Paris, 1903)

Shepard, J., 'When Greek meets Greek: Alexius Comnenus and Bohemond in 1097–98', *Byzantine and modern Greek studies* 12 (1998), 185–277

Sigoillot, A., 'Les *liberi homines* dans la polyptyque de Saint-Germain des Prés', *Journal des Savants* (2008), 261–71

de Sousa-Costa, A., *Studien zu volkssprachigen Wörtern in karolingischen Kapitularien* (Göttingen, 1993)

Spiegel, G., '"Defence of the realm": evolution of a Capetian propaganda slogan', *Journal of Medieval History* 3 (1977), 115–25

Spiess, K-H., *Das Lehnswesen in Deutschland im hohen und späten Mittelalter* (Idstein, 2002)

Stiegemann, C. and M. Wemhoff, eds., *Canossa 1077: Erschütterung der Welt* (2 vols., Munich, 2006)

Stock, B., *The implications of literacy: written language and models of interpretation in the eleventh and twelfth centuries* (Princeton, 1983)

Stone, R. *Morality and masculinity in the Carolingian empire* (Cambridge, 2011)

Bibliography

Stratmann, M., *Hinkmar von Reims als Verwalter von Bistum und Kirchenprovinz* (Sigmaringen 1991)

'Zur Wirkungsgeschichte Hinkmars von Reims', *Francia* 22 (1995), 1–43

Suchan, M., *Königsherrschaft im Streit: Konfliktaustragung in der Regierungszeit Heinrichs IV. zwischen Gewalt, Gespräch und Schriftlichkeit* (Stuttgart, 1997)

Suntrup, R., *Die Bedeutung der liturgischen Gebärden und Bewegungen in lateinischen und deutschen Auslegungen des 9. bis 13. Jahrhunderts* (Munich, 1978)

Symes, C., 'When we talk about modernity', *American Historical Review* 116 (2011), 715–26

Tada, S., 'The creation of a religious centre: Christianisation in the diocese of Liège in the Carolingian period', *Journal of Ecclesiastical History* 54 (2003)

Tanner, H., *Families, friends, and allies: Boulogne and politics in northern France and England, c.879–1160* (Leiden, 2004)

Tellenbach, G., 'Servitus und libertas nach den Traditionen der Abtei Remiremont', *Saeculum* 21 (1970), 228–34

Theuws, F., 'Landed property and manorial organisation in northern Austrasia: some considerations and a case study', in N. Roymans and F. Theuws, eds., *Images of the past: studies on ancient societies in northwestern Europe* (Amsterdam, 1991), pp. 299–407

Thiele, A., *Echternach und Himmerod. Beispiele benediktinischer und zisterziensischer Wirtschaftsführung im 12. und 13. Jahrhundert* (Stuttgart, 1964)

Tiefenbach, H., 'Ein übersehener Textzeuge des Trierer Capitulare', *Rheinische Vierteljahrsblätter*, 39 (1975), 272–310

Tischler, M., *Einharts Vita Karoli: Studien zur Entstehung, Überlieferung und Rezeption* (Hanover, 2001)

Tock, B.-M., ed., *La diplomatique française du Haut Moyen Age: inventaire des chartes originales antérieures à 1121 conservées en France*, 2 vols. (Turnhout, 2001). The charters this catalogue lists are now available in electronic edition on the Chartes originales website: see the list of websites above.

Trexler, R., 'Legitimating prayer gestures in the twelfth century. The de penitentia of Peter the Chanter', *History and Anthropology* 1 (1984), 97–126

Ullmann, W., *The Carolingian Renaissance and the idea of kingship* (London, 1969)

Vallange, un village retrouvé: les fouilles archéologiques de la Zac de la Plaine, no editor given (Vitry-sur-Orne, 2006)

Verhulst, A., *The rise of cities in north-west Europe* (Cambridge, 1999)

Vogtherr, T., 'Bischofsstäbe und Abtsstäbe im frühen und hohen Mittelalter', in *Kleidung und Repräsentation in Antike und Mittelalter* (Munich, 2005), pp. 83–90

Vones, L., 'Erzbischof Brun von Köln und der Reimser Erzstuhl', in *Von Sacerdotium und Regnum: Geistliche und weltliche Gewalt im frühen und hohen Mittelalter. Festschrift für Egon Boshof* (Vienna, 2002), pp. 325–46

Voss, I., 'La Lotharingie, terre de rencontres x^e–xie siècles', in D. Iogna-Prat and J-C. Picard, eds., *Religion et culture autour de l'an mil: royaume Capétien et Lotharingie* (Paris, 1990), pp. 267–72

Waas, A., *Vogtei und Bede in der deutschen Kaiserzeit*, 2 vols. (Berlin, 1919)

Wagner, A., *Gorze au 11e siècle: contribution à l'histoire du monachisme bénédictin dans l'Empire* (Nancy, 1996)

Wareham, A., *Lords and communities in early medieval East Anglia* (Woodbridge, 2005)

Bibliography

Watteaux, M., 'Archéogéographie de l'habitat et du parcellaire au haut Moyen Age' in J. Guillaume and E. Peytremann, eds., *L'Austrasie: sociétés, économies, territoires, christianisation* (Nancy, 2008), pp. 109–20

Watts, J., *Henry VI and the politics of kingship* (Cambridge, 1996)

Wedeen, L., *Ambiguities of domination: politics, rhetoric, and symbols in contemporary Syria* (Chicago, 1999)

Weiller, R., *Die Münzen von Trier, 6 Jahrhundert-1307* (Düsseldorf, 2008)

Weinfurter, S., 'Investitur und Gnade. Überlegungen zur gratialen Herrschaftsordnung im Mittelalter', in *Investitur- und Krönungsrituale. Herrschaftseinsetzungen im kulturellen Vergleich* (2005), pp. 105–23

'Lehnswesen, Treueid und Vertrauen. Grundlagen der neuen Ordnung im hohen Mittelalter', in Dendorfer and Deutinger, eds., *Das Lehnswesen*, pp. 443–62

Werner, K.-F., '*Missus – Marchio – Comes*. Entre l'administration centrale et l'administration locale de l'Empire carolingien', in W. Paravicini and K. F. Werner, eds., *Histoire comparée de l'administration (IVᵉ–XVIIᵉ siècles)* (Munich, 1980), pp. 191–239

'Untersuchungen zur Frühzeit des Französischen Fürstentums (9–10 Jahrhundert)', *Die Welt als Geschichte* 18 (1958), 256–89; 19 (1959), 146–93; 20 (1960), 87–119

Werner, M., 'Der Herzog von Lothringen in salischer Zeit', in *Die Salier und das Reich*, ed. S. Weinfurter (Sigmaringen, 1991), vol. I, pp. 367–473

West, C., 'Count Hugh of Troyes and the territorial principality in early twelfth-century Europe', *English Historical Review* 127 (2012), 523–48

'Principautés et territoires, comtes et comtés', in M. Gaillard, M. Margue, A. Dierkens and H. Pettiau, eds., *De la Mer du Nord à la Méditerranée. Francia Media, une région au cœur de l'Europe (c. 840–c. 1050)* (Luxembourg, 2011), pp. 131–50

'The significance of the Carolingian advocate', *EME*, 17 (2009), 186–206

'Unauthorised miracles in mid-ninth-century Dijon and the Carolingian church reforms', *Journal of Medieval History* 36 (2010), 295–311

White, S., *Custom, kinship and gifts to the saints: the* laudatio parentum *in western France, 1050–1150* (London, 1988)

'Debate: the Feudal Revolution: comment', *Past and Present* 152 (1996), 196–223

Re-thinking kinship and feudalism (Aldershot, 2005)

'Tenth-century courts at Macon and the perils of Structuralist history: re-reading Burgundian judicial institutions', in W. Brown and P. Gorecki, eds., *Conflict in medieval Europe* (Aldershot, 2003), pp. 37–68

Wickham, C., *Courts and conflict in twelfth-century Tuscany* (Oxford, 2003)

'Debate: the Feudal Revolution: comment 4', *Past and Present* 155 (1997), 196–208

'Defining the seigneurie since the war', in *Pour une anthropologie du prélèvement seigneurial* (Paris, 2004), pp. 19–35

'Le forme del feudalismo', *Settimane* 47 (2000), 15–46

Framing the early Middle Ages. Europe and the Mediterranean, 400–800 (Oxford, 2005)

The inheritance of Rome: a history of Europe from 400 to 1000 (London, 2010)

'Public court practice: the eighth and twelfth centuries', in S. Esders, ed., *Rechtsverständnis und Konfliktbewältigung: gerichtliche und aussergerichtliche Strategien im Mittelalter* (Cologne, 2007), pp. 17–30

Wightman, E. *Gallia Belgica* (London, 1985)

Wilkes, C., *Die zisterzienserabtei Himmerode im 12 und 13 Jahrhundert* (Munster, 1924)

Bibliography

Williams, J., 'Archbishop Manasses I of Rheims and Pope Gregory VII', *American Historical Review* 54 (1949), 804–24

Willwersch, M., *Die Grundherrschaft des Klosters Prüm* (Trier, 1989)

Wisplinghoff, E., 'Lothringische und Clunyazensische Reform im Rheinland', *Rheinische Vierteljahrsblätter* 56 (1992), 59–78

Wollasch, J., 'Reformmönchtum und Schriftlichkeit', *FMS* 26 (1992), 274–86

Wolter, H., *Die Synoden im Reichsgebiet und in Reichitalien von 916–1056* (Paderborn, 1988)

Wood, I., 'Entrusting Western Europe to the Church', *TRHS*, forthcoming
The Merovingian kingdoms 450–751 (London, 1994)

Wood, S., *The proprietary church in the medieval West* (Oxford, 2006)

Yante, J.-M., and Bultot-Verleysen, A.-M., eds., *Autour du 'village': établissements humains, finages et communautés rurales entre Seine et Rhin (IVe–XIIIe siècles)* (Louvain, 2010)

Yver, J., 'Autour de l'absence d'avouerie en Normandie. Notes sur le double thème du développement du pouvoir ducal et de l'application de la réforme grégorienne en Normandie', *Bulletin de la Société des antiquaires de Normandie* 67 (1963–4), 189–283

Zerner, M., 'Note sur la seigneurie banale: à propos de la révolte des serfs de Viry', in *Histoire et société, mélanges offerts à Georges Duby. Volume II. Le tenancier, le fidèle et le citoyen* (Aix-en-Provence, 1992), pp. 49–58

Zielinski, H., *Der Reichsepiskopat in spätottonischer und salischer Zeit, 1002–1125* (Wiesbaden, 1984)

Zotz, T., 'Die Formierung der Ministerialität', in S. Weinfurter, ed., *Die Salier und das Reich* (Sigmaringen, 1991), vol. III, pp. 3–50

INDEX

MANUSCRIPTS INDEX